The Life of Thomas Hardy

BLACKWELL CRITICAL BIOGRAPHIES

General Editor: Claude Rawson

The Life of
THOMAS HARDY

A Critical Biography

Paul Turner

First published 1998

Blackwell Publishers Ltd
108 Cowley Road
Oxford OX4 1JF
UK

Blackwell Publishers Inc.
350 Main Street
Malden, Massachusetts 02148
USA

British Library Cataloguing in Publication Data

A CIP catalogue record for this book is available from the British Library.

Library of Congress Cataloging-in-Publication Data

Turner, Paul, 1917–
    The life of Thomas Hardy : a critical biography / Paul D.L.
Turner.
        p. cm.
    Includes bibliographical references and index.
    ISBN 0–631–16881–8
    1. Hardy, Thomas, 1840–1928.   2. Authors, English—19th century—
Biography.   3. Authors, English—20th century—Biography.
I. Title.
PR4753.T87   1998
823′.8—dc21
    [B]   97–24557
                                                               CIP

Typeset in 10 on 11pt Baskerville
by Graphicraft Typesetters Ltd., Hong Kong
Printed in Great Britain by TJ International, Padstow, Cornwall

This book is printed on acid-free paper

To Jane Turner (1925–1992)

Contents

Contents

Illustrations

The illustrations appear between pages 158 and 159.

Preface and Acknowledgements

Like most writers on Hardy these days, I owe a great general debt to three pioneers of the subject, Richard Little Purdy, Michael Millgate, and Robert Gittings. Particular debts to them and other scholars I have tried to acknowledge in the notes. I owe further thanks to Christopher Sheppard for permission to read and quote from MS letters in the Brotherton Collection; to Sue Usher, the Oxford English Faculty Librarian, to the staff of the Bodleian Library, and to Tim Farmiloe of Macmillans, for giving me painless access to many publications; and to Richard de Peyer for kindly enabling me to use Hardy material in the Dorset County Museum. I am grateful to Val Sillery for sending me a postcard of the portrait reproduced on the dust-jacket; to Margaret Warrick for the indefinite loan of a rare but essential book; to Jill Hayes for alerting me to the appearance of an equally useful one; to Peter Streuli for information about the Victorian theatre; to Ginny Stroud-Lewis for vital help with the illustrations; to Andrew McNeillie of Blackwell Publishers, and Claude Rawson the series editor, for much patience and understanding; to 'troops' of other friends (as undeserved as Macbeth's would have been) for moral support and encouragement; and for all kinds of help and advice, to Park Honan.

I also owe both a debt and an apology to Thomas Hardy – for frequently borrowing the language of his letters, notebooks, and do-it-yourself biography; and for a type of approach that he would have ridiculed as 'rather imaginative', if not condemned as quite invalid. 'I cannot see', he wrote, 'how details of one's personal history, when certain books were read, &c., can be required for any legitimate literary criticism.'

Abbreviations

CH	R.G. Cox, ed. *Thomas Hardy: The Critical Heritage.*
CL	Hardy, *Collected Letters*, ed. R.L. Purdy and M. Millgate.
CM	*A Changed Man and Other Tales* (Alan Sutton, 1987).
COD	*Concise Oxford Dictionary of Current English.*
CP	Thomas Hardy, *Complete Poems* in NWE. Following number indicates page, unless prefixed by 'No' (= number of poem in CP).
CPW	Thomas Hardy, *Complete Poetical Works*, ed. S. Hynes.
CSS	*Thomas Hardy: Collected Short Stories*, ed. D. Hawkins.
D	*The Dynasts* (NWE).
DC	Longus, *Daphnis and Chloe*, tr. P. Turner.
DCC	*Dorset County Chronicle.*
DCM	*Dorset County Museum.*
DFB	D.F. Barber, *Concerning Thomas Hardy.*
DKR	D. Kay-Robinson, *The First Mrs Thomas Hardy.*
DNB	*Dictionary of National Biography.*
DR	*Desperate Remedies* (NWE).
EHD	*Emma Hardy Diaries*, ed. R.H. Taylor.
EL	F.E. Hardy, *The Early Life of Thomas Hardy 1840–1891.*
ELH	Emma Lavinia Hardy (née Gifford).
FBP	F.B. Pinion, *Thomas Hardy: His Life and Friends.*
FEH	Florence Emily Hardy (née Dugdale).
FMC	*Far from the Madding Crowd* (NWE).
G1	R. Gittings, *Young Thomas Hardy.*
G2	R. Gittings, *The Older Hardy.*
GND	*A Group of Noble Dames* (Alan Sutton, 1986).
HBH	'How I Built Myself a House', *Chamber's Journal*, 18 March 1865, pp. 161–4.

HC	F.B. Pinion, *A Hardy Companion.*
HE	*The Hand of Ethelberta* (NWE).
HPU	E. von Hartmann, *Philosophy of the Unconscious,* tr. W.C. Coupland.
HS	*Human Shows* (CP).
ILH	*An Indiscretion in the Life of an Heiress,* ed. T. Coleman.
ILN	*Illustrated London News.*
JOB	J.O. Bailey, *The Poetry of Thomas Hardy: A Handbook and Commentary.*
L	*A Laodicean* (NWE).
LEF	*Letters of Emma and Florence Hardy,* ed. M. Millgate.
LLI	*Life's Little Ironies* (Alan Sutton, 1987).
LN	*The Literary Notebooks of Thomas Hardy,* ed. L.A. Björk.
LUC	Lucian, *Satirical Sketches,* tr. P. Turner.
LW	*Life and Work of Thomas Hardy,* ed. M. Millgate.
LY	F.E. Hardy, *The Later Years of Thomas Hardy 1892–1928.*
M	M. Millgate, *Thomas Hardy: A Biography.*
MAT1	J.S. Cox, *Thomas Hardy: Materials.*
MAT2	J.S. Cox, *Thomas Hardy: More Materials.*
MC	*The Mayor of Casterbridge* (NWE).
MCN	M. Millgate, *Thomas Hardy: His Career as a Novelist.*
MSS	M. Seymour-Smith, *Hardy.*
NWE	New Wessex Edition (Macmillan).
OED	*Oxford English Dictionary.*
ORFW	*One Rare Fair Woman,* ed. E. Hardy and F.B. Pinion.
P	R.L. Purdy, *Thomas Hardy: A Bibliographical Study.*
PBE	*A Pair of Blue Eyes* (NWE).
PN	*Personal Notebooks of Thomas Hardy,* ed. R.H. Taylor.
PW	*Thomas Hardy's Personal Writings,* ed. H. Orel.
QC	*The Queen of Cornwall* (NWE).
RN	*The Return of the Native* (NWE).
SC	*Satires of Circumstance* (CP).
SMH	R. Gittings and J. Manton, *The Second Mrs Hardy.*
SR	Emma Hardy, *Some Recollections.*
SUP	Matthew Arnold, *Prose,* ed. R.H. Super.
TD	*Tess of the d'Urbervilles* (NWE).
TH	Thomas Hardy (1840–1928).
THJ	*Thomas Hardy Journal.*
THYB	*Thomas Hardy Year Book.*
TL	*Time's Laughingstocks* (CP).
TLS	*Times Literary Supplement.*
TM	*The Trumpet-Major* (NWE).
TT	*Two on a Tower* (NWE).
UGT	*Under the Greenwood Tree* (NWE).
W	*The Woodlanders* (NWE).
WB	*The Well-Beloved* (NWE).
WP	*Wessex Poems* (CP).

Introduction

In 1859, when Hardy was nineteen, Samuel Smiles published his best seller, *Self-Help*. It was all about men who had started near the bottom of the social scale, and worked their way up to the top. 'Masons and brick-layers can boast of Ben Jonson, who worked at the building of Lincoln's Inn, with a trowel in his hand and a book in his pocket.' If young Hardy ever read that sentence, he must have found it encouraging, for his father was a mason who ran a small building business. Certainly in any update of the book his own career would demand inclusion. Born in a remote country cottage, the son of a village builder and a cook, he made himself the most famous English author of his day, and was buried (for the most part) in Westminster Abbey.[1]

Apart from that astonishing achievement, he did nothing much out of the ordinary. A series of youthful love-affairs, a marriage that started well but ended badly, a quiet life, spent mostly in his study, a few short holidays in Europe, a heart-breaking bereavement, an unromantic but not wholly unsuccessful second marriage, a slow, sad progress through old age to death: such things are too common to be very interesting in themselves. What makes his life worth studying, as more than an *exemplum* of self-help, is its effect on his writings.

Obviously, that effect is hard to define, and varied from work to work. Neither the novels nor the poems were simple transcripts of his personal experience. They were all creative artefacts, shaping aspects of that experience in many different ways. But which aspects, and how? Those are the interesting questions, though few firm answers can be given.

To make tentative ones easier, I have focused each chapter on a single work, and divided it into two sections, one biographical, the other critical;

the first on what Hardy was doing and thinking in the run-up to publication, and the second on the work itself. Needless to say, this arrangement does not always work smoothly; for Hardy, like Wordsworth, often drew on thoughts and experiences 'from hiding-places ten years deep', and sometimes much deeper. For instance, certain childhood memories tend to recur throughout his long writing career. In such cases the current instalment of biography has had to be extended backwards, or the system otherwise modified.[2]

Here 'life' has to cover everything that went through Hardy's mind during the relevant period; not just what he did or had done to him personally, but also what he heard from other people, and especially what he read, or remembered reading. He needed no urging from Matthew Arnold in 1864 to 'know the best that has been thought and said in the world'. Instinctively, both to climb out of his class, and to equip himself as a writer, he began reading widely, and taking notes of what he read. His determined efforts towards self-education involved studying, besides English literature, the Greek and Roman classics. This was done with great difficulty in limited spare time. That he took such pains to read previous authors makes it all the more relevant to see what use he made of them.[3]

Hardy's works seem to show him processing, spontaneously and sometimes unconsciously, three types of raw material: his own first-hand experience, second-hand experience relayed to him in stories and traditions by his family and Dorset neighbours, and the products of his reading, which ranged from local newspapers to Greek tragedy. Such 'reading' must also be stretched to include his study of visual art; for this, with his habit of sketching, always inclined him to present events and feelings in pictorial terms.

And what of the mind that processed all this? In 'So Various', a poem written shortly before his death, Hardy reflected on the many different types of character that seemed to have made up his personality: 'I was all they'. His mind was equally various. But one permanent feature of his thinking was a special emphasis on knowledge. For him, like Browning's 'Grammarian', there was 'No end to learning', even when 'with the throttling hands of death at strife'. The day he died he was trying to read J.B.S. Haldane's latest book of popular science, *Possible Worlds*.[4]

This attitude to knowledge reflected a persistent sense of ignorance. Brought up as an Anglican, Hardy soon started moving towards Agnosticism in the religious sense of the word. But in a much wider sense *not knowing* was always central to his thought. 'I am utterly bewildered', he wrote in 1915, defending Herbert Spencer's theory of the Unknowable, 'to understand how the doctrine that, beyond the knowable, there must always be an unknown, can be displaced.'[5]

For convenience, I have labelled this concept of not-knowing, '*agnosia*'. The Greek word has a certain relevance, besides its linguistic link with *agnosticism*, for Thucydides once used it to describe a very Hardyan situation, where the majority opposed to a *coup d'état* at Athens did nothing to stop it, 'through not knowing one another (*dia ten allelon agnosian*)', i.e. because they did not know how few of them supported it. Hardy's fiction and poetry constantly feature similar ignorance. The plots of *Desperate Remedies* and *A Laodicean* both turn on the heroine's ignorance of the villain's parentage. In *Tess* it is the hero's ignorance of the heroine's character that precipitates the tragedy. Nearly all the 'Satires of Circumstance' tell stories of people who do not know the facts that affect them most deeply. The finest poems written after the death of Hardy's first wife are typically on the theme: 'if only I had known!' The historical characters in *The Dynasts* act like puppets, quite unconscious of what is really happening. And what happens is determined by 'It', the force that created and still runs the universe, but has no idea why.[6]

This preoccupation with *agnosia* appears even in Hardy's narrative technique. One of his favourite ploys was to prolong the reader's ignorance, not just of facts, but of identities. His novels often open with unidentified figures or objects. *Under the Greenwood Tree* begins with an unknown 'man' heard singing in the darkness; *The Return of the Native*, with a darkening landscape, and an 'old man' watching a 'moving spot' in the distance. *The Mayor of Casterbridge* starts with 'a young man and woman, the latter carrying a child', *The Woodlanders*, with 'a man' standing on an empty road, who does not know his way, and whose *agnosia* further increases the reader's. Such delaying of knowledge became almost habitual. Even when the characters in a novel have long become familiar, episodes still tend to open with an unidentified 'figure' or 'object'. Thus the fire that concludes *A Laodicean*, when all other secrets have been revealed, is started by an unnamed 'figure' that 'an eye might have noticed . . . flitting' to and fro.'[7]

Naturally, Hardy's works resulted from emotions as well as thoughts. If *agnosia* was central to his thinking, what was central to his feeling? At the end of the twentieth century, the answer generally assumed is, women. Certainly much of his fiction and poetry was about sexual love, increasingly in protest against Victorian prudery and the conventional view of marriage. Certainly throughout his life relationships with women were of crucial importance to him. Like most men, perhaps, he evidently needed some such relationship to stimulate his creativity.

But there was another notable feature of his emotional make-up which was far more individual: a special feeling for animals. This has often been dismissed as an amiable weakness, a neurotic symptom, or, in the case of his dogs and cats, a displacement-reaction to childlessness. It was actually a key-element in his personality, instinctive in childhood, but soon justified intellectually by Darwinism. As he explained in 1910: 'the most far-reaching consequence of the establishment of the common origin of all species is ethical . . . it logically involved a re-adjustment of altruistic morals by enlarging, as a *necessity of rightness*, the application of what has been called 'The Golden Rule' beyond the area of mere mankind to that of the whole animal kingdom.'[8]

Hardy has now come to be admired instead of vilified for pioneering what Matthew Arnold mocked as 'the great sexual insurrection of the Anglo-Teutonic race'. He was still more ahead of his time as a champion of animal rights. But he had no illusions on the subject. One reason he gave for his general pessimism was 'the tremendous responsibility thrust upon us – an impossibility almost, of doing right' by animals 'according to our new lights'.[9]

1

'How I Built Myself a House'

Building was in Hardy's blood. He was born (2 June 1840) in a house built by his great-grandfather, where his father still carried on the family building business. He himself became an architect, and went on to apply his structural instincts to verse-forms, fictional plots, and a massive historical drama. His writings illustrated what Matthew Arnold, following Goethe, thought the mark of the professional artist: '*Architectonicè* in the highest sense; that power of execution, which creates, forms, and constitutes'. Hardy's first surviving poem, 'Domicilium', a blank-verse description of his home written in his late teens, already showed an interest in structure and proportion, with its three six-line sections rounded off by one of eighteen lines.[1]

At twenty-five, he published his first piece of prose fiction, 'How I Built Myself a House'. About twenty years later he turned fiction into fact, when he designed and supervised the building, by his father and brother, of Max Gate, just outside Dorchester. But his first constructive act, one might say, had been to make his parents marry one another, less than five and a half months before his birth. Neither his mother, Jemima Hand, nor his father, Thomas Hardy Senior, was keen on the arrangement, though it created a good home for Thomas Hardy Junior.[2]

'Hardy's Cottage', as it is now called, still looks like the long, thatched, three-chimneyed building of his own pencil sketch, 'Higher Bockhampton, T. Hardy's Birthplace.' But the 'wilder scene' of the Heath behind it, as described in the third section of 'Domicilium', has been destroyed by the Forestry Commission. To imagine his childhood environment, we must picture a small island of family culture, linked to a scattered village community, on the edge of an empty wilderness. The immediate household included Mary Hardy, Hardy's widowed paternal grandmother, and eventually three other children: Mary, born 1841, Henry, 1851, and Katharine (Kate), 1856. Hardy's uncle, John Hardy, lived close by in Bockhampton, and in Puddletown, about $2\frac{1}{2}$ miles across the Heath, lived an assortment of aunts, uncles, and cousins.[3]

From his father Hardy inherited a gift for music as well as building. His grandfather had played the cello, his father was a violinist, his uncle James a cellist, and all three had belonged to the Stinsford Church 'choir', which provided both vocal and instrumental music for the services, and also played secular music in the neighbourhood for dances and celebrations. Hardy soon learned to play the violin too, and to 'tweedle from notation', as he put it, 'hundreds of jigs and country dance tunes that he found in his father's and grandfather's old books.'[4]

From his mother, Jemima Hardy, he seems to have got a tendency to pessimism, and a taste for reading. Brought up in extreme poverty, she had been given only a basic education. But she read all the books she could find, and was resolutely ambitious for her son. It was doubtless because of her that Hardy could read 'almost before he could walk'; and when, at eight, he started school, she gave him three books that profoundly affected his later writings: Johnson's *Rasselas*, Dryden's translation of Virgil, and an English version of Bernardin de Saint-Pierre's *Paul et Virginie* (1787). *Rasselas* offered him a model for a plot based on a series of disillusionments. The *Aeneid*, besides supplying many thoughts, quotations, and epigraphs, would suggest a key element in the plot of his first published novel. It also contained an incident that he would often adapt for his own love stories.[5]

Paul and Virginia was more than a pastoral tale of boy-and-girl love in an island-paradise, modelled on the Greek novel, *Daphnis and Chloe*. It was also a tragedy of inter-class love. Virginia's mother had been disowned and disinherited by her family for marrying beneath her. So, as it happened, had Jemima's. Paul's peasant-mother has been made pregnant and then deserted by a gentleman. The idyllic love-affair between Paul and Virginia ended in tragedy, because Virginia's snobbish aunt took her off to Paris to make a lady of her, and stop her marrying an illegitimate peasant. Paul's hopes of climbing up to Virginia's new class by studying to become a famous author, were promptly dashed by the assurance that his low birth would block every road to advancement.[6]

Paul's predicament must have seemed all too like Hardy's own just then; for he soon lost his heart to the 'lady of the manor', Mrs Martin of Kingston Maurward House, who had founded his first school at Stinsford, helped him with his reading, and grown 'passionately fond' of him. Her hugs and kisses evoked a disproportionate response. 'In fact', Hardy recalled, 'though he was only nine or ten and she must have been nearly forty, his feeling for her was almost that of a lover.'[7]

Apart from parental influences, Hardy's childhood was dominated by two things: the local church, and the natural world around him. Sunday services, regularly attended by the family, imprinted on his memory the interior of Stinsford Church, with all the details of its tombs and memorial tablets. He greatly enjoyed the music and drama of the services themselves, and on wet Sundays reproduced them at home, wearing a tablecloth, standing on a chair, and making everyone say that 'Tommy would have to be a parson, being obviously no good for any practical pursuit'. Though he gradually came to find Anglican theology incredible, he never lost his affection for the Church, and the Bible strongly influenced all his writing.[8]

As a small boy, he was far from hyperactive. The doctor who delivered him thought at first that he was dead. He disproved that diagnosis by surviving for nearly eighty-eight years; but he was initially undersized and sickly, taking life at a slower tempo than the average child. Wandering by himself over a small area of countryside, he got to know it intimately: how it looked in different weathers, how individual plants and trees sounded in the wind. Having no television to watch, he watched his natural environment, and found in it the kind of expressiveness that he observed in human faces.[9]

It was, of course, animal life that he watched with the greatest interest, and felt closest to. Unlike Heracles, who strangled snakes in his cradle, Hardy was once found in his, with 'a large snake curled up upon his chest, comfortably asleep like himself.' The picture was symbolic of a lifelong feeling, also suggested by his childhood memory of 'lying on a bank of thyme or camomile with the grasshoppers leaping over him.' He was fascinated by the spiders and sparrows in the thatch above his bedroom; and he never forgot the painful sensation of holding in his hand the starved corpse of a fieldfare that his father had casually thrown a stone at, 'possibly not meaning to hit it'. That kind of pain would become familiar. Taken briefly to London by his mother at eight or nine, he was horrified by the 'cries of ill-treated animals' at Smithfield cattle-market.[10]

His mother's ambitions for him demanded a better education than she had had. So after a year at the village school he was sent, at ten, to Dorchester, first to the British School, run by a Nonconformist society, and then to an independent 'commercial academy' started by his teacher, Isaac Last, where at thirteen he started taking Latin as an extra subject. In both cases he had to walk six miles there and back every day, an experience that possibly gave roads their special importance in his novels.[11]

His Dorchester school days (1850–56) gave him a new perspective. From rural isolation he had passed to a busy county town, from a timeless, static world to one in contact, through newsagents and bookshops, with all the latest developments, especially since the recent arrival of the railway. He was also made vividly conscious of the whole great sweep of time. At Bockhampton, old churches and prehistoric tumuli had spoken vaguely to him of the distant past; but Dorchester was still in outline a Roman city, with its Roman amphitheatre at Maumbury Rings, and Roman remains everywhere, making Latin seem anything but a dead language. The place also opened a window on to contemporary history, with a visit from Prince

Albert in 1849, demonstrations against 'Papal Aggression' in 1850, and
local involvement, through the Barracks, with the Crimean War from the
end of 1853. The Barracks had a special appeal for a boy with an artist's
eye and a musician's ear, as the source of colourful processions and military bands. There was more public drama when the Assize Judges arrived;
and in front of the prison occasional hangings took place, watched on one
occasion by an estimated three or four thousand people, from a total
population (1841)of only 3249. Not surprisingly, Hardy went along too.

At school, though 'always ready to help the other boys with their les-
sons', Hardy seems to have made no special friends. He found girls more
congenial. In retrospect, he rated himself a late developer 'in virility . . . he
was a child till he was sixteen'. But from fourteen onwards he fell in love,
more or less 'madly', with a long succession of girls, including village
beauties in Stinsford, cousins in Puddletown, and a 'total stranger' on
horseback who once smiled at him in Dorchester.[12]

After an 'Academy', the next stage in upward mobility, for a small
builder's son, was obviously to train as an architect. So the Stinsford vicar
must have thought when in 1856, with Hardy and his mother in the congregation, he preached a sermon against the presumption of using architecture as a ladder up to the professional classes. That year Hardy had
been articled to a Dorchester architect called John Hicks, who happened
to have 'read some Greek'. Hardy's work as an apprentice, mostly survey-
ing and measuring churches due to be restored, left him time to continue
his classical education, with Hicks's approval and help, though he had to
do most of his reading 'between five and eight in the morning before he
left home for the office.' He started teaching himself Greek, and set to
work on the *Iliad*, which still studying Virgil, Horace, and Ovid. Latin
became so familiar to him that he 'often caught himself soliloquizing' in
it, while walking his daily six miles. And an argument about Infant Baptism with a Baptist fellow apprentice called Bastow did wonders for his
koine – making him buy a new Greek Testament, and comb its text 'at
night' for useful debating-points next day.[13]

The cost in sleep and energy of all this spare-time scholarship was high;
but he got some help and encouragement from the self-taught philologist
and dialect poet, William Barnes, who lived next door to Hicks's office;
and a great deal more from a young man eight years older than himself,
who became his closest friend, Horace Moule. Horace was a son of the
Vicar of Fordington, on the south side of Dorchester. Though a fine
classical scholar, he had left both Oxford and Cambridge without a
degree, to become a freelance writer of reviews and articles in periodicals,
especially the *Saturday Review*. He would later become an alcoholic, but
then he seemed everything that Hardy most admired: musical, brilliant,
scholarly, charming, up to date with the latest thought, and in with the
literary set in London.

From about 1857 he became Hardy's unofficial supervisor, lending him
books, and generally directing his educational programme. Thus Hardy

started reading the *Saturday Review*, a new Liberal weekly sceptical in tone, and generally critical of the status quo. Within the next two years he also read three potentially subversive books, Mantell's *Wonders of Geology* (1838), J.S. Mill's *On Liberty*, and Darwin's *Origin of Species* (both 1859).

But reading, as he recalled much later, was only one part of his 'triple existence' just then. He was juggling with the 'three balls of architecture, scholarship, and dance-fiddling'. After 'reading the *Iliad*, the *Aeneid*, or the Greek Testament from six to eight in the morning, he would work at Gothic architecture all day, and then . . . rush off with his fiddle under his arm', sometimes with his father and uncle, to play dance music at some country festivity, 'not returning sometimes till nearly dawn'.[14]

In these conditions, while busy on 'the *Agamemnon* or the *Oedipus*', Hardy asked Moule if he ought to read some more Greek plays, but was sensibly advised to concentrate for the moment on architecture, as his only likely source of income. It was not the advice he had hoped for, but he followed it. He 'almost dropped' Greek language from then on, though he returned to the Greek dramatists later (doubtless reading them in translation with occasional references to the Greek text), and acquired 'substantial knowledge' of them. But for Moule's advice, he felt he 'might have ended his life as a Don', for he had 'every instinct of a scholar'.[15]

That he would end up as a famous author must then have seemed out of the question. But he had already started writing 'Domicilium', to mourn the death of his grandmother in 1857. She had been his chief source of family and general history, and of many stories and folk-songs. Though he would call the poem 'Wordsworthian', its blank-verse sections were possibly suggested by Tennyson's 'Tears, idle tears', published ten years before. There the stanzas were linked by a six-word refrain, and Hardy may have meant to link his quasi-stanzas by final lines that rhymed with one another, though only the first two did so.[16]

By 1860, when he finalized the poem, his thoughts were turning from versification to his immediate prospects in architecture. Having finished his apprenticeship, and then started working as Hicks's paid assistant, he decided to get more training and experience in London. He had no job to go to, but off he went (17 April 1862), with two letters of introduction and a return ticket (but no violin), to see what he could find there. Luckily a fashionable architect called Arthur Blomfield needed 'a young Gothic draughtsman who could restore and design churches', and Hardy was taken on. He found lodgings in Kilburn, still a semi-rural district, liked and joined the parish church, and travelled daily by horse-drawn omnibus to work in Blomfield's office, first near Trafalgar Square, then on the first floor of 8 Adelphi Terrace (now displaced by Shell-Mex House), overlooking the Thames.[17]

He soon returned to his music and his self-education. He sang tenor in Blomfield's office-choir. Instead of fiddling for country-dances he danced himself at Willis's Rooms in St James's. Then he bought an old violin, and fiddled tunes from Italian operas with a pianist fellow-lodger. He went to

the opera two or three times a week; and whenever in later life he heard
music from Verdi's *Il Trovatore*, it reminded him of this first year in London, when 'he was strong and vigorous and enjoyed his life immensely'.[18]

Blomfield, whose father had published editions of Greek poets, including Aeschylus and Euripides, encouraged Hardy's interest in classical and
English literature. Over the next few years, besides reading Dickens,
Thackeray, and Trollope, and a lot more Virgil and Horace, he put himself
through a course of English poets, possibly including the then unfashion-
able Donne. He particularly studied Shakespeare, both in the text and, as
often as he could, on the stage. Shelley impressed him deeply as a verbal
musician, and as a revolutionary. Against the title of *The Revolt of Islam*, in
a copy bought in 1866, Hardy wrote 'Hyde Park – morning' That may have
indicated, not just when and where he read it, but a mental association
with the Hyde Park riots of 23 July that year, started by the Reform
League, whose headquarters were immediately below Blomfield's office.[19]

Of contemporary poets, he responded most to Tennyson, Browning,
Meredith, and Swinburne. The first two then represented the poetical
establishment, the last two the maverick avant-garde. Meredith's *Modern
Love*, published during Hardy's first year in London, must have appealed
by the 'modernity' of its imagery, diction, and sexual ethics. Swinburne
shared Shelley's attraction of being a revolutionary – especially if Hardy
knew that the Reform League had asked Swinburne to represent them in
Parliament; and his *Atalanta in Calydon* (1865) doubtless interested Hardy
by its imitation of Greek tragedy, its seductive verbal music, and its protest
against 'The supreme evil, God.' This last, though quite in the spirit of
Euripides, had a new meaning after two works had come out in 1859: Darwin's *Origin of Species* (of which Hardy was 'among the earliest acclaimers')
and Fitzgerald's *Omar Khayyám*. In 1866 *Poems and Ballads* added to Swinburne's other charms an uninhibited attitude to sex, and an unpopular-
ity with the critics which won Hardy's instant sympathy. Perhaps it was
partly a wish to champion the underdog that made him walk through
'the crowded London streets' reading Swinburne, to the 'imminent risk of
being knocked down.'[20]

Besides this literary self-education, Hardy also taught himself some art-
history. Reading Ruskin's *Modern Painters*, he thought of writing art-
criticism for periodicals, as Thackeray had done in his youth. In 1862 he
went daily to look at the 3, 370 paintings collected in South Kensington for
the second International Exhibition. In 1863 he started a notebook systematically distinguishing 'Schools of Painting', and in 1865 began visiting the
National Gallery for 'twenty minutes after lunch' each day, to concentrate
on the work of one artist per visit.[21]

But his real interest was poetry, and he was busy writing poems himself.
One of them, 'Amabel' (1865), evidently reflected his shock when, calling
at Mrs Martin's town house soon after he arrived in London, he had
found 'the lady of his dreams – Alas' looking her full age, then over fifty.
When these poems were all 'rejected by editors', he thought of 'combining

poetry and the church' by becoming 'a curate in a country village'. Since that would mean getting a degree, he started saving up money to go to Cambridge. But apart from the practical snags about this 'visionary' project, there was the 'conscientious' one that, though still a regular churchgoer, he was ceasing to believe in orthodox theology.[22]

Meanwhile, though in 1863 he had won two small prizes in architectural competitions, he was not much enjoying his work, which was mostly mechanical, except for one bizarre task: supervising 'by the light of flare-lamps' the nocturnal removal of skeletons from a churchyard, to make way for a railway cutting. Feeling generally depressed, he found a little cold comfort in Stoicism. On the first day of 1865 Horace Moule had given him Long's new translation of Marcus Aurelius, inscribed with these words from the text: 'This is the chief thing: Be not perturbed: for all things are according to the nature of the universal'. In its context, the sentence ended: 'and in a little time thou wilt be nobody and nowhere, like Hadrianus and Augustus'. Faced in 1886 with the 'depressing' doubt whether Max Gate had been worth building, Hardy would remind himself of that sentence, and he kept the book by his bed all his life. Pater's *Marius* moved from Aurelian Stoicism towards Christianity; perhaps Hardy, moving away from it, was looking for a substitute religion.[23]

Ten pages before Moule's sentence Hardy may have noticed a more positive piece of advice: 'Within is the fountain of good, and it will ever bubble up, if thou wilt ever dig.' Anyway he kept on digging, and soon came up with a tiny nugget of success. Having established himself as the literary expert among Blomfield's 'pupils and assistants', he wrote for that captive audience a satirical sketch about architects and their clients. It went down so well that he sent it to *Chambers's Journal*, entitled, 'How I Built Myself a House'. Accepted, for a fee of £3.15s, it came out in March 1865. It was his first breakthrough.[24]

The sketch followed a comic formula first popularized in *Punch* by Douglas Jerrold twenty years before, in *Mrs Caudle's Curtain Lectures.* Mrs Caudle, personifying the bossy and unreasonable wife, demanded 'a nice little house somewhere at Brixton' or some other suburb; but once settled in the house she wanted, complained of being 'buried alive', of black-beetles, and of her husband's failings as a father: 'Much you think of the dear children'. Hardy's Mrs Caudle, renamed Sophia to stress her lack of wisdom, was equally critical of her husband's efforts to get a new house built for them. When it was already marked out on the ground, she insisted on lengthening the drawing-room by at least four feet; and when they had moved in, and gone to bed, delivered an authentic 'curtain-lecture' about her husband's lack of feeling for his 'poor little children': 'Why *did* you put the nursery on the second floor?'[25]

Jerrold's formula was oddly combined with Johnson's *Rasselas*. There the bored Prince and Princess escape from the Happy Valley to seek happiness elsewhere, but never find it. Tired of their 'Highly Desirable

Semi-Detached Villa', John and Sophia 'escape from it' to build a house which will make them both 'peculiarly happy ever afterwards', and cost 'just enough to fitly inaugurate the new happiness.' But the project merely brings out their incompatibility. The moment they start exchanging ideas about the arrangement of rooms – 'We soon found that there was no such thing as fitting our ideas together, do what we would.' The nature of their relationship becomes clear when Sophia, knowing John's terror of heights, shames him into climbing to the top of the scaffolding: 'My wife was picking daisies a little distance off, apparently in a state of complete indifference as to whether I was on the scaffold, at the foot of it, or in St George's Hospital.'[26]

The short piece is quite funny, but the jokes hint at Hardy's serious assumptions, not just about marriage, but about the inevitability of disappointment. Finding that the late addition of a porch would block a window, thus creating 'a trifling darkness, or rather gloom', which 'might tend to reduce' him and his family 'to a state of chronic melancholy', John bought a reflector 'advertised to throw sunlight into any nook almost'. But he found that 'the gloom was for all time, the patent reflector, *naturally enough*, sending the spot of light against the opposite wall, where it was not wanted, and leaving none about the landing, where it was.'[27]

2

The Poor Man and the Lady

Any euphoria induced by publication in March 1865 had evaporated by June. 'My 25th birthday', Hardy wrote in his notebook. 'Not very cheerful. Feel as if I had lived a long time, and done very little. Walked about by moonlight in the evening. Wondered what woman, if any, I should be thinking about in five years' time'. He was lonely in London, worried about his future, and approaching the end of an unsatisfactory love-affair with a Dorset girl called Eliza Nicholls, who had been in London as a lady's maid. Having calculated the cost, in time and money, of getting to Cambridge, he now gave up the country-curate idea. As he told his sister Mary, it would take him at least seven years to get a degree, and it seemed 'absurd to live on now with such a remote object in view'. But what was the alternative? £3.15s.0 from *Chambers's Journal* did not go far towards earning a living as a freelance journalist. Should he try writing blank-verse plays for the theatre? With that in mind, he gave himself a bit of stage-experience by appearing as an extra in a Covent Garden pantomime (December 1866). But the playwright soon went the way of the country curate.[1]

Eliza, to whom he had been more or less engaged, served to inspire some poems, notably the 'She to Him' sonnet-sequence (1866). But she was evidently not the woman he was looking for, and the relationship ended sadly in 1867. His love-affair with religion had also come to an end. Reading Newman's *Apologia* in 1865, with 'a great desire to be convinced by him', Hardy had loved his style, and his 'excellent chain of reasoning' from 'converging probabilities', but could find 'no first link' in it; 'Poor Newman! His gentle childish faith in revelation and tradition must have made him a very charming character'.[2]

Depression soon led to physical symptoms. By the summer of 1867 Hardy was looking ill, and feeling utterly exhausted. No doubt it was partly caused, as he thought, by the 'stench from the mud at low water' during office-hours, followed by six hours' reading every night at his new lodgings in Westbourne Park Villas, Paddington. Such a life-style naturally made him pine for his country home, and Blomfield himself advised him to go back there for a while to recuperate. So, as Hicks needed someone to help him with church-restoration, Hardy returned to Bockhampton in July, and within a few weeks was 'completely restored'.[3]

He had recently jotted down this thought in his notebook: 'The defects of a class are more perceptible to the class immediately below it than to itself'. He had also written a poem called 'Heiress and Architect'. Taken together, the note and the title might suggest that Hardy was now fantasizing about a love-affair, not with a lady's maid, but with a lady. Actually the poem parodied Tennyson's 'Palace of Art', in the spirit of *Rasselas*. Far from loving the Heiress, the Architect systematically demolished her dream of happiness in an ideal home that she proposed to build. Thus the comic theme of 'How I Built Myself a House' was transposed into a minor key.[4]

Still, the idea of a love-affair between an heiress and an architect must also have been in Hardy's mind by 1867, for within a few weeks of returning to Bockhampton, he started writing a novel finally entitled, *The Poor Man and the Lady; By the Poor Man*. Though it was never published, and no manuscript survives, the gist of its plot is known: a young Dorsetshire peasant, trained as a draughtsman and then employed by an eminent architect, falls in love with the daughter of the wealthy squire. When Hardy boiled the novel down into a magazine story eleven years later, he gave it a title reminiscent of the early poem: *An Indiscretion in the Life of an Heiress*. But by then the Architect had turned, like Hardy, into an author.[5]

As he realized later, his 'fitful yet mechanical and monotonous existence . . . in London lodgings' had prevented him from thinking clearly what he wanted to write. Back at home he was 'almost suddenly' able to ask himself the 'practical' question, what did he really know about? Two things, he decided: 'West-country life in its less explored recesses and the life of an isolated student cast upon the billows of London, with no protection but his brains'. That should give him quite enough material for 'a striking socialistic novel'. Why socialistic? – because in 1867, when the second Reform Act gave the vote to urban working classes, such a novel should hit the current mood of revolt against the social order, as demonstrated by the recent Hyde Park Riots. What better moment could there be to highlight the 'defects' of the upper classes, as perceived by the lower? Before leaving London in July Hardy may have seen Tom Robertson's topical comedy, *Caste*, which had opened that April. This satirized class-prejudice with a story of inter-class marriage – between the son of an unbelievably snobbish Marquise, and the daughter of a stage-Cockney drunkard, full of 'the wrongs of the workin' classes.' Hardy meant to treat the issue more realistically.[6]

The woman who helped to stimulate his creativity this time was one of his Puddletown cousins, Tryphena Sparks, then sixteen. She seems to have lived up to her Greek-sounding name, with its hint of softness and delicacy, and been pretty, bright, and amusing. He saw a lot of her that summer, though the theory that he promptly had a son by her sounds more picturesque than factual. But the relationship was clearly important to him and, with Tryphena as current Muse, he got his novel finished by June 1868. Next month, with a letter of introduction from Horace Moule, he sent it off to Alexander Macmillan, co-founder of the publishing firm. His own covering letter implied that the novel expressed 'strong feeling' against the 'upper classes', though 'inserted edgewise so to say; half concealed beneath ambiguous expressions, or at any rate written as if they were not the chief aims of the book (even though they may be)'. This, he hoped, would ensure that members of those classes would not 'throw down [the] volume in disgust'. He also implied that 'the main incidents of the novel' were concerned with 'questions of manners, rising in the world, &c'.[7]

Macmillan replied with a long, generally encouraging letter: 'If this is your first book I think you ought to go on.' But he was not prepared to publish it, thinking the satire on the upper classes so exaggerated that they would indeed 'throw down the book in disgust.' He enclosed further comments from John Morley, then editor of the *Fortnightly Review*, who believed in 'firmness' as a prime quality of good writing, and whose *On Compromise* (1874) would argue the need to call a spade a spade. Yet even he, while finding the novel 'very curious and original', and Hardy's writing 'strong and fresh', thought 'some of the scenes so wildly extravagant that they read like some clever lad's dream', and the story 'too loosely' constructed. A third opinion came from the poet of *Modern Love*, George Meredith, who read the MS for another firm, Chapman and Hall, and Hardy was invited to meet him, though not then told his name. Meredith was encouraging too, but warned Hardy 'that the press would be about his ears like hornets if he published the manuscript', and advised him to put it aside for a while, and write another novel 'with a purely artistic purpose' and 'a more complicated "plot"'. After trying one more publisher, Tinsley (who was only prepared to publish if insured in cash against loss), Hardy reluctantly took Meredith's advice, and let his first novel remain unpublished – though not uncannibalized for later ones.[8]

Judgement *in absentia*, on hearsay evidence, may be legally 'unsafe', and criticizing an unpublished novel in the absence of any manuscript has obvious dangers too. But enough is known of this work from Edmund Gosse's synopsis of the plot, as told him by Hardy in 1921, and from the 'Indiscretion of an Heiress' (1878), to make reasonable guesses at the novel's sources.[9]

The nearest Hardy himself had come to the *Poor Man*'s type of love-affair had been his 'earliest passion' for Mrs Martin; but author and hero had more than that in common. Their surnames, Hardy and 'Strong', were almost synonyms. Both trained as draughtsmen and joined the offices of eminent architects. Both won competition-prizes, with disappointing results. Hardy had been awarded an RIBA Silver Medal, but deprived of the cash-prize that should have gone with it, for inadequate treatment in his essay of a topic not originally prescribed. Will Strong had his award publicly retracted in a scene that Macmillan thought incredible.[10]

If, as seems true, the *Poor Man* and the 'Indiscretion' had roughly the same plot, there were several more links between Hardy and Strong. Hardy's home had been built by his great-grandfather, Strong's by his grandfather. Strong went to a church containing a marble monument with 'a winged skull and two cherubim', like the one in Stinsford Church. When the heiress broke off their relationship, Strong walked blindly from the West End to Kilburn, where Hardy had lived in 1862, and from 'the hill beyond' looked back on the lights of central London, as Hardy must often have done. Earlier in the story, the heroine got mortar on the trowel-handle while laying a foundation stone, and whispered to Will Strong, 'Take it, take it'. Hardy had heard the Crown Princess of Germany use those words for much the same reasons to Blomfield, when laying a foundation-stone at New Windsor in 1865.[11]

But the personal elements in *The Poor Man and the Lady* were evidently organized on lines suggested by Hardy's reading. Here poets were more important than novelists. Kingsley's *Alton Locke* (1850) had featured an educated working man turned Chartist, who made inflammatory speeches to his fellow-workers. George Eliot's *Felix Holt the Radical* (1866) was an eloquent left-wing politician. Hardy's Will Strong also became a radical, and held forth passionately to a crowd in Trafalgar Square. But there the resemblance to previous novels ended.[12]

The 'poor man–lady' formula, though first put in Hardy's mind by *Paul and Virginia*, must have affected the novel chiefly through Tennyson and Mrs Browning. The basic situation in *Maud* (1855) was thus summarized by the lover: 'Your father has wealth well-gotten, and I am nameless and poor.' Maud, like Hardy's heroine, was driven to her death by the conflict between her rich family and her poor lover. Hardy's plot came even closer to that of Tennyson's 'Aylmer's Field' (1864). There the lover, rejected by the heiress's snobbish parents, tried to qualify for her hand by solitary work in London, cheered only by a secret correspondence with her, until her parents stopped that too. Losing at last her will to live, she died of 'some low fever'. Hardy, having taken medical advice, made his heiress die less predictably of a pulmonary haemorrhage.[13]

In the 'Indiscretion' Will Strong became Egbert Mayne (Hardy strength persisting as might and main?), and the heiress was Geraldine' – presumably her original name, from 'Lady Geraldine's Courtship: A Romance of the Age' (1844), by Elizabeth Barrett, later Mrs Browning. This was a story (told mostly by the hero) of a 'poor poet', 'born of English peasants', 'Quite low-born! self educated!', who fell in love with 'an earl's daughter'.

literally'. In fact, he adapted that advice quite sensibly to his own situation. To justify the risk of switching from architecture to authorship he needed not just to get his next novel published, but to make it a money-spinner. When he had first started going to London theatres, he had possibly seen C.H. Hazlewood's popular melodrama, *Lady Audley's Secret* (1863), from the novel by M.E. Braddon (1862), and realized the commercial possibilities of the Sensational Novel. This new genre was also being exploited by Wilkie Collins and Mrs Henry Wood. A Victorian version of the eighteenth-century Gothic novel, it specialized in complicated plots full of crime, mystery, and horror. Like the twentieth-century detective story, it dealt with a largely artificial world, remote from ordinary life. Meredith had recommended a novel with a 'purely artistic purpose' and a 'more complicated plot'. In Hardy's financial circumstances, his best bet was probably to do exactly what he did: try to jump on to the Sensational bandwagon.[3]

So the novel that he started writing that autumn was as sensational as he could make it. To save time and effort, he recycled extracts from the *Poor Man* manuscript and, to make concentration easier, returned to Bockhampton in February 1870. By then most of Hicks's outstanding work had been dealt with, and Tryphena had moved to a teacher training college in London. Soon after he got home, Hardy was asked by Crickmay to 'take a plan and particulars' of one more job undertaken by Hicks, the rebuilding of a church near Boscastle, Cornwall, at a place called St Juliot. Though 'struck' by the name's 'romantic sound' (especially to the ear of a potential Romeo), Hardy refused to interrupt his writing just then. But by March he had practically finished the novel, and sent all but the last three or four chapters to Alexander Macmillan. Two days later (7 March 1870) he trailed off 'reluctantly' to St Juliot. It was a tiresome journey, which meant getting up at 4 a.m., walking 'by starlight . . . armed with sketch-book, measuring tape and rule' to Dorchester station, 'changing trains many times and waiting at stations' between there and Launceston, and then hiring a dogcart for the last sixteen or seventeen miles. He reached St Juliot, a tiny village on the Atlantic coast, well after dark, and rang the Rectory doorbell.[4]

From then on the place lived up to its name. He was welcomed, not by the Rector, who was in bed with gout, but by a 'very attractive' girl of about his own age (actually five months younger) with 'golden curls and rosy colour', dressed 'in brown'. She was Emma Lavinia Gifford, the Rector's sister-in-law; and even her middle name must have seemed promising: Virgil's Lavinia married the hero of the *Aeneid*.[5]

Born in Plymouth, the daughter of John Gifford, an alcoholic ex-solicitor from Bristol, she had been brought up in what she called 'a most intellectual' home. It was also a very snobbish one, especially after 1860, when the Giffords suddenly came down in the world, because John's mother's capital, on which they had always relied, turned out at her death to have been mostly spent. To save money, they had moved from Plymouth to Cornwall. Emma's sister Helen had married the elderly Rector of St Juliot, the Revd. Caddell Holder, and Emma had gone to live with them, and help with the work of the parish. Though she enjoyed living in that 'romantic spot', they all felt the lack of '*equals*' in the neighbourhood, and the sisters looked back regretfully to the 'life of quiet cultivated leisure' at Plymouth.[6]

The tastes and accomplishments acquired by Emma in those happier days included a love of reading, writing poems and stories, sketching, singing, piano-playing, and riding her 'beloved mare' Fanny in a 'wild fearless fashion', self-consciously picturesque with her 'hair floating on the wind.' Hardy must have found her irresistible, if sometimes tantalizingly unpredictable. She saw him first as a man 'much older than he was', with a 'yellowish' beard, a 'rather shabby great coat', and 'quite a business appearance', but soon afterwards as 'a perfectly new subject of study and delight', and finally as what Coventry Patmore would have called her 'predestinated mate' – though he would not long see her as the 'Angel in the House'. Of his three days at St Juliot, the first went on 'drawing and measuring' in the church, the second on driving with Emma and her sister to Boscastle, Tintagel, and the Penpethy slate-quarries 'with a view to the church-roofing'. On the third he went with Emma alone to the precipitous 'Beeny Cliff', 'She on horseback' and he walking beside her. After a 'Dawn . . . Adieu' to Emma he started home next morning, spent one night at Bockhampton, and then returned to Weymouth, to work on his St Juliot drawings.[7]

There, in April, he got his manuscript back from Macmillans: 'far too sensational . . . for us to think of publishing'. He promptly sent it off to the publishers of *Lady Audley*, Tinsley Brothers. They offered to publish it, when completed and slightly altered, if Hardy paid them £75 in advance. Thus encouraged, he gave up his job with Crickmay, and moved to London, where he supported himself by occasional work for Blomfield, and for another architect called Raphael Brandon. He also saw a good deal of Horace Moule who, after teaching for three years at Marlborough, had suddenly left the school for reasons unknown, but probably alcoholic. Otherwise Hardy drifted 'desultorily and dreamily' about London, mostly in museums and picture-galleries, doubtless thinking about Emma.[8]

They had been writing frequently to one another, and in August 1870 he returned to St Juliot, and spent three weeks of that very hot summer there with Emma, mostly out of doors. Despite what has been said of a Rectory conspiracy to get Emma married off, they both seem to have been genuinely in love, and both would look back on that period as a kind of golden age in their lives. Nor was Emma the type to be easily pressurized into marriage. 'When hints about marrying fell upon me from the officious,' she wrote, 'I would say "I prefer my mare to any husband"'. But Hardy evidently had the edge even on Fanny.[9]

Some time that autumn Hardy revised and finished his novel. He was then back at Bockhampton, where any hopes of literary success or marriage were doubtless discouraged by Jemima, for in October he noted: 'Mother's notion, & also mine: That a figure stands in our van with arm uplifted, to knock us back from any pleasant prospect we indulge in as probable.' But in December the novel went off to the publishers, in a fair copy written by Emma. Tinsley's reader now thought 'the book ought to sell', and Hardy finally produced his £75, out of savings totalling £123, perhaps originally meant to get him a Cambridge degree.[10]

On 25 March 1871 *Desperate Remedies* was published anonymously, and Hardy moved back to Weymouth to do some more work for Crickmay. The next month his 'mother's notion' was amply justified. After quite good reviews in the *Athenaeum* and the *Morning Post*, his novel was sternly denounced by the *Spectator*, for its immorality. Hardy was too upset to notice the incidental praise of the comic rustics, the fire, and the use of 'scenic and atmospheric effects' to suggest a 'corresponding mental condition'. Presumably the reviewer only meant to protest against the Sensational Novel itself, and urge this anonymous author not to 'prostitute' his obvious 'powers' to 'idle prying into the ways of wickedness'. But Hardy, reading the review 'as he sat on a stile . . . on his way back to Bockhampton', felt 'knocked back' from all he had hoped for, and 'wished that he were dead.'[11]

The most obvious links between Hardy's life and *Desperate Remedies* were topographical. Weymouth, where he had boated, flirted, and perhaps got more deeply involved with Tryphena, became Creston, where the hero, Edward Springrove, first kissed the heroine, Cytherea Graye, in a boat. Mrs Martin's house, Kingston Maurward, which stood on a 'knap' or hill beside a lake, became Knapwater House, the home of Cytherea's employer and namesake, Miss Aldclyffe. More generally, the novel started the development of 'Wessex', the fictional region based on the real topography of Dorset and the surrounding counties, though without yet establishing a coherent system of place-names. Thus Weymouth would end up as not 'Creston' but 'Budmouth'; and though the 'county town' was already called 'Casterbridge', from the Latin *castra* (camp) or *chester* in Dorchester's name, it was not yet recognizable in detail as Dorchester itself.[12]

For Cytherea's duties as 'lady's-maid' to Miss Aldclyffe Hardy doubtless relied on what he had heard from Eliza Nicholls. The multiple causes of the inn-fire have been traced to the report of a fire near Puddletown in the *Dorset County Chronicle*. But it was first-hand experience that made architecture figure so largely in the plot. Cytherea's father was an architect, who realized John's fears in 'How I Built Myself a House' by falling to his death from a building-scaffold. Her brother Owen worked in an architect's office at Creston, where Edward Springrove was the 'head draughtsman'. Edward, according to Hardy, was modelled on a colleague in Crickmay's office; but he closely resembled his author in being 'a man of rather humble origin', a 'thorough bookworm' who knew all about Shakespeare, and 'a poet himself in a small way', who had an 'unorthodox opinion about the subordination of classes'. Edward's experience had also taught him something very like 'Mother's notion': 'he had reached the period in a young man's life when episodic pasts, with a hopeful birth and a disappointing death, have begun to accumulate, and to bear a fruit of generalities'.[13]

One scene strikingly combined two items in Hardy's visual memory, one from childhood, the other from his recent study of art. Young 'Tommy' used to sit alone on the Bockhampton stairs, waiting for the 'chromatic effect' created by 'the evening sun' on the 'Venetian red' walls. Waiting in a 'blue gloom' to be interviewed by her future employer, Cytherea notices a 'very thin line of ruddy light' under the door to the next room. When the door opens, she is dazzled by 'the blaze of the afternoon sun', 'refracted' and 'heightened' by the crimson curtains, carpet and walls. She then makes out what looks 'like a tall black figure standing in the midst of fire'. It is Miss Aldclyffe – but it is also Turner's *Angel standing in the Sun* (1846).[14]

To such extracts from experience Hardy had added material from his reading. Though he seems to have bought instead of borrowing a copy of *The Woman in White*, Wilkie Collins was not the only Sensation Novelist to influence this book; and since Hardy himself described it as after 'the Miss Braddon school', it seems more relevant to ask what use he made of her bestselling novel, which was far less melodramatic than Hazlewood's stage-version of it. When he met her in 1879 he was struck by her 'thought-creased, world-beaten face . . . and always liked' her. There were several things about *Lady Audley's Secret* that he may have liked too. Its hero, Robert Audley, had the temperament of Tennyson's 'Lotus-Eaters' and lived in Tennyson's 'Audley Court', here built in a mixture of historical styles, planned by no 'mortal architect', but by 'that good old builder – Time'. It was in Dorset that Robert fell in love with the girl he married. His best friend's library contained 'an old Greek Testament', and the novel was full of other references to things that interested Hardy, poetry, Greek, architecture, pictures, and music.[15]

Besides many casual allusions to pictures, Miss Braddon used a 'Pre-Raphaelite' portrait of Lady Audley to identify her as the wife and supposed murderess of George Talboys. The 'almost wicked look' that the painter had given to her 'pretty pouting mouth' pointed to D.G. Rossetti, a specialist in sinister female portraits, from *Borgia* onwards. Hardy, too, peppered his narrative with references to visual art. He also made ironical use of Rossetti's pictorial poem 'The Blessed Damozel' (republished in 1870, though not yet to be seen as a painting). On her first evening at Knapwater House Cytherea leans out of her bedroom window 'like another Blessed Damozel'. Rossetti's dead heroine was unhappy in Heaven, despite her proximity to 'Lady Mary' and her 'five handmaidens', because her lover was not there too. Cytherea is equally sad because Edward is not with her, but also because her elevation to this upper-class heaven involves 'servitude'. She has no wish to be a Lady's handmaiden, and relinquish her own peculiar tastes to help on the wheel of this alien establishment'.[16]

Miss Braddon also used music to support characterization. Lady Audley was a 'very brilliant pianist' whose taste for 'sombre and melancholy melodies, so opposite to her gay, frivolous character' suggested the dark complexity of her nature. But when Clara, who would marry the hero, was heard improvising 'slow harmonies of a dreamy melody' on a church organ, the 'monotonous melancholy' of [her] performance implied that her personality was more consistent, and would have 'a soothing influence' on her husband. Hardy's villain, like Miss Braddon's, was an accomplished musician. It was by playing the organ in a storm that Manston first gained power over Cytherea. His taste for 'saddening chords' hinted at his own dark secrets, and his modulation into 'the Pastoral Symphony' (surely Beethoven's Sixth, with its mixture of storm and calm) warned that his complex nature threatened her simple love. His contempt, as an organist, for Cytherea's instrument, the piano, had similar implications for their relationship.[17]

Lady Audley's secret, apart from her insanity and two attempted murders, is that she has been married before and had a son. Miss Aldclyffe's is that she has had a son, but has not been married. Lady Audley pushes her first husband down a well, and tries to stop Robert Audley's investigations into her past, by setting fire to the village inn, where he is spending the night. Manston does not actually start a fire, but when the village inn burns down, and his first wife seems to have been burnt to death, he goes down on his knees in gratitude. Only when she turns up alive and starts nagging him, does he kill her – and even then by mistake: 'I furiously raised my hand and swung it round with my whole force to strike her. She turned quickly . . . By her movement my hand came edgewise exactly in the nape of the neck – as men strike a hare to kill it'. Thus Hardy's agnosticism rejected Original Sin, and transferred the guilt of both arson and murder from his villain to the nature of the universe. The inn-fire was caused by 'a strange concurrence of phenomena', the killing, by the concurrence of automatic responses to anger and fear.[18]

In cooking up the plot of *Desperate Remedies*, Hardy used the Sensational recipe, but his first ingredient was Virgil. While trying in 1869 to get his previous novel published, he had been reading 'Virgil's *Aeneid* (of which he never wearied)'. Its hero, the 'pious' Aeneas, suggested a good 'Christian' name for a hypocritical villain, especially as 'Dryden's *Virgil*' (which Hardy's mother had given him when he was eight) added to the Invocation the words here italicized: 'O Muse! the causes *and the crimes* relate . . .' The poem's first words, 'Arms and the *man*', supplied the surname, Manston. Virgil's Aeneas seduced and deserted Dido, who then committed suicide on a funeral pyre, leaving him to see the flames as he sailed away. Hardy's Aeneas tires of his first wife Eunice and on his way to to the railway-station, sees the flames in which she appears to have died. In the

Aeneid, the love-affair with Dido was engineered, with Juno's help, by Aeneas's mother Venus, there called Cytherea. The final trick was to send a storm of rain, to make Dido and Aeneas shelter in the same cave. In the novel, Aeneas's mother, Cytherea Aldclyffe, engineers a marriage between him and Cytherea junior, who happens to be the daughter of the man Miss Aldclyffe once wanted to marry. A storm makes Cytherea shelter in Manston's house, and the power of Venus and Juno is replaced by the divine power of music, which momentarily overcomes Cytherea's resistance.[19]

From such heterogeneous materials, Hardy built a novel which is, if nothing else, compulsive reading. The overall design, when finally grasped, is highly ingenious. Written at great speed, the book is often verbose, but cannot be skipped without risk of missing vital links in its chain of demystification. Nor must one lose momentum by making too much of individual links. At one point Miss Aldclyffe makes what nowadays look like Lesbian advances to Cytherea. Nothing could have been further from the author's or his publisher's mind. The point of the scene is simply to keep the reader guessing. Why is this lady behaving so oddly? Because, it turns out, she regards Ambrose Graye's daughter as virtually her own, and wants to make her at least a daughter-in-law. Nor do her attempts at anti-male indoctrination of Cytherea indicate Lesbian tendencies, any more than Miss Havisham's similar attempts with Estella in Dickens. She is simply dropping clues to her own past, when like Miss Havisham she was 'cruelly betrayed' by a man. All she wants of Cytherea is a substitute daughter who will refuse to marry anyone but her own illegitimate son.[20]

Looking back at this book, Hardy would say that its 'powerfully not to say wildly melodramatic situations had been concocted in a style which was quite against his natural grain'. The 'quite' is questionable. His maturest novels would occasionally verge on melodrama, and his last one, *Jude*, would seem to go over the edge with the hanging of the three children. Certain elements of his Sensation novel would also be rehandled. The two Mrs Manstons would be paralleled by the two Elizabeth-Janes in *The Mayor*, and Miss Aldclyffe's concealed seduction and motherhood by that of *Tess*.[21]

The early thriller also anticipated Hardy's more serious fiction in its allusive symbolism. Trapped into marrying Manston, Cytherea saw Edward gazing at her from the opposite bank of 'a narrow river . . . She stretched out her hand and fingers towards his, but not into them. The river was too wide.' The pathos of the scene had an extra dimension, for it echoed a famous line in Virgil, where dead 'boys and unmarried girls' stood waiting to cross the Acheron, the River of Sorrow in Hell, 'and stretched out their hands in love of the further bank (*tendebantque manus ripae ulterioris amore*)'. Miss Aldclyffe's first appearance as a black figure in sunlight alluded via Turner's picture to Revelation, where the 'angel standing in the sun' prefigured the final war against Satan, and where 'a woman clothed with the sun' did just what Miss Aldclyffe had done: 'brought forth a man child'. The 'chromatic effect' associated with the allusion was followed by several other uses of colour-symbolism, as when Cytherea, after telling

Edward never 'to see her face again', still hoped he would try to do so. Her inner conflict was reflected by the 'gloomy grey' light striking one side of her face from the window, and the 'yellow glimmer' that 'fluttered' on the other from 'the newly-lit fire', making her shadow dance 'like a demon, blue and grim.'[22]

One theme of the novel, the psychology of women, was clearly not handled by Hardy 'quite against his natural grain'. *The Poor Man and the Lady* came to him naturally enough, and he told Gosse that 'The only interesting thing about it was that it showed a wonderful insight into female character.' In *Desperate Remedies* he was always generalizing about women: 'So much more important a love-letter seems to a girl than to a man'; 'Women make confidences and then regret them'; 'His clothes are something exterior to every man; but to a woman her dress is part of her own body'; 'with women there's nothing between the two poles of emotion towards an interesting male acquaintance. 'Tis either love or aversion.' Since Hardy greatly admired J.S. Mill, he was lucky not yet to have read Mill's latest book, *The Subjection of Women* (1869), which made short work of all such wonderful insights: 'The most favourable case which a man can generally have for studying the character of a woman, is that of his own wife ... accordingly one can, to an almost laughable degree, infer what a man's wife is like, from his opinion about women in general.' Certainly Hardy's generalizations tell us less about female character than about his current girl-friends and himself – especially when he complains: 'a woman never seems to see any but the serious side of her attachment, though the most devoted lover has all the time a vague and dim perception that he is losing his old dignity and frittering away his time.'[23]

So much for women. As for life as a whole, the escapist nature of the genre did not conceal Hardy's grimly realistic outlook. 'Mother's notion' was paraphrased by Edward's father: 'There's a back'ard current in the world, and we must do our utmost to advance in order just to bide where we be.' It was also symbolized, when Edward, running as fast as he could to save Cytherea from a marriage he now knew to be bigamous, had to cross a ploughed field: 'The thaw had so loosened the soft earth, that lumps of stiff mud were lifted by his feet at every leap he took and flung against him by his rapid motion, as it were doggedly impeding him, and increasing tenfold the customary effort of running.'[24]

That Manston's efforts were ultimately impeded more than Edward's might suggest 'an arrangement of Providence' (which Manston once thought was on his side). Yet the reader gets the impression that everything has been planned, not by a benevolent god, but by one as irresponsible as the Zeus of the *Iliad*, or the 'It' of *The Dynasts*. Human beings are left completely in the dark. The heroine's brother had not the slightest 'adumbration' or 'presentiment' of an event 'as portentous' to them both 'as any, short of death itself, could possibly be'; and he was astonished 'ever afterward' at his *agnosia*: 'How unutterably mean', he often thought, 'must my intelligence have appeared to the eye of a foreseeing God.' But the last word on human life was given to the villain in the condemned cell, when Aeneas 'the man' became Man's representative: 'I am now about to enter on my normal condition. For people are almost always in their graves. When we survey the long race of men, it is strange and still more strange to find that they are mainly dead men, who have scarcely ever been otherwise.'[25]

4

Under the Greenwood Tree

In May 1871 Hardy was back at St Juliot to supervise the building opera-
tions. On his way home the day after his birthday, he found *Desperate
Remedies* being remaindered on Exeter station. His reaction was quite
positive: he promptly asked Tinsley to advertise the book better by quoting
extracts from the favourable reviews. His morale had been boosted, not
only by Emma's support, but also by having a new novel on the stocks.[1]

When writing to Macmillan about the *Poor Man* in 1868, Hardy had
added: 'I have been hunting up material for another tale, which would
consist entirely of rural scenes & humble life; but I have not courage
enough to go on with it till something comes of the first.' Nothing had
come of it, but in April 1871 he felt sufficiently cheered by the publication
of his second novel to outline a plot for his third. Not surprisingly, with
Tryphena in the last stage of teacher training, it was about a village girl
who became a schoolmistress.[2]

He wrote it up that summer at Weymouth and Bockhampton, again
borrowing passages from the *Poor Man*, notably one that Morley had thought
'really of good quality', the 'Christmas-Eve in the tranter's house'. In August
Hardy sent off the manuscript to Macmillan, explaining that this novel was
exclusively 'rural', because three reviewers of his last one had particularly
liked his treatment of peasant and village life.[3]

At the end of September, an unsigned review of *Desperate Remedies* by
Horace Moule appeared in the *Saturday Review*. Despite the book's 'rather
sensational' title, Hardy's friend was prepared to 'risk the downright opinion' that it was 'worth reading'. Though full of detailed praise, the review
was too coolly impartial in tone to impress the average novel reader.[4]

It also came far too late. When asked to quote from it in future advertisements, Tinsley doubted if any lending library could be induced to buy

a remaindered book. Nor did Moule's review have any effect on Macmillan, though Hardy naturally mentioned it, when trying to hasten a decision about his rural novel. The reply was disappointing. Macmillan liked the new story, but found it rather light-weight, and too short to publish in the usual three volumes. So he returned the manuscript, merely offering to reconsider it in the spring, if Hardy had not by then disposed of it elsewhere.[5]

Assuming, perhaps too soon, that Macmillan would never publish it, Hardy wrote to Tinsley, ostensibly to ask how *Desperate Remedies* was doing financially. He then mentioned that he had 'nearly finished . . . a little rural story', and 'proceeded a little way with another, the essence of which is plot, *without crime* – but on the plan of D.R.' Thus he opened negotiations for *Under the Greenwood Tree* and also for *A Pair of Blue Eyes*, which would fictionalize some of his recent experiences with Emma. Tinsley, he knew, really wanted a three-volume novel, so he tried to use that as a lever to get his short one published first, by adding, 'The result of the first venture would of course influence me in choosing which to work up with the most care –'.[6]

Tinsley's response was as depressing as Macmillan's. He warned Hardy not to expect all of his £75 back on *Desperate Remedies*, suggested that he should write another three-decker, but said nothing about either of the novels that Hardy had mentioned. Exasperated, Hardy told Emma that 'he had banished novel-writing for ever, and was going on with architecture henceforward.' By return of post, Emma urged him to stick to authorship, and so did Moule soon afterwards, making the practical point that Hardy's eyes might not always prove equal to the strain of 'fine architectural drawing'.[7]

But there was obviously no hope yet of earning a living by authorship, let alone supporting a wife. So just before Easter 1872 Hardy moved to London (4 Celbridge Place, Westbourne Park), to work for T. Roger Smith, who had been one of the judges in an architectural competition won by Hardy in 1863. Smith was now designing school buildings required to implement the 1870 Education Act. It took three letters to extract from Tinsley the £59 odd due to Hardy from the £75 he had paid to get *Desperate Remedies* published. Having come to expect even less, he was 'much gratified' to find that 'he had only lost his labour and £15 in money'.[8]

He had better reason to be pleased by the letter that came with the cheque, asking about his next book. After a talk at Tinsley's office, Hardy sent him in April the manuscript of *Under the Greenwood Tree*, promising, in effect, to finish the long novel as quickly as possible, if the short one was published first 'on liberal terms'. The terms that Tinsley offered were scarcely that – only £30 for the copyright, and no royalties. But by then 'caring nothing about the book', Hardy accepted them, and the novel was published anonymously in early June 1872.[9]

This time Hardy had made sure that a review-copy went to Horace Moule, but again his friend did not help much. It was more than three months before Moule's review appeared. Though generally enthusiastic, it must have irritated Hardy by implying distaste for Fancy's involvement with the vicar, and finding 'one definite fault in the dialogues', that the rustics occasionally spoke more like their author than themselves. On that point Hardy perhaps knew better than his middle-class critic. Luckily the *Athenaeum* and the *Pall Mall Gazette* praised the book far more promptly, and warmly enough to make Tinsley offer to serialize Hardy's 'new story' in *Tinsley's Magazine.*[10]

As a product of Hardy's life, *Under the Greenwood Tree* was an expanded version of 'Domicilium'. The home sketched in the poem became the Tranter's in the novel, 'a long low cottage with a hipped roof of thatch, having dormer windows breaking up into the eaves'; and in one of those windows, which belonged in real life to Hardy's bedroom, much of the book had been written. It filled in the details, not just of the house itself, but of its whole physical and cultural environment. Stinsford was pictured as Mellstock, and the scenes of the story were precisely located within the Bockhampton area. 'The Mellstock Quire' (the novel's original title) was the one in which Hardy's grandfather, father, and uncle had sung and played, and which a new vicar replaced by a harmonium.[11]

Music was thus the chief link between the novelist's family and the Tranter's. How far the Dewys, with their slightly henpecked paterfamilias, were otherwise based on the Hardys, can only be guessed. Dick, at any rate, was not much like his author except in playing the violin. Here Hardy's experience showed through in realistic details – strings going sharp in cold weather, chairs 'wriggled' out of place 'by frantic bowing'. He also used music to describe Fancy's appearance and inconsistent character. The legato suggestions of her eyebrows, 'like two slurs in music', were contradicted by a staccato quality in the 'bright sparkle' of 'each' eye. Her half-conscious singing hinted at her tendency to infidelity. When 'flitting thoughts' interrupted Dick's opening song, he had faithfully 'resumed at a point it would have reached had its continuity been unbroken'. But Fancy, while preparing dinner, was melodically promiscuous, 'singing the tips and ends of tunes that sprang up in her mind like mushrooms.'[12]

To old William, music meant more than life itself. To Fancy's father, 'her musical notes' were primarily a social asset, qualifying her to catch a 'gentleman' husband. To Fancy herself, music was a form of sexual display, which duly made the vicar fall in love with her. The real 'musicians' recognized the meretricious character of her first performance in church. They 'could not help thinking' that their own 'simpler notes' had suited the old church better than 'the crowded chords and interludes it was her pleasure to produce.'[13]

So far, the novel's materials came chiefly from Hardy's own life and family background; but its cynical undertones came partly from his reading of Shakespeare and Horace – for the book is not what it seems, a cosy love-story with a happy ending. It actually ends with a bride determined 'never to tell' her credulous bridegroom something very important about herself. The song in *As You Like It* from which Hardy took both his title and the triple 'Come hither' on his last page, had an equally cynical epilogue, capping the praise of country life with the comment that only a fool would go in for it: 'Ducdame ducdame ducdame: / Here shall he see gross fools as he'. 'Ducdame', glossed by Jaques as 'a Greek invocation to call fools into a circle', sounds more like Latin and French for 'Lead, lady' – to a lady of come-hitherish type. Perhaps Hardy took it so, and applied it to romantic love. Certainly when Fancy says 'Come hither', Dick is led by the nose. His final predicament, though he does not know it, is that of the flirt's lover in a Horace *Ode* familiar to Hardy both in Latin and in Milton's literal translation, who 'now enjoyes [her] credulous, all Gold, / Who alwayes vacant, alwayes amiable / Hopes [her]'.[14]

There is reason to believe that the novel was influenced much more by an ancient work of fiction. Hardy called his book an 'Idyll' (as Theocritus called his pastoral poems), and Moule described it as a 'prose idyl', i.e. a pastoral narrative, a genre pioneered by the short Greek novel that inspired *Paul et Virginie*, Longus's *Daphnis and Chloe*. Hardy could have read it either in the original (no harder than the Greek Testament), or in Courier's immensely popular French translation, or in one of two English versions, the first by Angel Day (1587). If Hardy ever came across a mention of that translator, the Christian name would have stuck in his mind, if only by recalling the one (later used in *Tess*) on the winged-skull memorial in Stinsford Church. The surname might then have stuck too, and suggested Fancy Day's. But there are far better grounds than that for suspecting that Hardy had somehow read *Daphnis and Chloe*. There is no external evidence that he ever did so; but, knowing Hardy's interest in Greek, in novels, and in *Paul and Virginia*, Moule would naturally have told him about this famous work, which Goethe called 'a masterpiece', and either given or lent him a copy. If so, the absence of any reference to the book, in the *Life* or in his letters, would be easily explained by its pornographic reputation. As late as 1856, Mrs Browning had referred to it as an 'obscene text'.[15]

Hardy's text, though far from obscene, was full of resemblances to *Daphnis and Chloe*. Longus claimed to be telling the story of a painting seen in Lesbos; Hardy subtitled his story, 'A Rural Painting of the Dutch School'. Longus's novel was in four seasonal Books, starting with spring, Hardy's in four seasonal Parts, starting with winter, plus a Conclusion (late in spring). Longus's names were mythical, literary, and symbolic. Daphnis, so named from having been exposed under a bay-tree (*daphne*), was the archetypal shepherd in Theocritus. Dick, from Shakespeare's 'Dick the shepherd', was first found in a wood, recognizing the 'voices' of individual trees. 'Chloe' means the green shoots of spring, 'Dewy' suggests the break of 'Day'. Thus both novelists emphasized their lovers' youth. 'Fancy', by recalling Shakespeare's song, 'Tell me where is fancy bred', and Keats's ode, 'Fancy', hints at the visual origin and roving character of sexual love, as personified in the heroine. Longus's love story was programmed by Eros;

thus when Daphnis and Chloe reached puberty, Eros 'made something serious flare up', by contriving for Chloe to see Daphnis 'washing his hair and his whole body.' Dick might 'just possibly' have got 'free' of Fancy, after she had wasted his half-holiday 'snipping and sewing' – 'But Venus had planned other developments'. Chloe was the daughter of a rich man, though brought up as a working shepherdess. Fancy was 'born to fortune' (estimated at £900), but brought up 'as if not born to it', and made to 'work . . . hard'.[16]

There were precedents in the Greek novel for several other features of the English one: for Dick's blunt approach to Mr Day: 'I've come to ask for Fancy', and for her father's feeling that she was too good to marry someone of Dick's class; for the lovers' talk under an apple-tree; for Fancy's bee-sting; for bird-liming as a lover's ploy; and for a wedding-reception associated with animals and snobbery: Longus's rich townees disliked the presence of the goats, Hardy's heroine criticized her father's 'thee' and 'thou', and the local habit of 'drawing the back of the hand across the mouth after drinking'.[17]

Longus's tone was affectionately satirical of his young lovers' sexual innocence, and he told their story from a safe distance: 'as for me, I hope that the god will allow me to write of other people's experiences, while retaining my own sanity.' Hardy took the same line. In his last two novels, he had clearly identified with the lovers. Here his tone was detached and humorous, especially when describing Dick's race with Shiner to fetch the 'sweet-oil-and-hartshorn'. On other subjects than love, this new tone enabled Hardy to express his own feelings more effectively. His protest against the upper classes, exaggerated in the *Poor Man*, was subtly subversive in the portrait of the vicar. Plainly inferior to old William and the Tranter in wisdom and humanity, he abolishes the old church-music out of trendiness, fear of the churchwarden, and sexual attraction to the organist.[18]

Here Hardy's religious scepticism, implicit in *Desperate Remedies*, came into sharper focus. His church-centred village community betrayed its underlying paganism in Mrs Penny's reference to 'the sky-folk'. The real complaint against Maybold was that he lacked his predecessor's virtue of inactivity: 'he never troubled us wi' a visit from year's end to year's end. You might go anywhere, do anything: you'd be sure never to see him.' Vicars, in fact, were superfluous: 'I don't believe twill make a penneth o' difference to we poor martels here or hereafter whether his sermons be good or bad, my sonnies.'[19]

Hardy's scepticism about marriage, too, came out more clearly. Jocular in 'How I Built Myself a House', it became sadder here with the apparently loveless relationship of Mr and Mrs Dewy, the chronic failure of communication between Mr and Mrs Day, and the final establishment of non-communication as a marriage policy, when Fancy 'thought of a secret she would never tell.'[20]

Two other important feelings of Hardy's were first expressed in this novel: his sense of past history, and his concern for animals. Seen against the night-sky, the profiles of the choir-members were like figures on 'Greek or Etruscan pottery'. They sang an ancient and time-worn hymn . . . in words orally transmitted from father to son through several generations, down to the present characters'. Their leader's Christmas greeting had been said at that hour and season for the previous forty years'. The Tranter's doorway was worn and scratched by much passing in and out'. Mr Day's 'window-board' was covered with black circles left by the cups of former drinkers. His two competing clocks emphasized the passing of time, and the good things that passed with it were the novel's central theme. Though the choir was magnanimously prepared to 'make room for the next generation', its supersession was presented, not as progress, but as vandalism.[21]

Animals figured both as intelligent thinkers and as victims of human and natural cruelty. The Dewys' horse was an inductive reasoner: 'Smart . . . had been lost in thought for some time, never dreaming that Dick could reach so far with a whip which, on this particular journey, had never been extended further than his flank . . .' While being stung by bees inside his shirt, Geoffrey Day still felt sorry for the 'lively young mortals', but could not think how to treat them fairly: 'The proper way to take honey, so that the bees be neither starved nor murdered, is a puzzling matter'. Nature had no such scruples: soon after the honey-taking 'the silence was . . . disturbed by some small bird that was being killed by an owl in the adjoining wood, whose cry passed into the silence without mingling with it.' These two feelings, for animals and for history, were neatly brought together when the human mating was celebrated under 'an ancient tree' which had sheltered countless generations of birds, rabbits, hares, moles, and earthworms. By implicit allusion to the 'entangled bank' and the 'great Tree of Life' in Darwin's *Origin of Species*, the 'Greenwood Tree' was thus made to enforce what Hardy thought the corollary of Darwinism: that the 'do as you would be done by' principle must be applied to 'the whole animal kingdom.'[22]

Hardy's second published novel also developed two narrative features very typical of him. The first was the window-picture. Though the one of Cytherea in *Desperate Remedies* had been suggested by Rossetti's 'Blessed Damozel', more interesting examples were to be found in Tennyson. 'The Miller's Daughter' (1832) was first seen at a window, reflected in the water, then as a shadow crossing a lighted blind. In *Enoch Arden* (1864) the husband returned to see, through a window from the darkness outside, 'all the happiness' of his wife's second marriage. Hardy's interest in this device doubtless stemmed from his own sketching and water-colour painting, perhaps also from viewing illuminated pictures through an aperture in the London dioramas (early precursors of the cinema), and probably even more from his theatre-going. Fancy was first seen at her window by the carol-singers. After an 'expectant stillness', her audience of thirty saw a light approaching behind the blind. Then the blind went up, to reveal the leading lady, holding a candle to her own charms. Finally the window opened, and she delivered her first line. The stagy effect gave an instant clue to her character.[23]

The second narrative feature may be briefly labelled 'eye-mind focus', i.e. the common tendency, which may have puzzled Hardy when watching adults as a child, to focus one's eyes on one thing while thinking of another. Thus Mrs Penny, after 'throwing her glance into past times', let her eyes 'stay idling on the past scenes just related, which were apparently visible to her in the centre of the room.' 'I always like to look things in the face', Reuben told Maybold, 'gazing hard at him . . . and then out of the window', so that Maybold and old William looked there too, as if the 'things' faces alluded to were there visible.' When Dick asked Mr Day 'for Fancy', both men's eyes were fixed on the 'whitish shadowy shape' of a pig.[24]

There the comic device was subtly adapted to satire on the marriage system, by the hint that the two men were actually negotiating a sale of livestock. It would be adapted to a very different purpose in 'The Self-Unseeing', where the eyes were focused on the immediate scene, but the mind failed to register the happiness that deserved more attention: 'Yet we were looking away!' In one more adaptation of the idea, where the mind's eye actually interfered with bodily vision, this early novel anticipated Hardy's later poetry. After Emma's death he would describe how 'visions' of the past 'Blotted to feeble mist . . . the customed landscape.' Upset by a window-picture of the vicar 'standing on some books piled in a chair' to hang up Fancy's canary-cage, Dick drove home, 'with the eye of reflection so anxiously set on his passages at arms with Fancy that the road and scenery were as a thin mist over the real pictures of his mind.'[25]

5

A Pair of Blue Eyes

Tinsley's offer to serialize Hardy's new novel (called 'A Winning Tongue Had He' until renamed *A Pair of Blue Eyes*) was too good to refuse. Serialization was the best form of advance publicity for a novel in book-form, and gave the author a regular salary while he was writing it. Reckoning that he 'could do it in six months', and could not earn more than £100 in that time by architecture, he prudently asked for a fee of £200, and got it. He also insisted this time on keeping his copyright. Twelve months after the three-volume edition all rights would revert to the author. He even had the self-confidence to put a clause in the contract entitling him to 'some fair additional allowance' in case the novel was a smash hit.[1]

Once committed, he got cold feet. It was now 24 July, and the first instalment had to be sent off in time to be illustrated and printed on 15 August. He would then have to meet eleven more such monthly deadlines, writing everything out in longhand, unaided by typewriter or computer. All he had to go on was a plot, and rough notes of the opening chapters. It was a formidable undertaking, but he went ahead with it. Having met his first deadline, he told his employer, Roger Smith, that he was taking an August holiday, and went off to Cornwall to continue the story of a younger architect called Stephen Smith.[2]

Thus Hardy stepped on to a treadmill, which would contribute largely over the years to the tensions of his first marriage. Nor did it yet make that marriage possible. When, on the strength of his £200, he asked Mr Gifford's permission to marry Emma, the answer was even ruder than Mr Day's to Dick. According to the second Mrs Hardy, Gifford 'was very contemptuous of Hardy's social position'. Though Emma stood firmly by him, the crucifixion image in the poem 'Near Lanivet, 1872' doubtless described her sense of conflicting loyalties. But the painful situation made excellent copy for the novel.[3]

In three other ways that Cornwall 'holiday' contributed to the story. His journey down by sea from London Bridge supplied material for chapter 29. The 'little starved green grass' that he noticed on the ledges of Beeny Cliff must have suggested the 'turf-covered slope' that Knight would slide down, and the 'last outlying knot of starved herbage' that just stopped him going over the edge. The idea of such an incident, involving the wind that struck 'the face of the rock', possibly came into Hardy's head on a visit to Tintagel, where Emma had earlier memories of the 'dangerous' wind. She had once been 'nearly blown into the Atlantic, and clung to the rocks frightened.'[4]

Though he saved a little time by adapting bits of the *Poor Man*, such as the scene in Rotten Row, Hardy's main problem was how to write fast enough, and the October instalment went off late on 7 September. He then returned to London, but finding he could not not 'get on with his novel' there, he finished it at Bockhampton, and sent Tinsley the last chapters (with a bill for the rest of his fee) on 12 March 1873.[5]

He had 'done it', not quite in six, but in less than eight months. Towards the end he had speeded up, for two good reasons. On 10 August 1872 he had burnt his boats architecturally by refusing an offer of further work, on 'any more liberal terms', from Roger Smith. And on 30 November Leslie Stephen, impressed by the anonymous *Under the Greenwood Tree*, and given the author's name and address by Horace Moule, had invited Hardy to write a serial for a much more prestigious magazine than *Tinsley's*, the *Cornhill*. Stephen's letter seemed as providential in its manner of arrival as in its contents. Casually dropped by some schoolchildren told to deliver it from the village post office, it was spotted in the mud and salvaged by a passing labourer.[6]

Fearful of missing such an opportunity, Hardy had replied that he was still busy on another serial, but if it would not be too late, he had thought of writing next a 'pastoral tale' called *Far from the Madding Crowd*, in which 'the chief characters would probably be a young woman-farmer, a shepherd, and a sergeant of cavalry.' Stephen had liked the 'idea' and the title, and been prepared to wait. So Hardy had got Tinsley's novel off his hands as quickly as possible. Having finished the serial version, he revised it, with large cuts in Chapter 1, for the three-volume edition, which appeared under his own name at the end of May 1873.[7]

While waiting for the reviews, Hardy had lunch and dinner with Horace in London, and visited him in Cambridge five days later. One 'never-to-be-forgotten morning' they stood together on the roof of King's College Chapel, and saw 'Ely Cathedral gleaming in the distant sunlight'. Hardy then joined Emma and a tactfully non-adhesive friend of hers at Bath for a holiday, which included trips to Tintern Abbey and Bristol. At Clifton the lovers were 'surprised' to see in a newsagent's the *Spectator's* 'commendatory' review of *A Pair of Blue Eyes*, by the critic whose attack on *Desperate Remedies* had made Hardy wish he were dead. Other reviews were equally satisfactory – though their highest praise was to compare him with George Eliot.[8]

Hardy denied that the novel was autobiographical, except for 'the lonely drive across the hills towards the coast, the architectural detail, and a few other external scenes and incidents'. Elfride was a bit like Emma 'in quite young womanhood, a few years before Hardy met her', especially in her instinct for horse-riding. 'But this is all that can be asserted, the plot of the story being one that he had thought of and written down long before he knew her.'[9]

The 'architectural detail' included the collapse of the church-tower. Hardy had heard of similar cases from Hicks and Blomfield. Under 'other external scenes and incidents' came Knight's reading of a lesson at Endelstow which Hardy had heard read at St Juliot in August 1870. And it was doubtless the heroine's association with Emma that made Hardy so fond of this particular novel. As for the prefabrication of the plot, its general theme of love thwarted by class prejudice certainly dated back at least to *The Poor Man and the Lady*.[10]

Here, though, that theme was fleshed out with details very close to Hardy's recent experience Mr Swancourt's snobbish rejection of Smith as a son-in-law seems to caricature Mr Gifford's contemptuous dismissal of Hardy. Was there not a hint of bitterness in making Smith's first gift of his earnings to his 'Own wifie' Elfride precisely £200, the amount of the fee from Tinsley on which Hardy had hoped to marry Emma?[11]

The characterization of Knight seems similarly edged. Moule must have recognized himself as the model, and possibly meant to disclaim Knight's cliff-top heroism when he commented, 'how gloriously you have idealized here and there'. He then complained of occasional 'slips of taste'. Perhaps Hardy had both Moule and Knight in mind when he wrote in September, 'One man is a genius in trifles, a fool in emergencies: another a fool in trifles, a genius in emergencies.' Away from the cliff Knight's folly is most in evidence. Dogmatic, fastidious, patronizing, and cruel, he is not an appealing character. Perhaps, beneath his grateful affection for Moule, Hardy shared Stephen's resentment at always being treated 'as a mere disciple'.[12]

He described his book as a 'Romance', a term with several meanings, but then commonly used to classify the works of the *Erotici Graeci*, i.e. the prose love-stories now usually called 'Greek novels'. Hardy's 'romance' gives further reason to believe that he had read the best of them, *Daphnis and Chloe*. Longus's lovers were children just reaching adolescence, and he emphasized their innocence. There was similar stress on the youth and inexperience of Stephen and Elfride: 'And now parting arose like a death to these children . . . Then the boy and girl beguiled themselves with words of half-parting only.'[13]

When Daphnis defeated his rival Dorcon, in a formal contest for the prize of kissing her, Chloe jumped up and kissed him for the first time. It was a kiss 'untaught and without technique (*adidakton kai atechnon*) but well able to warm the heart.' Elfride's first kiss was equally 'awkward and unused'. The proper technique was then described and her lack of it explained: 'Why? Because experience was absent. A woman must have had many kisses before she kisses well.' Longus's implication that good kissing technique must be 'taught' seems to underlie Knight's theory that 'experience teaches . . . and . . . the sweetheart who is graceful under the initial kiss must be supposed to have had some practice in the trade.'[14]

It was Chloe's initial kiss that made Daphnis fall in love with her, but her passion for him had been started by a more dramatic incident. While chasing a goat, Daphnis fell into a pit 24 feet deep, and could not climb out. In the absence of a 'long rope' Chloe took off her breastband (*tainia*) and let it down to him. Helped by Dorcon, she thus pulled Daphnis up, and in washing the mud off his body, first felt sexually attracted.[15]

While retrieving his hat, Knight nearly fell over a 650-foot precipice, and could not climb back. Elfride took off her underclothes to make a 'perfect rope' 18–21 feet long, and let it down to him. Though not much help in the rescue, Dorcon the defeated rival was there too in the person of Stephen, on board the *Puffin* far below. And the erotic effect of the washing in the spring was paralleled by the 'impulsive embrace in the rain', with Elfride in her 'meagre habiliments', rain-drenched, 'diaphanous', and 'clinging to her like a glove'.[16]

Contrastingly, Mrs Troyton was mocked by allusions to Horace and Virgil. Mr Swancourt's Horatian quotation identified her with the witch Canidia, credited elsewhere with uncut nails and black teeth. Her fingers, 'stiff with rings, like Helen's robe' in the *Aeneid*, implied that hers was *not* a face to launch a thousand ships. If Elfride's singing 'fired a small Troy, in the shape of Stephen's heart', it was Mrs Troyton's wealth that set Swancourt's heart on fire.[17]

Elfride's experience of love was patterned on the *Aeneid*. There Dido started as queen of Carthage, with Aeneas her humble suppliant, and ended as suppliant herself. Elfride suffers the same reversal of roles, only with different lovers. Queen to Stephen, whom she loves for being so 'docile', she ends in a state of dog-like devotion to Knight: 'He saw the stubble-field, and a slight girlish figure in the midst of it . . . Elfride, docile as ever, had hardly moved a step, for he had said, Remain.' Her incipient reduction to suppliant status was marked by a specific reference to Virgil. When she first entered Knight's London world, 'Elfride . . . like Aeneas at Carthage [when he first entered Dido's world as a shipwrecked refugee] was full of admiration for the brilliant scene'.[18]

Hardy's reading of 'Greek plays' was also put to good use in the novel. Elfride's guilty past pursued her in the person of Mrs Jethway, like the Furies pursuing Orestes in Aeschylus. Knight ruthlessly forced Elfride to confess the truth that he could not bear to hear, just as Oedipus forced

Jocasta and other witnesses to tell him things that would make him put out his eyes. The dramatic irony typical of the *Oedipus Tyrannus* was also reproduced in Elfride's early remark to Stephen about Knight: 'I don't want to know him, because he comes between me and you.'[19]

The concluding scene in the vault, with Elfride's husband stretched in grief over her coffin, recalls Antigone's fiancé clinging to her corpse in her 'marriage-tomb'. But the Greek play that probably influenced the novel most was Euripides' *Alcestis*. Turned into a narrative poem by Morris in 1868, illustrated by Frederic Leighton in 1871, translated by Browning with an imagined stage-performance in *Balaustion's Adventure* (1871), it had been discussed by Horace Moule in a review-article that November.[20]

Its theme, a wife dying for her husband, first surfaced in the novel when Elfride exclaimed on the cliff: 'O, I would have died instead!'. It was burlesqued when Knight said to Stephen, 'You have an idea that Elfride died for you, no doubt', and finally transferred to her husband: 'He'd have died for her, I believe.' Thus both husband and wife had the altruism of Alcestis, the lovers the selfishness of Admetus, which Browning's poem had underlined, and of which Moule had offered three possible interpretations.[21]

While denying that its ending was 'farcical', Moule had called the *Alcestis* 'a tragicomedy'. Hardy's novel was clearly that too, but more than its ending was probably modelled on a popular English farce, Morton's *Box and Cox: A Romance of Real Life* (1847). These famous lodgers have been living in the same room, but at different times. While still unaware of each other's existence, and appearing separately on the stage, they duplicate one another's actions like mirror-images. When they meet, the duplication continues in action and dialogue, and they both turn out to be engaged to the same woman. Having nearly fought a duel for the privilege of not marrying her, they hear that she has been drowned, and compete for the right to her money. She finally turns up alive, having married a Mr Knox.[22]

Hardy's 'Romance', which begins with a theatre programme giving 'The Persons' and 'The Scene', has an almost identical pattern. Smith and Knight live in turn at Endelstow Rectory, make love to the same girl, play chess with her, and sit with her on the same rock. When they realize they are rivals, they separately and surreptitiously take the same train down to Cornwall. The climax of farcical duplication comes at Chippenham: 'Stephen looked out. At the same moment another man's head emerged from the adjoining window. Each looked in the other's face. Knight and Stephen confronted one another.' Arriving to find Elfride dead, they imitate Box and Cox's argument about their relationships to the deceased. '*Your* intended? Come, I like that! Didn't you very properly observe just now, sir, that I proposed to her first?' '*Your* darling! . . . I know this. She was *my* darling before she was yours, and after too.'[23]

Like Box and Cox's 'intended', Elfride has married another man; but her death comes closer to the 'tragi-comedy' than the farce. The *Alcestis* begins with Thanatos (Death) rejecting all Apollo's arguments for letting Alcestis live and it is only by fighting Thanatos that Heracles brings her back to life. In the novel there is no Heracles, but death is twice personified. Hanging on the cliff Knight wondered: 'Was Death really stretching out his hand?', and Elfride told him later: 'Death stares me in the face in the person of that cliff.' Death pervades the novel, from Stephen's remark that his life is 'solitary as death', and the description of the churchyard, to young Jethway's tomb, Mrs Jethway's 'half-buried' corpse, Elfride's 'Harry, I shall soon die', and the third scene in the vault.[24]

The most terrifying manifestation of Thanatos had a nearer literary source than Euripides. For readers of the serial it was doubly a cliff-hanger. With Knight 'literally suspended by his arms' in February 1873, they had to wait until March for Elfride to come back with her 'rope'. Knight's ordeal in the interval closely resembled one imagined by Leslie Stephen in 'A Bad Five Minutes in the Alps'.[25]

Published in the month that Stephen had first written to Hardy, this fictional article presented the agnostic climber hanging by his hands 200 feet above a rocky torrent. Like Knight, he had got there by 'slithering downwards'. The strain on his arms was slightly relieved by one foothold, as with Knight by a 'third in one' gradient, and he knew that 'the strongest man cannot hold on by his arms alone for more than five minutes'. Knight thought his hands would 'not hold out ten minutes'. So hanging, Leslie Stephen thought about life, death, and the theories of theologians, philosophers, and scientists, including Darwin and the geologists. Knight's eyes met those of a fossilized 'creature' just in front of him, and he pictured the whole history of Darwinian evolution.[26]

Hardy had promised Tinsley 'plot, *without crime* – but on the plan of D.R.', and Sensationalism survived in the pointless mystery of the shadows on the blind and the kiss heard on the lawn. More typical of Hardy's mature narrative method was the symbolism of the falling tower (Knight's failure to prove Elfride's 'strong tower against the enemy'); and a striking use of the 'unidentified object'. Just back from India, Stephen sees two 'moving specks' in the distance, one white and the other black. They are Elfride and Knight, fresh from their embrace in the rain. Thus Hardy marked a shift of perspective, as Elfride's first lover returned to stage centre.[27]

A new trick of narrative was the duplication of incident, not just between the two lovers, as in *Box and Cox*, but in the sequence of events. After nearly falling from the tower-parapet, Elfride tells Knight of her feeling 'that the moment has been in duplicate, or will be . . . I felt on the tower that something similar to that scene is again to be common to us both.' The cliff-scene duly followed. Besides acting as rhymes in the poetic structure of the plot, such duplications had various other functions. The two chess-games stressed the heroine's fall from dominance to subservience, and also gave early warning that her health was 'as inconsequent as her actions'. The two rock-seat sessions, linked by the lost earrings, confirmed Knight's jealousy. The first two vault-scenes, while simulating a verse-couplet that became a conclusive triplet, and advancing the plot in several ways, progressively developed the thought that, in a world 'where death is so emphatically present', sexual rivalry is ridiculous.[28]

That thought explains the apparent change of tone in the last four chapters. It is disconcerting at first to find the lovers reduced to figures of farce, and for Elfride's coffin to travel down with them to Cornwall seems rather a sick joke. But it would be wrong to infer that Hardy had ceased to take the novel seriously, in his haste to finish it, and write another for the *Cornhill.* There was no real inconsistency. Like the King's death in *Love's Labour's Lost*, the long prepared-for triumph of Thanatos made the lovers look suddenly silly.[29]

Though Knight's behaviour had best illustrated the epigraph, 'Jealousy is cruel as the grave', 'the selfishness of love and the cruelty of jealousy were fairly exemplified' by both men. Both were unreasonably possessive in their love for Elfride, Knight obsessively so. Neither recognized her unique value as an independent person. It was against this type of love that Elfride made her bitter protest:

> 'Am I such a – mere characterless toy – as to have no attrac – tion in me, apart from – freshness? Haven't I brains? . . . Haven't I some beauty? . . . You have praised my voice, and my manner, and my accomplishments. Yet all these together are so much rubbish because I accidentally saw a man before you!'[30]

The 'romance', in fact, was a satire on romantic love. Sending Tinsley an extract from the *Spectator* review for use in advertisements, Hardy rightly excised the remark that the title was 'perhaps the weakest point in the book'. For the title summed up the satire. In Sheridan's drinking song, any woman would serve as 'an excuse for the glass': 'Here's to the girl with a pair of blue eyes, / And here's to the nymph with but one, sir.'[31]

6

Far from the Madding Crowd

Refreshed by his holiday with Emma, Hardy returned to Bockhampton in July 1873, to concentrate on his novel for the *Cornhill*. As he later told Leslie Stephen, it was easiest to write it there, within walking-distance of 'the district in which the incidents are supposed to occur [i.e. the Puddle-town area]. I find it a great advantage to be actually among the people described at the time of describing them.' He saw as much as he could of local sheep-farming, walked to the sheep fair at Woodbury Hill, and thought of a shepherd he knew called 'Maniel' Riggs, who had recently been found dead: 'A curious man, who used to moisten his lips between every two or three words.'[1]

The next news of death was more traumatic. Horace Moule, whose 'last smile' Hardy had seen on Cambridge station on June, had three months later killed himself by cutting his throat with a razor. Reasons suggested for the suicide include a broken engagement, an illegitimate child, alcoholism, and chronic depression exacerbated by a deeply depressing job, for Moule had recently become an inspector of workhouses.[2]

The pain of Hardy's grief was doubtless intensified by feelings of guilt. While he had been going up in the literary world, Moule, his chief teacher, had been coming down. In a poem of 1866, 'A Confession to a Friend in Trouble', Hardy had felt guilty at merely wishing to distance himself from Moule's problems. Now he had repaid his friend's kindness by implicitly satirizing him in *A Pair of Blue Eyes*. And Moule had heaped coals of fire on his head by a generous review of that novel in the month before he died.[3]

Hardy coped with these feelings, as he would cope with rather similar ones at Emma's death, by grimly continuing to write. Some of the grimness got into the new novel. A 'pastoral tale' would not normally include madness or murder; and though the poem that supplied the title did mention the possibility of being 'crazed with care, or cross'd in hopeless love', there was no one like Boldwood in the list of probable characters first offered to Leslie Stephen, despite his demand for striking 'incident', if not quite for 'a murder in every number'. So perhaps the whole Boldwood sub-plot was a later response to Moule's 'suicide while in a state of temporary insanity'.[4]

On the strength of about ten chapters, which went off to him at the end of that month, Stephen definitely accepted the novel, to start publication in the spring. The appearance of the first instalment was then brought forward to December, which committed Hardy to another race with the printers. Some of the writing was done out of doors, where 'naturally enough' his best ideas came to him when he had no paper, and he had to use dead leaves or odd pieces of wood, slate, or stone instead. He also did sketches of costumes, buildings, and equipment, to send his illustrator, with 'a hope that the rustics, although *quaint*, would be made to look 'intelligent, & not *boorish* at all.'[5]

He could now negotiate with the publishers, Smith, Elder & Co, from a position of strength: 'the value of my writing has changed', he told them, 'since I made my last agreement for a story.' His serial fee changed too, from £200 to £400. Once on with the new publisher, there remained the slight problem of how to be off with the old one. Tinsley's request for another serial was met by a certain economy with the truth: 'a friend . . . more than a year ago asked me for my next after the Greenwood Tree.' Tinsley still felt ill-used. Hardy, politely apologizing for any 'a breach of courtesy', assured him it was 'quite unintentional', and tried to keep on good terms; but Tinsley nursed his grievance, and later got his own back, by refusing to sell the copyright of *Under the Greenwood Tree* for less than ten times what he had paid for it.[6]

Leslie Stephen did indeed become 'a friend', but when Hardy called him so, to excuse his change of publisher, the two men had never met. It was a fortnight later that he first visited his new editor at his house in South Kensington. There he also met Stephen's sister-in-law Anne Thackeray, daughter of the novelist, and a novelist herself. Next month he wrote a letter that would embarrass him shortly before his death, by being auctioned at Sotheby's. In it he confessed to finding 'a peculiar charm' in 'the society of educated womankind', the more so from its 'having been denied by circumstances until very lately'. 'Educated womankind' was a category that excluded Eliza and Tryphena. It had to be stretched a little to admit Emma herself.[7]

Gender apart, Stephen put Hardy in touch with the London intelligentsia, and as an editor gave him what he then most needed, encouragement (e.g. 'You are original and can stand on your own legs'), and technical advice. Tinsley was a business man, definitely not a member of 'educated mankind', and his editorial comments were so silly that Hardy once had to tell him: 'Always notice whether the words are the author's own, or those of a character speaking.' Stephen was a distinguished author and thinker who could teach the tricks of the magazine writer's trade: 'for the present', Hardy told him, 'circumstances lead me to wish merely to be considered a good hand at a serial.' When Stephen interfered, as in wanting to 'omit' Fanny's baby, he did it without questioning Hardy's literary judgement: 'I object as editor, not as critic, i.e. in the interest of a stupid public, not from my own taste.'[8]

Hardy spent that Christmas at St Juliot with Emma. On his way back, he bought the January *Cornhill* at Plymouth station, and found his novel starting on page one, still anonymously, but with a splendid illustration by Helen Paterson. When he met her four months later, her 'peculiar charm' was enough to make him wish, at sixty-six, that she had married him instead of William Allingham. But now he sent the magazine to Emma, 'to give her a pleasant surprise', and show how right she had been to make him stick to authorship. Sure enough, the new novel was immediately welcomed by the critics, and the *Spectator*, after wondering if it could be by George Eliot, found out and published the real author's name.[9]

Hardy stayed at Bockhampton until he had finished writing the novel. That was in July, when he noted down two things that Emma had said in a letter: 'My work, unlike your work of writing, does not occupy my true mind much . . . Your novel seems sometimes like a child all your own & none of me.' Both remarks suggest that she felt cut off from him by his creative work. Yet such work, especially against deadlines, demanded exclusive concentration. Marriage, which at least brought physical proximity, must have seemed the best solution. It was now financially possible, and Emma had apparently talked her father round. But living with a husband whose thoughts were usually elsewhere would prove hardly better than physical separation.[10]

However, like Stephen and Elfride, the poor 'children' of thirty-four did what they could. On 17 September 1874 they were married at St Peter's, Elgin Avenue, Paddington, by Emma's clerical uncle, Dr E.H. Gifford. Her brother Walter was the only other member of either family present. After a night at a London hotel, and three at Brighton, they travelled via Dieppe and Rouen to Paris for their honeymoon. How they got on in bed is no business of ours, but Emma's diary, illustrated with tiny drawings, shows that Paris fascinated her. She found the cats 'superb', the children 'sportive & charming', the people 'very nice', 'Les Latrines Publiques most strange for English eyes & notions', and even the three bodies in 'La Morgue' ('middle one pink – Their clothes handing above them') 'Not offensive but repulsive.' Hardy told his brother Henry he was going there 'for materials for my next story', but there is no reason to doubt that he enjoyed himself too.[11]

Returning to London in October, they rented rooms in Hook Road, Surbiton, then a remote surburb, where Hardy knew a music-teacher from Weymouth. Emma's father made the proper gesture of turning up at the house to see them move in. Next month (23 November 1874) *Far from the Madding Crowd* was published in two volumes. It had been serialized in America as well as England, and now, at Hardy's request, his name appeared on the title-page, as the author of his last two novels, though not of *Desperate Remedies*.[12]

Henry James, who had not yet produced any major novel himself, dismissed Hardy's latest as a poor imitation of George Eliot. Finding it 'hard to read', much too long, and written in 'an ingeniously verbose and redundant style', he concluded: 'the only things we believe in are the sheep and the dogs.' But the rest of the reviews were good. Better still, the book went down well with ordinary readers, as Hardy and his wife began to realize when, on their trips into London, they kept seeing 'ladies carrying about copies of it with Mudie's label on the covers.'[13]

By then Hardy, like Oak, must have learnt 'to say "my wife" in a wonderful naterel way'. Apart from the similar connotations of their surnames, hero and author were most like each other in their marriages. Having danced at Bathsheba's 'skittish heels . . . for many a long mile, and many a long day', Gabriel had finally climbed into her social class, and married her. Hardy, though less single-minded in his devotion, had done much the same thing with Emma over the last four years. His rise to the status of author matched 'Oak's Advancement' to the control of two farms, his royalties corresponding with Oak's prized 'share of the receipts'.[14]

Bathsheba came closest to Emma as the 'Girl on Horseback', who 'dexterously dropped backwards flat upon the pony's back'; and as 'she, back there upon the pony' after the fire, where Gabriel's humble address to 'the slight female form in the saddle' recalled Hardy's pedestrian courtship of Emma. 'She on horseback', he had noted in his diary. The dominance thus implied had been stressed in the previous novel when Elfride spoke to Stephen 'in a didactic tone justifiable in a horsewoman's address to a benighted walker'.[15]

Otherwise, Bathsheba was 'drawn from' Hardy's handsome aunt' Martha Sharpe, whom he had known for three or four weeks at the age of eight or nine. As 'a woman farmer', Bathsheba was possibly modelled on a friend of Tryphena's who ran a farm near Weymouth after her husband's death. Here Hardy doubtless hoped to exploit the current interest in feminism. In 1869 J.S. Mill had condemned the exclusion of women from jobs they could do quite as well as men, and the early feminist Mary Wollstonecraft had mentioned 'regulating a farm' as a job that might have saved many women from a lifetime of discontent.[16]

Troy's real-life model was Martha Sharpe's husband John, an ex-army farmer, whose military glamour and gift of the gab had dazzled young Hardy in 1849. Troy's heartless womanizing came from the 'soldier' with the 'winning tongue' in M.G. Lewis's song. 'The Banks of Allan Water', which had supplied the first title for *A Pair of Blue Eyes*. That soldier's 'lovely' victim, found on the 'Banks' in a snowstorm, became a 'spot' on a river-bank, throwing 'morsels of snow' at Troy's window in the barracks. The spot was called Fanny Robin, presumably after Emma's 'beloved mare'. *Tess* would more clearly show Hardy's tendency to associate seduced women with birds and horses.[17]

But it was more through setting than characters or plot that Hardy's own experience entered the novel. Here he first named as 'Wessex' the 'horizons and landscapes' of the 'partly real, partly dream country' where his stories were located. In this one the 'real' part centred on Puddletown ('Weatherbury'). Though that was Tryphena's home, the novel's chief attraction has little to do with her. It came from Hardy's love of the surrounding countryside, as he wandered about it by himself in early youth. What one remembers most is Gabriel Oak 'standing alone on a hill' beneath the stars. Rhythmically, his name was an echo of Maniel Riggs, the shepherd recently 'found dead' as Gabriel nearly was. But the initial impulse to write about a shepherd probably came form Hardy's own taste for solitude in a natural environment.[18]

Part of the Wessex conception, then very popular, was the wit and wisdom of the local inhabitants. With changed expectations of social classes and regional speakers, Hardy's rustic dialogues, like Shakespeare's, have lost some of their intrinsic charm, and may even tempt one to skip. But they were now becoming strictly functional. Cain Ball's choking-fit, irritating in itself, added suspense to the shock of Bathsheba's involvement with Troy; and the much funnier conversation at the Buck's Head served as foil to Fanny Robin's tragedy, while keeping her above ground long enough to figure in her big scene, 'Fanny's Revenge'.[19]

By a 'pastoral tale' Hardy meant not just a tale about a shepherd, but a contribution to the pastoral tradition from Theocritus, Virgil, and Longus to Milton and Matthew Arnold. Was Troy's failure to drown a sardonic gloss on the famous lines: 'Weep no more, woful shepherds weep no more, / For *Lycidas* your sorrow is not dead, / Sunk though he be beneath the watry floor'? The 'Pastoral Tragedy' had more obvious literary roots. The 'chalk-pit' that killed Oak's sheep, thanks to an over-zealous sheepdog, was like the 'pits' in *Daphnis and Chloe*, designed to protect the flocks from a wolf, but only managing 'to kill a great many sheep and goats'. The dog's inability to distinguish 'between doing a thing well enough and doing it too well' had its counterpart in Longus too, when the sheepdogs started biting the wolf-skin that Dorcon was wearing, and continued to bite when they 'got at Dorcon himself'.[20]

As Hardy pointed out in a footnote, Gabriel called his missing sheep 'in Latin'. He was then compared to the *nautae* in the *Eclogues*: 'He called again: the valleys and furthest hills resounded as when the sailors invoked the lost Hylas on the Mysian shore; but no sheep.' Neither Virgil in that passage, nor Theocritus in its original source called the shore 'Mysian'. That detail could have been found in a classical dictionary, but possibly came from the *Argonautica* version of the same story, which did name the country. There the only person to hear Hylas's cry for help, as the nymph dragged him down to his death, was the Argonaut Polyphemus, aptly associated with the idea of danger to sheep: 'Like a wild beast that hears the voices of sheep in the distance, and goes hungrily after them, but finds no flocks, for the shepherds have already got them into the sheepfold . . . so Polyphemus grieved greatly . . .'[21]

In Theocritus the Cyclops Polyphemus, transformed from a cruel monster into a pathetically ugly shepherd, falls in love with the sea-nymph Galatea. If the Argonaut contributed to the 'Pastoral Tragedy', the Cyclops probably helped in the 'Description of Farmer Oak'. Visually grotesque, especially when getting his watch out, Gabriel's multiple moral character 'in the scale of public opinion' made him etymologically, too, a Polyphemus, i.e. someone of whom may things are said.[22]

As lovers Oak and Polyphemus have much in common. Polyphemus serenades Galatea from a rock on the beach. Oak oils his 'sandy' hair until it looks like 'wet seaweed round a boulder after the ebb.' Polyphemus offers Galatea a list of inducements to live with him, including milk, cheese, iced water, and music: 'I can play the pipe better than any Cyclops here'. Oak's list, while including a gig and a cucumber-frame, starts with a piano – 'and I'll practise up the flute right well to play with you in the evenings.' Both shepherds' dogs are involved in the courtship. Galatea pelts Polyphemus's dog with apples, as he barks at the sea. Bathsheba calls Gabriel's dog 'a nasty brute'. Polyphemus is told of Galatea: 'She runs away from you when you try to love her, and runs after you when you don't.' That is almost literally how Bathsheba reacts to Oak's proposal. Polyphemus studies his reflection in the water, and decides that he is not so ugly as people say. Bathsheba looks at herself in a mirror, and smiles with satisfaction. Here the male's action was transferred to the female, but the initial model for the Gabriel-Bathsheba relationship was clearly that of the Cyclops and the slippery sea-nymph, taken almost allegorically: Oak had no eye for any woman but one.[23]

The pastoral mixture was thickened with a dash of philosophy. Hardy had been reading Comte, in a translation given him by Moule. Comte's Positivism promised what Hardy needed, a 'satisfactory synthesis of all human conceptions', incorporating science and social reform, without sacrificing imaginative or spiritual feeling. It replaced Christianity by 'The Religion of Humanity', and looked for support from 'Women' and 'the Working Classes', since women naturally relied on 'Feeling, the most influential part of human nature', and the working classes' 'high intellectual and moral qualities' made them 'a most important source of moral power.'[24]

Comte saw Humanity struggling to improve things, against 'the defects of the External Order', 'the immutable Necessity of the external world', e.g. 'the phenomena of the Solar System'. Oak's struggle starts against that immutable background of the stars. Enter Woman, '*mutabile semper*', according to Virgil, but to Comte 'the spontaneous priestess of Humanity'. Oak's love for Bathsheba makes him an altruist. 'The heart,' wrote Comte, 'cannot throw off its original selfishness, without the aid of some complete and enduring affection.' Thus Gabriel achieves what Comte called 'the real happiness of man, pure and disinterested love', crowned by a marriage of 'good fellowship – *cameraderie*'. For Comte, while admitting that sex had usually 'something – to do' with marriage, insisted that 'all the best results' of marriage might follow from a 'union . . . as chaste as that of brother and sister', 'a perfect ideal of friendship'.[25]

Philosophical pastoral was finally spiced with theatrical melodrama. The Hazlewood *Lady Audley*, for instance, used two stock features of the genre, the resurrection (when a character thought dead suddenly comes on stage) and the tableau (when the actors freeze into a dramatic picture). Just as the Lady is charged with her husband's murder, the husband makes his entrance and 'Omnes' cry 'Alive!' Her confession of insanity is then followed by the stage-direction: *'falls – dies – music – tableau of sympathy'*. The first device was reproduced when Bathsheba's husband, supposedly drowned, 'advanced into the middle of the room, took off his cap, turned down his coat-collar, and looked Boldwood in the face.' The second was imitated when she and her husband stood on either side of Fanny's open coffin, and he, from a stance of 'well-nigh congealed immobility', bent down in slow motion to kiss the corpse. A third feature of melodrama was recognizable behind the murder. In *The Factory Lad* (1832) the heartless factory-owner was shot dead by one of the accused across a crowded court-room. The hero of Tom Robertson's *Birth* (1870) was similarly shot in a crowd-scene, but predictably kept alive for a surprise entrance 'with his arm in a sling'. Troy, shot in the middle of the Christmas party, hardly qualified for a second resurrection.[26]

Such heterogeneous materials were individualized by Hardy's personality, especially in the presentation of animals as victims of injustice. The young dog was shot for doing his job 'too well'. The dog that played Good Samaritan to Fanny was stoned for his pains. Bathsheba's pony was presumably 'beloved' like Emma's, but the 'restive' circus horse existed only to be publicly 'tamed' by Troy. Tenderly nursing a new-born lamb in the small hours, Oak looked the very picture of a Good Shepherd. But he was always worried by the thought that 'his flock ended in mutton – that a day came and found every shepherd an arrant traitor to his defenceless sheep.'[27]

This aspect of the pastoral theme was summed up by the 'multitudes' of terrified sheep 'bleating piteously' on their journey to the Fair, 'a tall shepherd rising here and there in the midst of them, like a gigantic idol amid a crowd of prostrate devotees.' For them even the sheep-shearing, which showed Oak's technical skill, was a painful ordeal, as he 'put down the luncheon to drag a frightened ewe to his shear-station, flinging it over upon its back with a dexterous twist of the arm.' For humans the ovine strip-tease, 'like Aphrodite rising from the foam' might have sexual suggestions, and the snipping in the groin showed that Bathsheba had 'wounded the ewe's shearer in a still more vital part.' But the real victim was the ewe.[28]

In *Far from the Madding Crowd* Hardy proved himself 'a good hand at a serial'; but no serial written against time can be perfectly shaped, and this one lacked the structural elegance of *Under the Greenwood Tree*. Henry James was wrong, though, to call the movel defective in 'composition'. Bathshheba's three lovers, for instance, were arranged in a neat chiastic pattern, with Gabriel as alpha and omega bracketing the other two.[29]

The transitions between the love-affairs were delicately managed through visual, musical, and Biblical symbolism. Just when Oak, by putting out the night-fire, seems set to make progress with Bathsheba, he meets an unknown girl in the darkness, later identified as Fanny, Troy's victim and harbinger. Boldwood is first introduced as an unseen visitor with a 'deep voice', asking about Fanny. His ousting of Gabriel is marked by the shearing-supper, where the farmer joins Bathsheba inside the candle-lit room, leaving the shepherd in the twilight outside. Translated into music, Boldwood's stronger position is expressed by the contrast between his 'profound' bass and Gabriel's 'dulcet piping'. But Bathsheba's song, 'The Banks of Allan Water' portends her experience with Troy, and the picture of her listeners, reclining 'against each other as at suppers in the early ages of the world' suggests that for Boldwood this is a Last Supper before a betrayal. 'The same night' (the Prayer Book phrase), Bathsheba gets 'entangled' with Troy, who suddenly appears from the darkness, 'like the sound of a trumpet [from] silence', 'brilliant in brass and scarlet', outshining both the night-fire of Oak's first success and the candle-lit window-picture of Boldwood's. The subdued character of Gabriel's final triumph was also shown visually and musically. The wedding was carefully kept dark, took place on a Foggy Morning', and was celebrated, not with a trumpet, but with the 'venerable worm-eaten instruments' of the village band.[30]

Despite its happy ending, the novel's world was not a happy place. Human beings ill-treated animals and each other, while Comte's 'External Order' ill-treated human beings. The 'Pastoral Tragedy' was no one's fault: it was in the nature of things. A good man was sent mad, by the natural thoughtlessness of the young, and hanged for murder. A bad man's pathetic attempt to reform was instantly frustrated by 'The Gurgoyle', a 'horrible stone entity' aptly representing the humorous malice of external forces. Having sought refuge from human misery in Nature, the heroine found she had slept on the edge of a 'malignant' swamp that seemed to exhale 'the essences of evil things in the earth, and in the waters under the earth'. The echo of the Ten Commandments implied, not that Bathsheba was being punished for idolizing Troy, but that religion was no more comfort than Nature – a thought repeated when the passing schoolboy made nonsense of the collect he was learning.[31]

Comfort was only to be found in human solidarity. Comte called it 'universal Love'. Hardy still thought of it in Christian terms, as Charity or loving-kindness, and here he expressed it in the 'transient little picture of Liddy crossing the swamp' to comfort Bathsheba. Details were added to the picture as if to illustrate the Gospel text: 'For I was an hungred, and ye gave me meat: I was thirsty, and ye gave me drink . . . Naked, and ye clothed me': 'Liddy vanished, and at the end of twenty minutes returned with a cloak, hat, some slices of bread and butter, a tea-cup, and some hot tea in a little china jug.'[32]

7

The Hand of Ethelberta

When the *Cornhill* serial ended in December 1874, Leslie Stephen asked for another, to start in April. Hardy agreed to produce one for July. Even so, as he later explained, he had no time to think what sort of book he really wanted to write. He knew his last novel had been popular, and since he now wrote for a living, popularity was important. But what had that novel contained of genuine 'value . . . on which to build a career as a writer with a real literary message'? Commercially, he might do best to cash in on his 'reputation for a speciality'; but he did not want to be typecast as a 'sheepfarming' or even a rustic novelist.[1]

To show he could do something quite different, Hardy 'put aside a woodland story he had thought of', and deliberately surprised his public and his publishers, by producing 'a comedy, or satire, on the fusion of classes', over a third of it set in London. Despite Smith, Elder's dismay at this change of course, he managed to negotiate much better terms than last time: £700 for the English serial and volume, and £550 more for serialization in America. That was in March 1875. The same month he sent off the first instalment, and then, as he told his publisher, moved 'to Town for three months on account of Ethelberta', i.e. to new furnished rooms in Newton Road, Westbourne Grove, not too far from the 'house on the north side of Hyde Park' where Ethelberta would first appear in fashionable society. Perhaps it was also on account of Emma, who after Paris may have been finding Surbiton a little dull.[2]

While writing the novel, Hardy made notes for future poems, notably 'an Iliad of Europe from 1789 to 1815.' By way of preliminary research he visited Chelsea Hospital on 18 June, and talked to a Pensioner who had fought at Waterloo, exactly sixty years before. He also accepted two invitations that marked his new standing as an author. He joined a deputation to Disraeli calling for a Parliamentary inquiry into the law of copyright; and he replied to the toast of 'Literature' at an Oxford undergraduate club dinner. A third invitation indicated his growing friendship with his editor. This was to witness Leslie Stephen's signature to a deed renouncing his clerical status. Ordained in 1855 simply to qualify for a Cambridge fellowship, he was now too conscientious an agnostic to remain even technically a clergyman. After the formal business of that late-night meeting, the two sceptics had a cosy chat about 'theologies decayed and defunct, the origin of things, the constitution of matter, the unreality of time, and kindred subjects.'[3]

Having got the feel of Ethelberta's 'Town' environment, Hardy turned to her Wessex one, and in late June started 'house-hunting' in Dorset. Finding nothing suitable at Shaftesbury, Blandford, or Wimborne, he took Emma in July to Bournemouth, where after her death he would remember sitting with her at a window, staring out at the pouring rain: 'We were irked by the scene, by each other . . .' Typical seaside weather, and a very normal reaction to it; but Hardy's irritability may have had other causes. Besides the frustrations of trying to write a book while house-hunting, Emma had invited his mother to Bournemouth, so that they could get to know each other, but Jemima had got Kate to reply: 'she is so very busy just now that she cannot possibly come.' She evidently wanted them to come to Bockhampton instead.[4]

A few days later they found and moved into rooms in West End Cottage, Swanage. There they had a splendid view over the bay, and a landlord, Captain Masters, who told them 'strange stories' about his life at sea. Short of having a home of their own, they could hardly have found a better place to live. They 'walked daily on the cliffs and shore', which inspired Emma to start writing her long story, 'The Maid on the Shore'. As for Hardy, the Swanage area gave him a suggestive setting for Ethelberta's later history. A 'Breakfast Picnic' at Corfe Castle in September neatly combined authorial business with pleasure; for Hardy's sisters Mary and Kate came too, and got on well with Emma. Her lively sketch of the outing ended enthusiastically: 'A splendid day – fine breeze, fine hills, fine trees. A most beautiful road.'[5]

In November the *Examiner* offered to serialize Hardy's next novel, but this time he was not going to commit himself too soon: 'My intention is to suspend my writing – for domestic reasons chiefly – for a longer time than usual after finishing *Ethelberta*, which I am sorry to say is not nearly done yet.' Ostensibly, 'domestic reasons' meant the search for a permanent home, but they probably included a realization that writing under constant pressure spoiled his relationship with Emma. It made him go through life in blinkers, missing what mattered most. The 1917 poem subtitled '(Bournemouth 1875)' would express bitter regret for his blindness in thinking there was 'Nothing to read', when there had been so much to read in his wife. Yet even that November he had noted: 'He has read well who has learnt that there is more to read outside books than in them.'[6]

The last instalment of the serial went off in late January 1876, and in March the Hardys moved into rooms at 7 St Peter Street, Yeovil, Somerset, 'to facilitate their search for a little dwelling' in north Dorset. When the novel came out in two volumes (3 April 1876), it was quite well reviewed, but less enthusiastically than its predecessor. Still, all but sixty-one of the thousand copies printed were sold in two years. Matthew Arnold, not a great reader of modern novels, put this one on his reading-list. That Emma never opened a copy inscribed to her by 'the Author' is best explained by assuming that she had made a fair copy of it, and knew the text only too well already. As she told a friend in 1910: 'My husband's books have not the same kind of interest for me as for others. I know every word of the first edition – in MS sitting by his side.[7]

The most obvious effect of Hardy's life upon the book was topographical. Named after the chief ruler of the Anglo-Saxons, and a village near Weymouth, Ethelberta Chickerel was first seen in the Saxon town of Wareham ('Anglebury'), stepping out of the Red Lion inn (its real name). The life-size statue of a chained Black Bear above the next inn door probably suggested the grim thought that Ethelberta had been trained to be a lady, just as 'a bear may be taught to dance.' From London she retired to Swanage ('knollsea'), and joined the Hardys in their 'cottage . . . on a high slope above this townlet', sharing their view and their seafaring landlord. With them she visited Corfe Castle ('Corvsgate'), repeated their honeymoon trip to Rouen, and ended up living at Encombe House ('Enckworth Court'), on the road that had brought the Hardys from Wareham station to Swanage.[8]

In Shelley's *Julian and Maddalo*, Julian was Shelley himself, and Christopher Julian was in some respects Hardy. Playing the piano for the dance, he virtually re-enacted Hardy's early 'adventures with the fiddle', his fingers 'tingling' afterwards just as Hardy's 'finger-tips' had tingled 'from pressing the strings'. Like his author, he was intensely susceptible to the charm of 'the female form', 'sometimes read as he walked', and was apt to obscure 'the scene before his eyes' by subjective 'visions'. More generally, he appears to have represented the plus and minus sides of Hardy's self-image. 'A born musician, artist, poet, seer, mouthpiece . . . of Nature's oracles', he was handicapped by 'his too general habit of accepting the most clouded possibility that chances offered'. Finally ineffectual, the hero seems almost a caricature of his author.[9]

As a 'Professed Story-teller', who sat 'in a chair – as if she were at her own fireside', Ethelberta was a revised version of Hardy's paternal grandmother, whose fireside stories had entranced him as a child. Her method of housing and supporting her family in London was suggested by his mother's plan to become a London 'club-house cook'. Her experience, judged 'impossible' by the critics, of being waited on by her father at a dinner-party, was adapted from an awkward one of Hardy's. Only the year before he had been waited on at dinner by the father of an ex-girlfriend, Cassie Pole.[10]

But Ethelberta had more important connections with Hardy. As a working-class intellectual who had climbed into a higher social bracket, she felt vulnerable to snobbish talk about her background. Hardy had recently suffered from 'quizzing personal gossip', including a newspaper report that he was 'a house-decorator', like Ethelberta's brother Dan. She began as a poet, ended 'writing an epic poem' ('an Iliad of Europe'?), and 'felt that to write prose would be an uncongenial occupation'. Her first published poems were 'playful' (Lady Petherwin called them 'ribald'), with 'a single mournful' one 'at the very end'. Hardy was about to publish his first poem, 'The Bride-Night Fire' (so ribald that it had to be 'Bowdlerized for the magazine'), and the mournful ones would remain unpublished until the very end of his career as a novelist, or 'Professed Story-teller'.[11]

Ethelberta's mother thought her performances 'an impossible castle-in-the-air sort of trade for getting a living by'. After a 'triumphant opening' Ethelberta herself saw audiences getting smaller, and feared that this method of supporting her family might fail. With parents of sixty-four and sixty-two, two younger sisters, and a class-conscious wife to support, Hardy was probably feeling just as anxious. Perhaps *Far from the Madding Crowd* had been a one-off 'happy accident'. Meanwhile dreaming up stories to meet monthly deadlines must often have felt almost like improvising them before a live audience. How long could he keep it up?[12]

Besides practical anxiety, there was an element of self-disgust. Family responsibilities forced Ethelberta into prostitution, literally when she married Lord Mountclere, almost literally when her audience-appeal was enhanced by 'the brilliant and expressive eye of a handsome woman', and metaphorically throughout her campaign to charm London society – especially when she used Milton's denunciation of Mammon to further her mercenary ends. Her self-disgust surfaced in two animal-contexts: the first when she found that Neigh's social status was based on starving horses before slaughtering them, and sensed that he and she were 'cattle of one colour'; the second when she disowned the donkey that had carried her to Corvsgate Castle: 'My God, what a thing am I!'[13]

Hardy had analogous feelings. A born poet, he was writing the sort of prose that magazine readers wanted, simply to make money. By instinct a 'solitary' countryman who disliked 'going about to dinners and clubs and crushes as a business', he was doing so in pursuit of his novel-writing 'trade'. Wanting to live his life 'as an emotion', he was treating it as 'a scientific game'. He had become ' a good hand at a serial', just as Ethelberta was 'a rare hand at contrivances', but they were both getting sick of it. Both probably felt disloyal to their families. Socially, Ethelberta was 'of no family', and had to hush up the Chickerels; but they were what she cared about most. And much of Hardy would have endorsed Julian's conclusion: 'The only feeling which has any dignity or permanence or worth is family affection between close blood-relations.'[14]

The novel was subtitled *A Comedy in Chapters*. The chapter headings gave scenes, not summaries of incidents, and the presentation was generally theatrical. As in Sheridan's *The Rivals,* the first characters were introduced by a street-dialogue between servants. Upper-class dialogue was often laboriously witty, as in Restoration Comedy. At the Rouen hotel there was more *Box and Cox* farce, when two suitors popped their heads simultaneously out of adjacent windows, to see a third popping the question on the balcony below. And the story ended with a stagy lighting effect, when Mountclere struck a match in a dark carriage to show Ethelberta his face. The supposed rescuer from marriage revealed as the chuckling husband was an idea already tried out in Hardy's first short story (1874), but here it was reworked to create pure melodrama.[15]

The novel's theatricality expressed its theme: Ethelberta was acting a part, and so were most people in fashionable society. The Belmaines, for instance, were 'perfectly ... practised in sustaining that complete divorce between thinking and saying which is the hall-mark of high civilization.' Hence the epigraph: '*Vitae post-scenia celant*', 'they hide what goes on behind the scenes of life.' But the quotation meant something more specific. It came from Lucretius's warning against the illusions of sexual love, and his advice on how to cure the 'madness'. One remedy suggested was to realize that the glamorous beauty is a perfectly ordinary woman 'behind the scenes', though she takes great pains to conceal it. Ethelberta's ordinariness consisted chiefly in her family background, but the Lucretian prejudice against sexual love itself coloured the whole novel.[16]

That passage in Lucretius was the germ of Ovid's *Remedies for Love,* and Ethelberta's 'gay and amatory verse' was noticeably Ovidian. It began with an *Ars Amatoria,* given the feminist slant of the *Heroides*: 'a series of playful defences of the supposed strategy of womankind in fascination, courtship, and marriage'. It ended with a *Tristia,* Ovid's 'single mournful poem'. While Hardy was reading Ovid around 1856, he had started to read Homer. Ethelberta's character was precisely that of Odysseus: a stoical adventurer, devoted to home life, but meanwhile fairly promiscuous, and above all '*polumetis*', 'of many contrivances'. Her return to Enckworth Court neatly paralleled his to Ithaca: 'When she first entered the house, everybody was against her. She had to fight a whole host of them single-handed.' Odysseus put paid to his wife's suitors. Ethelberta quickly disposed of 'the *other* Lady Mountclere' and all the other 'women' in her husband's life. She even had a Homeric precedent for being 'occasionally too severe with the servants'. Odysseus hanged twelve of them on a single rope.[17]

There were also Victorian precedents for the novel's conclusion. Ethelberta's abortive flight from her husband followed the pattern of Marie Antoinette's 'Flight to Varennes', in Carlyle's *French Revolution.* The secret communication through a window, the carriage waiting in the dark, and the messages forged by the husband, probably came from Browning's *The Ring and the Book.* There Pompilia, another woman 'of no family', ran away from her cruel husband, Count Guido, only to be murdered by him later. Ethelberta survived, but her attractive personality did not. Transformed into a domestic tyrant, and last seen firmly in the driving seat, she fully justified her lover's final reaction: 'He stood a long time thinking; but he did not wish her his.'[18]

Her transformation parodied an early Tennyson poem about 'the fusion of classes', 'The Lord of Burleigh' (1842). Posing as a poor 'landscape-painter', the Lord married a 'village maiden', only then revealing his social status. Ethelberta played much the same trick in reverse, while her suitor Ladywell repeated the painting without the poverty: 'he has a pretty good private income beyond what he gets from practising his line of business'. Faced with 'the burthen of an honour / Unto which she was not born', the village maiden sickened and died. Ethelberta lived and dictated. With 'everybody respecting her', there was no reason to think that 'the people loved her much', or that she ever 'loved [her husband] truly'. Still, as 'steward, and agent, and everything' she carried out all too literally Lady Burleigh's original resolve: 'She will order all things duly, / When beneath his roof they come.'[19]

According to the 1895 Preface, the story was 'somewhat frivolous', and meant to be be read with 'a certain lightness of mood'. It seems, however, to express the sadness of exile – not, like Ovid's *Tristia*, from civilization, but from home, natural life, poetry. Prosaic in most of its subject-matter, the novel made two moves towards poetry. The first was the symbolic prologue about the hawk and the duck. This was clearly suggested by the fights between an eagle and a snake in the *Iliad* and *The Revolt of Islam*, by Penelope's dream about the eagle and the geese in the *Odyssey*, and possibly by Lycaenion's story of the eagle and the goose in *Daphnis and Chloe*.[20]

In the *Iliad* the snake's escape from the eagle is taken as a warning to the Trojans not to bite off more than they can chew, but Hector scorns to 'trust birds': 'The best of all bird-omens is to defend one's fatherland.' That will be Ethelberta's attitude towards her family. In Shelley the snake means resistance to tyranny, and its death marks the failure of the French Revolution. In the *Odyssey* the eagle's slaughter of twenty geese predicts Odysseus's slaughter of the suitors, which Ethelberta will parallel when disposing of her husband's 'women'. In Longus the story of the goose abducted by the eagle is merely an Ethelberta-type 'contrivance' of Lycaenion's to get Daphnis to herself. All these meanings were relevant to Ethelberta's history; but in Hardy's account of the hawk-duck conflict, the predator was ultimately out-manoeuvred by its prey. Thus 'the great cruel bird' aptly represented Mountclere and the tyranny of the social system, while the casting of Ethelberta as a 'harmless duck' anticipated the irony of the book's conclusion. Meanwhile the duck's ultimate refuge was 'a hole through to a nether sky', a wonderfully suggestive image for the limitless resources of this maiden in distress.[21]

The other episode that verged on the multiple significance of poetry was Ethelberta's donkey-ride to Corvsgate Castle. Her view from the ridge of two weathers 'wrestling for mastery immediately in her pathway' struck her as 'typical of her own fortunes', but the full implications of that idea were left for the reader to work out. Corvsgate was the meeting-ground of two cultures, the 'civilized' and the spontaneous. They had met on page one, when Ethelberta had flung off her 'diadem-and-sceptre bearing', released her 'animal spirits', and actually started running. Now they met again, when a ring of passengers from 'shining carriages' gathered round her donkey. But the two weathers were also her own 'versatile moods'. In one of self-confidence she had decided that going by donkey was socially acceptable as an 'unconventionality – almost eccentricity' to be expected in 'a poetess'. Now she was 'suddenly overcome with dread to meet them all single-handed as she stood', and the donkey would not do.[22]

Yet that 'faithful beast' had more than social connotations. From the ridge the Channel looked like 'a New Jerusalem', and from one point of view Corvsgate Castle seems very like the old one. Her entrance into it, riding on a 'humble ass', recalls that of Jesus into Jerusalem, 'lowly, and riding upon an ass'. The association was justified by her genuinely Christian motives. Everything she did was 'to benefit her brothers and sisters', including her final act of self-sacrifice, the voluntary crucifixion of marrying Lord Mountclere. But when asked in so many words how the donkey 'could have got up' there, she virtually repeated Peter's 'I know not the man': 'Many come and picnic here . . . and the animal may have been left till they return from some walk.' Realizing what he had done, Peter 'went out and wept bitterly.' Ethelberta gave 'a groan'.[23]

She groaned at the 'inconsistency' between her altruistic ethics and her natural egotism, 'the pride and emulation which had made her what she was'. That conflict was implicit in the novel's punning title. *The Hand of Ethelberta* meant her hand in marriage; the hand dealt to her in the 'scientific game' of her life, i.e. her 'stock of saleable originality'; and her Odyssean resourcefulness, as 'a rare hand at contrivances'. Since the Preface called the book 'a drama . . . wherein servants were as important as, or more important than their masters', there may also have been a private allusion to the surname of Hardy's ex-cook mother, Jemima Hand and her servant relatives.[24]

But the *Hand* of the title meant something more. *The Mayor of Casterbridge* would feel that he was 'in Somebody's hand', and Ethelberta liked playing Providence. Gabriel Oak had liked playing it too, but only in a humble way, as Bathsheba's guardian angel. Comte had actually recommended human beings to take over that role: 'the conception of man becoming . . . the arbiter . . . of his own destiny, has in it something far more satisfying than the old belief in Providence'. Picotee, at least, was fully satisfied with Ethelberta's performance in the part. The book ended with Julian's amusement at 'Picotee's utter dependence, now as ever, upon her sister, as upon an eternal Providence.'[25]

For other people the Hand of Ethelberta qua Providence proved less satisfactory. Like King Ethelbert, the Viscount followed his wife into the Christian church – but only by being marched off there 'every Sunday as regular as a clock'. Ruling him and his whole household with a rod of iron, she imposed a régime of joyless efficiency. That she marked 'the trees to be felled' reminds us of her first tree-felling exploit. What she had enjoyed then was 'the sense of novel power . . . A landscape was to be altered to suit her whim', and the exercise of such power had finally become an addiction. As for her own relations, she had long been 'the prime ruler of the courses of them all', and had married for their benefit. But she had not made them happy: 'She might have pleased her family better by pleasing her tastes'. And the chief result of her educational programme was that Joey now knew all about the sex-life of 'that pagan apostle Jupiter', and thus qualified for 'genteel living' as a parson – or even a bishop.[26]

8

The Return of the Native

Hardy had now published five novels in as many years, and he needed a break. After finishing the fifth, he had told his publisher: 'I do not wish to attempt any more original writing of any length for a few months, until I can learn the best line to take for the future'. As a first step towards collecting his thoughts and generating new ones, he got Emma to copy into a leather-bound notebook entitled 'Literary Notes I' all the extracts he had made from his reading since 1863. He then started reading more systematically, and within a few months had added at least 850 items to that notebook.[1]

The second step was a holiday abroad. In May 1876, after a fortnight in London, they went off on a round trip to Holland, the Rhine, and Brussels. Apart from the change of scene, the tour was useful to Hardy in three ways. From Brussels he was able to 'explore' the Waterloo battlefield, with a view to his 'Iliad of Europe'. Germany gave him some some good settings for episodes in his later fiction. And at Heidelberg he saw something that clearly affected the conception of his next novel:

> looking west one evening from the top of the tower on the Königsstuhl, Hardy remarks on a singular optical effect that was almost tragic. Owing to mist the wide landscape itself was not visible, but 'the Rhine glared like a riband of blood, as if it serpentined throught the atmosphere above the earth's surface.'[2]

By that time poor Emma was past caring about optical effects. Her 'occasional lameness, suffered from early childhood', had made the climb to the tower in hot weather, 'by rugged steps and slippery places' an exhausting ordeal. Tough and courageous as she normally was, just then she was nursing an infection. It came out a few days later at Strasbourg, with 'fever' and and an 'ulcerated throat'. Hardy thought he had 'set her right in a day or two', with a 'thick brown mysterious fluid' bought at an Italian chemist's. But she was only just convalescent when they got to Brussels.[3]

Before they left London, Hardy had told a friend: 'We are ... on our way to Brussels &c'. Knowing his priorities, Emma gamely helped him research the Waterloo area on foot, enjoying all she could of it herself – the 'glass of delicious milk each (black stove, huge wardrobe)' at La Belle Alliance, the 'basket of skulls – teeth perfect' at La Haye Sainte, and the 'little child [that] ran into the garden and gave me flowers'. But next day she wrote: 'I am still greatly fatigued, & Tom is cross about it.' He was perhaps more cross with himself than with her, for having made her walk so far.[4]

In *Ethelberta* Hardy had mentioned the type of rainy day when 'clerks' wives hate living in lodgings'. Now Emma wrote despondently: 'Going back to England where we have no home and no chosen county.' Next month (3 July 1876) they got both – a 'pretty cottage overlooking the Dorset Stour – called Riverside Villa ... at Sturminster Newton ... It was their first house and, though small, probably that in which they spent their happiest days.' The semi-detached house is still attractive, with a fine view over the river; but of the two things they hoped to produce there, a book and a baby, the second came only by proxy. Their maid, spotted one night with a man in the outhouse, and 'ordered' back to bed, disappeared before morning through the dining-room window, and two months later was reported pregnant. 'We hear that Jane, our late servant, is soon to have a baby. Yet never a sign of one is there for us.'[5]

The book did materialize, but not immediately. Passing through London, fresh from Waterloo, Hardy had revisited Chelsea Hospital, talked again to the Waterloo survivor John Bentley, and thought about the Napoleonic wars. Back in Dorset, he started planning a novel about the return of a native, set in the immediate neighbourhood of his own birthplace. Taking Emma to Bockhampton that Christmas must have seemed a good way of getting his wife and parents to know each other, while reminding himself of the place and its atmosphere. There is no hard evidence that Jemima and Emma hated each other on sight, but there is no sign either of any warm feeling between them.[6]

The other object of the visit was more evidently realized. Once back at Sturminster after Christmas, with a sharpened picture in his mind of the heath behind the Bockhampton cottage, Hardy started writing about 'the vast tract of unenclosed wild known as Egdon Heath'. By April 1877 he had written thirteen chapters – but then came the problem of finding a publisher. Disappointed by *Ethelberta*, Leslie Stephen refused to commit himself about the *Return*, until he could see the whole novel. He feared 'the relations between Eustacia, Wildeve, and Thomasin might develop into something "dangerous" for a family magazine'. *Blackwood's* rejected the story because of its slow start: there was 'hardly anything like . . . Novel interest' in the opening scenes. *Temple Bar* turned it down too, and after extensive rewriting Hardy finally got it accepted by a rather down-market magazine called *Belgravia* (edited by the author of *Lady Audley*), at a fee of only £240 for the twelve instalments.[7]

He had wanted the book-version out by May 1878, but rewriting and finding a publisher delayed its appearance until November. This caused financial difficulties in the interval, especially as both his new publishers, Chatto and Windus in London, and Harpers, who were serializing the novel in New York, proved unpunctual in paying his monthly fees. Money was so tight that the Hardys were glad of £9 for a short story in a Christmas annual, 'The Thieves Who Couldn't Help Sneezing'.[8]

Set in Blackmoor Vale north of Sturminster, it shared several features with the novel that Hardy was writing: the darkness and solitude of the opening scene; the initial reference to 'elderly gentlemen's walking-sticks', like that of the 'old man' who first represented 'Humanity' in the *Return*; the 'yeoman's son' hero recalling Clym's surname. But the sound of 'wind, rain, and sea battling in a hurricane' threatened no triple drowning. It merely described the response of three horse-thieves to snuff in a cupboard. And the 'Cheerfulness' of the hero's final reunion with his beloved horse, unlike the final union of Thomasin and Venn, was unclouded by any doubts of its 'artistic' propriety.[9]

A more serious cash-raising expedient was the hasty compression of the *Poor Man* into a magazine story. The need for such hack work was probably the main factor in Hardy's decision 'that the practical side of his vocation of novelist demanded that he should have his head-quarters in or near London.' So in March 1878 they reluctantly ended their 'Sturminster Newton idyll', and moved on a three-year lease into 1 Arundel Terrace, Trinity Road, Upper Tooting. This fairly new house, with a laburnum tree in its not too small garden, seemed exactly what they needed. From Wandsworth Common station, just down the road, they could get quickly into central London, while the Common itself, close by, gave a pleasant sense of being almost in the country. 'We might have ventured on Kensington', Hardy told a new friend who lived there, 'but for such utter rustics as ourselves Tooting seemed town enough to begin with.'[10]

Thus Hardy's return to his native county had ended before *The Return of the Native* came out in book form (4 November 1878). Clym had finally 'found his vocation'; but Hardy, according to the reviews, had certainly not found his. The result of his deliberate efforts to 'learn the best line to take for the future' was judged by the *Athenaeum* 'distinctly inferior to anything' he had written before. The novel meant to express his mature view of life, 'all that a man learns between 20 and 40', was disparaged by the *Saturday Review* as a fiction constructed for himself, 'rather than for other people'. His calculated attempt at tragic poetry in prose seemed to the *Spectator* 'less than tragedy – dreariness, rather than tragedy'. And in the *Academy* the poet of 'Invictus', W.E. Henley, gratuitously bloodied

Hardy's head: 'rare artist as he is, there is something wanting in his personality, and he is not quite a great man.' Even before that attack, Hardy had noted: 'November 28. Woke before it was light. Felt that I had not enough staying power to hold my own in the world.'[11]

'I got to like the character of Clym before I had done with him', wrote Hardy in 1912, after proofreading the novel for the Wessex Edition. 'I think he is the nicest of all my heroes, and *not a bit* like me.' Clym's niceness is not very obvious on 'a Black Morning', and his unlikeness seems even more overstated. In situation, feelings, and environment he clearly came close to Hardy. Both 'natives' had returned disillusioned with the lucrative urban jobs they had got for themselves, Clym's success in 'the nick-nack trade' matching Hardy's in catering for magazine readers. Clym's plan 'to get properly qualified' by systematic reading was equivalent to Hardy's, and Clym's eye-trouble recalled those 'floating specks' seen by Hardy in 1872, soon after Moule's warning that something might 'happen to his eyes'.[12]

Eustacia was quite unlike Emma except for her feeling about Paris; but Clym's period of happiness with her 'in their little house at Alderworth' paralleled 'our happiest time' at Sturminster. Neither Clym's nor Hardy's mother came to her son's wedding. Though little is known for certain about relations between Jemima and Emma, Hardy was undoubtedly devoted to his mother, and must have felt somewhat torn between her and his wife. According to his friend Sydney Cockerell, Mrs Yeobright was actually based on Jemima. Certainly Hardy's 'sketch-map of the scene of the story' put Mrs Yeobright's home, Blooms-End, roughly where Jemima was living, at Higher Bockhampton.[13]

Several other features of the narrative may be traced to Hardy's recent life. The 'dance on the green' that restarted Eustacia's affair with Wildeve was probably derived from the 'dancing on the green at Sturminster Newton' in June 1877. The baby conceived at Riverside Villas had not been Emma's, and the novel contained a similar irony: the baby called Eustacia was not Eustacia's. The 'froth of the waves' that concealed Clym's drowning wife was like the 'froth' of the 'flooded river' under the Sturminster bridge in November, described by Hardy in terms strongly suggestive of drowning: 'then the arch chokes, and after a silence coughs out the air and froth, and gurgles on.' The game of dice by the light of glowworms was adapted from the story of how Hardy's grandfather once posed as the devil 'reading a list of his victims by glow-worm light.' Perhaps Hardy had been reminded of the story by an optical effect he noticed in 1876: 'Cowslips under trees. A light proceeds from them, as from Chinese lanterns or glow-worms.'[14]

But the 'singular optical effect' at Heidelberg left more significant traces. The 'tragic' 'riband of blood' that 'glared' and 'serpentined through the atmosphere above the earth's surface' reappeared as 'the riband of bright firelight' that crossed Eustacia's path on the night she died, the 'red ribbon' used to identify her wax image, and the quasi-supernatural reddleman serpentining through the action, a 'blood-coloured figure' whose firelit van glared with 'a sinister redness', 'dull and lurid like a flame in sunlight'.[15]

And what of Hardy's recent reading? Philosophically, the novel owed something to an article of 1876 on 'The Ethics of Suicide', to Matthew Arnold's lecture on 'Pagan and Mediaeval Religious Sentiment' (1864), and to Walter Pater's *Renaissance* (1873). The article contrasted the pagan with the Christian view of suicide: Christians condemned it, pagans positively admired it. The proud pagan attitude was found epitomized in Swinburne's words: 'I kneel not, neither adore, *but, standing, look to the end.*' Eustacia (etymologically, 'well standing') has 'Pagan eyes' and takes the pagan view: 'Why should I not die if I wish?' Clym, a Christian in ethics if otherwise a a Comtist, says 'I . . . ought to have drowned myself', but does not do so. The article ascribed the increasing freqency of suicide to modern scepticism, which produced 'a gloom and dreariness of mind'. Hence, in the novel, the tragic expression of the 'modern type' face.[16]

Arnold's lecture contrasted Christianity with Hellenism. The Greeks were 'never made to be serious, never made to be sick or sorry'. But their 'ideal, cheerful, sensuous, pagan life' proved finally inadequate. The human condition demanded 'a religion of sorrow', like Mediaeval Christianity. At Sturminster the Hardys had read Keats together; and the epigraph from *Endymion*, which set the mood of the novel, repeated Arnold's point, that sorrow was inseparable from human life. Pater found fault not with Hellenism but with Christianity, for its 'crushing of the sensuous, the shutting of the door upon it, the flesh-outstripping interest'. Eustacia, with a mouth 'formed less to speak than to quiver, less to quiver than to kiss', was Hellenic in her sensuousness. Clym, whose 'love' for her 'was as chaste as that of Petrarch for his Laura', shut the door on that aspect of her nature.[17]

Such intellectual influences on the novel were reinforced by visual ones. The idea of the unbeautiful 'modern' face probably came from J.S. Mill's, seen with 'cameo clearness' in 1865, and recalled by G.F. Watts's portrait of him (1873). Eustacia, 'full-limbed and somewhat heavy', with 'extinguishing' dark hair, eyes 'full of nocturnal mysteries', and 'oppressive lids and lashes' sounds like a D.G. Rossetti painting, particularly his most recent one, the sinister *Astarte Syriaca* (1877). After such a description Hardy had no right to complain that his illustrator had made Eustacia look insufficiently 'youthful in face, supple in figure'.[18]

The picture most relevant to the novel's conception was Holman Hunt's *The Light of the World* (1853–6). This illustrated a Biblical passage containing the elements both of Clym's blindness and of Mrs Yeobright's attempt at reconciliation.

Thou art . . . blind . . . anoint thine eyes with eye-salve, that thou mayest see . . . Behold, I stand at the door, and knock: if any man hear my voice, and open the door, I will come in to him, and will sup with him, and he with me.

Explaining the picture's elaborate symbolism, Ruskin had pointed out 'the creeping tendrils of ivy, showing that [the door] has never been opened.' Hardy had borrowed that idea in *Far from the Madding Crowd* to disprove Troy's claim that he went to church through 'the old tower door'. Here, the the visual image of knocking at a closed door became central, not only to the plot's conclusion, but to its symbolism.[19]

As the title of Book Fourth, 'The Closed Door' referred specifically to Mrs Yeobright's experience, but it pointed to other things too: the final rift between two closed minds, the 'crushing of the sensuous', Clym's eviction of his wife. From her point of view it meant the exclusion of all options but suicide. Every other door seemed closed to her. Expelled from her new home, she returned to her old one, and 'found the front door closed and locked.' Wildeve seemed to offer a possible escape-route, but that was also barred: he was 'not *great* enough' to justify adultery. Susan's door was 'ajar', but inside was nothing but hatred. Only one door was opened for her, by the reddleman; but by then 'the cruel obstructiveness' of all about her' had determined her course.[20]

Neither thinkers nor painters, however, did as much for the novel as poets. Matthew Arnold's 'Scholar-Gipsy' (recently caricatured in Edward Lear's 'Dong with a Luminous Nose', 1877), offered precedents for Venn's mysterious comings and goings. Virgil and Theocritus supplied, in the witchcraft theme, a new metaphor for scepticism about love. Damon Wildeve took his first name from the shepherd in *Eclogue* viii. This poem, partly adapted from *Idyll* ii, enacted an incantation with a wax image melted in a fire, to bring back an unfaithful lover. Horace's witch Canidia (already alluded to in *A Pair of Blue Eyes*) also attempted it in *Epode* v, and D.G. Rossetti had adapted the theme in 'Sister Helen'. Eustacia was said to be 'a witch', and used a fire to 'recall' Wildeve. Like Rossetti's Helen she was helped by a small boy who had no idea what she was up to. She later became the target of the wax-image process herself, with another small boy involved. As the title of Book Third, 'The Fascination' was used in the Latin sense of the word, to mean 'the bewitching', with specific reference to Eustacia's effect on Clym, but also covering 'the fantastic nature of her passion' for him. She too was bewitched, 'in love with a vision' as unrealistic as Christian's 'fascinated' view of those 'magic machines' the dice. Thus love and gambling were presented as equivalent types of compulsive behaviour.[21]

Arnold's comparison of paganism with Christianity began with a translation of Theocritus, and ended with one from the *Oedipus Tyrannus*, having put Aeschylus and Sophocles among the 'four great names' offering guidance to 'the modern spirit'. Hardy's new reading programme had included them both. Of the *Prometheus Vinctus* he noted: 'Prometheus is bound down in a cleft of a rock in a distant desert of Scythia.' In character and in situation Eustacia resembled him. A figure of 'smouldering rebelliousness', she was imprisoned, 'as one in a desert', on Egdon Heath, 'her Hades', and 'eternally unreconciled thereto.' The tragedy ended with thunder, lightning, whirlwinds, 'air confounded with sea', and Prometheus protesting: 'You see how unjustly I suffer'. Eustacia's story ended with a 'chaos of the world without', a storm of wind and rain that seemed to utter 'the prologue to some tragedy', and she was last heard crying: 'I do not deserve my lot!'[22]

The bonfire 'Custom' was ascribed to 'spontaneous Promethean rebelliousness' against the darkness of winter, but the novel's fiery prologue came from another Aeschylus play, the *Agamemnon*. Whether or not Hardy had already read it around 1860, as he later suspected, FitzGerald's and Browning's translations of 1876 and 1877 would have made him read it then. It opens with a Watchman waiting through the night for a signal-fire to announce the fall of Troy. When he sees it, Clytaemnestra is called, and locates all the other fires that have been lighted to bring the news to Argos, including one on the Aegean island of Lemnos. From Rainbarrow at night 'thirty bonfires' were visible, 'the locality of each fire' identifiable 'by its angle and direction, though nothing of the scenery could be viewed.' At daybreak the lower hills round Rainbarrow looked like 'an archipelago in a fog-armed Aegean'. Eustacia first appeared in a place 'full of watchful intentness' as a figure waiting in the darkness, like the Watchman. Her use of fire-signals then associated her with Clytaemnestra – aptly enough, for she had her Aegisthus in Wildeve, and would prove lethal to her husband.[23]

But the *Oedipus Tyrannus* was a more pervasive influence. 'Humanity appears upon the Scene' as 'an old man' with 'a walking-stick which he used as a veritable third leg'. The answer to the Sphinx's riddle was Humanity (*anthropos*), which 'when old presses down a stick as a third leg'. As Jebb, the Victorian expert on Sophocles, put it: 'In reference to a Greek tragedy, we cannot properly speak of "Acts"; but the *parodos* and the *stasima* mark the conclusion of chapters in the action. The *Oedipus Tyrannus* falls into six such chapters.' Hardy divided his novel into six 'Books'.[24]

The title of the fifth, 'The Discovery', was the usual translation of Aristotle's technical term for a structural feature of tragedy, *anagnorisis* (recognition). This he defined as 'the change from ignorance (*agnoia*) to knowledge in the characters marked out for good or bad fortune, causing either friendly or hostile feeling.' He found the finest example of it in the *Oedipus*, where the tragic hero discovers that he has killed his father and married his mother. That knowledge causes such hostile feeling that he rushes off to kill her as well. Clym discovers that he has caused his mother's death, and his hostile reaction causes his wife's death too. Though he has not literally married his mother, his love for Mrs Yeobright is enough to destroy all his love for Eustacia.[25]

Clym echoed Sophocles' Oedipus in several other ways. He was faced by a 'riddle of death', his mother's last reported words. He blinded himself, if only temporarily by excessive reading. His blindness was mental as well as physical: 'You are blinded', his mother told him. After learning the truth, he even looked like Oedipus in 'imaginatively rendered studies' of him. And at one point his words were heavy with Sophoclean irony. 'I never saw him', says Oedipus about his father. 'Why didn't she come to my house?' asks Clym about his mother. 'My door has always been open to her.'[26]

Such detailed imitation of Greek tragedy, in structure, themes, plot-elements, and dramatic technique, had its dangers. It might have resulted in an academic exercise like Matthew Arnold's *Merope*. And to express a modern world-view in such archaic terms as the Oedipus myth seems, *pace* Freud, asking for trouble. To Aristotle the *Oedipus Tyrannus* was evidently the finest specimen of its genre. To readers and playgoers it is still a splendid piece of theatre, at some points amazingly true to their own psychological experience; but morally it has ceased to make very good sense. All Oedipus's efforts to evade disaster are frustrated, not by bad luck, which we could understand, but by Apollo's pointless 'I told you so.' Hardy escaped these dangers by skilful selection. He transplanted only those elements of Greek tragedy that were viable for a modern mind, excluding the supernatural, but letting its aura persist in vestiges of witch-craft, and the vaguely numinous figure of the reddleman, not entirely spoilt by making him double as Thomasin's faithful lover. The tragedy was caused by common factors of human experience: mismatching of temperament with situation, incompatibility of partners in sexually deter-mined marriages, built-in marriage problems where husbands are wedded to their work or devoted to dominant mothers.

Greek tragedy served, in fact, not to side-track Hardy into an alien world of the past, but to inspire new ways of expressing his insights into the present. Even Aristotle's abstract definition of tragedy as producing 'pity and fear' seems to have prompted one of the most poignant passages in the novel, where the small boy finally leaves Mrs Yeobright to die:

> He was not so young as to be absolutely without a sense that sympathy was demanded, he was not old enough to be free from the terror felt in child-hood at beholding misery in adult quarters hitherto deemed impregnable; and whether she were in a position to cause trouble or to suffer from it, whether she and her affliction were something to pity or something to fear, it was beyond him to decide.[27]

The novel's after-image owes much of its clarity to those three Greek tragedies, adapted to suit the Victorian theatre. After an overture per-formed in semi-darkness, musical in feeling if not always in language, the footlights go up with the Aeschylean bonfires, to be finally extinguished by the Aeschylean storm. The visual link between beginning and end is Sophoclean. Oedipus is first seen as a standing figure addressing seated suppliants as 'Children of Cadmus', and using his authority to comfort them. This *de haut en bas* attitude is finally replaced by its opposite: he himself becomes the suppliant to authority, his own 'children' his only comfort. The novel starts with the morally suspect Eustacia, standing motionless on Rainbarrow. It ends with her husband (who has 'driven two women to their deaths') standing on the same spot, preaching to a 'reclining or sitting' congregation on 'morally unimpeachable subjects'.[28]

Such was the tragi-comic epilogue to the Heath's larger symbolism. Egdon was 'a place perfectly accordant with man's nature'. Old as earth itself, it represented earth as man's mother. The first figure on the breast-like 'semi-globular mound' of the barrow was 'a necessary finish' to the landscape, implying that Humanity was 'the only obvious justification' for the planet's existence. Yet earth's offspring, to judge by the two samples given, was inherently flawed. The beautiful pagan on the prehistoric tomb was born for misery and death. The product of Christian civilization with the ravaged 'countenance of the future' was still half-blind, and his 'Sermons on the Mount' would do no more good than their prototypes had done in nearly two thousand years.[29]

9

The Trumpet-Major

The move to London served its immediate purpose. It put Hardy more in touch with editors, publishers, and other authors. He met some of them when he and Emma went to a garden-party at Alexander Macmillan's large house half a mile away. He also made new contacts through the Savile Club, of which he was made a member in June 1878, and the Rabelais Club, founded in 1879 to promote 'virility in literature'. This he was asked to join 'as being the most virile writer of works of the imagination then in London'. On that score Henry James was not invited, though Hardy met him later. While living at Tooting he also met Tennyson, Browning, Matthew Arnold, Thomas Huxley, whom he greatly liked, the actor Henry Irving in his dressing-room ('naked to the waist – champagne in tumblers'), and the critic Edmund Gosse, who became a close friend.[1]

So far, so good – but there the good points of that London home ended: 'it was in this house', Hardy would recall, 'that their troubles began'. What troubles he did not say, though 'A January Night (1879)' suggests that some of them were caused by the builder: 'Through the joints of the quivering door / The water wheezes.' Two years later Hardy would note: 'Driving snow . . . creeps into the house, the window-plants being covered as if out-of-doors.'[2]

But the poem was not really about physical discomfort. It recorded some emotional 'incident' linked to a general sense of disillusionment: 'they seemed to begin to feel that "there had passed away a glory from the earth."' What that meant we can only guess. After their splendid view over the Stour, the one from 'The Larches' must have seemed dreary enough. After the success of *Far from the Madding Crowd* the relative failure of the *Return* was deeply discouraging. Worse still, the switch from architecture to authorship had not made their lives any happier. Hardy had done what he meant to do, and made himself known as a distinguished novelist. Yet here he was in another rat race, endlessly competing for contracts, sales, and reviews, while meeting his competitors too often to forget about their existence.[3]

Emma had parallel problems. At Sturminster she had had to compete for her husband's attention with his reading, thinking, and writing, but at least he was there, and it was a pleasant place to live. Now, in a suburban house that was not even weatherproof, she was often left alone while Hardy was out making useful social contacts. Though she sometimes went with him to the British Museum, and helped with his research there, she must have felt increasingly isolated. Resultant tensions between them were possibly reflected in 'The Fellow-Townsmen' (1880), a short story about an unhappily married couple.[4]

Hardy was facing his own 'troubles' in the spirit of Mark Tapley, determined to be 'jolly' 'under circumstances that would make other men miserable'. For the clouds of 1879 he invented a silver lining: 'A perception of the FAILURE of THINGS to be what they are meant to be, lends them, in place of the intended interest, a new and greater interest of an unintended kind.' He wrung what amusement he could from a conversation heard in a bookshop, studied jokes in *Punch*, and later suggested one for George du Maurier to illustrate. The policy worked well enough to produce the delightful comedy of another short story, 'The Distracted Young Preacher' (1879).[5]

A larger product of Tapleian jollity was *The Trumpet-Major*. Trying to combine the 'rural' novel that his public wanted to read with the Napoleonic theme that he wanted to write about, Hardy had set to work, by February 1879, on a 'tragical-comical-historical-pastoral' about the 1804 invasion-scare in Dorset. Grandfer Cantle had mentioned it in the *Return*, and his 'cumulative cheerfulness', there almost lost in the 'gloom' of which that novel's reviewers complained, was to saturate its successor. Thus the book could be offered to editors as 'above all things a cheerful story, without views or opinions, & ... intended to wind up happily'.[6]

Even so, three editors had turned the novel down before he got the Revd Dr Donald Macleod to serialize it in *Good Words*, with a caveat against 'anything – direct or indirect – which a healthy *Parson* like myself would not care to read to his bairns at the fireside ... everything likely to offend the susceptibilities of honestly religious & domestic souls.' Under such constraints he wrote *The Trumpet-Major*, planning to restore in the book-version anything expurgated from the serial. Meanwhile he indulged his own theatrical ambitions by turning *Far from the Madding Crowd* into a play. Henry Irving, on the night Hardy met him, had been acting Dickens's Jingle. Why not Hardy's Oak, Troy, or Boldwood?[7]

In January 1880 the new novel started appearing in *Good Words*. In April Hardy consulted his brother Henry about finding a building-plot in Dorchester. He had evidently started to question 'the wisdom of his decision, considering the nature of his writing,' to live in London. The change of mind might have been guessed from his recent review of William Barnes's poetry (October 1879). There he described 'the slow green river Stour', beside which he and Emma had so lately lived, as 'the dearest river' of the Dorset poet's 'memories, and the inspirer of some of his happiest effusions'. While thus identifying the country round Barnes's 'early home' as the 'precise source' of the poems' 'inspiration', Hardy was probably feeling that he too needed his native landcape to inspire him.[8]

Shortly before the new novel was published in three volumes (26 October 1880) Hardy began to show symptoms of stress. London, overwork, financial worries, and 'our troubles', whatever they were, combined to induce a sense almost of nightmare. He was 'sometimes haunted' by 'an eerie feeling, a horror at lying down' close to 'a monster whose body had four million heads and eight million eyes.' Mrs Tennyson, when visited, 'was lying as if in a coffin'. A funny take-off of well-known actors at a party seemed 'ghostly', because each actor was 'then in his grave'. The 'intense pathos' of an article about nightingales caged 'in a dirty street' troubled him 'all day'. On a Normandy holiday with Emma in July, everything about their Havre hotel seemed 'gloomy', 'sinister', and 'queer'. Their bedroom floor looked 'bloody red', and for some time they lay in bed with a light on, 'waiting' for someone to break in. At Cambridge in October, the candles of King's College chapel made Hardy think of shrouds and ghosts, and he felt 'an indescribable physical weariness'. It was not indeed all in the mind. When the reviews of *The Trumpet-Major* came out in November, he was flat on his back with a painful illness then called a 'bladder inflammation', but now conjecturally diagnosed as some type of stone. The healthy parson's prescription for the novel, 'humour . . . character . . . manly bracing fresh air . . . honest love-making and stirring incidents', had not done the novelist much good. Nor did the book's sales match the approving reviews. It was remaindered within two years.[9]

Praising the objectivity of Hardy's characterization, a review of *The Trumpet-Major* added: 'Yet it can be hardly doubted that he likes his hero.' Yes and no. As a model of cheerful courage John Loveday doubtless represented what Hardy was trying to be at the time. But John went so far against his natural instincts that nothing was really left for him but death. Hardy's Tapleian policy did similar violence to a temperament not naturally 'jolly', and ended in serious illness. John's altruism, too, had its counterpart in Hardy's own situation. The pressure to make money, which had prompted the move to London, arose from the need to support his parents, sisters, and wife. Having married above him, he probably felt an extra obligation to raise Emma's standard of living, and cater for her social tastes: 'oh what parties we had at Plymouth everywhere!', she would write in 1910. She probably enjoyed the London ones far more than he did, and found urban life less uncongenial.[10]

While admiring John, Hardy may have sympathized more easily with Bob. The brothers possibly reflected a current conflict in their author, between monogamous and polygamous impulses. On trains 'from Tooting to Town' his eye roved in search of types for heroines, noting the contrast between a 'statuesque girl' with 'absolutely perfect' features but a smile confined to her lips, and 'a girl of sly humour – the pupil of her eye being mostly half under the outer side of her eyelid.' But perhaps his interest was not purely professional.[11]

Other traces of his own feelings were excluded from this novel, or oddly distorted. His concern for animals surfaced only in Champion's 'amazement' when Anne leapt on to his back. Hardy's love of music presumably determined John's job, but though the trumpet-major's 'musical pursuits had refined him, educated him, and made him quite poetical' in Anne's eyes, his approach to music seems purely technical. He can argue about the exact pitch of a bell, but shows no feeling for music itself, except as a means to military discipline. Ousted by the trumpet, and even the Aeolian harp, Hardy's own instrument was reduced to a source of 'discordant screeches'. 'Bob's shattered nerves' would not bear 'the inevitably jarring effect of fiddles'.[12]

Hardy's characteristic ideas were less completely suppressed. Though the story was meant to be free from 'views or opinions', his scepticism about religion and ethics came out in passing jokes. 'How can you think of such trifles as churchgoing at such a time as this?' asks the drill-sergeant. In the farcical scene where John resists all Anne's efforts to make him kiss her, he finally takes refuge in St Paul's advice against marrying. 'Fie, John, pretending religion!' she replies. 'It isn't that at all. It's *Bob*!' It was actually both, for John was doing quite literally what St Paul had told him: 'Be kindly affectioned one to another with *brotherly* love; in honour preferring one another'. He 'preferred' Bob's happiness to his own, and thus, to Anne's annoyance, 'rated her happiness as of meaner value than Bob's'. Sure enough, the result of his Christian self-denial and brotherly love was to leave Anne in the same predicament as Grace in *The Woodlanders*, tied for life to an incorrigible womanizer.[13]

Perhaps, as an almost unpublished poet only five foot six and a half inches tall, Hardy was making a small personal point when he called his villain 'a fine fellow as to feet and inches', and named him after *Festus*, an immensely long bad poem which had just gone into its tenth edition. But the novel's most personal feature was its historical setting. As a small boy, Hardy had been told all about that invasion-scare by his paternal grandmother, whose husband had joined the Puddletown Volunteer Light Infantry at the time. The boy had grown up among relics of the crisis: 'bullet-holes' left by 'firelock practice when the landing was hourly expected', ruins of a beacon-keeper's hut, 'worm-eaten shafts and iron heads of pikes for . . . those who had no better weapons', 'ridges on the down thrown up during the encampment, fragments of volunteer uniform'. At eight he had found in a cupboard a contemporary magazine *History of the Wars*, full of exciting pictures. And just visible from his birthplace was the monument to Thomas Masterman Hardy, Nelson's Captain at Trafalgar, whom the Hardys regarded as a distant relative. Hardy even detected 'a family likeness' between him and his own father.[14]

To family traditions and childhood imaginings Hardy added much scholarly research at the British Museum from May 1878 onwards. The 'Trumpet-Major Notebook' contains all the material he collected from such sources as the *Annual Register*, local histories, contemporary newspapers and magazines, and army regulations. Not content to get his facts and dates exactly right, he made sketches of uniforms, civilian fashions in clothes and hairdos, and current designs for fire-grates, teapots, and cream jugs. An advertisement told him that 'Real India Long Shawls' were 'now the most fashionable articles of dress for ladies of distinction'. So it was 'a lovely shawl' that Mrs Garland first noticed in Bob's box. 'Dash my wig, then,' cried Festus when Anne refused to let him in. That was presumably the nearest Hardy's editor would let him go to the 'oath of the period' recorded in a *Morning Chronicle* for 1805: 'Damn my wig'.[15]

For this first step towards an 'Iliad of Europe', Homer contributed the proleptic obituary, and the relationship between the two brothers. Nastes went to war dressed in gold, 'but that did not save him from a miserable death at the hands of Achilles in the river'. Sergeant Stanner sang 'a satirical song' about the war, but – 'Poor Stanner! In spite of his satire, he fell at the bloody battle of Albuera . . . being mortally wounded and trampled down by a French hussar'. John's attitude towards Bob was precisely that of Hector towards Paris in *Iliad* vi, sternly critical of his brother's womanizing but still deeply affectionate and protective. Herodotus, the historian of the Persian Wars, also helped. 'Xerxes', Hardy had noted, from a social history of Greece, 'at the review of his vast forces, burst into tears, that not one of the multitude would be alive in 100 years. (Herod.).' Seventy-six years after the 'grand review' of the troops by George III, Xerxes' thought was rephrased in the novel: 'but the King and his fifteen thousand armed men . . . how entirely have they all passed and gone! – lying scattered about the world as military and other dust . . .' Had Hardy looked up the passage in Herodotus, he would have found something even more to his taste: 'Why worry?' said Xerxes' uncle. 'Nobody gets through human life anyway without often wishing he were dead.'[16]

As if to justify his membership of the Rabelais Club, Hardy used the Rabelaisian comic catalogue to describe how 'They make Ready for the Illustrious Stranger', and modelled the wedding-feast menu on that of the 'Gastrolaters' sacrifice'. The most recent book to affect the novel was probably Walter Pater's *Renaissamce* (1873), which referred to 'the individual in his isolation, each mind keeping as a solitary prisoner its own dream of a world.' Hardy transferred the idea to the 'straight lines of red, straight lines of blue' seen in the 'military manoeuvres': 'Who thought of every point in the line as an isolated man, each dwelling all to himself in the hermitage of his own mind?'[17]

But the chief Victorian influence was Tennyson. 'The Lord of Burleigh' posed as 'but a landscape-painter' to marry the village maiden. Parodying

Tennyson's social model, Hardy started his own study of inter-class marriage with 'a landscape-painter's widow'. As such, Mrs Garland 'occupied a twilight rank between the benighted villagers and the well-informed gentry', so in marrying the miller she repeated the Lord of Burleigh's mistake. Anne Garland thus became the miller's step-daughter, and like Tennyson's 'Miller's Daughter', presented a candle-lit window-picture for John to gaze at across the mill-pond. John himself was a 'neglected heroic man' like that 'strong heroic soul', Enoch Arden. At the sight of his wife living happily with another man, Enoch resolved 'not to tell her, never to let her know' that he was alive. At the sight of Anne and Bob 'locked together' in a passionate embrace, John determined never to let either of them know how he really felt.[18]

So he 'set his features to conceal his thought . . . instructed his tongue to do likewise . . . threw fictitiousness into his very gait . . . adhering to the part he meant to play'. Such histrionics were typical of the whole novel. Written in the year that Hardy dramatized *Far from the Madding Crowd*, it was full of theatrical references and ideas. Bob's Matilda was an actress of easy virtue, pretending to be respectable. Festus was a coward pretending to be a hero. Bob, the merchant seaman, dressed up as a 'beau' to take Anne to the Theatre Royal, where John encouraged their belief that he was in love with Matilda. And he gave a farewell performance virtually in his brother's role, that of the sailor with a wife in every port: 'Who knows that you won't hear of my attentions to some Spanish maid before a month is gone by?'[19]

Bob uses nautical language out of context like a stage sailor in Douglas Jerrold's *Black-Eyed Susan* (1829), calling Anne a sweet little craft', and offering to 'pilot' her down a stony path. But that was just one of the plays that affected the novel. 'Thrift, thrift, Horatio!' said Hamlet of his mother's wedding. 'The funeral bak'd meats / Did coldly furnish forth the marriage tables.' Anne's mother married the miller 'that the wedding victuals may not be wasted'; and for Bob's sake the festivities were made 'just like a funeral'. In his grossness, his drinking-party, and his impatience for his uncle's wealth Festus was a Tony Lumpkin straight out of Goldsmith's *She Stoops to Conquer*. The *Box and Cox* pattern was used once again for the two brothers' alternating courtships. T.W. Robertson's *Ours* (1866), about the Crimean War, contained a tableau of parted lovers meant to look like Millais's *The Black Brunswicker*. John's final parting from Anne was similarly posed, and illustrated in the serial: a candle-lit figure in full military uniform standing against a background symbolically black.[20]

For the Players in *Hamlet* 'Plautus' was not 'too light.' Nor was he too light to serve as chief dramatic source for Hardy's cheerful 'historical-pastoral'. The sordid miser Farmer Derriman, his pretended poverty, his buried treasure, and the transfer of his precious 'box' from one hiding-place to another all came from the *Aulularia*. The *Trinummus* offered precedents not only for the hidden treasure, but also for its final conversion into a dowry for Anne. The *Mostellaria* (*The Ghost*) added a hint for

Uncle Benjy's momentary appearance as a 'ghostly intruder'. And the *Miles Gloriosus* (*The Boastful Soldier*) supplied Festus's whole character, including his violent assault on Anne: Plautus's villain kidnaps a girl during her lover's absence. There too the lovers live in adjacent houses and get together through a hole in the wall. Hence Bob's sudden appearance in Anne's room, 'with the saw in his hand.' The *miles* is suitably punished. Lured by a prostitute posing as a rich lady, he is beaten up and nearly castrated. Festus was similarly lured into marrying Matilda, but otherwise got off much too lightly, with a good 'smacking'.[21]

The Trumpet-Major is a clever piece of historical reconstruction, but a dull novel. The characters and plot are too theatrical to be convincing. Intended to be a '*good* woman', the heroine turns out a rather silly one. Worse than marrying 'the wrong man', as Leslie Stephen complained, she can even react to the unspeakable Festus with '*not altogether unrelished* fear and excitement.' The humour is often forced, and Hardy's real 'views and opinions' are too obliquely expressed to make much impact. Altogether the novel seems unworthy of him, chiefly because so much of him was deliberately kept out of it. But at least the promise of a happy ending was not kept. John's final fate, left uncertain in the serial, was brought closer in the book-version to Hardy's temperament, and the realities of war: 'he . . . went off to blow his trumpet till silenced for ever upon one of the bloody battle-fields of Spain.'[22]

10

A Laodicean

In April 1880, while still writing *The Trumpet-Major*, Hardy had arranged for his next novel to be serialized in a European edition of *Harper's New Monthly Magazine*, to be launched in London that November. Since the success of the new venture would depend largely on his story, he felt able to ask for £100 per instalment. By then he must have decided what the novel would be about. But the only clue to the date of its first conception is the inclusion of notes on two of its themes, gambling and infant baptism, in the 'Trumpet-Major Notebook' (1878–9). Perhaps, as he jotted them down, he was already getting tired of historical research and resolving to make his next book *A Story of Today*.[1]

'I see no difficulty', he now told Harpers, 'in having the manuscript for the first monthly part ready & in your hands by Oct 1'; and more than three instalments were in type before the end of that month. But then the 'difficulty' began. On the 23rd he fell ill, with violent pain and signs of internal bleeding. Faced by the doctors with a choice between 'a dangerous operation' and a long period in bed, lying 'on an inclined plane, with the lower part of his body higher than his head', he naturally opted for bed. He stayed there for five months, and in those frustrating conditions composed the last three-quarters of his novel. Unable to write, he dictated instalments to Emma, who 'worked bravely both at writing and nursing', not to mention housekeeping in a cold and leaky house, and giving much-needed moral support. Miraculously, they met all deadlines, and on 1 May 1881 he was able to write the conclusion himself 'in pencil'. *A Laodicean* was not one of Hardy's best novels, but as a product of his relationship with Emma, it certainly represented 'their finest hour'.[2]

In this period of extra 'leisure' (his own euphemism for enforced bedrest) Hardy's mind did some free-wheeling. He contemplated the cornless beauty of his unused feet, 'shapely as those of a Greek statue', and roughed out a theory of history based on postures of Society, 'upright', 'oblique', 'prostrate', 'drooping', or 'inverted'. He found another silver lining: 'troubles coming in battalions . . . neutralize each other.' He thought about Carlyle and George Eliot, 'vanished into nescience while I have been lying here'; about Comte's 'religion of Humanity', which would have caught on much faster if Christ had been included among Comte's 'worthies'; about Matthew Arnold, 'wrong about provincialism', which was really 'of the essence of individuality', but right about 'the imaginative reason', which gave insight into '*the heart of a thing*', to produce a deeper kind of 'realism'.[3]

As for himself, he determined in November 'to resume poetry as soon as possible.' He then thought of tackling his Napoleonic theme in a 'Great Modern Drama'. That brought him closer to the idea of *The Dynasts* (1903–8), and in March he outlined its 'philosophic scheme or framework': 'Mode for a historical Drama. Action mostly automatic, reflex movement, etc. Not the result of what is called *motive*, though always ostensibly so, even to the actors' own consciousness.' He had evidently read some account of Hartmann's *Philosophy of the Unconscious* (1868), though it had not yet been translated into English. In May he struck out a notion that would figure both in *The Dynasts* and in several of his later poems. 'After infinite trying to reconcile a scientific view of life with the emotional and spiritual', he concluded that human beings were the victims of 'overdoing' by natural 'Law'. They should have been mere machines, as unfeeling as the process that evolved them. 'The emotions have no place in a world of defect, and it is a cruel injustice that they should have developed in it.'[4]

That month he was well enough to go for his first walk by himself. He stood in the sunshine on Wandsworth Common, quoting Gray aloud, and feeling all the delight of 'the wretch that long has tost / On the thorny bed of pain', when able to 'breathe and walk again.' Free at last from illness as well as the novel, he decided, 'for reasons of health and for mental inspiration', from then on to live in the country, visiting London 'for a few months only each year'. Town life, he found, 'tended to force mechanical and ordinary productions from his pen.'[5]

After some more house-hunting in Dorset, the Hardys found one that would do for the moment in Wimborne. From 23 June 1881 they were again living by the Stour, not quite in sight of it this time, but only five minutes' walk from its bank, at 'Lanherne', The Avenue (now 16 Avenue Road), Wimborne. In date and style more like Riverside Villa than the 'cottage' that Hardy called it, 'Lanherne' boasted a coach-house, a garden full of fruit and flowers, and a small lean-to conservatory, from which they saw 'the new comet' on the night they moved in. It was one of four comets observed that year, and the first to be successfully photographed. So the poorest imitation of an observatory had a special appeal for Hardy just then. He had recently consulted a urologist who happened to be a keen amateur astronomer, and would later set up a real observatory at his house.[6]

Late in August the Hardys went off for a holiday in Scotland. If meant to complete Hardy's convalescence, it was not a great success, for at Stirling they were both 'laid up with colds.' But they returned via the Lake District to a warm September at Wimborne, where Hardy sat under their vine correcting proofs of the book-version *Laodicean*, and doubtless remembering Marvell's 'green Thought in a green Shade': 'The sun tries to shine through the great leaves, making a green light on the paper . . .' When the novel came out in three volumes (December 1881), it was badly reviewed, especially in the magazine that had originally published it, and remaindered within two months. But Hardy had the best of consolations for such things. Asked in September for a serial by a prestigious literary journal in New England, the *Atlantic Monthly*, he was already busy writing another book.[7]

Hardy said that *A Laodicean* contained 'more facts of his own life than anything he had ever written'. Nor was this simply because, composing 'prostrate', he had to rely chiefly on materials already in his head. The thirteen chapters written 'upright' were equally based on personal experience. As a young 'architect's pupil', he recalled, 'I used to be sent round to sketch village churches as a preliminary to their restoration – which mostly meant destruction'. The novel opened with a 'young draughtsman' sketching a 'village church', as a preliminary to restoring a castle, which was finally destroyed by his 'assistant', a 'would-be student of architecture'. Named after a county next to Dorset, George Somerset then took over Hardy's moustache, 'all-sufficient to hide the subtleties of his mouth', his 'Institute medal (if Havill's snide guess was right), his nostalgia for 'west-gallery . . . church-music', his potential ordination, his early arguments about infant baptism, his rejected poems, his 'return to architecture' as a 'practical' source of income, and his instinctive resistance to 'the general tide of opinion.' His adolescent ordeal of being denounced from a pulpit was transferred to Paula Power, his heroine, and her imagined reactions became the focus of the hero's first thoughts about her: 'For Somerset there was but one scene: the imagined scene of the girl herself as she sat alone in the vestry.'[8]

All these personal materials had been exploited before Hardy's imagination was cut off in October 1880 from external sources of inspiration. He then did his best to fictionalize his own frustrations. The 'long illness' that was keeping him out of circulation was transferred to Abner Power, to explain why nothing had been heard of him for ten years. Hardy's 'troubles coming in battalions' were passed on to the rival architect, Havill. Imprisoned in his bedroom, Hardy made Somerset feel 'so well walled in by circumstances that he was absolutely helpless'. His own sense of impotence developed a plot where the hero, excluded from the scene of action, could only wait and suffer injuries inflicted on him from 'nine hundred miles' away, by a group of opponents aptly named 'the Powers'.[9]

While physically immobilized, Hardy probably became more conscious of his emotions. 'Captain de Stancy was a changed man.' The sudden increase in that character's drive and creativity, when his policy of sexual repression broke down, was vividly enough described to suggest some basis in the author's own experience. Had he too adopted at marriage 'a system of rigidly incarcerating within himself all instincts towards the opposite sex', only to find that 'the love-force that he had kept immured alive was still a reproducible thing'?[10]

Clearly there was personal feeling of another kind behind Hardy's choice of villain. Conscious of his short stature, he had made Festus a giant. Socially insecure and highly sensitive to criticism, he now gave William Dare all the brazen effrontery implied by his surname. There he re-sembled Don Pacifico, a Portuguese Jew born in Gibraltar who in 1850 had got the coast of Greece blockaded for his benefit, thus nearly starting a European war, comparable to the literal conflagration started by Dare. Of course, Gibraltar was an obvious place for an army officer to father an illegitimate son. But the real point of Dare's Gibraltarian origin was his character as 'cosmopolite'. 'I am at home anywhere!' cried Dare, after drinking too much 'old port'. Hardy was not. And just then he was feeling very home-sick for his native Dorset.[11]

Meanwhile, for lack of other material, he fell back on memories of foreign travel. When Paula's 'horizontal position' at Strasbourg restricted her view to the 'dormered house-tops' opposite her window, Hardy was not just thinking how little he could see from his bed, but remembering how Emma had been 'laid up' in Strasbourg, presumably on that same 'red velvet couch'. The 'shining . . . blood-red worm' of 'the distant Rhine' seen by de Stancy from the Königsstuhl was the 'riband of blood' seen by Hardy, and Paula's loss of 'interest' through 'fatigue' after climbing up to the tower was evidently based on Emma's. At Karlsruhe the Hardys had 'attended a fair, and searched for a German lady Hardy had known in England, but were unable to find her.' That search was reproduced by Somerset in a series of foreign cities, as 'his business – or fatuity – of discovering the elusive lady'. The last of the series was Karlsruhe. There Somerset, having tried in vain to find the Paula he had known in England, used the 'animated environment' of the fair as a temporary anaesthetic for the pain of Paula's coldness.[12]

Predictably, since 'Writing Under Difficulties', Hardy borrowed all he could from his early reading. Somerset and Paula had their first love-scene while sheltering from the rain in a summer-house – the latest version of the cave in the *Aeneid*. There the love-making is witnessed by two goddesses, 'Earth and Juno promoter of marriage'. Here the unseen witnesses were Havill and the all too earthly Dare, intent on promoting a marriage between Paula and his father, a character consciously descended from Horace's *Odes*.[13]

Dare was partly modelled on 'the Etruscan youth, Tages' in being a boy with, seemingly, the wisdom of a sage'. Hardy must have read about Tages in Ovid's *Metamorphoses*, one of which was the transformation of a 'fatal clod of earth' into this human figure. Tages apparently fused in Hardy's mind with Tennyson's 'one low churl, compact of thankless earth, /The fatal byword of all years to come', who 'Boring a little auger-hole in fear, / Peeped' at Lady Godiva. So Dare arranged a peep-show for his father in Paula's gymnasium. Ovid mentioned that Tages 'taught the Etruscans to reveal future chances (*casus*)'. Hence the 'theory of chances and recurrences' that Dare explained to Somerset at the Casino.[14]

Hardy's bedside Marcus Aurelius naturally came in handy, when the words inscribed in it by Horace Moule were exasperatingly used by Paula to excuse her own shilly-shallyings: 'This is the chief thing: Be not perturbed; for all things are of the nature of the Universal.' Longus seems also to have helped. Four important plot-elements of *Daphnis and Chloe* appeared in thin disguise, the bath, the pit, the beauty-contest, and the finally magnanimous rival. Chloe's passion for Daphnis began when she watched him washing himself in the spring, Somerset's for Paula when he watched her standing 'on the brink' of the baptismal 'pool'. Daphnis fell into a pit, from which he was rescued by Chloe: Somerset fell into the bottom of a turret, from which he 'pictured Paula . . . ascending to deliver him . . . by her own exertions', only to be replaced by 'a dreary footman'. The beauty competition with Dorcon was echoed first by the 'intellectual tournament' with the Baptist minister, and then by the architectural competition with Havill. In both cases the defeated rival showed magnanimity, the minister in becoming Somerset's friend, and the architect in withdrawing from the competition and wanting 'to be friendly with' Somerset. Dorcon finally told Chloe how to rescue Daphnis from the pirates. Havill told Somerset about Dare's parentage, which should have helped him to rescue Paula from marrying the father and accomplice of the 'young criminal'. But it made a better ending for the information to reach her by another route.[15]

To English authors the novel owed a wide range of ideas. The castle theatricals came from Jane Austen's *Mansfield Park*, with *Lovers' Vows* replaced by *Love's Labour's Lost*, where four lovers break vows like de Stancy's, to keep away from women. *Romeo and Juliet* was drawn on for de Stancy's gag, with its extra piece of business, and *A Midsummer-Night's Dream* for Paula and Charlotte's 'friendship of Hermia and Helena', complete with their different 'statures', Paula being 'rather tall than otherwise' and Charlotte 'almost dumpy'. Thomas Lodge supplied a poem for de Stancy to recite. It was possibly shown to Hardy by Edmund Gosse, who was busy editing Lodge's poems when he came to Hardy's 'bedside'. Milton's Satan, whose 'face / Deep scars of Thunder had intrencht' in his war against God, probably suggested Abner Power's 'face which had been the plaything of strange fires' from his own terrorist bomb.[16]

In his 'ennui' and disillusionment De Stancy descended from Byron. His quotation from *Don Juan* stopped just before the line that anticipated his threat to Paula (and Ethelberta's threat to Lord Mountclere). After

'Seen beauties brought to market by the score' the text continues: 'Sad
rakes to sadder husbands chastely taming.'[17]

But the chief poetic influences were Victorian. Hardy's chapel recalls
Browning's in *Christmas-Eve*, with the vision of 'Him' in 'a sweepy garment,
vast and white' replaced by the view of Paula 'in an ample robe of flowing
white'. Browning's trick in *The Ring and the Book* of telling the same story
from different angles was briefly copied in the summer-house love-scene,
described first from Somerset's, and then from Havill and Dare's view-
point. Clough, whose poetry was represented during Hardy's illness in
T.H. Ward's *English Poets*, may have contributed much more. His *Amours
de Voyage* was an epistolary verse-novel about a lover who 'really is too *shilly-
shally*'. Deciding too late to take his own feelings seriously, he pursues the
girl in question through a series of foreign hotels, always arriving after
her departure. In Hardy's love-story, often told through letters and telegrams, the frustrated-search pattern was repeated by Somerset when he
tried to see Paula in Nice, and by Paula, when she tried to find him in
Normandy.[18]

Clough's *Dipsychus* was a male 'Laodicean', who in one of Ward's
extracts deplored his 'woman's heart, / Fain to be forced, incredulous of
choice', his 'double self', his temperamental reluctance 'To do anything,
/ Distinct on any one thing to decide'. Paula seems just like that. 'I won't
be compelled!' she tells de Stancy, but next morning she feels forced to
say 'Yes'. Dipsychus is tempted by a Mephistopheles who mocks his conventional morality. That is how Dare treats de Stancy: 'You are quite a
Mephistopheles, Will', said his father, and on his wedding-day 'was as full
of apprehension as one who has a league with Mephistopheles.'[19]

As a 'sketcher', if not actually a 'landscape-painter', Somerset is thought
'a possible Lord of Burleigh', and Tennyson may frequently be seen
behind the novel. The 'peeper' at Godiva was struck blind: 'So the Powers,
who wait / On noble deeds, cancelled a sense misused.' Paula Power, who
would not 'be a party to baseness', made the gymnasium-peeper look like
'a man who had died', and cancelled their engagement. Maud's brother,
like Paula, gives 'a grand political dinner' to which her lover, like Paula's,
is 'not invited'. There 'Maud will wear her jewels, / And the bird of prey
will hover, / And the titmouse hope to win her'. With his 'raven black'
hair, and his cousin Jack Ravensbury, de Stancy reflected the first fortune-
hunter-image, and Paula's jewels, though worn by Charlotte at the Hunt
Ball, served his predatory purposes in the play.[20]

Paula resembles *The Princess* in her independent power, her mediaeval
setting, her modernist and feminist ideas, her plans to found a new town
(recalling Ida's college), and her final acceptance of her lover when he
lies 'pale and interesting' on a sickbed. But the Prologue to Tennyson's
poem offered more than the 'tale' itself. The incongruity of the telegraph-
wire entering, through an 'arrow-slit', a 'fossil of feudalism' bought by a
railway engineer followed Tennyson's juxtaposition of 'A Gothic ruin and
a Grecian house' with the latest technology, including 'A petty railway'
and a 'telegraph' that 'flashed a saucy message to and fro'. Hence, in part,

Paula's idea of adding a 'Greek court' to her castle, and perhaps her regrettably 'saucy composure' just before promising to contact Somerset from Nice by telegraph.[21]

Another prominent figure in the novel's background was Matthew Arnold. 'The Forsaken Merman' 'climbed on . . . the stones worn with rains' to gaze at his Margaret through 'the small leaded panes' of the 'little grey church'. Somerset climbed on to the 'plinth' of the ugly 'red brick' chapel, holding on to the 'iron stay' of the 'stove-chimney', to gaze at Paula through the 'plate glass' window. The contrast between the two buildings supported Arnold's case in *St Paul and Protestantism*, that Dissenters were Philistines who cut themselves off from the beauty of the national church. That beauty was an aspect of Hellenism, which Arnold had opposed to Hebraism in *Culture and Anarchy*, an opposition dramatized in the debate between Mr Woodwell ('strictness of conscience') and Somerset ('spontaneity of consciousness'). Paula naturally oscillated between the two poles. Her name associated her with St Paul, seen by Arnold as the source, though misinterpreted, of Dissenting theology, and with the Hebraists. But she also claimed to be 'Greek', and told Charlotte to call Greek pottery 'Hellenic'. In practice, her spontaneity, though strictly controlled, proved too great for her lover's comfort.[22]

Matthew Arnold also combined with Hardy's own experience to make Paula a Baptist. If Mr Woodwell was modelled on the Dorchester Baptist minister Frederick Perkins, Paula, 'the fair Puritan', was related to the seventeenth-century Puritan family satirized in Arnold's recent essay, 'Equality' (1878), who gave a dinner-party to discuss the 'error of the paedobaptists'. 'Whereupon' their latest baby 'was not baptized.' Arnold also mentioned the fate of 'nine Raphaels, eleven Correggios, twenty-eight Titians': all those representing the Virgin Mary were 'forthwith burnt' by the Puritan Parliament. Dare, though no Puritan, did the same with 'a Raffaelle Virgin-and-Child, a magnificent Tintoretto, a Titian, and a Giorgione.'[23]

According to Comte, all women's 'social sympathies are given to the Middle Ages'. So Paula's last words were: 'I wish my castle wasn't burnt, and I wish you were a de Stancy.' But that 'Mediaeval Sentiment' qualified her offer to represent what Arnold had called 'the main element in the modern spirit's life . . . the imaginative reason.' Here she mocked her own Laodiceanism, and to some extent Arnold himself; for by calling him 'a finished writer' she implied that these were just fine phrases. Hardy had mocked him too, after their first meeting: 'Arnold . . . had a manner of having made up his mind upon everything years ago, so that it was a pleasing futility for his interlocutor to begin thinking new ideas, different from his own, at that time of day.' Nor did Arnold's constant presence in the novel imply acceptance of his thought. Hardy was merely using Arnold's ideas and terminology to structure his own.[24]

He also used themes from the theatre. The social conflict between modern and mediaeval had been dramatized in Taylor and Dubourg's *New Men and Old Acres* (1869). Set in a ruined abbey full of 'old family pictures', the home of an 'ancient family' but 'mortgaged up to the hilt', it dealt with two prudential marriages between 'rank and money', like Paula's engagement to de Stancy. One of the 'New Men' was 'a self-made man' called Bunter, like Paula's father a Nonconformist, and like Havill a hypocrite. While boasting of his 'Cheristian principles', he contributed a 'lot of beautiful bricks', rejected as unsaleable, to the building of a new chapel. His daughter Fanny was like a caricature of Paula in her pursuit of Arnoldian culture: 'Give me art and intellect, sweetness and light, you know . . . a lovely landscape and the "Stones of Venice." Oh, I could live upon Ruskin!'[25]

In Tom Robertson's *Progress* (also 1869) another abbey, the home of an 'old lord' and his 'ruined' family, was threatened with demolition to make way for a railway-station. The railway-engineer, who finally married into the family, claimed to represent modern progress: 'it is I – the engineer, the motive-power – who leads the way.' His words probably suggested, not only John Power's surname, but also Somerset's tactless remark about him: 'To design great engineering works . . . requires no doubt a leading mind. But to execute them, as he did, requires, of course, only a following mind.' And Paula's purchase of a clock with a second-hand, because 'time, being so much more valuable now, must of course be cut up into smaller pieces', may also be traced to Robertson: 'engineers are the heroes of the hour – I should say of the minute – for the present age goes so fast that we have to count in minutes.'[26]

The continuing inspiration of *Box and Cox* showed in the names of Somerset's 'draughtsmen, Bowles, Knowles, and Cockton'. Knowles took precedence later, possibly because the architect J.T. Knowles had recently founded the *Nineteenth Century*. The alternating lodgers became Paula's 'sentry-box' architects: 'when Havill walks out, he'll walk in, and not a moment before.' The ludicrous correspondences between the two tenants' actions suggested a more literal mirror-image when Somerset's search for Paula in the south was 'inversely imitated' by her search for him in the north. Box and Cox's abortive duel became the vestry confrontation between Abner and Dare, where both men drew pistols and tried to blackmail each other, but finally agreed to do nothing: ' "I cry quits, if you care to do the same." Dare assented, and the pistols were put away.'[27]

That scene illustrates the novel's weaker side. The schematic dramatization of conflicting cultures makes an intellectually attractive opening, where Paula seems a character of potential interest and charm. But the larger perspective soon gives place to a melodramatic love story which gradually loses momentum. De Stancy's persecuting courtship grows as tiresome to the reader as it does to Paula, whose irresolute gullibility can be equally irritating. But patience is rewarded by an ending almost as delightful as the beginning, with the same unobtrusive humour. John Power, who desired his daughter's immersion in the 'cold and dark and fearful' water of the chapel 'pool', died 'from a chill caught after a warm bath.' Paula, condemned, like the seventh church of Asia (Laodicea), for being 'neither cold nor hot', vainly searched seven churches in Normandy. In the seventh, where the 'seven candles burning' mimicked St John's 'seven golden candlesticks', she found not Somerset but Cockton. Only when, 'sick and tired' like her lover, of 'holy places', she moved on to unholy Étretât, did she find him – shamelessly dancing with another young lady.[28]

After the subtle comedy of Paula's recantation, Dare's fire seems melodramatic, but its function was quite complex. It rounded off the love story with a spectacular window-picture, viewed from indoors by a hero who had long been an outsider. With a 'powerful irradiation' (like that of the electric bulbs installed that year in the Savoy Theatre) it floodlighted the opening scene of the drama, 'the brick chapel in which Somerset had first seen the woman who now stood beside him as his wife.' The fire marked the end of the De Stancy threat, but gave Paula a chance to show, by her final 'wish', that she was still *A Laodicean*.[29]

She had just confessed to being one in 'creed':

> But of course that's a sub-species – I may be a lukewarm anything. What I really am, as far as I know, is one of that body to whom lukewarmth is not an accident but a provisional necessity, till they see a little more clearly.

She then 'whispered a name' which Mr Woodwell had also 'whispered' about her. The only name that fits both contexts is 'Agnostic'. Thus Hardy whispered the dreadful truth about himself.[30]

11

Two on a Tower

The comet seen from his new home in June 1881, the star-gazing urologist, and the pre-Copernican astronomical clock in Wimborne Minster all probably combined to turn Hardy's thoughts towards astronomy. His earlier attraction to it, clear from Gabriel Oak's contemplation of the stars, had made him buy R.A. Proctor's *Essays on Astronomy* (1872), which discussed the Transits of Venus expected in 1874 and 1882. That of 1639 had been predicted by Jeremiah Horrocks, whose career had 'always been interesting' to Hardy. A farmer's son, educated by a country schoolmaster, Horrocks had taught himself astronomy, with a telescope bought for half-a-crown, and later become a curate. He nearly missed his precious Transit, because it happened one Sunday afternoon, when he had to be in church. But he got back just in time to see 'the disc of Venus already entered upon the sun' and wrote it all up in his *Venus in Sole visa*. He then suddenly died before he was twenty-three, and was praised on a 'marble scroll' in Westminster Abbey (1875) for not neglecting his 'greater' clerical duties to deal with his astronomical 'sideline (*parerga*)'.[1]

So the Transit of Venus would be a good subject for a novel in 1882, and the title of Horrocks's book (Venus seen in the sun) suggested the germ of a plot: love, or a beautiful earthly body, coming between an astronomer and his heavenly one, like the mouse that got into the telescope in Samuel Butler's 'The Elephant in the Moon'. Horrocks's life suggested a possible hero: a precocious self-taught astronomer, poor and country-bred, working with inadequate equipment. It also suggested a conflict between him and the church, and another between orders of magnitude, between love, for instance, and astronomy: 'the less must give way to the greater'.[2]

Where could such a hero set up his telescope? In July 1881 the Hardys hired a 'wagonette' to see an Iron Age hill-fort called Badbury Rings. On

the way there the driver 'pointed out Charborough', a private estate containing a tower with stairs inside, and remarked that the 'present owner
lives there alone – a quiet little lady – keeps no company.' There was
'Venus' and the observatory. But would the tower really answer that purpose? In November Hardy applied to visit Greenwich Observatory, to
'ascertain if a hollow memorial pillar, with a staircase inside, can be adapted
for the purpose of a small observatory'. The crafty wording implied that
the fictional project was a real one of his own: 'I have no Observatory . . . but
am sketching plans for one'. After briefly researching the technique of
lens-grinding, he was ready in January 1882 to finalize his agreement with
the *Atlantic Monthly*, and by March he had sent the Boston editor the first
nine chapters of *Two on a Tower*.[3]

Meanwhile he had had a brush with the London theatre. When the critic-
playwright Comyns Carr suggested a stage version of *Far from the Madding
Crowd*, Hardy sent him the one he had made in 1879, entitled '*The Mistress
of the Farm* – A pastoral drama'. Improved for theatrical purposes by Carr,
it was provisionally accepted by the St James's Theatre, 'actually put in
rehearsal . . . and then rejected.' A year later (December 1881) the same
theatre put on Pinero's *The Squire*, a 'new and original play' clearly derived
from Hardy and Carr's. In the press controversy that followed, Hardy
himself was accused of plagiarism in two of his novels. Carr cashed in on
the publicity by drastically revising *The Mistress of the Farm*, and getting it
staged, as *Far from the Madding Crowd*, first in Liverpool and then at the
London Globe. It ran for 114 performances, though not quite as long as
The Squire.[4]

Despite that small success, Hardy had not enjoyed the episode. Trying
to put it in perspective, perhaps after watching the mechanical Grenadier
strike his bells outside Wimborne Minster, he thought of writing 'A history
of human automatism . . . an account of human action in spite of human
knowledge' (another step towards *The Dynasts*). He also decided that his
'only way of keeping up a zest' for writing was 'by not mixing with other
workers of the same craft.' Only so could he be true to his own vision. 'As,
in looking at a carpet, by following one colour a certain pattern is suggested, by following another colour, another; so in life the seer should
watch that pattern among general things which his idiosyncrasy moves
him to observe, and describe that alone.' But Hardy felt most himself in
his earliest environment, so on 21 March 1882, he applied for a building
site 'at Stinsford Hill, near Dorchester.'[5]

Still, Wimborne had its uses for the current novel. Its prehistoric origins
fostered the image of a modern woman 'sitting aloft on a lonely column,
with a forest groaning under her feet, and palaeolithic dead men feeding
its roots.' Known in the eighth century for its Benedictine nunnery housing five hundred novices, Wimborne suggested a heroine 'under solemn
oath' to 'live like a cloistered nun' in her husband's absence. Dominated
by the Minster, it sharpened Hardy's satirical view of the clergy. And its
prudish residents must have seemed almost asking for a book to shock
them. After a Shakespeare reading with some of his neighbours Hardy

recorded: 'The General reads with gingerly caution, telling me privately
that he blurted out one of Shakespeare's improprieties last time before he
was aware, and is in fear and trembling lest he may do it again.' Hardy's
plot, by contrast, was deliberately improper, ending with a 'reckless *coup
d'audace*' at a Bishop's expense.[6]

He sent off the last part of the serial to Boston in September, and then
went off with Emma to Paris for a holiday, not bothering to revise the
novel for the book-version, which came out in London at the end of
October 1882. Viviette's *coup* of marrying the Bishop to legitimize her
child by Swithin did not go down well with the critics. The *Saturday Review*
found it 'repulsive', and the *Spectator* used the same word about Viviette's
whole 'passion for Swithin'. But the Rabelais Club presumably liked
the book's 'virility', and 'the public', Hardy thought, 'by their buying, &
enthusiastic letter-writing' showed more interest in the novel than in anything he had recently published.[7]

'Remarkably fine boy', said the vicar about Swithin's son, 'and yet he was
a seven months' baby.' With equal inaccuracy Hardy might have been called
a five-and-a-half months' baby. His father, like Anthony Green, had married
to save a domestic servant 'from unborn shame'. By now the novelist felt
enough self-confidence to make private jokes about his own background.
Other personal material was handled more seriously. His paternal grandmother figured as Swithin's 'maternal grandmother', Mrs Martin. The
real-life Mrs Martin, 'the lady of his earliest passion as a child', must have
suggested one of the novel's themes, the problems of a love-affair with an
older woman. Though the age-gap of thirty years was reduced to 'nearly
ten', Swithin's reaction to Viviette's appearance on his return from the
Cape was just like Hardy's to Mrs Martin's in London.[8]

Swithin at first seems more like a child than a 'youth', in taking Viviette
for granted as an all-providing mother-figure, and grumbling when she
fails to do quite enough for him: 'O, Lady Constantine! How could you
serve me so!' He shows no more interest in her as a person than Hardy
showed in Emma on 'That Swithin's day' in Bournemouth. Did Swithin's
egotism anticipate 'We Sat at the Window' in expressing some regret for
Hardy's own attitude towards Emma? Did he feel he had been childish in
taking all she gave him, as wife, housekeeper, secretary, and nurse, and
still wanting something more? Clearly another theme of the novel, the
conflict between marriage and professional work, was one of his own
problems, So was the conflict between female piety and male scepticism.
Having persuaded Swithin to 'observe the church's ordinances' and be
confirmed, Viviette even urged him to 'give up this astronomy till the
confirmation is over', so as to devote his 'attention exclusively to that
more serious matter.' While thus paraphrasing the words of the Horrocks
memorial, she also reflected Emma's scale of priorities, and her dislike of
Hardy's agnosticism.[9]

The prior publication of Swithin's 'amazing discovery' by another astronomer recalled Wallace and Darwin's independent discoveries of natural

selection; but it also had its traumatic parallel in Hardy's recent life, when his own stage-version of *Far from the Madding Crowd* was forestalled by Pinero's. Much earlier experiences, too, went into the novel. The birds in the thatch above Hardy's Bockhampton bedroom were heard by Swithin 'scratching the back of the ceiling over his head'. The vicar's sermon against Hardy's social presumption became the Bishop's churchyard rebuke to Swithin for 'infringing the first principles of social decorum'. Hardy's uneasy sense of oscillating between two classes produced a hero with 'two stations of life in his blood.' While staying at Bockhampton in October 1870 Hardy had noted down 'Mother's notion, & also mine' of a figure waiting 'to knock us back from any pleasant prospect'. His next note summarized a story he had just heard, of a woman whose husband treated her 'roughly, left her, and went to America. She pined for him. At last he sent for her to come with the children. She died of joy at the news.' The 'notion' and the story were transferred to Viviette. When the hurricane delayed her marriage: 'I thought something would occur to mar our scheme!' And when Swithin finally got back from South Africa and said he would marry her, 'Sudden joy after despair' was too much for her 'over-strained heart'.[10]

Swithin went to the Cape to complete the observations made there by 'the younger Herschel', on whom he seems to have been partly modelled. Proctor's *Essays on Astronomy*, published the year after Herschel's death, emphasized his 'mental purity', i.e. his freedom from emotional prejudice. Swithin looked at Viviette with 'speculative purity' in his eyes, and his 'inexorably simple logic' precipitated Viviette's death. Herschel returned from the Cape after 'four years and a quarter'. Swithin started home shortly after hearing that Viviette's child was 'between three and four years of age'. Herschel was quoted as saying that 'the sun's rays are the ultimate source of almost every motion which takes place on the surface of the earth.' That is why Swithin, found totally absorbed in watching a 'cyclone in the sun', first registers Viviette as 'somebody unusual' when she asks, 'Will it make any difference to us here?'[11]

In April 1882 Hardy attended Darwin's funeral. He had recently translated some words from *The Origin of Species* into Dorsetshire dialect. Darwin had mentioned 'the strange fact that every particle of food and drink which we swallow has to pass over the orifice of the trachea, with some risk of falling into the lungs'. Hezekiah Biles defined the design-fault more feelingly: 'I'd move every man's wyndpipe a good span away from his glutchpipe, so that at harvest time he could fetch breath in's drinking, without being choked and strangled as he is now.' Another favourite author of Hardy's youth, J.S. Mill, contributed to a turning-point in the plot, when an unholy alliance of Christian and Utilitarian ethics forced Viviette to 'immolate' herself by refusing to legalize her marriage: 'ought a possibly large number, Swithin included, to remain unbenefited because the one individual to whom his release would be an injury chanced to be herself?'[12]

The intellectual theme of the novel was partly derived from Thomas Huxley and Matthew Arnold. In 'Science and Culture' (1880) Huxley had argued that 'real culture' could be acquired just as well by an 'exclusively scientific education' as by an 'exclusively literary one', and that 'classical education', the 'ordinary smattering of Latin and Greek', was for scientists at least 'a mistake', Hardy liked and admired Huxley. But he had worked hard to gain such a 'smattering' himself, and had found it very useful. So he responded with a hero who, 'having been reared, or having reared himself, in the scientific school of thought' was insensitive and unimaginative. In June 1882, when the first nine chapters had been published, Arnold made his own response to Huxley in *Literature and Science.* There he argued that Greek was an essential 'part of our culture', and that 'humane letters' were indispensable for 'engaging the emotions', and 'helping us to relate the results of modern science to our need for conduct, our need for beauty.' In short, he 'would rather have a young person ignorant of the moon's diameter' than capable, like one training-college student, of paraphrasing 'Can'st thou not minister to a mind diseased?' as 'Can you not wait upon the lunatic?'[13]

The comparison of astronomical knowledge with semantic awareness was highly relevant to Hardy's novel, and the contrast between scientific and artistic temperaments was from then on made more explicit. Swithin was 'not only too young in years, but too literal, direct and uncompromising in nature to understand such a woman as Lady Constantine, and she suffered from that limitation in him . . .' She suffered most when he failed to see what she meant by telling him to go away. 'He was a scientist, and took words literally.'[14]

Some debt to earlier novels may also be suspected. Swithin's sexual innocence recalls that of Daphnis, which was also ended by an older woman. Under Viviette's influence Swithin 'had become a man': Lycaenion told Daphnis, 'I made a man of you'. In Saint-Pierre's pastoral Virginia's mother was called Madame de la Tour: Viviette was literally the lady of the tower, and her honeymoon with Swithin in the 'cabin' among the 'firs', with the birds hopping round the open door, was like Virginia's idyll with Paul in the cottages among the palm-trees near Port Louis, where all the birds 'advanced promiscuously' for her to feed them. Had Hardy by then discovered that the 'cottages' were originally '*cabanes*'? And did Port Louis suggest the name of Viviette's brother?[15]

The astronomer in *Rasselas* was thought at first to be 'happy' in his 'turret'. Having checked that an equatorial is the one thing Swithin needs to make him 'quite happy', Viviette buys him one, and then asks 'Now are you happy?' Johnson's astronomer thinks he can regulate the weather, and make it rain whenever he likes, but cannot yet control the winds. Swithin's name implies some influence over rainfall, but a 'circular hurricane' upsets all his plans.[16]

Hardy considered himself a novelist in the tradition of Fielding, while thinking him snobbish in his treatment of Molly Segrim, 'as worthy a creation of Nature as the lovely Sophia'. Molly's 'philosopher' lover was found hiding behind the rug that served as 'curtains' to her bed. The lovely Lady Constantine was placed in the same 'ridiculous' situation herself, when the bishop spotted her behind the 'curtains' of Swithin's bed. But it was not Hardy's line to borrow from contemporary novelists. Nor did he (as has been suggested) need George Eliot to tell him, in *The Mill on the Floss* (1860), that the Latin grammar he had been using since 1852 contained these suggestive words: 'astronomus *an astronomer* exosus *hating* mulieres *women* ad unam (mulierem) *to one,* that is, *in general*'. Hence, perhaps, Swithin's initial statement: 'I shall never marry . . . a beloved science is wife enough for me.' As Hardy probably knew, those born under Saturn were traditionally 'haters of women, and cursers of conjugal love'. To Swithin Saturn was 'by far the most wonderful [world] in the solar system.'[17]

Poets, as usual, influenced the novel most. Picturing Swithin as an Odysseus sailing the night sky, when not distracted by some 'Circe or Calypso', Viviette prefigured her own role as an unmarried Penelope waiting for a husband who, even when back in Ithaca, could be distracted by Tabitha Lark. The hallucination that told her she was pregnant implicitly cast her as a Dido, sacrificed to her lover's empire-building: 'in a dusky vista among the fir-trunks she *saw, or thought she saw,* a golden-haired, toddling child.' The words in italics came from Virgil, where Aeneas dimly sees the shade of Dido, like a moon rising through clouds. Mr Torkingham's Horatian tag subtly predicted Viviette's death on the tower: 'Yes, pale death knocks at the cottages of the poor and the palaces of kings . . .' 'Palaces' suited the Bishop's death; but Horace's word was 'towers'.[18]

The Wimborne reading of *The Tempest* left traces in the novel: a storm that wrecked, if not a ship, a means of 'nocturnal sailings' by an astronomer who had slept there 'like a sailor in the maintop'; an 'island in the midst of an arable plain'; and a 'youth as 'beautiful' as Ferdinand, living 'in a primitive Eden of unconsciousness, with aims towards whose accomplishment a Caliban shape would have been as effective as his own'. Other Shakespearian works contributed too. The Bishop was a Malvolio, gulled by Louis into believing that Viviette loved him. Swithin was a Berowne, converted from study to love by the educative power of 'women's eyes'. 'Your eyes are to be my stars for the future' he told Viviette, paraphrasing from the *Sonnets*: 'Not from the stars do I my judgment pluck; / And yet methinks I have astronomy . . . But from thine eyes my knowledge I derive . . .' He had started as an 'Adonis-astronomer', responding sulkily to the advances of his Venus. 'My horse is gone', grumbled Adonis, 'and 'tis your fault I am bereft him so'. 'My object-glass broken!' cried Swithin. 'My great telescope won't work!'[19]

Milton suggested one touch of irony. 'The *Occidental* had just sailed' with the father of Viviette's unborn baby, and 'the sun rested his chin upon the meadows'. In Milton's 'On the Morning of Christ's Nativity', 'the Sun in bed . . . Pillows his chin upon an Orient wave'. But Viviette is not 'the Virgin blest' of the next sentence. She has not yet found a Joseph to marry her, and the Orient-Occidental contrast hints that her sun, far from rising, is setting to its death. The 'Romance' drew more heavily on the

Romantic poets. Byron's 'Darkness' was probably one reason why Swithin saw the sky as 'a horror'. 'The bright sun was extinguish'd, and the stars / Did wander darkling in the eternal space . . .' 'Imagine them all extinguished', said Swithin, 'and your mind feeling its way through a heaven of total darkness'. The scene with Donna Julia in *Don Juan* was amusingly adapted when Louis tried to catch Swithin in Viviette's bedroom: instead of emerging 'half smother'd, from the bed', the missing astronomer crept upstairs from a bit of 'nocturnal sailing'.[20]

Meeting Shelley's son in 1879, Hardy had for the third time 'impinged on the penumbra of the poet he loved' – an astronomical image doubtless suggested by *Prometheus Unbound* Act iv. As 'the lonely philosopher at the column', Swithin recalls Shelley's Laon, chained naked on the 'platform' of a 'column', until rescued by a hermit whose 'lonely home' was a 'gray tower'. But he is even more like descriptions of Shelley himself in his 'blonde hair, ardent eyes, and eloquent lips', his remoteness from real life, and his physical clumsiness. Invited, after his lunch in Viviette's library, to have some fruit in another room, Swithin rushes off after her, 'walking over his napkin'.[21]

Keats's *Endymion* and Lemprière did most for the novel's plot. Swithin's beauty was virtually blamed on 'the 'Classical Dictionary', for Lemprière, having mentioned Endymion's eternal youth and his licence from Jupiter 'to sleep as much as he would', told how the moon-goddess Diana saw him sleeping naked on Mount Latmos, 'and was so struck by his beauty that she came down from heaven every night to enjoy his company.' Diana, who took up hunting 'to shun the society of men' became Lady Constantine, who belonged to the hunting classes, had promised to avoid male society, and finally agreed to marry beneath her. The nightly assignations were bowdlerized into Viviette's 'rape of a lock' from Swithin's head, when she found him lying asleep in the sun, and succumbed to his 'physical attractiveness'. Lemprière interpreted Endymion's 'amours' to mean that he was really an astronomer, who used Mount Latmos as an observatory. In Keats, Endymion's union with the 'golden'-haired moon-goddess was not completed until he felt compassionate love for her earthly incarnation, the 'black'-haired, sorrowful, Indian maid. Swithin, obsessed with the heavenly bodies, had the goddess's 'very light shining hair': Viviette, as her human avatar, had hair 'black as midnight'. But despite their sexual intercourse, the union was never really consummated. Swithin did not approach compassionate love, or 'loving-kindness' as he called it, until it was too late.[22]

Hardy's favourite Victorian poets also helped. Tennyson's 'Palace of Art', quoted on Proctor's title-page, supplied one simile for the stars seen from the Cape, and a precedent for Swithin's descent from his tower to 'a cottage in the vale', whether his grandmother's 'thatched house' in the 'dell', or the 'cabin' where he lived with Viviette. Viviette's bigamy after the supposed death of her unpleasant husband abroad parodied the theme of *Enoch Arden*. Browning's *Red Cotton Night-Cap Country* had used *Turf and*

Towers to symbolize a conflict like Viviette's between religious and sexual impulses, and its hero jumped to his death from a tower, as she once thought of doing. Swithin was given the 'corn-coloured' hair of 'The Blessed Damozel' (as Louis pointed out) and on his return from the Cape played the dilatory lover of Christina Rossetti's 'The Prince's Progress', though he arrived in rather better time for the lady's funeral.[23]

Swinburne's just published *Tristram of Lyonesse* offered both an aptly astronomical quotation to mark the lovers' parting, and an oddly arithmetical type of kiss. Why, at Viviette's agreement to marry him, should Swithin have 'pressed his *two* lips continuously on hers'? He could hardly have kissed her with one. Presumably because in Swinburne, when the lovers drank the potion, 'their four lips became one burning mouth'; and when Iseult kissed Tristram 'newly dead', 'their four lips became one silent mouth.' Thus the allusion foreshadowed the moment when Swithin would hold Viviette, whose name suggested life, 'newly dead' in his arms. But to enjoy the effect sufficiently one needs to admire Swinburne as much as Hardy did.[24]

Swithin ended like Candide, reunited with his Cunégonde, and prepared to marry her, but not really wanting to do so, since she 'had grown so ugly'. The influence of Voltaire, perceptible in passing comments on Torkingham and Helmsdale, culminated in the last sentence: 'The Bishop was avenged.' That, however, was the weakest point in the book. If anti-clerical satire had been its main purpose, the flippant conclusion would have been apt enough: as a final absurdity, the exponent of the Christian ethic got his revenge. But the novel's real thesis was that human life was more important than the 'stellar universe', that 'of these contrasting magnitudes the smaller might be the greater'. It is only the adolescent Swithin who thinks otherwise. When he tells Viviette that astronomy will 'reduce' her anxieties, 'by reducing the importance of everything', she rightly laughs at him: 'I will endeavour to sink down to such ephemeral trivialities as human tragedy'. But her tragedy is trivialized only by that last sentence. Impatient to get the book finished, Hardy did not care quite so much how he did it. As he later confessed to Gosse: 'though the plan of the story was carefully worked out, the actual writing was lamentably hurried . . . It would have been rewritten for the book form if I had not played truant and gone off to Paris.'[25]

Of course there are other weak points. Coincidence strains credulity, especially in the timing of the hurricane, of Swithin's uncle's letter, and of Viviette's husband's death. The heroine's tiresome brother, like the uncle in *A Laodicean*, seems more a plot-component than a character. But the central relationship between Swithin and Viviette is entirely convincing, and moving. How, one wonders for a moment, could Swithin be so careless as to let Viviette see the letter about his uncle's conditional bequest? But such carelessness was typical of his 'young man's inattention to issues', his Shelleyan willingness to live in a 'litter' of 'books and papers', his one-track 'scientific' mind: 'the vastness of the field of astronomy reduces every terrestrial thing to atomic proportions.' And once she found that letter, he had no option but to show her the more damaging one. Given her religious leanings, her self-denying reaction was equally inevitable.[26]

Hardy called *Two on a Tower* a 'slightly-built romance', but it carried a great weight of bleakly realistic thought. Its 'stupendous background of the stellar universe', with the two young people in the foreground, was pictorially delightful, like the first part of Hopkins's recently written but still unpublished sonnet, 'The Starlight Night'. But in contrast with that poem's religious sestet, the novel vividly expressed Hardy's mature view of the human condition: inexplicably dumped in a vast, empty world where 'nothing is made for man', which makes one feel, which Viviette, 'that it is not worth while to live'. Putting such a message in such an enjoyable form was a type of conjuring trick that now became Hardy's speciality.[27]

12

The Mayor of Casterbridge

Finding no suitable building-site at Stinsford Hill, Hardy had applied for one about a mile east of Dorchester. He signed the lease for it in June 1883, and that month they moved to the 'county town', the 'Caster-bridge' of Wessex. While waiting for the lease to start in October, and the new house to be built, they rented what Gosse called 'a queer rambling old' one, accessible only through a passage between buildings and with no view except of the Prison. But its situation, close to Shire Hall, the Town Hall, and the Corn Exchange, would have done very nicely for 'The Mayor'.[1]

After their river-level home at Wimborne, the 'bracing air' of 'upper' Dorchester brought the Hardys 'health and renewed vigour'. Though Emma would come to hate living in Dorchester, Hardy's immediate reaction to the move was 'exhilaration'. But his underlying mood was grim. The death of Emma's brother-in-law at St Juliot in November had made 'the scene of the fairest romance of their lives' seem a thing of the past. Before leaving Wimborne, Hardy finished 'a short hastily written novel' called 'The Romantic Adventures of a Milkmaid'. It treated romantic love with sardonic humour, as a quasi-magical interrupter of real life. The Milkmaid's 'brief encounter' with the mysterious, morbidly depressive Baron ended with a tolerably happy marriage to her rustic fiancé, whose job as a lime-burner made him 'an incarnation of salubrity'. Some time in 1883 Hardy wrote a poem abjuring romantic love as a juvenile delusion: 'But – after love what comes?/ A scene that lours,/ A few sad vacant hours,/ And then the Curtain.' His next novel would be the first in which such love did not play a central role.[2]

August found Hardy at the deathbed of a friend from his early days with Hicks, Hooper Tolbort. Praising the dead man, two years his junior, he implied his own disillusionment: 'Tolbort lived and studied as if everything in the world were so very much worth while.' Another friend from the Hicks period, William Barnes, was unlikely to live much longer, and death was just beneath the surface of Hardy's own building-site: 'in digging the foundations', he reported, 'we found . . . three human skeletons in separate and distinct graves.' 'Here and everywhere', Henchard would think, 'be folk dying before their time . . .'[3]

Untimely death was made material for black comedy in the 1883 short story, 'The Three Strangers', about a hangman who sat drinking with his intended victim. The same year Hardy contributed an essay on 'The Dorsetshire Labourer' to the current agitation for the rights of agricultural workers. Trying 'to describe the state of things without political bias', he first insisted that farm workers were 'infinite in difference; some happy, many serene, a few depressed; some clever, even to genius . . .' Thus he defended in advance his choice of a hay-trusser hero. He also included a description of an old shepherd at a hiring-fair, which would be recycled for his next novel.[4]

One more clue to the state of mind from which that novel developed was a boys' adventure story written that year, 'Our Exploits at West Poley'. Its 'sufficiently apparent' moral, voiced by 'The Man who had Failed', was this comment on two boys' experiments in diverting the course of a river: 'Quiet perseverance in clearly defined courses is . . . better than the erratic exploits that may do much harm.' The 'Man', who spoke in a 'poetico-philosophic strain', and had failed 'from want of energy', sounds like Hardy mocking himself, perhaps even regretting his diversion from architecture to authorship. One of the boys hated the thought of being a farmer all his life, like his father. But he ended up a very successful one, 'remarkable for his avoidance of anything like speculative exploits'. Erratic and speculative exploits would be the *Mayor*'s speciality.[5]

In March 1884 Hardy started prospecting for plot-material in back-numbers of the *Dorset County Chronicle*. Among other suggestive news-items, he came across 'a labring man' who sold his wife for £5, and a 'public nuisance' who transformed himself into 'a respectable tradesman' by swearing off alcohol for seven years. After that term's expiry, and just one bender to celebrate, he renewed his oath for twelve years more. Hardy had recently read the querulous autobiography of a man who had written for the *Chronicle*, the self-taught poet and playwright J.F. Pennie, and commented: 'He was, seemingly, a man who had chiefly himself to blame for the vicissitudes of his life . . .' Pennie had ruined himself by hiring a theatre to stage one of his plays, quarrelled with all his theatrical managers, founded a school that went bust, and had barely got out of debt before he died in a cottage on a heath. Like Henchard he confirmed Hardy's reflection of March or April 1884: 'Every error under the sun seems to arise from thinking you are right yourself, and other people wrong, because they are not you.'[6]

Thus equipped with ideas for his first two chapters, and a model for his hero's character and career, Hardy started writing the novel. On Friday 17 April 1885 he noted: 'Wrote the last page of "The Mayor of Casterbridge', begun at least a year ago, and frequently interrupted in the writing of each part.' The main source of interruption had been his new house, Max Gate. It was really Mack's Gate, after the former keeper of a nearby toll-gate; but Hardy liked to think of it as 'Porta Maxima', the chief gate into the Roman town. He had designed the house himself, and closely super-vised its building by his father and his brother Henry. In October 1883 he had marked out a spot for a well. On New Year's Eve he had started planting two thousand Austrian pines (of which only two have survived). In March 1885 the house, like the novel, was 'nearly finished', and in June the Hardys slept there for the first time. Apart from its primitive plumbing (water had to be pumped daily from the well by hand), Max Gate proved what a house-agent might rightly call a desirable country residence, stand-ing in its own grounds of one and a half acres. Though not quite 'The House Beautiful' of Oscar Wilde's Dorchester lecture (September 1883), it now looks a very pleasant place to live.[7]

But it made neither Hardy happy. Emma would rather have lived in her own 'native county' of Devon, or at least not so close to her Bockhampton in-laws. And Hardy, according to a visitor in August, 'recoiled' from the house, 'preferring the freedom of rooms in an attic'. Just before moving in, he had compared the people of London to 'caged birds'. He evidently felt like one himself. The end of 1885 found him 'sadder than many previous New Year's eves have done'. Had the building of Max Gate been 'a wise expenditure of energy?'[8]

He must have asked himself the same question about *The Mayor of Casterbridge*. Serialized in the *Graphic*, and *Harper's Weekly*, then revised and partly rewritten, it had finally appeared as a book (10 May 1886). But neither critics nor readers had realized the novel's greatness. The *Saturday Review* called it 'a disappointment', its story 'very slight, and singularly devoid of interest'. The *Spectator* complained of its 'pagan reflections' and 'fashionable pessimism'. Yes, Henchard was Hardy's most 'powerful study' yet, but what could the subtitle, A Story of a Man of Character, possibly mean? Surely 'character' was the one thing Henchard lacked? It meant, of course, that Henchard's story was determined by his character, or 'uncon-scious propensity', as Hardy had recently put it in a comment on his-tory (20 October 1884). With American readers the book was popular enough to be widely pirated; but in England it was remaindered within eight months.[9]

Casterbridge was Dorchester. Armed with a suitable pamphlet, one can still walk round the town, precisely locating most of the scenes in the novel. How far was Hardy *The Mayor*? Though he never held that office, he did start sitting as a magistrate while at work on the story, and must sometimes have felt, like Henchard, that he was 'no better' than the people he was there to judge. He had not Henchard's drink problem, nor had he sworn off alcohol. But he found it unhelpful for his work, and had recently claimed, with 'rare exceptions', to have 'taken no alcoholic liquor for the last two years.' He had not sold Emma for 'five guineas', but had perhaps spoiled his marriage to increase his literary earnings. Henchard walked to Weydon-Priors, 'reading, or pretending to read, a ballad sheet', and totally ignoring his wife. While exploring Waterloo Hardy had possibly treated Emma in much the same way, intent on his 'Ballad of the Hundred Days'. Henchard later reflected that 'his attempts to replace ambition by love' had been 'foiled' by his 'wronged wife'. Had Emma's growing resentment already frustrated some attempt by her husband to re-establish a more loving relationship?[10]

Like Henchard, Hardy had 'worked his way up from nothing'. If not quite 'a pillar of the town', he had certainly put Wessex on the map. Yet bad reviews, like the complaints about Henchard's 'bad corn', indicated that his position was still precarious. Henchard at his 'fall' was 'not much over forty': Hardy was nearly forty-four when he began the novel. In physique Henchard was Hardy's antithesis, but in temperament not unlike him. Both men were intensely susceptible to music and suffered from 'gloomy fits'. Hardy was not outwardly bad-tempered, but perhaps with him too there was 'unruly volcanic stuff beneath the rind'. If so, the strain of preventing an eruption was expressed in Elizabeth-Jane, when 'keeping in all signs of emotion till she was ready to burst.' Into her character and history went also his early efforts at self-education, now seen as faintly ludicrous, and his present sense that life was of only 'moderate value', that marriage was 'no dancing matter', and that 'happiness was but the occasional episode in a general drama of pain.'[11]

Fragments of personal material were scattered all over the novel. The 'Dorset Hardys' were said to come from Jersey, which Hardy had visited in August 1884; and his maternal grandmother's maiden name was Swetman, Lucetta came from Jersey, and her maiden name was Le Sueur, i.e. 'Sweat', the feminine noun made masculine to suit the Dorset Hardys' ancestor, Clement le Hardy. The dead fieldfare of Hardy's childhood became the 'little ball of feathers' found by Elizabeth-Jane. Prince Albert's brief visit to Dorchester, which Hardy had probably seen at nine years old, was used to humiliate Henchard. One of the village girls for whom Hardy had written love-letters in his school days grew up into Mother Cuxsom: 'getting a schoolboy to write ours for us; and giving him a penny . . . not to tell other folks what he'd put inside'. During his 'pupillage' with Hicks, Hardy had once trained a telescope on the distant gallows and seen a 'white figure' drop downwards – so suddenly that 'the glass nearly fell from [his] hands'. Identifying a 'masculine figure' on the Budmouth road as Newson's, Henchard 'dropped the glass', feeling 'like a condemned man'. Finally, the skeletons found at Max Gate popped up in the Roman substratum of Casterbridge: 'It was impossible to dig more than a foot or two deep . . . without coming across some tall soldier . . . lying . . . like a chicken in its shell.' The simile had been less neatly worded in a 'scholarly' paper read to the local Antiquarian Field Club: 'the tight-fitting situation being strongly suggestive of the chicken in the egg shell'.[12]

On Easter Sunday 1885 Hardy praised the 'perfect art' of 'Bible nar-ratives'. They had clearly affected the novel he was just finishing. 'Like Job', said Henchard, 'I could curse the day that gave me birth', and that was the gist of his 'Will'. He was most like Job in his cumulative afflictions, and in such 'comforters' as Alderman Tubber and 'another good-natured friend'. Farfrae's flair for business was compared to Jacob's for sheep-breeding, and he lived up to Jacob's name throughout, successively 'supplanting' Henchard in love, trade, local government, house, furniture, and Elizabeth-Jane's affection.[13]

When visiting Wide-oh, 'Henchard felt like Saul' consulting Samuel. Saul's relationship with David influenced the novel more. David gave Saul music-therapy for his 'evil spirit', and Saul 'loved him greatly'. Henchard, who also suffered from 'visitations of the devil', heard Farfrae singing, and thought, 'how that fellow does draw me!' David solved Saul's Goliath-problem and was made his general. Farfrae solved Henchard's problem of 'grown wheat' and became his manager. Saul then grew jealous of David's success, and tried to kill him. So did Henchard with Farfrae. Told that Henchard was her father, Elizabeth-Jane 'was troubled at his presence, like the brethren at the avowal of Joseph'. Their 'trouble' was largely guilt, at having sold their brother for 'twenty pieces of silver'. Hers was an intuition of Henchard's guilt, at having sold his wife for five guineas.[14]

The New Testament was drawn on too. Lucetta's biblical knowledge was too 'limited' for her to have grasped why Henchard thought her 'wise in her generation', i.e. like the Unjust Steward. But the reader was expected to grasp it, and also to register her identification with Peter. Anxious not to be recognized as 'the young Jersey woman who had been Henchard's dear comrade', Lucetta stopped using French words 'with the suddenness of the weak Apostle at the accusation, "Thy speech bewrayeth thee!"' She later re-enacted Peter's triple denial, when Farfrae 'had laid hold on' Henchard 'and led him away' from the royal carriage: 'he distinctly heard her deny him – deny that he had assisted Donald, that he was anything more than a common journeyman.' He went on to die as if on a cross, with a self-condemning 'superscription': 'Upon the head of his bed he pinned a piece of paper', 'Michael Henchard's Will'. But his only resur-rection was in the new life of his stepdaughter, 'suddenly irradiated' with 'daybeams' of brief happiness, 'after the Capharnaum in which some of her preceding years had been spent.' The image came from Isaiah, quoted by Luke ('The people which sat in darkness saw great light'), and the spelling of Caperneum (where the miracles started), from Hardy's Greek Testament.[15]

As a *Durnovariad*, or 'Iliad of Dorchester', the novel might have been subtitled 'The Wrath of Henchard'. 'Temper' cost him his wife, and was still to be seen in his face nearly twenty years later. Achilles had been educated by a centaur or man-horse, and all he really knew about was fighting. Henchard was nearly as illiterate, and the 'idiosyncrasy . . . which had ruled his courses from the beginning' was an animal 'instinct of opposition'. Having caused the death of his friend Patroclus, Achilles felt he was 'a useless burden on the earth', and wanted to die. After nearly killing his friend Farfrae ('no man ever loved another as I did thee'), Henchard felt 'an encumberer of the ground', living on against his will.[16]

So far, Henchard was Achilles; but in the epic quarrel he played Agamemnon, the bad general jealous of his brilliant young lieutenant, to Farfrae's 'swift-footed Achilles'. As a dancer Farfrae earned that epithet by showing everyone the 'nails in the soles of his boots', and as manager he was 'so cursed quick in his movements as to give old-fashioned people in authority no chance of the initiative.' In Homer the quarrel stemmed from Agamemnon's abduction of a slave-girl allotted to Achilles; in Hardy, from Henchard's rough treatment of a workman under Farfrae's management. If not exactly a girl, 'Poor Abel . . .'ithout breeches', his shirt 'fluttering' below his waistcoat, did not look much 'like a man'. Henchard's last Homeric model, when 'wandering' round Wessex, 'an outcast . . . wanted by nobody, and despised by all', was Bellerophon: 'when hated by all the gods, he wandered alone about the Land of Wandering, eating his heart out, avoiding the paths of men'.[17]

But the primary Greek influence was Sophocles. The Aeschylean doctrine of *pathei mathos* (learning by suffering) was briefly dismissed: 'Misery taught him nothing more than defiant endurance of it.' To quote a recent classical dictionary, 'Sophocles' heroes and heroines give the impression that it is their innate characters that initiate the action, and that they could not have behaved otherwise.' For Hardy (November 1885) 'a tragedy exhibits a state of things in the life of an individual which unavoidably causes some natural aim or desire of his to end in a catastrophe when carried out.' Sophocles' Oedipus does all he can to avoid the catastrophe of killing his father and marrying his mother, but circumstances combine with his nature to force him into it. Henchard tries his best to make up for the shameful 'deed' of his youth, but everything he does goes wrong.[18]

The *Oedipus Tyrannus*, which Hardy had probably studied in Greek a quarter of a century before, touched the novel at many points. Each hero was a choleric, 'overbearing – even brilliantly quarrelsome' character, who had arrived in the town as a stranger and become its chief citizen by signal service to the community – Oedipus by saving it from the Sphinx, Henchard, as 'one of the chief stimulants' to the town's 'development'. Each man's position was undermined by a matrimonial secret of his youth. When this came out each became subservient to a partner in authority with whom he had recently quarrelled. And both partners, Creon and Farfrae, belonged to the same type: correct, reasonable, even generous, but coldly unsympathetic.

Oedipus blinds himself, and goes into voluntary exile, led by his daughters. Henchard starts drinking again, and is led by his step-daughter out of the pub, walking 'blankly, like a blind man'. But she does not share his exile. His last wish 'That no man remember me' comes close to what Oedipus asked for: to be 'thrown where no mortal man can speak to me'.[19]

That Hardy had the *Oedipus* in mind seems confirmed by the echo of the '*triplais hamaxitois*' (triple waggon-ways) where Oedipus killed his father. As Jebb had explained in his recent edition of the play (1883), this meant the junction of a path from Daulia with the Delphi-Thebes highway. Henchard's and Farfrae's waggons collided at a similar junction between an 'arched thoroughfare' from Bull Stake Square and the High Street.[20]

The Virgilian tag. '*videt aut vidisse putat*', was used again, with its connotations of death, when Elizabeth-Jane 'saw – or fancied she saw . . . her step-father slowly raise his hand to a level behind Farfrae's shoulders'. Her own meeting with Farfrae in the granary during a rainstorm, contrived by her mother to make them marry each other, was Hardy's latest version of the Dido–Aeneas cave-sequence. A subtler use of the *Aeneid* was the simile for Henchard's espaliers: 'writhing in vegetable agony, like leafy Laocoöns'. Laocoön's agony with the sea-serpents was his punishment for warning the Trojans: 'do not trust the horse'. Henchard had just welcomed Farfrae into his business and his home, where his new friend would proceed to operate just like the Trojan Horse.[21]

As a bankrupt on a bridge, who after his 'mad attack' on Farfrae and 'mad lies' to Newson was strangely saved from suicide, Henchard replicated Horace's 'mad' Damasippus, except for being converted to a belief in Providence rather than Stoicism. Bede's simile for human life, a sparrow flying through a lighted hall, had been elaborated by the working-class poet, Alexander Smith, just before Hardy first went to London; and he seems to have borrowed its symbolism for the swallow that interrupted the wife-sale in the furmity-tent. Amusingly, Farfrae said of the corn-drill almost exactly what Dante's Beatrice said of the Great Wheels: 'Each grain will go straight to its intended place'. Confronted by his own 'image' the Mayor was like Shelley's Magus, who 'met his own image walking in the garden . . .'[22]

Apart from such vague precedents as Lear and Cordelia, *Samson Agonistes*, *Empedocles on Etna* ('The brave impetuous heart yields everywhere/ To the subtle, contriving head'), and the 'Enoch Ardenism' of which one reviewer complained, English literature did unusually little for this book. In fact, *Enoch Arden* merely suggested a mechanism for shuffling the tiresome Newson on and off stage – unless it was Enoch's costly funeral that made Henchard so anxious not to have one. The important literary influence was that of Greek epic and tragedy, and the result was Hardy's finest novel yet.[23]

Just before it came out in book-form, Hardy saw Gladstone in Parliament, and commented: 'Large-heartedness *versus* small-heartedness is a distinct attitude which the House of Commons takes up to an observer's eye.' *The Mayor of Casterbridge* gives the same impression. Henchard is a hero of epic or tragic stature, surrounded by characters who justify the 'local exclamation' heard and noted down by Hardy the previous December: 'Everything looks so little – so ghastly little!' Farfrae's littleness, first revealed in his bogus passion for his 'ain countree', was summed up by his reaction, worthy of the feeblest chorus-leader, to the news of the tragic hero's death: 'Dear me – is that so!' Lucetta was his counterpart. Though not quite as humourless and literal-minded as her husband, she matched his sentimental singing with her 'picturesque' posturing, and his absorption in business with her commercial attitude to marriage: 'I knew I should lose Donald if I did not *secure* him at once'. Elizabeth-Jane, potentially a much larger personality, was fatally diminished by her self-righteous intolerance. 'Any suggestion of impropriety was to Elizabeth-Jane like a red rag to a bull. Her craving for correctness of procedure was, indeed, almost vicious.' Her snap judgement on Lucetta's moral dilemma ('there is only one course left to honesty. You must remain a single woman') foreshadowed her heartless and unimaginative condemnation of her step-father: 'I could have loved you always . . . But how can I when I know you have deceived me so . . . !'[24]

Henchard's greatness in a world of such 'ghastly little' people was enhanced by identification with great natural forces. He was the sun to Farfrae's moon, both in his 'strong warm gaze upon' Lucetta, and when the hay-wagon marked with Farfrae's name' filled the room with 'reflected sunlight'. He was a volcano, a 'great tree in the wind' a tiger, a lion, a buffalo and, at the royal reception, 'a bull breaking fence'. Here Hardy's horror of animal suffering, which made the tragedy culminate in a starved bird, added to Henchard's miseries the connotations of Bull Stake Square, i.e. North Square, Dorchester, where 'oxen had been . . . tied for baiting with dogs to make them tender' before slaughter. Thus Henchard was implicitly identified with the runaway bull that he had immobilized in the barn, by violently wrenching the ring welded 'through the gristle of his nose', and reducing him from a menace to a sufferer 'to be pitied'. The tragic hero would undergo a similar reduction, baited by little people.[25]

The real bull 'perhaps rather intended a practical joke than a murder'. If so, it was one of a series of such 'practical jokes' in the novel. Henchard's offer to sell his wife, his plans to 'do for' Farfrae ('I am a fearful practical joker when I choose'), his 'horse-play' with Lucetta's letters, and his lie to Newson, all are envisaged as 'jokes', and the lethal skimmington-ride is a 'great jocular plot'. The hero himself is the butt of another such plot. The moment he tells Elizabeth-Jane that she is his daughter, he learns that she is not. First his sports and then his finances are ruined by tricks of the weather. Just when he starts to dream of 'a future lit by [his step-daughter's] filial presence', her father knocks at the door. Even when he tries to commit suicide, he is preserved for more suffering by a caricature of himself.[26]

Why this odd emphasis on perverted humour? Perhaps it was one more development from Sophocles: Oedipus was clearly the victim of an elaborate practical joke by Apollo. Though they liked Farfrae's singing, the jocular drinkers at the Three Mariners found something 'ludicrous' in his 'odd gravity'. 'But no?' said poor Farfrae, 'gazing round into their faces with anxious concern', when told they are 'hardly honest sometimes'. Surrounded by jokers, he could not see a joke. That, according to *The Mayor of Casterbridge*, was the human situation. For the most 'fearful practical joker' of all was the one that Hardy would celebrate in *Satires of Circumstance* (1914).[27]

13

The Woodlanders

'Do not be induced to write too fast', Hardy warned Gissing, after publishing two long novels in just over ten months. In October 1884, when half way through the *Mayor*, he had been asked for a serial by *Macmillan's Magazine*. Terms were agreed in March 1885: £600 for 12 instalments, the first to appear in March or April 1886. But he had problems with the plot, and it was not until eight months later that he went 'back' to his 'original' one, i.e. that of the 'woodland story' he had 'put aside' in 1874. By then he was very short of time: 'Am working from half-past ten a.m. to twelve p.m., to get my mind made up on the details.' At the end of November 1885 the story had still 'hardly passed out of the chaotic stage'. So he found himself racing with the printers on both sides of the Atlantic, since the novel was to appear in *Harper's* as well as *Macmillan's*. One instalment had to be completed in a village pub, and ten of the twelve had been published serially before he got the novel finished (2 February 1887). 'Thought I should feel glad', he noted, 'but I do not particularly – though relieved.'[1]

Writing at such speed increased his dissatisfaction with his own work. When the *Mayor* first appeared in the *Graphic*, he had told himself: 'I fear it will not be so good as I meant'. Praise of it had only made him think how much better it would have been, 'if the story had been written as it existed in my mind, but, alas, was never put on paper'; or 'if my novels had been exact transcripts of their original irradiated conception, before any attempt at working out that glorious dream had been made'. This sense of failure to realize his own conceptions would be generalized into a central theme of the new novel: 'the Unfulfilled Intention, which makes life what it is'. And that novel too would disappoint him: 'It would have made a beautiful story if I could have carried out my idea of it: but somehow I come so far short of my intention that I fear it will be quite otherwise'.[2]

He had started writing *The Woodlanders* during 'a fit of depression, as if enveloped in a leaden cloud'. Through 1886 it seldom lifted. Whatever its inner causes may have been, besides literary frustration, outward circumstances did not help. His father was crippled with rheumatism. William Barnes was 'quite bed-ridden' and would die that October. Leslie Stephen, also ill and getting deaf, though Hardy did not realize it, seemed anxious 'to express sympathy' but could only make 'caustic' remarks 'showing antipathy instead'. Had Emma become like that too? If so, it would partly explain Fanny Stevenson's comment on her (August 1885): 'What very strange marriages literary men seem to make!'[3]

There were, of course, more cheering things: a new friendship with 'a most clever & interesting woman' called Mary Jeune, a judge's wife distantly related to Emma; an offer from Robert Louis Stevenson to dramatize the *Mayor*; some quiet reading at the British Museum, near which the Hardys took lodgings in the spring and summer of 1886; a brief visit by Gosse to Max Gate, and a much longer one by Emma's small niece Lilian, whom Hardy liked enough to draw comic scenes from the classics to amuse her; a 'pleasant week' with Emma at Lady Portsmouth's country house in Devon; London concerts, Impressionist exhibitions and parties full of distinguished people, who at least gave Hardy practice in verbal caricature: Walter Pater's 'manner is that of one carrying weighty ideas without spilling them.'.[4]

But the leaden cloud hung around, to condense in Hardy's notebook: 'The Hypocrisy of things. Nature is an arch-dissembler. A child is deceived completely: the older members of society more or less according to their penetration; though even they seldom get to realize that *nothing* is as it appears.' (21 December 1885). At the British Museum (May 1886) he came across Hegel's dictum that 'real pain is compatible with a formal pleasure': 'But it doesn't help much. These venerable philosophers seem to start wrong; they cannot get away from a prepossession that the world must somehow have been made to be a comfortable place for man.'[5]

He was more impressed that August by an article in the *Revue des deux mondes* on 'L'Homme Automate'. This questioned the current theory that Man was just a machine, that human consciousness, thoughts, and feelings were merely automatic responses to the functioning of the physical organism. It also discussed the suggested analogy with dreams and the 'mental state' during sleep. In December Hardy noted: 'I often view society-gatherings, people in the street, in a room, or elsewhere, as if they were beings in a somnambulistic state, making their motions automatically – not realizing what they mean.' That idea had already gone into *The Woodlanders*, and soon after finishing it he suggested a possible compromise between the traditional and the scientific theory: people might be divided into 'the mentally quickened, mechanical, soulless; and the living, throbbing, suffering, vital. In other words into souls and machines . . .'[6]

But one type of machine might actually contribute to the life of souls. In his obituary of William Barnes (16 October 1886), Hardy had quoted the philologist's 'death-bed' protest against the word 'bicycle': 'Why didn't they call it "wheel-saddle"?' A month before, Hardy had written to Gosse about a possible expedition to the Cotswold village of Broadway: 'On a tricycle you might do wonders . . . why did we not talk of tricycles? I am much exercised about them – not on them as yet.' It was actually an ordinary 'wheel-saddle' that would later prove his great resource, not only for transport and physical exercise, but also for spiritual refreshment. That was his great need now, so the day before *The Woodlanders* was published by Macmillans as a book (15 March 1887) he started off with Emma for a holiday in Italy.[7]

Back in London (27 April) he found the novel had got better reviews than anything he had published since *Far from the Madding Crowd*. The *Spectator* thought Fitzpiers should not have been allowed to get away with it. Coventry Patmore misunderstood the ending, and complained that one was 'expected to believe in that incredible event, the abiding repentance and amendment of a flippant profligate'. But the general verdict was favourable, and Hardy's hope that the book was 'romantic' and 'rural' enough to sell better than its predecessor was not disappointed. Sales eventually reached 5,000 copies, against the *Mayor*'s six hundred plus.[8]

'We are going straight to Italy', said Mrs Charmond's coachman. Hardy had long planned to do so. Her affair with Fitzpiers started at Heidelberg, where the Hardys had stayed on their so-called 'second honeymoon'. Fitzpiers, a villain 'of a philosophical stamp', was found reading 'a German metaphysician', and was 'primarily . . . an idealist'. Hardy had read Hegel's 'dictum' that 'the idea is all', before deciding that such 'philosophers' 'started wrong'. Marty, minus her hair, had 'three headaches . . . a rheumatic headache . . . a sick headache . . . and a misery headache'. Her author, when deciding on the plot, had suffered from deep depression and 'sick headache.' In 'hag-riding' Grace's horse to visit his mistress, Fitzpiers resembled the man Hardy met in a train, who 'wore out seven sets of horseshoes in riding from Sturminster Newton to Weymouth when courting a young woman'. Marty's father died from an obsession about a tree that 'sprouted up when he was born' and was now 'threatening [his] life'. William Barnes, obsessed with his native language, 'would . . . instance any natural object, *such as a tree*' to prove the richness of the Dorset dialect, and 'became quite indignant' on his deathbed about the latest threat to pure English.[9]

But the novel touched Hardy's life at more important points. Though he changed the topography in later editions, 'Great Hintock' was originally Melbury Osmond in north-west Dorset, and 'Little Hintock', as he told Gosse (5 April 1887), was 'a hamlet anywhere within 2 miles of the former.' Melbury Osmond, which gave Grace Melbury her surname, was where Jemima had lived in great poverty as a child, when her mother, Betty Swetman, had been disowned by her parents for marrying beneath her. So Marty's hard life, and Grace's sufferings from parental snobbery, were probably based on Jemima's stories about her childhood.[10]

Giles Winterborne lost his 'dwelling-place' and his 'Grace' because he was a life-holder. His tenure depended on a lease 'for three lives', the last of which was a member of his mother's family, Mr South. The Bockhampton cottage was held on a similar lease: Hardy's father was the last of the three 'lives', and when he died, his family would lose their home, unless (as fortunately happened in 1892) the landlords allowed them to stay on as rent-payers. In 'The Dorsetshire Labourer' (1883) Hardy had 'deplored' the current tendency of landlords to evict lifeholders, and 'pull down each cottage as it falls in'. That was what Mrs Charmond did to Giles. Earlier in the article Hardy had pointed out that the modern labourer's gains in personal freedom involved the loss of that 'intimate and kindly relation with the land' experienced by 'a serf who lived and died on a particular plot, *like a tree.*' South felt so closely related to the tree on his plot that he died when it was felled.[11]

In the previous novel Elizabeth-Jane's laborious efforts to educate herself had been gently satirized, as if symptomatic of her 'craving for correctness'. Here education proved positively harmful. Its immediate effect was to alienate Grace from her natural environment, her parents, and the man who really loved her. In return, it brought her a fleeting friendship with Mrs Charmond, and lifelong 'bondage' to Fitzpiers. Hardy had invested a huge amount of time and energy in educating himself. But now ('*nothing* is as it appears') had it been worth it? Though it never alienated him from his family, it must have made conversation with them less spontaneous. If he talked to his father about the books that interested him, as Grace to Giles about 'Méry's style', he probably got much the same reply: 'Suppose you talk over my head a little longer?'[12]

Obviously, Grace's marriage was not based on the current stage of Hardy's, but there were points of contact between them. The *Spectator* was shocked to find in the novel 'a vein of positive liking' for Fitzpiers, despite his 'good-natured profligacy'. There was at least some fellow-feeling. Hardy, who that year celebrated 'The forty-seventh birthday of Thomas the Unworthy', was conscious of not being an ideal husband. Apart from a roving eye, and a growing tendency to prefer the company of other women, he knew that when writing or trying to write, i.e. for most of his waking hours, he left his wife on her own. There Grace's situation was like Emma's, only worse: 'her life with Fitzpiers had brought her no society; had sometimes, indeed, brought her deeper solitude than any she had ever known before.' And Hardy felt lonely too: 'Our life here is lonely & cottage-like', he told Gosse, when pressing him to come down for a week-end. Loneliness pervades the novel, from the 'solitude' of the 'deserted highway' on the first page to the 'solitary and silent girl' on the last, standing alone by the grave of the man she loved, who had never loved her.[13]

While writing the novel, Hardy had been thinking about the future of 'novel-writing as an art'. Having progressed from mere story-telling to psychological analysis, it must go 'still further in that direction. Why not by rendering as visible essences, spectres, &c. the abstract thoughts of the analytic school?' The idea was not to be fully implemented until *The Dynasts*, but he tried it out right away in the scene where Melbury was on tenter-hooks for Fitzpiers to propose to Grace: 'Could the real have been beheld instead of the corporeal merely, the corner of the room in which he sat would have been filled with a form typical of anxious suspense, large-eyed, tight-lipped, awaiting the issue.'[14]

Meanwhile Hardy's view of the human predicament was further defined by his latest reading. Already in Chapter Six, the notion of human auto-matism was implicit in the doctor's remark that 'no man's hands could help what they did, any more than the hands of a clock'. But in chapter Twenty-Eight, published three months after the article on 'L'Homme Automate', Giles started acting like one with Grace: 'Almost with the abstraction of a somnambulist he stretched out his hand and caressed' the 'flower that she wore in her bosom.' A few paragraphs later Grace's mind made 'an automatic leap of thought' to her husband's story of 'tooth-drawing', and within the next twenty-three pages Giles was found working 'like an automaton', Grace walking 'as by clockwork', and Fitzpiers riding home fast asleep. In managing not to fall off, the 'philosopher' virtually duplicated the experiment in 'animal automatism' described at the start of the article. This was 'Mr Huxley's frog-philosopher' which, though 'de-prived of both cerebral hemispheres, did a prodigious balancing-act, to save itself from falling off a hand that was being turned in various directions.'[15]

The Impressionist paintings that Hardy had recently seen struck him as 'more suggestive' for literature than art. Their 'principle', he thought, was to highlight '*what appeals to your own individual eye and heart in particu-lar*', and to 'omit to record' everything else. Only one thing about Marty really interested 'Barber Percomb', so his window-picture of her was 'an impression-picture of extremest type, wherein the girl's hair alone . . . was depicted with intensity and distinctness', and the rest was 'a blurred mass of unimportant detail lost in haze and obscurity.' On the same principle the 'illumined face of Fitzpiers' appeared to Grace amid the darkness of the wood, where she herself was later highlighted by the moonlight, among the 'weird shadows and ghostly nooks of indistinctness'. The same prin-ciple was used in reverse, when her receding figure melted into the land-scape, 'a sylph-like greenish-white creature, as toned by the sunlight and leafage'; and when she saw Giles 'diminishing to a faun-like figure under the green canopy and over the brown floor.'[16]

Soon after starting the novel Hardy had noted: 'Winter. The landscape has turned from a painting to an engraving.' He elaborated the thought in Chapter Seven: 'Angles were taking the place of curves . . . A sudden lapse from the ornate to the primitive on Nature's canvas . . .' A month before finishing the story, he had written that realistic 'scenic-paintings' were 'interesting no longer'. He did not want to see 'the original realities – i.e. as optical effects', but 'the deeper reality underlying the scenic'. What interested him now was 'the much-decried, mad, late-Turner rendering'.

The Woodlanders was full of such interpretative 'scenic painting'. Like 'In a Wood' (begun 1887), the novel pictured the deeper reality of the woodlands as the Darwinian 'struggle for existence', but outdid the poem in stressing the cruelty of the process: the ivy that 'slowly strangled to death the promising sapling', the 'corkscrew shapes' produced by 'the slow torture of an encircling woodbine'. Grace was a sapling similarly warped by the constrictions of 'social law'. Her hopeless 'revolt' against it 'may have showed in her face' when she and Giles were gazing at a Turner-type sunset. The setting was possibly suggested by one of Turner's very last paintings, *The Visit to the Tomb* (1850), which pictured a non-Virgilian visit by Dido, Aeneas, and Cupid to the tomb of her husband, Sychaeus. Fitzpiers was not dead, and Giles would never desert his Grace; but the two scenes were otherwise analogous, and the title of Turner's MS poem, which supplied the epigraph, was as relevant to Grace as to Dido: 'The Fallacies of Hope'.[17]

Grace was highly educated because her father had been laughed at for not knowing 'Who dragged Whom round the walls of What?' Fitzpiers came to Little Hintock because of 'Achillean moodiness after an imagined slight'; and the comic scene where the three 'wives' of Fitzpiers weep together round his empty bed seems almost to parody the great moment in the *Iliad*, where the old enemies Priam and Achilles weep together for their dead. The climax of the *Odyssey* was more obviously burlesqued. Reunited with Odysseus after twenty years, Penelope 'sat opposite him in the firelight' while he 'sat waiting for her to say something . . . But she sat silent for a long time'. After twenty-four years' separation, the couple in the bark-ripper's story sat on opposite sides of the fire, and promptly fell asleep, 'not having known what to talk about at all.'[18]

That travesty of epic functioned like the satyric plays that concluded Greek performances of tragedies. Litle Hintock was potentially a stage for 'dramas of a grandeur and unity truly Sophoclean'. Marty's thought that newly planted trees 'sigh because they are very sorry to begin life in earnest – just as we be' was Sophoclean too: 'Not to be born is best . . .' Sophocles, according to Aristotle, introduced 'the third actor and scene-painting'. The novel had scarcely more major characters than the *Oedipus Tyrannus*, and made extensive use of 'scenic paintings'. The fatal quarrel about right of way between Oedipus and his father was re-enacted by Giles and Mrs Charmond, when his waggons met her carriage. Marty's unswerving devotion to Giles's grave echoed Antigone's determination to bury her brother, with Grace, when she failed to keep her appointment at the churchyard, playing the unreliable sister Ismene, who 'loves only in words'. The hero of Sophocles' *Trachiniae* died in agony from an illness unwittingly caused by his wife. So, but for an Unfulfilled Intention to marry, did Giles.[19]

The Preface (1912) implied that the novel was about the rights and wrongs of divorce. No doubt it was wrong, if marriage was 'a distinct covenant or undertaking, decided on by two people fully cognizant of all its possible issues'. But suppose they got married without such knowledge? When Grace knew her husband's real character, she wondered 'how far a person's conscience might be bound by vows made without at the time a full recognition of their force.' In Euripides' *Hippolytus*, which Hardy knew well in translation, her point was made more briskly: 'It was my tongue and not my mind that swore'.[20]

This line was quoted defensively by Diogenes in Lucian's 'Auction of Lives', i.e. of philosophies of life. In another amusing dialogue Diogenes was the spokesman for a crowd of angry philosophers, armed with sticks, who wanted to beat up Lucian. They included the 'Peripatetic' Aristotle. Hardy's classical drawings for Lilian had been dominated by Diogenes, but also showed some 'Peripatetics' walking past trees, led by 'Aristotle delivering his lectures'. The tone and subjects of the drawings suggest that Hardy, fed up with 'venerable philosophers', had turned for amusement to Lucian's satires on them. If so, one result was the scene where the 'auctioneer . . . like some philosopher of the Peripatetic school' led through the trees a crowd of men with 'walking-sticks', sometimes using his own to hammer 'a little boy's head', as though it were Lucian's.[21]

Giles teased Fitzpiers with 'Socratic *eironeia*'. Was Plato also behind the remark that Giles's and Grace's heads 'bent towards each other' in the gig, 'drawn together, no doubt, by their souls; as the heads of a pair of horses well in hand are drawn in by the rein'? The *Phaedrus* pictures the soul as a 'rein-holder' trying to control two horses, a good one, who 'restrains himself from leaping upon the person loved', and a sex-mad bad one, who has no such inhibitions. Grace certainly had to cope with two such types, Giles and Edred. Virgil, Horace, and Ovid left clearer traces. Giles's sad thoughts on the site of his demolished cottage were those of Meliboeus, evicted from his cottage in the *Eclogues*. The cave that sheltered Dido from the rain turned up twice more, first as the doctor's porch and sitting-room, and then, with tragic irony, as Giles's hut. Mrs Charmond felt inclined 'to run mad with discretion' – Mrs Montagu's version, apparently, of a famous phrase in Horace's *Satires*. 'The Daphnean instinct' made Grace run away from her husband. Like Ovid's Daphne, she ran into 'the darkness of the woods'; had a father who virtually told her, 'Daughter, you owe me a son-in-law'; and was pursued by a lover almost vain enough to boast: 'Medicine is my invention'.[22]

English literature was drawn on too often for more than a few cases to be mentioned. Fitzpiers undermined his last declarations of love for Grace by a quotation from *Measure for Measure*, which linked him with the lying Lucio. Sleep-riding on Grace's placid Darling, he travestied Byron's *Mazeppa*, tied naked to a wild horse as a punishment for adultery. By spouting Shelley he associated himself with the poet's regrettable love-life, recently publicized in Dowden's biography (1886). The 'reclining philosopher' played *Alastor* when the 'lovely form' of Grace 'seemed to have visited him in a dream'. Quoting from *Epipsychidion* on his way to Mrs Charmond, he implemented that poem's anti-monogamous 'doctrine': 'True love in this differs from gold and clay / That to divide is not to take away.' It was then paraphrased by his author: 'The love of men like Fitzpiers is unquestionably of such quality as to bear division and transference.'[23]

Giles, contrastingly, had the stoicism of Horatio in *Hamlet* ('As one, in suffering all, that suffers nothing') and, as 'Autumn's very brother', the patience of Keats's Autumn, watching 'by a cyder-press'. But Giles was also a 'frustrate ghost' from Browning's 'The Statue and the Bust', wasting his chances of happiness, and dying a martyr to conventional morality. Tennyson's *Maud* added a touch of irony: 'She is coming, my own, my sweet', cried Maud's would-be husband. 'Oh – he is coming!' cried Edred's wife, 'and in her terror sprang clean out of bed upon the floor.'[24]

Though the germ of the story went back to 1874, its development was apparently affected by Tennyson's last play, staged in 1882, *The Promise of May*. Like the 'fair promise' of the apple-blossom gazed at by Giles, the title symbolized the blighting of hopes for the rustic heroine. Pretty, and 'eddicated' by her 'feyther . . . to marry gentlefolk', she was seduced by a philandering 'gentleman' from 'Lunnun', very like Fitzpiers. First found reading a book 'proving man / An automatic series of sensations', he had 'a smattering of science', never went to church, and suggested marriage at a registry office. Both seducers followed Walter Pater's advice 'to catch at any exquisite passion'. Tennyson's lived for 'sensations', / Pleasant ones'; Hardy's, 'a subtlist in emotions, cultivated as under glasses strange and mournful pleasures'. And Pater's horrible account, in *Marius the Epicurean* (1885), of flaying a man's leg at the Roman Circus, as a form of 'practical joking upon human beings', must have prompted the picture of tree-barking as a 'flaying process', which left the 'executioner's victim' standing 'naked-legged' and 'ridiculous'.[25]

Giles died because he let Grace use his hut as a refuge from her husband. The idea for this may have come from Boucicault's *The Colleen Bawn*. Tennyson's play was a flop, but this one had been a great success, just before Hardy first arrived in London. The playwright had acted Myles, an altruistic rogue in love with the wife of a man who for social and financial reasons thought he had been 'mad to marry her'. He did reject an offer to murder her, but like Fitzpiers wished he were free to marry someone else. When Myles let her hide in his hut, he went out to sleep on the mountain-side, with 'a cloud round [him] for a blanket.' Giles did much the same, only the cloud burst.[26]

Rereading *The Woodlanders* in 1912, Hardy wrote: 'I think I like it, *as a story*, the best of all. Perhaps that is owing to the locality and scenery of the action, a part I am very fond of.' Except for the 'South Carolinian', dragged in to dispose of Mrs Charmond, the story was beautifully contrived to economize on plot-material, by making each item serve several purposes. Thus Mrs Charmond's wig rapidly defined her selfishness and artificiality, revealed Marty's poverty and love for Giles, and finally

served, through the 'complications' of Marty's motivation, to separate
Mrs Charmond from Fitzpiers, thus leaving her an easy target for her old
lover's gun.[27]

The man-trap theme was also given plenty to do. First, as Mrs Charmond
pointed out, the man-traps in her house implied that she was a menace
to men. Later, the reader was made to feel that Fitzpiers was a similar
menace to women. At the end of the novel the 'cobwebbed object' found
by Tim Tangs revived Grace's love for her husband and so prolonged
her 'bondage' to him. The man-trap had now become a metaphor for
marriage itself, outdated but still lethal. Her rendezvous with Fitzpiers
was 'her engagement', and 'Midway between husband and wife was the
diabolical trap, silent, open, ready.' Her marriage had proved just such a
trap, and she was about to be caught again.[28]

The theme also served to frame two larger concerns of the novel:
cruelty and automatism. These were presented as central features of the
human predicament. Like the trees, 'disfigured with wounds resulting from
their mutual rubbings and blows', men and women were programmed to
make each other miserable, a process exacerbated by marriage. But all
human beings were 'wrestling for existence' in a vast Darwinian machine
powered by hunger and sex, which forced them to be cruel to one another.
This automatic cruelty was epitomized, as so often in Hardy, by their treatment of animals. Shortly before sacrificing his own life to love, Giles was
found making a burnt offering for supper, with 'his eyes on the roasting
animal' – a phrase chosen for its hint of torture, to remind readers how
even the kindest people were programmed to get their protein.[29]

In such a world what were people to do? The novel's answer was
bleak. Christian self-sacrifice was ill-adapted to the struggle for existence.
In Giles's case, as in the Trumpet-Major's, it only made things worse for
the woman he loved. Another Christian virtue, 'lovingkindness', shown by
Mrs Charmond to the bleeding Fitzpiers, and by Grace to Giles after her
marriage, still had its value, though motivated by sex. But best of all was
Marty's blend of Christian and Stoic ethics. Nothing went right for Marty,
but she still loved and endured. That is why she spoke last, as poor Humanity's representative: 'she touched sublimity at points, and looked almost
like a being who had rejected with indifference the attribute of sex for
the loftier quality of abstract humanism.'[30]

14

Wessex Tales

'The year has been a fairly friendly one to me', wrote Hardy at the end of 1887. 'It showed me and Em the south of Europe – Italy, above all, Rome, and it brought us back unharmed and much illuminated.' One threat of harm was averted by Emma herself when, showing 'her usual courage,' though actually in 'a dreadful fright', she saved him from being mugged in Rome. Her own illumination, endearingly recorded in her travel-diary, included the discovery of 'Italian suavity', when she 'resolved to speak' to a Florence cabman about the poor condition of his horse, and did not get the 'offensive reply' she expected.[1]

And what did Italy do for Hardy? 'The Profitable Reading of Fiction', written soon after he got home, suggested that fiction, like travel, might give 'relaxation and relief when the mind is overstrained or sick of itself', and should also give 'mental enlargement'. He had clearly got both from Italy. Rome, where he seemed to hear Horace pursued by the 'bore' in the *Satires*, and to see 'a chained file of prisoners', including St Paul, 'plodding wearily along' the Appian Way, inspired four poems. Milan reminded him of Napoleon's coronation there, and 'in later years' he thought he had 'conceived' the coronation scene in *The Dynasts*, while sitting with Emma on the Cathedral roof. Venice, Milan, and perhaps the sight of Emma writing her travel-diary gave ideas for his next short story, 'Alicia's Diary'.[2]

Another short story may have germinated in Italy too. Rome's 'measureless layers of history' seemed to lie upon him like a physical weight'. 'I am so overpowered', he wrote to Gosse, 'by the presence of *decay* in Ancient Rome that I feel it like a nightmare in my sleep.' He was using the word *nightmare* literally: 'an evil spirit (incubus) once thought to lie on and suffocate sleepers'. 'The Withered Arm' started with just such a nightmare:

Gertrude sitting on Rhoda's chest, making her feel 'nearly suffocated by pressure'. And that 'incubus', like Rome in decay, had 'features shockingly distorted, and wrinkled as by age'.[3]

Back in London at the end of April 1887, the Hardys spent three months there 'gaily enough', going to parties in that 'brilliant Jubilee-year'. Hardy's own socializing began with a Royal Academy dinner, at which he heard Huxley and Morley make speeches, talked to Browning about 'The Statue and the Bust', but occasionally felt snubbed: 'I spoke to a good many; was apparently unknown to a good many more I knew. At these times men do not want to talk to their equals, but to their superiors.' The immediate effect of such 'gaiety' was to hold up his work. 'I dare say you are still producing', he wrote to a poet friend in June, '– which I, alas, am not doing just now.' But that month he agreed to supply Tillotson's Newspaper Fiction Bureau with a new serial novel for a thousand guineas; and in August he returned with Emma to Max Gate, to start, as he said, 'clearing off some minor sketches which I have long promised to some of the magazines.'[4]

Having cleared off 'Alicia's Diary', he set to work on 'The Withered Arm'. Short stories, originally tackled as pot-boilers, had now begun to interest him. That winter, in 'The Profitable Reading of Fiction', he 'dwelt . . . particularly' on the importance of 'construction': 'to a masterpiece in story there appertains a beauty of shape, no less than to a masterpiece in pictorial or plastic art'. There, while discussing novels, he virtually defined the essence of the short story. That genre compelled him to concentrate on producing 'a well-rounded tale', a 'well-knit interdependence of parts', which obeyed Addison's Aristotelian rule for the epic: 'nothing should go before it, be intermixed with it, or follow after it, that is not related to it.'[5]

The same article stated that every author 'has a specialty', an 'especial gift', not necessarily the one for which he is best known. Thus the popular humorist may show 'startling touches of weirdness'. That was to be Hardy's own specialty in short stories. He told *Blackwood's* that 'The Withered Arm' was 'of rather a weird nature', which might not be a bad thing, since 'the taste of readers seems to run in that direction just now'. Le Fanu's bestselling collection of creepy stories, *In a Glass Darkly*, had been republished in 1884, *Dr Jekyll and Mr Hyde*, by Hardy's friend Stevenson, had proved instantly popular in 1886. The Society for Psychical Research had been founded in 1882 to investigate stories of 'apparitions, clairvoyance, haunted houses, hypnotism, thought-reading, and spiritualistic phenomena' – just the type of story that Hardy had heard as a child from his grandmother, and could still hear from his parents. Weirdness was the obvious vein for him to work. In September 1887 he recorded a local superstition about pigeons' hearts, in January decided that 'A "sensation-novel" is possible in which the sensationalism is not casualty but evolution; not physical but psychical'; and in February noted down 'a story of a farmer who was "overlooked" [malignly affected] by *himself*'.[6]

What, meanwhile, about 'The Profitable *Writing* of Fiction' in short-story form? In 1880 Leslie Stephen had suggested a book of 'prose-idyls about country life – short sketches of Hodge & his ways', and Hardy was now intent on keeping 'the name *Wessex*' as his own trademark. The two ideas came together in the conception of *Wessex Tales*. On the last day of February 1888 he sent Macmillans five short stories (including 'The Withered Arm'), which had already appeared in magazines, and asked if they could be brought out as a book. The publishers agreed, offering £50 in advance, another £50 for a Colonial edition, and royalties of one-sixth on all copies sold. The English edition was published in two volumes on 4 May 1888. At the end of that month Harpers brought the book out in America, embellished with a portrait of the author.[7]

In the final edition of 1912 there were seven *Wessex Tales*, but now in 1888 there were only five: 'The Three Strangers', 'The Withered Arm', 'Fellow-Townsmen', 'Interlopers at the Knap', and 'The Distracted Preacher'. Written as one-off pieces over a nine-year period, they had little in common but the hangman that figured in two of them, and the women in two others who refused proposals of marriage. So they are best considered separately.[8]

'The Three Strangers' was set in 'a lonely cottage' about the same distance from Dorchester as Bockhampton, with a twelve-year-old boy enjoying one of those 'adventures with the fiddle' that Hardy had 'loved' at that age, and coping with a problem that must have faced Hardy too: 'his fingers were so small and short as to necessitate a constant shifting for the high notes, from which he scrambled back to the first position with sounds not of unmixed purity of tone.' At one point Mrs Fennel 'touched the fiddler's elbow' to stop the music, just as Hardy had once been stopped by 'his hostess clutching his bow-arm'. The second Stranger had to start work at eight next morning. It was the hour when Hardy had once seen a hanging through a telescope, and the Dorchester hangman had been a friend of the Hardy family. So the picture of that 'ominous public officer' as a genial drinking companion sprang naturally from Hardy's early social environment.[9]

The irony of the hangman's sharing a table with the man he was to execute reminds one of Sophocles: Oedipus shared a bed with the widow of the man he had killed. But the most obvious literary influence was Shakespeare's. The 'sworn constable' came straight out of *Much Ado about Nothing*, complete with a crying baby. 'If you hear a child cry in the night', Verges told the Watch, 'you must call to the nurse and bid her still it.' In Hardy it was the constable and his 'able-bodied men' that made the baby cry: 'disturbed by the noise . . . the child who had been christened began to cry heart-brokenly in the room overhead.'[10]

Written soon after the staging of *Far from the Madding Crowd*, 'The Three Strangers' was clearly conceived as a play, with almost all the action confined to the cottage interior, and the hangman's song thrown in to entertain the audience and keep them guessing. In 1893 Hardy would make a stage version of the story, which ran for a week at a London theatre. Meanwhile 'The Three Strangers' neatly exploited his old interest in *agnosia*, and its shapely version of the *Three Bears* archetype realized his new ideal of a 'well-rounded tale'.[11]

'The Withered Arm' was 'founded on fact.' The 'cardinal incidents', he told William Blackwood, 'are true, both the women who figure in the story having been known to me.' In telling it he had drawn on his own as well as their experience. In October 1887 he had noted that the thorn bushes battered by the gale at Rushy Pond looked like angry human beings. From there Gertrude saw far away 'a white flat façade' with 'specks ... moving about' on its roof. Coming nearer, she saw that the specks were erecting a gallows. From Bockhampton Hardy had seen in the distance 'the white stone façade of the gaol', but not the gallows or the man hanging from it, until he brought the scene closer with a telescope.[12]

He also remembered being told by his father of 'a stripling of a boy of eighteen' who was hanged just for watching a rick being burnt by pro-testers, and later confided to a friend: 'Nothing my father ever said to me drove the tragedy of Life so deeply into my mind.' Gertrude learned from Davies (the real name of the Dorchester hangman whom the Hardy family knew) that the condemned man was only eighteen, and had been 'present by chance when the rick was fired.'[13]

Rhoda was 'called a witch', and her dialogue with her young son over the fire suggests that Rossetti's 'Sister Helen' was still in Hardy's mind; but his main sources were oral, not literary, and his main purpose, to construct 'a neat thing in *weird* tales'. 'The Withered Arm' was certainly that: the final discovery that the hanged man was Rhoda's son brilliantly combined surprise with inevitability. Yet the story was more than 'creepy' and cleverly contrived. Its 'sensationalism', as in Hardy's note about a 'sensation-novel', was 'psychical' (about souls) rather than 'physical'. Rhoda was badly treated, but made to feel 'like a guilty thing' for resenting it. Ger-trude was equally innocent, but made to suffer from Rhoda's involuntary feelings, and then be unjustly accused: 'Hussy – to come between us and our child now!' Both women behaved naturally, only to be punished by the supernatural. That, as Hardy had come to see it, was 'the tragedy of Life'.[14]

Written at Upper Tooting, where 'our troubles began', 'Fellow-Townsmen' was the tale of an unhappy husband. Hardy, like Barnet, 'was a man with a rich capacity for misery'. Like him, he had married above his class, and in times of 'trouble' had perhaps thought wistfully of a former girl-friend. As an architect, he probably meant to build a house for himself one day – though not to call it 'Chateau Ringdale'. When working up these bits of personal experience into a story that had, he felt, 'more human nature in it' than 'The Three Strangers', Hardy took hints, as usual, from Virgil and Homer. The Port-Bredy harbour was 'like the Libyan bay which sheltered the shipwrecked Trojans'. The allusion to the *Aeneid* heralded the shipwreck that nearly killed Mrs Barnet – last seen sitting in a carriage, a 'stiff erect figure' with a 'boldly-outlined face' like one of Virgil's 'nymphs' on their 'seats of living stone'.[15]

Before and after deciding to try and resuscitate his wife, Barnet glanced at the smoke from Lucy's house. Before entering Circe's palace, and soon afterwards her bed, Odysseus twice saw the smoke from her fire. Barnet was an Odysseus who, after 'twenty years' of travel, would return to Circe, hoping to make her his Penelope. Circe's regular response to lovers was to turn them into animals. Lucy's was to make an ass of him: 'such an impracticable thing – I won't say ridiculous, of course, because I see you are really in earnest, and earnestness is never ridiculous to my mind.'[16]

Their reunion reversed the situation of Gilbert's comedy, *Sweethearts* (1874). There Harry, having failed even to recognize his 'sweetheart' after thirty years in India, is shown a 'withered rose' that she has kept in her pocket-book ever since he gave it her. Here Lucy, who made Downes marry her by threatening to go to India, has never even guessed why Barnet went away. Hardy thought 'Fellow-Townsmen' 'rather good'. Its three best points were the subtly satirical portrait of Lucy, whose veneer of 'common-sensed rectitude' over ruthless self-interest increased the futility of Barnet's passion for her; the passage where her image briefly interrupted his 'mechanical movements' to resurrect his unloved wife; and his symbolic response to Lucy's marriage: helping the sexton finish off a grave by 'treading in the dead man'.[17]

'Interlopers at the knap', Hardy told his photographer friend, Hermann Lea, was the only one of his stories where he 'was thinking entirely of Melbury Osmond'. By then (1911) the house and the 'sycamore tree' had disappeared, but the village was always important to him, as the place where both his grandmother and his mother had been born and married. Betty Swetman, disinherited by her family for marrying a drunken 'servant' called George Hand, and reduced to extreme poverty, was dimly reflected in Helena, 'left penniless' by her uncle because she 'disgraced' herself by marrying Philip Hall, whose death from an 'infernal cough' matched George Hand's from consumption. Darton's initial journey to marry Sally Hall, including the signpost-climbing and his lack of enthusiasm for the marriage ('Hanging and wiving go by destiny'), was based on Hardy's father's journey to marry Jemima Hand.[18]

Like Hardy when a boy, Philip's son was 'entered as a day-scholar at a popular school at Casterbridge', though he commuted the 'three or four miles' on a 'forest-pony', not as Hardy had done, on Shanks's. Like Emma's father, Helena's snobbish uncle was 'a solicitor', and like Emma herself, she sometimes 'spoke regretfully of the gentilities of her early life'. When Hardy wrote the story (1884), was he already beginning to fear that, like Darton with Sally, 'he had worn out his welcome' in Emma's heart?[19]

Apart from such personal sources, the tale owed most to the theatre. Darton's previous love-life was suddenly presented as a tableau:

Two people appeared before her . . . a pale, dark-eyed, ladylike figure . . .
standing up, agitated; her hand was held by her companion – none else
than Sally's affianced . . . upon whose fine figure the pale stranger's eyes were
fixed, as his . . . upon her. His other hand held the rein of his horse, which
was standing saddled as if just led in.

Another stage trick followed. 'He is gone – gone!' cries Lady Audley, after
pushing her second husband down the well', 'and no one was a witness to
the deed!' 'Except me!' says Luke. '*You* belong to another', Darton told
Helena, 'So I cannot take care of you.' 'Yes, you can', said his fiancée,
suddenly appearing beside them. 'You can, since you seem to wish to.'[20]

Despite such melodrama, there was humour and human interest in the
story, with implicit satire on male complacency. Darton begins by explaining that he has 'decided' to go down market and marry Sally, because she
is 'a comely, independent, simple character'. He ends up inventing wrong
reasons why she refuses to marry him. The real reason is that she is too
'independent' to need him: 'The truth is, I am happy enough as I am, and
I don't mean to marry at all.'[21]

But for the demands of 'the English magazine at the time of writing',
as Hardy explained in 1912, Lizzy would have refused just as firmly to
marry 'The Distracted Preacher'. In 'the true incidents of which the
tale is a vague and flickering shadow', she actually married her fellow-
smuggler, and they 'both died in Wisconsin between 1850 and 1860.' Hardy
had doubtless heard about them from his grandmother. His grandfather,
like Lizzy's, 'used to do a little in smuggling', and 'sometimes had as many
as eighty "tubs" in a dark closet . . . little elongated barrels . . . of thin staves
with wooden hoops', one of which Hardy remembered having been turned
into a bucket. Such details, noted down in 1871, proved useful when Lizzy
was showing Stockdale how best to cure his cold. The source of the apple-
tree cache was an ex-smuggler employed by Hardy's father, and Hardy
himself had known 'several, now dead, who shared in the adventurous
doings along that part of the coast fifty or sixty years ago.'[22]

He had noticed two books at the British Museum (1878–9), called *The
Smuggler: A Tale*; but apart from the Rabelaisian comic catalogue of the
places searched by the 'Customs-men', his own tale of smuggling owed
little to previous literature. The Bible, though, naturally contributed.
'Distracted' (in the Latin sense of being torn apart) by 'the attractive Lizzy'
and his nonconformist conscience, Stockdale 'often said Romans for
Corinthians in the pulpit'. Those epistles, both dear to dissenters, held the
seeds of his 'dilemma'. Romans put the question: 'thou that preachest a
man should not steal, dost thou steal?' It then elaborated the antithesis
between 'faith' and 'law', and the doctrine of 'justification by faith'. But
could a preacher be justified in helping a woman to 'side with men who
break the laws'? Corinthians was even more worrying: 'It is good for a man
not to touch a woman'. Still, it did offer a let-out: 'But if they cannot
contain, let them marry: for it is better to marry than to burn.' Stockdale

could not contain: 'He set a watch upon his tongue and eyes for the space of one hour and a half, after which he found it was useless to struggle further'. So he would have to marry – once he had 'a furnished house to live in, with a varnished door and a brass knocker'.[23]

'The Distracted Preacher' is far the most enjoyable story in the book. Though the plot is quite simple, the action is exciting, and Stockdale's gradual slide from blissful ignorance to the relative wisdom of supporting his neighbours' folly is very funny. The climax of his own folly, one might think, was his 'last sermon . . . particularly directed against Lizzy' – another adaptation of Hardy's youthful experience in Stinsford church. But was that sermon included in 'the ending that would have been preferred by the writer'? We do not know. One great attraction of the story as we have it is the sunny tone of its satire on church- and chapel-goers, and on the young minister himself. The warm glow of his feeling for Lizzy comes through, undimmed by his own absurdity; and though his eyes are 'without a ray of levity', she has more than enough for two: 'You dissent from Church, and I dissent from State. And I don't see why we are not well matched.'[24]

15

A Group of Noble Dames

After a holiday in Paris, the Hardys spent a month in London, at 5 Upper Phillimore Place, Kensington, close to where Walter Pater was then living. By the end of July 1888 they were back at Max Gate and there, while planning his novel for Tillotsons, Hardy wrote more short stories. The first, set in the time and place of *The Trumpet-Major*, ended with the heroine seeing her lover shot by a firing-squad. The second, a contemporary tale about 'the ambitions of two men, their struggles for education, a position in the Church, & so on', plunged Hardy 'up to the elbows in a cold-blooded murder'. The third, about the early history of the Ilchesters, of Melbury House near Melbury Osmond, began with the bitter wrangling of a married couple, and ended with what promised to be a similar marriage, arranged purely to accumulate wealth and prestige. Thanks, however, to the husband's cold-blooded diplomacy, and the wife's self-interested deceit, it worked out quite well. 'People said in after years that she and her husband were very happy. However that may be, they had a numerous family...' This story, 'The First Countess of Wessex', set the tone for Hardy's next collection, *A Group of Noble Dames*.[1]

'Rather a frivolous piece of work', he called the book later, 'which I took in hand in a sort of desperation during a fit of low spirits'. The connection between low spirits and history was implied by a note made after 'a rheumatic attack' in London:

> if there is any way of getting a melancholy satisfaction out of life it lies in dying, so to speak, before one is out of the flesh, by which I mean putting on the manners of ghosts, wandering in their haunts, and taking their views of surrounding things. To think of life as passing away is a sadness; to think of it as past is at least tolerable.[2]

Life was passing away. The great modern thinker of Hardy's youth had suddenly become 'the late Mr M. Arnold', whose attempts to delay the death of religious dogma had been mere 'hair-splitting'. For God, as 'an external personality', was also on his way out. 'I have been looking for God 50 years', Hardy would write eighteen months later, 'and I think that if he had existed I should have discovered him.' The latest modern thinker, their London neighbour Walter Pater, had reduced all human experience to 'the passage and dissolution of impressions, images, sensations . . . that continual vanishing away . . .'[3]

Hardy's parents, already seventy-seven and seventy-five, would vanish before long, as his friend Gosse's father did next month; and perhaps the Emma that he had loved seemed to be vanishing too. When relationships go wrong, causes and effects tend to be indistinguishable. But Hardy's notes around this time suggest that his eyes and thoughts were increasingly drawn towards other women, from the 'interesting' one met at Pater's dinner-party, whom 'one would be afraid to marry', to 'that girl in the omnibus' with 'one of those faces of marvellous beauty which are seen casually in the streets, but never among one's friends . . . Where do these women come from? Who marries them?' Some such 'interesting women' were 'Noble Dames': Lady Coleridge, for instance, who 'could honestly claim to be a beauty', or Lady Portsmouth, looking 'like a model countess . . . her black brocaded silk fitting her well and suiting her eminently . . . one of the . . . very few women of her own rank for whom I would make a sacrifice . . .' Extrapolating, presumably, from his own experience of marriage, Hardy coined a dismal epigram: 'Love lives on propinquity, but dies of contact.'[4]

So much for the 'low spirits' that generated the book. What of the 'desperation'? Hardy was driven to it chiefly by editorial censorship, which threatened to prevent him from publishing the serious fiction that he now wanted to write. 'The besetting sin of modern literature', he noted in October 1888, 'is its insincerity . . . particularly in morals and religion.' The novel he was writing for Tillotson's would be different. In February 1889 he read Plato's *Cratylus*, a dialogue about language which claimed that falsehood was impossible, since all words were naturally appropriate to the things they described. Hardy disagreed: 'The fact is that nearly all things are falsely, or rather inadequately, named.' His novel would conscientiously call a spade a spade. By then it was well under way, and was due to start serialization that year. In September 1889 he sent Tillotsons 'about one-half' of the MS of 'Too Late Beloved' (as *Tess* was originally entitled), and it was duly printed.[5]

But when Tillotsons' editors saw it in proof, they demanded drastic bowdlerization. Hardy refused, and at his suggestion the contract was cancelled. The novel was later rejected by both *Murray's* and *Macmillan's* magazines, because of its 'improper explicitness'. Hardy expressed his frustration in two ways. First he cocked a snook at Mrs Grundy by writing stories for *A Group of Noble Dames* that were clearly designed to shock her.

Then he tried to reason with her in *Candour in English Fiction*. The defiant gesture proved counter-productive, but the article must have begun to make people realize the absurdity of a situation where fiction 'for adults' was unpublishable, because magazine editors and circulating libraries thought it 'unsuitable' for 'household reading', i.e. for the ears of the young. Such 'censorship of prudery', he pointed out, could only lead to 'a literature of quackery'.[6]

In April 1889 Hardy had promised the *Graphic* a 'Christmas Story' for £125. In May 1890 he sent them *A Group of Noble Dames*. Apart from the snow in the framing narrative, nothing could have been less Christmassy, especially as the first of the six stories was the horrible 'Barbara'. Predictably, the *Graphic* doubted if fathers would care to read aloud to their families 'a series of tales almost every one of which turns upon questions of childbirth, and those relations between the sexes over which conventionality is accustomed (wisely or unwisely) to draw a veil.' This time Hardy was forced to bowdlerize, sometimes enough to destroy the whole point and coherence of his plot. Thus mangled, the 'Tale of Tales' came out in the Christmas Number of the *Graphic* on 1 December 1890. A more or less unexpurgated version appeared in America (*Harper's Weekly*, 29 November to 20 December); and the original text of the six stories, with four more added, and the narrative frame altered, was published as a book on 30 May 1891.[7]

Boccaccio, Chaucer, Morris, and Clough had all written 'tales of tales' where a group of people, forced by circumstances to spend time together, killed it by telling stories. Hardy adapted the pattern to his own recent experience. He had long been a member of the Dorset Natural History and Antiquarian Field Club, and in January 1889 he was elected to the council of the Dorset County Museum. So the *Graphic* stories were told by members of the Mid-Wessex Field and Antiquarian Club, snowed up after a meeting in a 'Museum' like the old one in Dorchester. In the book-version they were 'storm-bound' in a 'museum of the town', more suggestive of the present Museum building, opened in 1884. The 'crimson maltster' knew that his fellow-members, now so friendly, would tomorrow 'pass him in the street . . . with the barest nod of civility'. Was that Hardy's experience with the Field Club, or was it only at the Royal Academy dinner that people he knew had 'apparently' not known him?[8]

The stories told gave fleeting glimpses of the author, as the 'plain-looking young man of humble birth' who married 'a lady' in 'The Marchioness of Stonehenge', and perhaps as the 'man of eight-and-forty' in 'The First Countess' who 'was unhappy when near his wife'; as the husband inadequately grateful for his wife's devoted nursing in 'The Honourable Laura'; and in the same tale, as the 'man who arrived on a tricycle' at a country hotel. 'I wish you would *tri*cycle', he had urged the illustrator of 'The First Countess'. 'We would then scour the country.' Negative snapshots of Hardy were also presented by two repulsive antitypes: Barbara's husband 'had a phlegmatic dislike of dancing', and the Duke of Hamptonshire 'argued doggedly with the parson on the virtues of cock-fighting and baiting the bull.'[9]

But Hardy's life probably affected the stories most in the recurrence of certain themes: love that 'was only skin-deep'; the 'wish for a lineal descendant'; and the miseries of marriage. 'Won't you be a fright!' cried the horrified lover, when the girl he had just eloped with showed symptoms of small-pox. Barbara ran panic-stricken from her once handsome husband when horribly disfigured by burns. Was Hardy satirizing his own tendency to look for beauty on buses, now that Emma had lost her looks?[10]

Barbara was the victim of her second husband's desire for a 'lineal successor'. So, though less traumatically, was Lady Icenway. Squire Petrick actually got his son disinherited, 'to dish the intruder' into the Petrick line. Concern with pedigree was part of the aristocratic stereotype, but part of Hardy too. Fascinated by his family's history, he was sad to be, not just childless, but the last of his branch of the Hardys. Was he trying to argue away that feeling, by picturing childlessness as a lucky escape – telling himself that any child of his and Emma's would have suffered like Betty Dornell, Lady Mottisfont's Dorothy, or Petrick's Rupert, from its parents' disagreements, competing interests, or foolish snobbery? Even so, he may sometimes have felt like Lady Icenway's first husband, bigamous but 'now almost to be pitied', who loved 'vaguely and imaginatively only . . . a child who did not know him', and 'a woman who had ceased to love him.'[11]

In 'Candour in English Fiction' Hardy had contrasted 'honest portrayal' of real-life sexual relations with the 'false colouring' of the 'regulation finish that "they married and were happy ever after"'. On that score the stories were ruthlessly 'honest'. Only in the first and the last did marriage lead to anything like happiness. 'People said' that Betty and Reynard were 'very happy', but the author suggested otherwise. Laura and James had their first child after a twelve-year separation. If they were happy after that, it must have been because her masochism neatly fitted his sadism. Besides, the story was told by a young 'Spark' who preferred 'lively', 'modern' melodrama to realism. Lady Audley's husband was pushed down a well, only to reappear as good as new. James was pushed over an eighty-foot waterfall one snowy night, by an operatic baritone as incredible as any character in opera, but within 'a few weeks' was 'little, if any, the worse' for it.[12]

Such debunking of marital bliss, in fiction allegedly historical, was presumably an outcrop of Hardy's private life. This was kept well below the surface in the book's opening story. 'Betty Dornell', 'The First Countess of Wessex', was Elizabeth Horner (1723–1792), wife of Sir Stephen Fox ('Stephen Reynard'), who became the first Earl of Ilchester. They had lived at Stinsford House, next to Stinsford Church, where their daughter Lady Susan O'Brien and her actor husband were buried. But Hardy's family history came closer to the Ilchesters' than that. His grandmother and mother came from Melbury Osmond, the Ilchesters' country seat, and

Jemima had worked as a cook, first for the third Earl's uncle, and then for his brother-in-law. She was doubtless the source of the Ilchester family 'legend' that Hardy used in this story, and the fifth Earl was 'angry with' him for doing so.[13]

Such legends, taken 'from the lips of aged people', and the 'pedigrees of our county families . . . on the pages of county histories', were Hardy's acknowledged sources for *A Group of Noble Dames*. The pedigrees were in his copy of Hutchins's *History of Dorset* (where he also investigated the genealogy of the Dorset Hardys). Yet Hutchins provided little more than dates of births, deaths, and marriages. His only contribution to 'Barbara' was her death in Florence. He quoted Lady Baxby's ultimatum to her brother, 'you will find the bones of your sister buried in the ruins', but made no mention of her subsequent transformation 'from the home-hating truant to the strategic wife'. He told the funny story of Lady Penelope Darcy who, unlike her namesake in Homer, married all her suitors; but gave no hint of a tragic ending. Towards 'Squire Petrick's Lady' he supplied only the grandfather's insistence on walking 'over every single acre' of a property before buying it, and the will that he made in his elder grandson's favour. As for 'The First Countess', he quoted her husband's epitaph and, by giving his real surname', suggested his foxy character. That was all.[14]

The Preface admitted that the gap between 'these reticent family records' and the stories themselves had been bridged by imagination: 'Anybody practised in raising images from such genealogies finds himself unconsciously filling into the framework . . . motives, passions, and personal qualities . . .' That process apparently involved sardonic adaptation of literary precedents. In its title and general conception *A Group of Noble Dames* implicitly parodied Chaucer's 'Legend of Good Women', and Tennyson's 'Dream of Fair Women'. It ended with a burlesque of the *Odyssey*, when Laura's husband came home after twelve years abroad. Odysseus called first on the swineherd, then walked on to his palace disguised as a beggar. Northbrook went first to 'the servants' quarters', looking like 'a drenched wayfarer not too well blessed with this world's goods.' After making sure in the kitchen that his wife had no suitors, he 'walked round to the front door', rang the bell, and 'ceremoniously' asked to see her.[15]

'The Marchioness of Stonehenge' picked up a village lover, because she was bored with the men of her own class, and jealous of the village girl to whom 'he had paid some attentions'. The perversity of her choice was stressed by reference to Aristophanes' comic theory of sexual attraction in Plato's *Symposium*: the surprised villager soon responded to her advances, for 'a time comes when the stupidest sees in an eye the glance of his other half'. Her seduction of the villager was further satirized by calling her rival Millie a 'woodman's daughter'. That was the title of a poem by Coventry Patmore, made famous by Millais's painting, about a 'cottage-girl' who was seduced and impregnated by the 'rich Squire's son'. She therefore drowned her 'shame' in a weedy pool. In Hardy's tale the seducer herself was left holding the baby. So she farmed it out to her rival, and when it had grown up, tried to get it back. It rightly refused to come, making its 'corporeal mother' react like King Lear to 'a thankless child': 'The anguish that is sharper than a serpent's tooth wore her out soon.'[16]

Chronology rules out any causal link between the mutilated portrait in 'Barbara' and Wilde's almost contemporaneous *Picture of Dorian Gray*, but Hardy's story had more probable literary sources. Half-blinded by falling beams in a fire, while bravely rescuing other people, Edmund Willows almost duplicated the experience of Rochester in *Jane Eyre* and Romney in *Aurora Leigh*; and Barbara's inability to meet such a challenge to her love reads like a realistic comment on the idealized fidelity of Jane and Aurora.[17]

In Juvenal's lengthy *Satire* on women, the Empress Messalina stole out of bed, the moment her husband was asleep, to her cubicle (*cella*) in a brothel. The Latin word could also mean a chapel containing a divine image. Barbara similarly left her second husband's bed to 'kiss' and 'embrace' her first husband's statue. Messalina was always the last and the most reluctant of 'the girls' to 'shut her cell'. Lord Uplandtowers first guessed the contents of the 'tabernacle' when he 'heard the shutting of a door, and the click of a key'.[18]

Having finally caught his wife 'with her arms clasped tightly round the neck of Edmund, and her mouth on his', the noble lord proceeded to 'cure' her by 'virtuous tortures' differing only in their greater cruelty from those used by Petrucchio to 'tame' his wife. In 1888 Hardy had been much moved by 'the Shrew of Miss Ada Rehan . . . when her husband wears out her endurance . . . at first she hears the cracks of the whip with indifference; at length she begins to shrink at the sound of them.' Barbara was finally brainwashed into 'hating' her first husband and 'loving' her second one, 'as if dreading lest the scourge should be applied anew.'[19]

The death of the 'Poet' in Shelley's sad self-portrait, *Alastor* (written just before his first wife's suicide enabled him to marry his second), was neatly synchronized with the setting of the moon behind 'the jaggéd hills'. The 'unhappy' bigamist in 'The Lady Icenway' died 'as the sun was going down behind the garden-wall.' His job as 'under-gardener' associated him with a more notable sufferer than Shelley. Since his initial 'misdemeanour' he had developed from 'a free and joyous liver' with 'a foreign twist in his make' into 'a man of strict religious habits, self-denying as a lenten saint'. Not so his equally bigamous wife, Maria. Unlike the biblical 'sinner' who was forgiven because 'she loved much', Maria 'had now no conscious love left' for Anderling, and never forgave him. After first 'supposing [Jesus] to be the gardener', her gospel namesake joyfully recognized her resurrected 'Master'. When this Maria's husband, reported by her to have 'died of malignant ague', turned up in a conservatory as one of her under-gardeners, her first thought was to sack him.[20]

The theme of the earliest story in the book, 'The Duchess of Hamptonshire', was that of 'The Statue and the Bust': a promising passion aborted by moral scruples. The curate's refusal to rescue his Emmeline from a husband that 'tortured her' was evidently meant to disappoint expectations raised by the young priest's rescue of Pompilia in *The Ring and the Book*. The clerical lover's cruelty was emphasized by association with Bill Sikes, when Emmeline silently followed him 'through the darkness, like a poor pet animal that will not be driven back.'[21]

Like Clough, after resigning his Oxford fellowship on conscientious grounds, Alwyn then set up as a 'respectable scholar and gentleman' in America. The first poem in Clough's first volume seemed to recommend the motto, 'I will do my duty', but a few pages later he satirized 'duty' as 'Sacrificing aye the essence / Of all that's truest, noblest, best'. Having sacrificed the girl he loved, and unknowingly officiated at her funeral, Alwyn 'lived on' at Boston, 'exerting himself solely because of a conscientious determination to do his duty.' But the most typical use of literary material in these stories was the skit on *Silas Marner* in 'Squire Petrick's Lady'. Silas was an embittered miser humanized by fatherly love for little Eppie. Petrick seemed to be repeating that pattern with young Rupert – until he realized that the boy was his own son, and not, as he had guessed from his Christian name, a Duke's bastard. 'I'll Rupert thee, you young imposter! Say, only a poor commonplace Petrick!'[22]

That, in its way, is quite funny. But the humour seems contrived, and rather sour. The same applies to the book's other comic effects: the elopement in reverse, when Phelipson takes Betty back up the ladder, for fear of catching her smallpox; Lady Icenway's grief at her first husband's premature death, just when she has thought of using him to satisfy her second husband's need for an heir; the tug of war for the wedding-ring when Lady Caroline finds she is pregnant by the dead husband that she has shuffled off on to Milly. Technically, *A Group of Noble Dames* was a brilliant display of complex plotting, ironical surprise, and grim farce; but for all its cleverness, Hardy had no reason to be proud of it. Haste, depression, exasperation with editors, and preoccupation with *Tess* combined to trivialize the book. At the risk of agreeing with T.S. Eliot, we must admit that 'Barbara' is merely revolting. Nor need one share the *Graphic*'s prudery about childbirth and sexual relations to endorse the editor's tactfully worded comment that the stories were only 'too much in keeping with the supposed circumstances of their narration', i.e. with the jocular atmosphere of an all-male 'Club smoking-room'.[23]

16

Tess of the d'Urbervilles

Hardy's disappointing *Dames* had only just appeared in book form, when a 'mutilated' serial version of his finest novel opened in the *Graphic* (4 July 1891). He had started work on *Tess* in the autumn of 1888, but its elements had been assembling in his mind since at least 1871. *Desperate Remedies* had begun with the first Cytherea refusing to marry Ambrose, though she obviously loved him. Tess would puzzle Angel Clare in the same way, for much the same reason. Cytherea had been seduced and left with an illegitimate child. When Ambrose came along, she 'perceived what it was to be loved in spirit and in truth! But it was too late. Had he known her secret he would have cast here out.' That was Tess's problem with Angel. So the manuscript sent to Tillotsons in 1889 was entitled 'Too Late Beloved' – words originally addressed by Shelley to a girl in a convent, but sardonically paraphrased by Hardy in 1890, when Lady Icenway promised, for a '*reason*' of her own, to be nicer to her first husband in future: 'Too late, my darling, too late!' murmured the dying man. 'Too late, too late!' Tess would cry, when Angel finally found her at Sandbourne.[1]

To this theme of belated true love, blighted by previous false love, Hardy's experience had gradually added details. At Marnhull (Tess's native 'Marlott') in 1877, 'The prime of bird-singing . . . thrushes and blackbirds . . . pleading earnestly rather than singing', probably suggested his heroine's association with birds, initially singing bullfinches. At Sturminster Newton he watched 'dancing on the green': 'The pretty girls, just before a dance, stand in inviting positions on the grass.' Angel would find one of them more inviting than Tess at 'the May-Day dance'.[2]

The next night the Hardys' servant 'Jane', whom they 'liked very much', was seen coming out of 'the outhouse with a man' who had made her pregnant, and she later 'vanished'. Hardy asked after her at her father's

cottage, and 'Found them poorer than I expected (for they are said to be
an old county family).' She was apparently the Jane Phillips whose two-day-
old son Tom was buried at Sturminster that December. Hardy's namesake,
like his own mother, had been privately baptized. There, already, were
precedents for Tess's seduction after a dance, her d'Urberville ancestry,
and her christening of 'Sorrow'.[3]

Her bird-connection first became tragic, when she spent a night with
her 'kindred sufferers', the pheasants. That came from a gamekeeper's
account of a *battue*, given to Hardy in January 1882. In June Hardy's
mother told him how 'the son of Parson F.' (actually the nephew of the
Melbury Osmond vicar), had 'worked with the labourers and yarn-barton-
wenches ... in the yarn-barton'; and that August he described the behaviour of 'blackbirds and thrushes' during a heat-wave at Wimborne, in a
note later adapted to describe the hot August when Parson Clare's son
worked in the 'barton' at Talbothays.[4]

In 1886 Hardy got a sociological perspective on his theme from his new
friend Mary Jeune's articles about her voluntary work with 'the fallen
women of London'. There he learnt that only very few of them had been
'ruined by "gentlemen"' – but Tess would be no Londoner, and Alec a
gentleman only in just such inverted commas. 'These women', wrote Mrs
Jeune, 'are invariably untruthful' – so Tess had 'the woman's instinct to
hide', 'her instinct of self-preservation was stronger than her candour'.
'She alone bears the consequences ... the man escapes altogether' – so
Phases four and five were 'The Consequence' and 'The Woman Pays'. Mrs
Jeune thought these mothers had mixed feelings towards their children,
but she had found 'the maternal instinct' usually dominant, and 'seldom
seen more genuine grief than that of many an erring mother when her
babe died.' On the harvest-field Tess would subject hers to 'an onset which
strangely combined passionateness with contempt', yet its death 'plunged'
her into 'misery'.[5]

Mrs Jeune also gave grounds for the subtitle, *A Pure Woman*: 'The poorer
girl is not necessarily impure because ... she belongs to a class where
there is no strong public feeling in favour of women being pure, and
where the parental authority is not enforced'. And the article's conclusion
virtually invited Hardy to make his fallen woman a saint: 'as to individual
cases in one's experience ... there are some that stand out prominently as
beacons across the dark night of human sin and suffering ... characters
and dispositions as fine and noble as have lived on the earth.'[6]

At a concert in 1887 Hardy 'saw Souls outside Bodies'. The soul-body
antithesis was involved in the true-false love theme, and also in religion;
religious satire probably joined the novel's ingredients around March 1888,
when Hardy stayed at a temperance hotel in London, full of 'religious
enthusiasts of all sorts', who opened 'fresh views of Christianiy by turning
it in reverse positions'. Thus the obsessive text-painter would turn 'the
religion of loving-kindness' into one of terror, and the 'wicked' seducer

would become a 'ranter pa'son'. That month in the British Museum Hardy saw 'Souls . . . gliding about . . . in a sort of dream – screened somewhat by their bodies, but imaginable behind them.' A year later he wrote: 'In a Botticelli the soul is outside the body, permeating the spectator with its emotions. In a Rubens the flesh is without, and the soul (possibly) within.' Angel would first notice Tess when she said: 'our souls can be made to go outside our bodies when we are alive.' At one stage the novel's title was 'The Body and Soul of Sue'.[7]

In July 1888 Hardy started a short story in which a drunken father threatened his daughter's marriage. That character, possibly based on the author's grandfather, George Hand, merged with 'a tipsy man' who once 'swaggered past' Hardy in a small Dorsetshire town, 'singing "*I've-got a-great family-vault-over at-*" (&c., as in the novel', to produce 'Sir John' Durbeyfield.[8]

The same July Hardy noted the 'sad, impotent resignation' of Ada Rehan's *Shrew* when she heard 'the crack of the whip', and of some horses seen in London: 'What was it on the faces of those horses? – Resignation. Their eyes looked at me, haunted me. The absoluteness of their resignation was terrible.' Their eyes still haunted him in 1890, when he noticed at a ballet 'the air of docile obedience on the faces of some of the dancing women, a passive resignation like that of a plodding horse, as if long accustomed to correction'. That was how he had come to picture his heroine. Her sufferings would begin with the death of a horse, and her increasingly desperate struggles would be like those of the 'omnibus horses' on the slippery surface of Ludgate Hill in December 1888: 'The poor creatures struggled and struggled but could not start the omnibus.' Hardy's guilt at not having got out to reduce the load (as 'Em would have done' if she had been there) would be felt by Tess, when Prince was killed: 'she regarded herself in the light of a murderess.'[9]

One more note of July 1888 would be paraphrased to introduce Tess's 'Rally': 'Thought of the determination to enjoy. We see it in all nature . . . achieved . . . under superhuman difficulties . . . Even the most oppressed of men and animals find it . . .' The narrative purpose of the rally was to make Tess all the more sensitive to subsequent pain. Perhaps Hardy was remembering his father's recent account of floggings, where the operator did not 'flog fair', i.e. 'he waited between each lash for the flesh to recover sensation, whereas . . . by striking quickly the flesh remained numb through several strokes.'[10]

Thus the novel was slowly emerging from Hardy's life. As the tale of a woman's battle against poverty and social prejudice, it came also from accounts of his maternal grandmother, Mary Head. But what of the woman herself? Hardy is quoted as saying that he first imagined Tess when he saw a girl called Augusta Way working as a milkmaid on the Kingston Maurward estate. By the end of September 1888 (when she was eighteen) he had invented names for the Blackmoor and Frome valleys, 'The Valley of the

Great Dairies' and 'The Valley of the Little Dairies', and prospected some of the ground on foot, thinking of his own as well as Tess's genealogy: 'The decline and fall of the Hardys much in evidence hereabout . . . So we go down, down, down.'[11]

That October he had a thought that would twice recur in *Tess* (when the three Durbeyfields zigzagged home from the pub, and when the dairy-man made a joke of a problem like Tess's): 'If you look beneath the sur-face of any farce you see a tragedy . . . if you blind yourself to the deeper issues of a tragedy you see a farce.' In December he sketched the novel's philosophy as a kind of grammatical paradigm: 'He, she, had blundered, but not as the Prime Cause had blundered. He, she, had sinned, but not as the prime Cause had sinned. He, she, was ashamed and sorry; but not as the Prime Cause would be ashamed if it knew.' The unknowing neuter, 'It', would dominate *The Dynasts*. In *Tess* it would still be masculine, as the playful 'President of the Immortals'.[12]

By September 1889 half the novel had been written. When three editors had found it too 'explicit' to publish, Hardy found a way round. As if inspired by the recent Revised Version of the Bible (1881–5), he decided to produce two versions of his novel too, but in reverse order – first a revised, i.e. bowdlerized version to get serialized, then an authorized one to publish as a book. The 'plan' was ingenious, but painful to implement. Whatever 'cynical amusement' it gave him, it meant 'mutilating' his own best work the moment he had written it, on a system that proved 'sheer drudgery'. If only he could have had a computer! As it was, he had to write 'modified' passages in 'coloured ink', to facilitate their replacement in the book-version, and often felt 'it would have been almost easier for him to write a new story altogether.' The exasperating process must have made him quite impossible to live with. No wonder, about this time, Emma started writing bitter comments on him in her diaries. Her father had just died, and she probably wanted more support from her husband than he was then able to give her.[13]

But the plan worked. The 'modified' version was duly accepted and serialized by the *Graphic* (4 July – 26 December 1891), and the real, three-volume *Tess of the d'Urbervilles* was published by Osgood, McIlvaine & Co in the week of 29 November 1891. A signed copy went to the author of 'Helping the Fallen'. After 'reading the final proofs', Hardy had added the defiant subtitle. The reviews were generally admiring. The *Athenaeum* called the novel 'not only good, but great'. Two hostile critics spoilt their case by using the same trite formula to sum it up. 'Mr Hardy'. said the *Saturday Review*, 'tells an unpleasant story in a very unpleasant way'; 'the novelist', said the *Quarterly*, 'has gratuitously chosen to tell a coarse and disagreeable story in a coarse and disagreeable manner.' The second critic, then editor of *Macmillan's Magazine*, was doubtless trying to convince him-self that he had been right not to to serialize the novel. There were, of course, the usual complaints about Hardy's gloomy outlook, awkward style, dubious morality, and anti-religious philosophy; but for most critics and readers, *Tess* was a triumph. It gave Hardy enough self-confidence to jettison his beard and, but for a small moustache, bare his face to the world.[14]

Like Tess's Sorrow, Hardy was the product of extramarital sex, and if he was really 'thrown aside as dead' when born, might never have been baptized. The 'venerable "boy" of sixty' who drove Tess and Angel to their wedding was in real life William Young, who had driven Hardy and Emma to Badbury Rings. Talbothays, where Angel and Tess fell in love, was a farm owned by Hardy's father. And Jack Durbeyfield's pride in his pedigree simply burlesqued his author's. But Hardy had closer ties with his major characters. Alec was his own precise antithesis: 'tall', 'handsome', 'bold'-eyed, thick-skinned, unscrupulous, and cruel to animals. He boasted of having 'nearly killed' his horse and if Tess had not been around, would doubtless have enjoyed killing rats at the wheat-rick, instead of just watching them being killed.[15]

Angel was in some ways a positive version of Hardy. He had his Mrs Martin in 'the Squire's wife', and gave up his chance of going to Cambridge from the same 'conscientious feeling' that made Hardy stop trying to go there – feeling too much of a sceptic to make an honest clergyman. The subversive-book episode was an experience of Horace Moule's, whose father was one model for Mr Clare; but Hardy himself must have felt the same credal 'divergence' between himself and his parents as Angel felt at the Vicarage. No member of Angel's family attended his wedding: Hardy's had been similarly boycotted. Like Hardy, Angel tried to find comfort in Marcus Aurelius' advice: 'Be not perturbed . . .', regarded 'his own existence with the passive interest of an outsider', and played music. Hardy's instrument, the 'fiddle' was 'best' in the down-to-earth life of Trantridge and Talbothays; but Angel's name and otherworldly character naturally made him a harpist.[16]

Tess, too, had Hardy's 'innate love of melody', and much else of him besides. Her father, like his, was 'the last of the three lives' that determined the lease of the family home. Like Hardy, she 'spoke two languages; the dialect at home, more or less; ordinary English abroad and to persons of quality'. She also soon adopted his disillusioned outlook. Only a few weeks after moving with Emma into their 'first house' together, Hardy had written: ' "All is vanity", saith the Preacher. But if it were only vanity, who would mind? Alas, it is too often worse than vanity; agony, darkness, death also.' Eight months after joining Angel 'under their own exclusive roof-tree', Tess had the same thought, in almost the same words.[17]

As an agricultural worker, she suffered from the situation described in 'The Dorsetshire Labourer' (1883), which anticipated many of her special problems: minimal wages, 'turnip-hacking', 'feeding the threshing-machine', eviction as a life-holder 'in the interests of morality', and the removal of the family furniture, including the spasmodically striking clock. Among several passages transferred almost verbatim from the article to the novel was Angel's discovery that the 'unvarying Hodge' did not exist.

Such cannibalizing of a single text was simple enough compared with the mysterious process by which ideas from the distant and recent past combined to create one of Tess's private ordeals, her burial by Angel in his sleep.[18]

Knight had linked burial with personality-change in *A Pair of Blue Eyes* (1873): 'If she could but be again his own Elfride – the woman she had seemed to be – but that woman was dead and buried'. Thinking the same about Tess ('You were one person; now you are another'), Angel acted out the burial metaphor. Unconsciousness and somnambulism had been added to the compound by the 1884 translation of Hartmann's *Philosophy of the Unconscious,* and by 'L'Homme Automate' (1886). Somnambulism was next associated with a mistaken view of reality (like Angel's) in a note of 1887: 'people are somnambulists . . . it is because we are in a somnambulistic hallucination that we think the real to be what we see as real.' In January 1888 Hardy reverted to the idea of changing personalities: 'Different purposes, different men. Those in the city for money-making are not the same men as they were when at home the previous evening. Nor . . . when lying awake in the small hours'. – as Tess would lie, where Angel 'carefully laid' her. The cluster of ideas was completed by the Abbot's coffin at Binford Abbey, conveniently close to the Turberville manor-house at Wool; and by an odd picture remembered from a lunch-party in 1880: 'When I arrived Mrs Tennyson was lying as if in a coffin, but she got up to welcome me.' 'Tess sat up in the coffin.'[19]

Elsewhere in the novel, too, the theme of personality-change was often handled pictorially. The general effect of Hardy's visit to 'the Old Masters., Royal Academy' in January 1889 was to multiply allusions to works of art, and descriptions clearly conceived as landscapes or genre-paintings, like the view of Blackmoor Vale, 'so tinged with azure that what artists call the middle distance partakes also of that hue'; the candle-lit midnight-christening; the garlic-hunt with 'the soft yellow gleam . . . reflected from the buttercups into their shaded faces, giving them an elfish, moonlit aspect, though the sun was pouring upon their backs in all the strength of noon'; the 'sad yellow rays' of the 'morning candles' at the dairy, 'in contrast with the first cold signals of the dawn without'.[20]

But the Academy visit must also have suggested a train of thought which went into the novel: 'Turner's water-colours: each is a landscape *plus* a man's soul.' Tess was an attractive feature of a landscape, pictured by Angel as his soul-mate, but objectively quite 'another person'. 'What [Turner] paints chiefly is *light as modified by objects.' The Angel Standing in the Sun* (1846) shows a figure almost invisible against a background of light. Tess was too dazzled by 'a divine being' called Angel Clare to see what he was really like. '[Turner] said, in his maddest and greatest days: "What pictorial drug can I dose man with, which shall affect his eyes somewhat in the manner of this reality which I cannot convey to him?"' Each lover had just such a heightened picture of the other, which still conveyed something of that other's real character – for even the 'misnamed' Angel rose to the occasion at Sandbourne.[21]

For them, the 'pictorial drug' was sexual passion, but the Durbeyfield parents and the Trantridge dancers had another one, alcohol. In terms of Turner's *Angel* both drugs caused 'irradiation'. In gospel terms this might be called 'transfiguration': 'his face did shine as the sun, and his raiment was white as the light'. And in modern terms, for the drinkers, it was a 'halo-effect': 'Each pedestrian could see no halo but his or her own, which never deserted the head-shadow ... but adhered to it, and persistently beautified it ...'[22]

Forms of 'irradiation' marked critical points in the narrative. The sex-charged atmosphere before Tess's seduction was 'a faint luminous fog' that 'enveloped' her and Alec. At the christening her 'ecstasy of faith almost apotheosed her ... set upon her face a glowing irradiation'. Just before meeting Angel at the dairy she moved in 'an ideal photosphere', and her later love for him 'enveloped her as a photosphere, irradiated her into forgetfulness of her past sorrows'. Her brief happiness with him was implicitly compared to the 'brief glorification' of the gnats, 'irradiated' in the November sunshine. On the way to the wedding, she 'knew that Angel was close to her; all the rest was a luminous mist' Leaving the church, she 'felt glorified by an irradiation not her own, like the angel whom St John saw in the sun'. After her confession 'she knew that he saw her without irradiation'. From then on only Alec saw her 'irradiated by the brassy glare' of the burning couch-grass.[23]

Turner's *Angel* came from Revelation, where he invited the birds to 'supper': 'that ye may eat ... the flesh of horses ... and the flesh of all men'. Hardy's Angel was like that too. He celebrated his first 'supper' with Tess by condemning her 'sin' of the flesh, and was ultimately responsible for feeding that flesh to the gallows. In thus desecrating 'their *Agape*' after confessing his own 'dissipation with a stranger', he was like the Greek Testament 'dreamers' who after 'defiling the flesh' infiltrated the Christian community, as 'rocks in your feasts of charity (*agapais*)'. *Agape* in St Paul's definition was notably shown by Tess: 'she sought not her own; was not provoked; thought no evil ...'. But the parson's son had none of it.[24]

Such use of the Bible implicitly endorsed Christian ethics, but the use was more often ironical. The Durbeyfield cot flung the baby 'from side to side like a weaver's shuttle' – Job's simile for the shortness and hopelessness of his life. The 'pillar of cloud' that shielded and guided the Israelites exposed Tess on the allotment to threats of new bondage from Alec. The pair then parodied the gospel conversation at Jacob's well, with 'The Convert' playing Jesus, and Tess, the polygamous Samaritan woman: 'I have no husband' – 'It is quite true – in the sense you mean'. The allusion points forward to the moment when her real husband will find her living with a man 'who is not [her] husband.' Waiting to be carried over the pool, Izz quoted Ecclesiastes: 'There's a time ... to embrace and a time to refrain from embracing; the first is now going to be mine.' The second would be Tess's, when Angel refused to kiss her goodbye. At the pool he had whispered: 'Three Leahs to get one Rachel.' Now he had married his

Rachel, but 'behold it was Leah' i.e. 'Another woman'. It was one of the 'three Leahs', Izz, that he later propositioned in the gig.[25]

From a literary angle the novel was Tess's *Odyssey*, ending with the bloody slaughter of a suitor. When her marriage was wrecked, Tess slept on a bed of leaves like the shipwrecked Odysseus – to be woken, not by the cries of girls at play, but by 'strange noises' due to a blood-sport. 'Sometimes it was a palpitation, sometimes a flutter . . .' 'What is this fluttering of birds that I hear near me?' asked Aeschylus' Prometheus, tortured like Tess by 'the President of the Immortals (*makaron prutanis*)' for his kindness to human beings. His last words, as he disappeared in storms and whirlwinds, were: 'You see how unjustly I suffer.' The same kind of 'Justice' was done on Tess.[26]

But Tess had another Aeschylean prototype. In the month that Hardy 'settled down daily to writing' the novel, he noted: 'When a married woman who has a lover kills her husband, she does not really wish to kill the husband; she wishes to kill the situation. Of course in Clytaemnestra's case it was not exactly so, since there was the added grievance of Iphigenia, which half-justified her.' It was not exactly so with Tess either, for Alec was her husband only 'in a physical sense', and the lover was her real husband; but she had an added grievance too. Clytaemnestra's husband had sacrificed her 'dearest child' to his own ambition. Alec had sacrificed Tess to his own lust, and exploited her feeling for the children to get what he wanted. A month before the Clytaemnestra note, Hardy had quoted in Greek from Sophocles' *Oedipus Tyrannus*: 'And if there be a woe surpassing woes it hath become the portion of Oedipus'. On that incremental principle Tess's tragedy was constructed, and it needed a touch of Clytaemnestra to produce the final term in her series of Promethean sufferings.[27]

To the last, her husband was 'still . . . her Apollo', her Angel and God of the sun, who played a lyre-like instrument, and would tell her at Stonehenge about sacrifices to the sun. Like Apollo in Euripides' *Alcestis*, he had, 'though a god', condescended to 'eat with labourers', and 'tend cattle'. But he was really more like that play's Admetus, in letting his wife die for him; and Tess's farewells to the dairy recall those of the dying Alcestis, who 'gave her hand to each one, nor was any too low (*kakos*) for her to speak to and be answered by'. Tess, going even lower, 'bade all her favourite cows good-bye, touching each of them with her hand.' Doing dairy-work near Port-Bredy, she imagined herself back at Talbothays with 'the tender lover . . . who, the moment she had grasped him . . . had disappeared like a shape in a vision'. Hardy was probably remembering Milton's vision of his wife, 'Brought to me like *Alcestis* from the grave . . . But O as to embrace me she enclin'd / I wak'd, she fled, and day brought back my night.[28]

By quoting Horace, of all people, as an authority for sexual 'purity', Angel was made to betray his obtuseness on that subject; and the Horatian metaphor, '*post equitem sedet atra Cura* (black Care sits behind the horseman)' was literal when Tess, having once 'scrambled into the saddle behind' Alec, decided to steer clear of 'gentility': 'from that direction . . . Black Care had come.'[29]

Her 'Rally' was partly a response to the springtime 'stir of germination': it moved her, as it moved the wild animals . . .' Daphnis and Chloe were similarly moved by the flowers, bees, birds, and lambs of spring: 'now that all things were possessed by the beauty of the season, these two tender young creatures began to imitate the sights and sounds around them.' Their sexual love was later stimulated by spring-flowers, nightingales, skipping lambs and mating goats. Angel and Tess's 'passion' grew under the influence of 'flowers, leaves, nightingales, thrushes, finches', and 'arborescence', when 'the rush of juices could almost be heard below the hiss of fertilization'. Here the Talbothays idyll surely owed something to Longus's pastoral – especially as Angel Day's translation had just been republished (1890).[30]

English novelists also helped. Alec's 'ambush' for Tess in his mother's bedroom reproduced Mr B.'s for Richardson's Pamela. The scene where Car stripped off her bodice to fight Tess, thus revealing her 'faultless rotundities', copied one in Fielding's Tom Jones. And Alec drove fast to impress Tess, as Thorpe would have done to impress Catherine in Jane Austen's Northanger Abbey, had not his horse imposed a speed-limit of 'ten miles an hour'. But English poets, as usual, contributed much more. As Alec pointed out, he played Satan in Paradise Lost to Angel's Adam and Tess's Eve; and his sudden appearance in the firelight was probably suggested by Milton's simile (just after the lines he quoted) comparing Satan to a 'wandring fire' that misleads and destroys the 'Night-wanderer'.[31]

Marvell's 'Coy Mistress' (as well as the Woodlanders mantrap) probably lay behind Tess's impulse at Talbothays to 'snatch ripe pleasure before the iron teeth of pain could have time to shut upon her'; and Blake's 'Auguries of Innocence' behind her sense that 'the thread of her life was . . . distinctly twisted of two strands, positive pleasure and positive pain'. Certainly the truth of Blake's note, 'To generalize is to be an Idiot', finally came home to Angel: his 'mistake' about Tess 'had arisen from allowing himself to be influenced by general principles to the disregard of the particular instance.' If Tess was thinking of 'a phrase in . . . Genesis' when she called her baby 'Sorrow', Hardy was thinking of Keats: 'Sweetest Sorrow!/ Like an own babe I nurse thee on my breast'. The children's 'gnat-like wail' at the christening came from Keats too: 'Then in a wailful choir the small gnats mourn'. While 'living as a stranger and an alien' in her own home, Tess had gone 'harvesting' – with 'the sad heart' of Keats's 'Ruth, when, sick for home,/ She stood in tears amid the alien corn.'[32]

There were several quotations from Swinburne, and perhaps his 'Les Noyades' prompted Tess's thought of being drowned with Angel, 'so tightly clasped together that they could not be saved'. But the Victorian poets that most affected the novel were Browning and Tennyson. Angel 'emended' the optimistic line from Pippa Passes, just after doing the opposite of what

Jules did in that poem – for Jules decided to be kind to his bride, despite her being so different from what he had thought her. Angel's shift of feeling on his wedding-night was ironically marked by a quotation from 'By the Fireside' celebrating the 'infinite moment' that created a happy marriage; and Alec, as 'extremest antinomian', acted out the repulsive implications of Johannes Agricola's 'Meditation'.[33]

The roses-blood colour-symbolism was adapted from *Maud* when Alec, 'the blood-red ray in the spectrum of her young life', loaded Tess with strawberries and roses, and a thorn 'pricked her chin'. 'Dead, long dead' cried Maud's lover from his 'shallow grave': 'Dead! dead! dead!' murmured Angel, as he laid his wife in one. 'There was hardly a touch of earth in her love' for him: 'who loves me must have a touch of earth', said Tennyson's Guinevere, complaining that her husband had 'no fault at all'. Tess identified herself with 'Queen Guinever' in a ballad, and Angel behaved like Arthur in the *Idylls*. Both men 'forgave' their wives, and then abandoned them. 'Lo! I forgive thee, as Eternal God / Forgives', the 'blameless king' assured Guinevere, before stalking out with a face 'as an angel's'. 'I do forgive you', the 'perfect' Angel Clare told Tess, 'but forgiveness is not all.' 'Well is it', said the King, 'that no child is born of thee': 'Think of years to come', argued Clare, 'and children being born to us . . .' But Hardy's mind-set showed itself by one great departure from Tennyson: giving his hero the excuse of unconsciousness. 'Let no man dream but that I love thee still', declared Arthur, implausibly. Having packed Tess off, Angel 'hardly knew that he loved her still.'[34]

Tess was named after a cousin and a saint. The cousin, Teresa Hardy (1844–1928) lived with her mother at Higher Bockhampton. After her father's death in 1880 they were very hard up, their only known source of income being the £1.10 a quarter that she earned by playing the church organ – hence, perhaps, Tess's fondness for 'chanting' and church-music. The saint was the 'Admirable Saint Teresa' of Crashaw's 'Hymn', who 'never undertook to know / What death with love should have to doe; / Nor has she e'er yet understood / Why to show love, she should shed blood'. Tess sheds Alec's blood, not her own, but she certainly 'travel[s] to a Martyrdom', and otherwise lives up to Crashaw's conception: 'though she cannot tell you why, / She can LOVE, and she can DY.'[35]

Like Crashaw, Hardy stressed his Teresa's inability to understand or explain; and he did it largely by comparing her explicitly or implicitly, to a dumb animal. She was 'caught' by Alec 'during her days of immaturity like a bird in a springe', trapped like the small animals 'huddled together' in their 'shrinking' refuge on the harvest-field, or the rats 'uncovered from their last refuge' in the wheat-rick. Under Clare's first interested gaze she felt 'the constraint of a domestic animal that perceives itself to be watched'. She listened to his harp 'like a fascinated bird', reacted to his 'elaborate sarcasms' as 'a dog or a cat' might have done, and followed him, dog-like, 'with dumb and vacant fidelity'. Between the 'Amazons and the farmer' she was 'like a bird caught in a clap-net'. She glared at Alec with 'the hopeless defiance of the sparrow's gaze before its captor twists its neck.' That was after suddenly lashing out with the gauntlet – for her eyes had originally stared at him 'like those of a wild animal', and she had later shown 'something of the habitude of the wild animal in the unreflecting instinct with which she rambled on'. Her sudden savagery at Sandbourne was thus presented as an innocent form of animal behaviour.[36]

But this animal imagery was more than a ploy to win sympathy and indulgence for Tess. It was also a protest against animal suffering. The protest would become louder with the pig-killing in *Jude*, but was clear enough here from the comments on pheasant-shooting, and from one textual amendment. In the *Graphic* Alec called Tess 'as weak as a field-fare' – from that childhood memory of the starved bird killed with a stone. In the first edition this became 'a bled calf' – predating by over a century the 1995 demonstrations against cruelty in the veal-trade.[37]

17

Life's Little Ironies

Hardy's next book followed a period of 'Intermittent Writing' – poems, short stories, a play, a serial version of one novel, and a large part of another. The poems marked a new departure contemplated on Christmas Day, 1891: 'While thinking of resuming "the viewless wings of poesy" before dawn this morning, new horizons seemed to open, and worrying pettinesses to disappear.' The short stories were meant for the new collection, *Life's Little Ironies*. The play was *The Three Wayfarers*, dramatized from 'The Three Strangers' at Barrie's suggestion, and successfully produced in London (3 June 1893). The first novel, serialized as *The Pursuit of the Well-Beloved* (October–December 1892), dissatisfied Hardy, so he revised it thoroughly before publishing it as a book in 1897. The second novel was *Jude the Obscure.*[1]

The writing was 'intermittent' for several reasons, of which the first was *Tess*. 'The unexpected success of my new novel', he told Tillotsons in January 1892, 'has brought upon me a mass of correspondence which . . . has quite checked my quiet progress on your story', i.e. the *Pursuit*. The correspondence included a request for a short story to teach working boys and girls 'how the trifling with the physical element in love leads to corruption'. Hardy got out of it neatly: 'To do the thing well . . . all details should be clear & directly given', but 'This I fear the British public would not stand just now'. *Tess* 'was also the cause of Hardy's meeting a good many people of every rank during that spring, summer, and onwards', and of new 'adventures in the world of fashion at dinner-parties, crushes, and other social functions', which further interrupted his work.[2]

In June he told a friend, 'I feel unable to write or read.' This time the reason was more serious. His father was terminally ill. For two months Hardy was 'engaged in going to & fro' to Bockhampton, and by mid-July he was visiting his father 'almost daily' – only to miss the afternoon he suddenly died (20 July 1892): 'Thus, in spite of his endeavours, Hardy had not been present.' He was worried about his mother too: 'she looks at the furniture and feels she is nothing to it. All those belonging to it, and the place, are gone, and it is left in her hands, a stranger. (She has lived there these fifty-three years!)'[3]

His own sense of losing his past was sharpened by seeing Stinsford House, where his mother had worked as a cook and his father had played the violin, nearly burnt down that September: 'a bruising of tender memories for me'. In October he went to Fawley, where his 'gentle, kindly grandmother' had once lived: 'Though I am alive with the living, I can only see the dead here . . .' That month Tennyson died, and at Westminster Abbey Hardy 'looked into the grave' of the poet who had fathered so much in his own writing. Even his publisher had recently died: 'We buried Osgood this afternoon. The grave was in wet clay – and before we left it was more than half filled in. Very sad.'[4]

'My wife and I have each lost a near relative', he had told someone in August, but it had not brought them any closer together. Revisiting their Swanage home in September they had been invited to go in, but Emma had not done so, perhaps not wishing to be reminded of the happier days they had spent there. Next spring, for the first time, they rented 'a whole house' in London; but their 'adventures' in high society probably increased their estrangement, with Hardy surrounded by admirers, mostly female, and Emma just tagging along, or being left behind. In May they set off for Dublin, to stay with Lord Houghton, the Lord Lieutenant. On the way there they 'drove round Great Orme's Head. Magnificent deep purple-grey mountains, the fine colour being on account of an approaching storm.' In the poem, 'Alike and Unlike', the storm was made to symbolize something 'Tending to sever us thenceforth alway' – for the next day at Dublin (20 May 1893) they met 'a charming, *intuitive* woman' in whom Hardy seemed almost to recognize his other half.[5]

Mrs Florence Henniker was the daughter of Tennyson's friend Monckton Milnes, the minor poet who edited Keats. Before she was seven, and before she could write, she had dictated Blake-like poems to her elder sister. Now, at thirty-seven, she had already published three novels, 'felt acutely', like Shelley, 'the amount of suffering in the world', and shared Hardy's horror of cruelty to animals. She was happily married to an army officer said by his men to be able 'to see through a brick wall'.[6]

Back in London, Hardy started writing to her, and made every opportunity to see her – taking her to Ibsen plays, teaching her about architecture, advising her on fiction, and even collaborating in a short story. She soon made it clear that she was not the 'enfranchised woman' he thought her, and disappointed him by her 'conventional views', 'retrograde superstitions' and 'belief in ritualistic ecclesiasticism'. But the hope he expressed that June 'to number you all my life among the most valued of my friends' was fully, if too literally, realized. She delicately marked the transition from 'one-sided' romance to literary friendship by the gift of a silver inkstand engraved: 'T.H. from F.H. 1893'.[7]

His side of the relationship was expressed with equal delicacy in several
poems. Of those dated 1893, 'A Thunderstorm in Town' best suggests how
he felt about her then. 'Heaven only knows', he told her in July, 'when I
shall [begin to write again] – I feel much more inclined to fly off to
foreign scenes, or plunge into wild dissipation.' In September, though, he
was 'doing penance for the frivolities of the summer by trying to clear off
a few pressing contracts'. By October nine short stories, already published
separately, had been 'fastened together to be despatched to the publisher', and on 22 February 1894 they came out again as *Life's Little Ironies*.
Next day Hardy asked John Lane, his first bibliographer, not to mention
where the stories had first appeared. Otherwise lending libraries might
spoil the book's sales by 'pacifying subscribers' with the magazine versions.
Lane should call these 'modified and bowdlerized' – i.e. the real thing
could only be got for six shillings.[8]

'An Imaginative Woman' did not join the volume until 1912; but I shall
consider it here, since Hardy thought *Life's Little Ironies* 'more nearly its
place' than *Wessex Tales* (where he put it first), and this is where it belongs
in his life – for in December 1893 he 'Found and touched up a short story
called "An Imaginative Woman" ', and some 'touches' were clearly suggested by recent events.[9]

'Solentsea' was Southsea, where the Hennikers were living. Like Florence, Ella read Shelley, wrote poetry, and deplored human cruelty to
animals, but had married a man of no 'refinement', in the killing 'trade'.
Marchmill had a military-sounding name, manufactured guns, and thought
his wife's interest in poetry 'somewhat silly'. Major Henniker had 'studied
poetry' only when 'he was getting engaged to Mrs H. – at which time he
bought a copy of Byron, & read him manfully through. He then got
married, & has never read any since.' Ella's poet-idol, Trewe, was originally Crewe, Mrs Henniker's mother's maiden-name. A 'pessimist' with a
'luxuriant black moustache', Trewe caricatured Hardy in his 'unlimited
capacity for misery', his over-reaction to unfair criticism, and his 'mournful ballad on "Severed Lives", matching Hardy's poem, 'The Division'
(1893). Ella's one-sided 'correspondence' with him seemed to satirize
Hardy's with 'dear Mrs Henniker', while hinting that she was the 'Woman
Unknown' of his dreams.[10]

The heroine of 'The Son's Veto' (which opened the volume in 1894)
had a chronic version of Emma's 'occasional lameness'. Her longing for
her native village was increased by the sight of 'country vehicles' taking
vegetables to Covent Garden. Hardy had watched them too, from his
Kensington bedroom in 1888; and personal experience lay behind the
story's theme: the social gulf created by education between a son and
his mother. 'The Fiddler of the Reels' (1893) developed from Hardy's
early passion for dancing, and 'adventures with the fiddle'. His laborious
self-education, as a step towards Cambridge and ordination, was transferred to the clerical parricides in 'A Tragedy of Two Ambitions' (1888).

They disposed of their father (a tiresome alcoholic like Jemima's father, George Hand), in a way probably suggested by the drowning in the Frome of another, unrelated, Thomas Hardy. Our Hardy had once written love-letters for village girls: 'On the Western Circuit' (1891) exploited the tragic potential of such vicarious love-making. And the theme of 'For Conscience' Sake' (1891), the mistake of trying to make late amends for treating a girl-friend badly, possibly stemmed from 'thoughts of Phena' (Tryphena), whose death in 1890 had inspired a poem with that title.[11]

There was personal material, too, in the final 'tale of tales', 'Some Crusted Characters' (1891). This retailed local stories told on the return of a native after thirty-five years. Hardy had been away for only twenty-one, but had probably felt equally out of touch with local affairs when he returned to Dorchester in 1883. Fiddling, and the replacement of the old Stinsford Choir by a 'barrel-organ' were treated humorously in 'Old Andrey's Experience as a Musician', and 'Absent-Mindedness in a Parish Choir'. 'The History of the Hardcomes' ascribed a tragicomic wife-swap to the emotional effect of dancing, of which Hardy had been 'wildly fond'. The small boy in 'The Winters and the Palmleys', literally frightened to death when 'something came out from behind a tree' in the dark, recalled Hardy's childhood terror, 'thinking that Apollyon was going to spring out of a tree'. And the problem of life-tenancy, already serious at Bockhampton that year before his father died, was flippantly but resourcefully solved in 'Netty Sargent's Copyhold'.[12]

When 'The Fiddler' came near, Car'line 'would start from her seat in the chimney-corner as if she had received a galvanic shock, and spring convulsively towards the ceiling'. The unlikely movement possibly bur-lesqued Hunt's *The Awakening Conscience* (1852), where a fallen woman, seated on her lover's knee at an upright piano, suddenly leaps up to register 'startled holy resolve'. The pictorial allusion hinted that Car'line had already 'fallen' for Wat, but had no such holy qualms.[13]

'A Tragedy of Two Ambitions' was equally ironical about the Church and the Bible. For the would-be ordinands, the 'sharp thorn of their crown' was the loss of £900. The 'cloud no bigger than a man's hand' heralded, not rain from Heaven, but their father's return from Canada. The Epistle to the Hebrews, which they studied in Greek, urged patience under 'the chastening of the Lord', as under that of an earthly father; but their impatience with theirs was enough to make them kill him. As Cornelius realized too late, through not 'despising the shame' of having an alcoholic father, they 'endured the cross' of lifelong guilt.[14]

Literary material was adapted no less sardonically. Sophocles' Antigone got herself buried alive in what she called her 'tomb and bride-chamber' for conscientiously trying to bury her dead brother. Wishing, 'For Conscience' Sake', to keep a promise 'made twenty years ago', Milborne married a woman he had made pregnant and then deserted. By thus performing the last rites on a long-dead love-affair, he spoiled both their lives, and was finally forced to bury himself under a false name in Brussels. There he was 'burdened with the heavy thought which oppressed Antigone, that by honourable observance of a rite he had obtained for himself the reward of dishonourable laxity.' Sophocles had put it more neatly in four words: '*ten dussebeian eusebous' ektesamen* (by acting piously I have got the reward of impiety)'.[15]

Milton's Satan, watching Eve in Eden, turned up 'On the Western Circuit' as the young lawyer, 'full of vague latter-day glooms', watching Anna at the fair, 'as happy as if she was in a Paradise.' The 'Fiddler' emulated Browning's 'Pied Piper'; while specializing in women, he could also 'make any child in the parish, who was at all sensitive to music, burst into tears', and disappeared with one of them – the one he had fathered on Car'line. Ella, 'The Imaginative Woman' 'possessed of her fantasy' about Trewe, was partly Tennyson's Elaine, who 'lived in fantasy' about Lancelot, 'read' [his] naked shield' and 'guessed a hidden meaning in his arms', almost as Ella studied Trewe's 'scribblings', and tried on his 'mackintosh'.[16]

In 'To Please his Wife', Shadrach was a satirical version of *Enoch Arden*. Like Annie his Joanna proved a poor shop-keeper. But his purpose in going to sea was quite unlike Enoch's. It was not to save his wife and children from 'miserable lives of hand-to-mouth', but to gratify Joanna's social ambitions; not just to 'Have all his pretty young ones educated', but to help her compete with her neighbour, by sending her sons to 'College'. Enoch's faith in God (Cast all your cares on God: that anchor holds') was finally justified: he did come safely home. Shadrach, once 'providentially' saved from shipwreck like his Biblical namesake from the 'burning fiery furnace', was not this time 'plucked out of the burning'. 'No', the 'skeleton of something human' was told after six years, 'nobody has come.'[17]

The speaker of Swinburne's 'Les Noyades' was glad to be 'Bound and drowned' with his beloved: 'I shall drown with her, laughing for love; and she / Mix with me, touching me, lips and eyes'. In 'The History of the Hardcomes' the romantic regretters of the wife-swap were washed ashore 'tightly locked in each other's arms, his lips upon hers'. The speaker of Swinburne's 'Laus Veneris' asked: 'Yea, what if sapless bark wax green and white, / Shall any good fruit grow upon my sin?' The two colours suggested a specific tree. 'A Tragedy of Two Ambitions' ended with 'something [that] flashed white on the spot' where Joshua had hidden his father's walking-stick. 'From the sedge rose a straight little silver-poplar, and it was the leaves of this sapling that caused the flicker of whiteness.' In the legend, the blossoming of the Pope's staff meant that Tannhaüser's 'sin' was forgiven after all. Papa's blossoming stick meant that his, like *il Papa*'s, errors were venial, but his parson sons would never feel forgiven.[18]

The volume's title and contents presented '*Life*' as a spiteful practical joker. The unimaginative husband of an imaginative wife grew fanciful enough to think that her child was not his. An uneducated mother lost her one chance of happiness through the snobbishness of her educated son. By dutifully marrying a woman he had deserted, a born bachelor nearly ruined her and her daughter's lives. Two clergymen, after letting their father drown to facilitate their social climbing, found they were on the wrong ladder anyway: 'the Church is a poor forlorn hope for people without influence'. Through writing love-letters for her illiterate maid, a good employer created the conditions for two unhappy marriages. Meaning 'To Please his Wife', a 'good and honest man' made her a childless widow. And a kindly man was punished for adopting his wife's illegitimate child, by having it abducted by its natural father: 'he was nearly distracted by his passionate paternal love for a child not his own.'[19]

This central theme was slightly obscured by the inclusion (until 1912) of two stories about the Napoleonic wars, and also by the generally lighter tone of the concluding sequence, 'A Few Crusty Characters' (1891). But one of these anecdotes, 'The Winters and the Palmleys', conformed all too well to the general pattern: its hero was hanged for stealing his own love-letters to a girl who had turned him down for writing and spelling so badly. The framing story, too, confirmed life's irony: John Lackland justified his name by finding himself, after thirty five years' absence, 'an absolute foreigner' in his own birthplace. Such significant proper names formed another link between the 'tale of tales' and the preceding short stories. The nominal 'Wisdom' of Sophie, the ignorant mother who let her son bully her out of remarriage, matched the 'Unity' of Tony Kytes's fiancée, who found herself sharing a waggon with two of his other girl-friends.[20]

The collection was further integrated by its satirical targets: socially divisive education, sexual attraction, marriage, and the Church. The first was shown ending in parricide and judicial murder. The second was said to lead 'so often . . . to passion, heartache, union, disunion, devotion, overpopulation, drudgery, content, resignation, despair.' Marriage was typically 'mismating', as when a 'fastidious urban' was 'chained to work for the remainder of his life' with an 'unlettered peasant, chained to his side.' And the least repellent Reverend in the volume was Mr Toogood, who had 'been in at the death of three thousand foxes.'[21]

Technically, the tales show Hardy at his narrative best. Their economic structure, dry humour, and subtle suggestion make them very readable; but one can understand the criticism (1938) that his short stories were generally marked by 'improbability and unpleasantness', and this particular volume by 'extreme nastiness'. Tastes have changed since then, and nastiness has become a literary virtue – but what of improbability? Certainly Sod's Law never operates in real life with such concentrated efficiency as it does in this book. But that was quite in accordance with Hardy's theory of art (August 1890): 'Art is a disproportioning – (i.e. throwing out of proportion) of realities, to show more clearly the features that matter in those realities, which, if merely copied or reported inventorially, might possibly be observed, but would more probably be overlooked. Hence "realism" is not Art.'[22]

The 'improbability' of the stories was also implicitly defended by the Longpuddle story-tellers themselves, in 'adhering to their own opinion that the remarkable was better worth telling than the ordinary' – or, as Hardy put it in a note of February 1893:

> A story must be exceptional enough to justify its telling. We tale-tellers are all Ancient Mariners, and none of us is warranted in stopping Wedding Guests (in other words, the hurrying public) unless he has something more unusual to relate than the ordinary experience of every average man and woman. The whole secret of fiction and the drama – in the constructional part – lies in the adjustment of things unusual to things eternal and universal.[23]

18

Jude the Obscure

'I am creeping on a little with the long story', Hardy told Mrs Henniker in January 1894, just before his book of short ones came out. He had 'jotted down' the 'scheme' of *Jude* in 1890, 'revisited' the 'scenes' in October 1892, outlined the plot in 1892 and early 1893, and been writing it out since August. It had grown 'from notes made in 1887 and onwards, some of the circumstances being suggested by the death of a woman' in 1890.[1]

So much he explained in the Preface. The scenes revisited were at his grandmother Mary Hardy's birthplace, Fawley ('Marygreen'). Notes of June 1887 and March 1888 recorded the sight of 'Souls outside Bodies', and 'Souls ... screened somewhat by their bodies'. Sue would be a 'spirit ... disembodied ... no flesh at all', and Arabella, a soul almost invisible behind the screen of her body, 'a complete and substantial female animal, no more, no less'. Her dimple-trick came from another note made that March: 'Youthful recollections of four village beauties ... Rachel H –, and her rich colour, and vanity, and frailty, and clever artificial dimple-making'. The woman who died in 1890 was probably Tryphena Sparks. If so, she suggested Sue's training and work as a teacher, her cousinship to Jude, and Arabella's marriage to a pub-keeper (Tryphena married one called Gale).[2]

In April 1888 *The Times* reported a Commons speech urging the 'great need' in 'agricultural districts' for 'effective secondary day schools'. Without them there was no adequate 'ladder from the primary schools to the University' for 'that section of the working class who might fairly hope by their talents to rise to a superior position.' After two quotations from Matthew Arnold (who had died thirteen days before), the speech concluded: 'there were large numbers among the working classes who could be helped to rise to most important positions ... and we ought to beware of stifling talent among them.'[3]

That day Hardy noted:

> 'A short story of a young man – "who could not go to Oxford" – His
> struggles and ultimate failure. Suicide . . . There is something . . . the world
> ought to be shown, and I am the one to show it to them – though I was
> not altogether hindered from going, at least to Cambridge, and could have
> gone up easily at five-and-twenty.'

The idea of using a pig-breeder's daughter to interrupt the young man's
studies may have come from the MP's joke about one private school,
which offered to educate a butcher's daughter 'on reciprocal terms', i.e.
fees payable in meat.[4]

In July 1889 Hardy thought of calling the novel that became *Tess* 'The
Body and Soul of Sue'. The name was finally kept for his next heroine, to
whom the body-soul dichotomy was equally relevant. Jude was originally
Jack, probably after John Antell, the Puddletown shoemaker whose widow,
Hardy's aunt, had died in November 1891. Antell's character and career
as a 'self-made scholar' with academic ambitions frustrated by poverty
and alcohol, suggested some aspects of Jude, whose surname, originally
Head, after Hardy's grandmother, Mary Head, became Fawley, after her
birthplace.[5]

Having revisited the 'Marygreen' scenes there in October 1892, Hardy
went off in June 1893 to see Oxford ('Christminster') as an 'outsider'. 'It
was during the Encaenia, with the Christ-church and other college balls,
garden-parties, and suchlike bright functions, but Hardy did not make
himself known, his object being to view the proceedings entirely as a
stranger.' Jude's 'trade' there was 'possibly' suggested by Hardy's recent
contact with a stonemason, when designing his father's tombstone; and
Sue's Hellenist dislike of her trade in Gothic 'church fal-lals' was tried out
in November 1893 as the theme of a poem, 'The Young Glass-Stainer'.[6]

Meanwhile some of the novel's recurrent themes – matrimonial problems, animal sufferings, and human misery – were being suggested or
reinforced by Hardy's experience. One sign of disillusionment with his
own marriage was that this, according to Emma, was the 'first novel . . .
he . . . published without first letting her read the manuscript'; and his
doubts about marriage in general were probably strengthened by a discussion with three Ladies and a Duchess (July 1893): 'All four of us talked of
the marriage-laws, a conversation which they started, not I; also of the difficulties of separation, of terminable marriages where there are children . . .'[7]

Concern for animal welfare, previously a bond with Emma, had now
become one with Mrs Henniker: 'I think more cruelties are perpetrated
on animals by butchers, drovers, & cab-people, than by vivisectors', he told
her in January 1894. 'I wish you & I could work together some day for the
prevention of such barbarities.' Meeting a big-game hunter in March 1894,
Hardy 'wondered how such a seemingly humane man could live for killing'. In May he felt something like Jude's guilt about the pig, when he had

to catch and re-cage another Lady's green linnet '– reluctantly, but feeling that a green linnet at large in London would be in a worse predicament than as a prisoner.' And in July a war-correspondent told him 'a distressing' story of a horse with no under jaw, laying its head upon his thigh in a dumb appeal for sympathy, two or three days after [a] battle'.[8]

As for human misery, it had been discussed at length with one more Lady in August 1893: '[we] sat down on the edge of a lonely sandpit and talked of suicide, pessimism, whether life was worth living, and kindred dismal subjects, till we were quite miserable.' In the novel, as here, the gloom would be tinged with humour. Phillotson, for instance, was sacked in circumstances 'farcical yet melancholy'; and when the sole wedding-guest regaled the happy couple with a tale of a husband hanged and a wife that went mad, her choice of anecdote was subtly ridiculed as 'this exhilarating tradition from the widow on the eve of the solemnization.'[9]

The novel was due to be serialized in *Harper's Magazine* but, as the story developed, Hardy realized that the editor would find it unprintable. Having failed, in April 1894, to get his contract cancelled, he was finally reduced to repeating the tiresome *Tess* routine of bowdlerizing his text for the serial, while writing it for the book. This time conditions were even worse. While preparing the two versions, he was also busy arranging and revising his novels for a Colonial Edition by Macmillans. In July he put his back out by pulling a trunk downstairs. In September he started revising and writing Prefaces for the first collected edition of his works, Osgood McIlvaine's *Wessex Novels*. And throughout the autumn and winter he had builders at Max Gate, making extensions and alterations, partly designed to let the discordant couple get away from one another. The changes included two new attic-rooms, to which Emma would eventually withdraw.[10]

Despite such difficulties, Hardy completed his novel in March 1895, three months after it had started appearing in *Harper's*. There, among countless other concessions to the family reader, the pig gave no 'shriek of agony'; Arabella's 'plan' to catch Jude involved no pretended pregnancy; Sue shared no 'sitting-room' with her undergraduate boy-friend, nor did she ever share a house with Jude, but lodged in one just opposite, so that they could 'talk across the street'; Jude had no 'midnight contiguity' with Arabella after meeting her in the pub; the 'triplet of little corpses' was reduced to a 'pair'; on Jude's last visit to Sue there was no kissing; nor did she ever do her conjugal 'duty' by Phillotson. No wonder Hardy told a friend: 'Please don't read it in the Magazine . . . It will be restored to its original shape in the volume.'[11]

The restoration had to compete with other activities: dramatizing *Tess* (since several actresses had volunteered to play the heroine); moving into a Westminster flat for the London season, where Emma did some successful entertaining; 'going to teas on the terrace of the House of Commons'; proof-reading for *The Wessex Novels*. 'I am getting quite worn out', he told Winifred Thomson (who was painting his portrait) in July, 'the drudgery of hunting after printers' errors being anything but exhilarating'. Then he got 'English cholera' and spent four days 'confined to bed and dosed with medicine & iced brandy'. When he finally got down to debowdlerizing his novel, he confessed to Mrs Henniker: 'Curiously enough I am more interested in this Sue story than in any I have written.' But when, at the end of August, he sent it off to the publishers, he was still not happy about it: 'On account of the labour of altering "Jude the Obscure" to suit the magazine, and then having to alter it back, I have lost energy for revising and improving the original as I meant to do.'[12]

Before it came out (1 December 1895) as Volume Eight of *The Wessex Novels*, Hardy had given himself the advice once given to Jowett, the iconoclastic Master of Balliol College, Oxford: 'Never retract. Never explain. Get it done and let them howl.' The howling started promptly. Even Gosse's first review called it 'a grimy story'. The *Pall Mall Gazette* retitled it 'Jude the Obscene'. The Anglican *Guardian* called it 'a shameful nightmare', and the American *World* headed its review, 'Hardy the Degenerate'. In *Blackwood's* Mrs Oliphant described it as a 'nauseous tragedy' 'intended as an assault upon the stronghold of marriage', and almost ran out of words like 'foul', 'shameful', 'disgusting', 'sickening', 'unsavoury', 'filth', 'garbage', and 'depravity'. An Australian reader sent Hardy 'a packet of ashes, which the virtuous writer stated to be those of his wicked novel'. The Bishop of Wakefield burnt his copy too, and got the book quietly withdrawn from W.H. Smith's lending library.[13]

Other reviews, like Gosse's second one, were more balanced, and the bad ones proved good publicity, for twenty thousand copies were sold in three months. Swinburne had been quick to congratulate Hardy on 'The tragedy . . . equally beautiful and terrible in its pathos', calling him what Aristotle called Euripides, 'the most tragic of poets', and assuming that 'The man who can do such work can hardly care about criticism or praise'. But Hardy did care. When a literary agent asked for a new serial, Hardy replied. 'I am absolutely vague about a serial story. I will let you know if ever I have one to offer.' He never did have one. The 'howls' at *Jude* had put him off novel-writing for good.[14]

Jude was not, as 'some paragraphists knowingly informed the public', 'an honest autobiography', but Hardy was stretching the truth when he said that 'no book he had ever written contained less of his own life.' Jude's childhood reflections under 'his straw hat' closely resembled Hardy's, and so did Jude's fears of Apollyon when walking in the dark. Hardy had always felt that 'magic thread of fellow-feeling' with animals that made Jude useless as a rook-scarer or pigsticker, unable to kill a worm or bear the cries of a trapped rabbit, and more outraged to see a cab-horse kicked in the belly 'at college gates in the most religious and educational city in the world', than by Christminster's sins against himself. In that spirit Hardy offered the pig-killing scene 'gratuitously' to *The Animals' Friend*, for propaganda purposes.[15]

Hardy's programme of self-education had been very like Jude's. He never read Roman authors while delivering bread, though he once met a 'youth' who was doing so; but his 'soliloquizing in Latin' while walking matched Jude's 'imaginary conversations therein'. Both seem to have read the same 'passages' of the *Iliad*, both bought themselves 'Griesbach's text' of the Greek Testament, and both were slightly thrown at having to learn 'a new dialect', *Koine*. Had Hardy, too, once hoped to master Latin and Greek by some simple conversion-formula, some 'law of transmutation'?[16]

When Phillotson was ill, Sue showed him a sunset in a mirror: Margaret Macmillan had done that for Hardy when he was ill in 1881. The 'brown depression' where Jude scared rooks, 'trodden now by he hardly knew whom, though once by many of his own dead family', was presumably the 'ploughed vale' near Fawley that Hardy had called 'The Valley of Brown Melancholy ... I can only see the dead here.' The Ten Commandments on the wall of Fawley church probably suggested Jude and Sue's 'relettering of the Ten Commandments in a little church' at Aldbrickham. The strange picture of the 'boy' in the 'third-class carriage', also used for a poem, 'Midnight on the Great Western', was 'undoubtedly a figure Hardy had seen and recorded'. His sisters, Mary and Kate, had both done time in 'the species of nunnery known as the Training-School at Melchester' (Salisbury), and its harsh treatment of Sue was evidently modelled on Kate's accounts of 'how badly we were used'. 'St Silas' church' (St Barnabas'), where Jude found Sue 'prostrate on the paving', had been designed by Hardy's ex-employer and 'very old friend', Blomfield.[17]

The recurring theme of a married or quasi-married couple living separately in the same house (first Sue and Richard, then Sue and Jude, then Arabella and Jude) possibly came from the current situation at Max Gate. And 'Susanna Florence' owed more to Mrs Henniker than a Christian name. She used this pointedly when writing as Phillotson's fiancée or wife, to freeze Jude off. Here Hardy was doubtless thinking of Florence Henniker. 'I had some regret,' he had told her, while reading *Epipsychidion*, 'at thinking that one who is pre-eminently the child of the Shelleyan tradition – whom one would have expected to be an ardent disciple of his school and views – should have allowed herself to be enfeebled to a belief in ritualistic ecclesiasticism.' The reference to *Epipsychidion* seems to imply that he had expected her to accept its 'doctrine' of free love. She had certainly disappointed him as a freethinker. Hence perhaps Sue's final relapse into what Jude called 'mysticism or Sacerdotalism, or whatever it may be called ... which has caused this deterioration in you.'[18]

Hardy's anti-church novel drew heavily on the Bible, starting with the Apocrypha. Having collected enough knowledge and money to go to Christminster, Jude met Arabella, and promptly justified these words of Esdras: 'if men have gathered together gold and silver', or any other goodly thing, do they not love a woman which is comely in favour and beauty? And letting all those things go, do they not gape, and even with open mouth fix their eyes fast on her?' After the mini-massacre of her children, Sue did what Esther did at the threat of genocide: 'humbled her body greatly' and 'prayed unto the Lord God' saying, 'we have sinned before thee'. But where Esther's piety averted a tragedy, Sue's created one. She also played the Apocryphal Susanna, with Jude as her 'honour-able' husband Joakim, and Phillotson and Gillingham as the two elders, who 'perverted their own mind' and conspired to make her 'lie with' them. With Sue the plot succeeded, if only for Phillotson, who perverted his originally 'humane instinct' into accepting Sue's 'fanatic prostitution'.[19]

The Old Testament was often used prophetically. Christminster reminded the carter of the Tower of Babel because of its 'foreign tongues'. Jude would find it a Babel in another sense, as a great project abandoned: 'and they left off to build the city'. The 'picture of Samson and Delilah' in the first pub Jude entered with Arabella, predicted how she would disable him. While trapping him into a second marriage, she would find 'her shorn Samson . . . asleep'. The burdock leaves that covered Sue's 'so very naked' statuettes parodied Adam and Eve's fig-leaves, thus foreshadowing Jude and Sue's expulsion from their Spring Street Eden. Jude's first Christminster lodgings were in Oxford's Jericho: like the walls of the Bib-lical city his castle in the air would 'fall down flat'. Hardy called the district Beersheba, after the 'wilderness' where Hagar saved her son Ishmael from dying of thirst: Jude would die alone, gasping, 'Water – some water – Sue – Arabella!' Sue claimed to have an 'Ishmaelite' inside her ('he will be a wild man; his hand will be against every man, and every man's hand against him'). Her wildness only came out long enough to make her and Jude social outcasts, before it was tamed by 'true religion'.[20]

Apart from Samson, Jude's chief Old Testament prototypes were Joseph and Job. 'You are Joseph the dreamer of dreams, dear Jude', said Sue. '. . . You'll suffer yet!' Joseph's sufferings matched Jude's at one point, when his brothers left him to die in a pit with 'no water in it.' Yet he treated them kindly when they were dying of famine, just as Jude did Arabella when she appeared on his doorstep 'lonely, destitute, and houseless'. But Joseph's dreams were realized: Jude's were not. Besides following Job's general pattern of undeserved suffering, Jude consciously identified with him. His chalked response to cold comfort from the Mas-ter of Biblioll College was Job's reply to his comforters. Jude pictured his son wishing, in Job's words, that he had not been born; and he himself died whispering those words, and much of the speech that followed them. But even Job was luckier than Jude. His curses ended in his being 'blessed' – among other things with a daughter called, like Hardy's mother, Jemima.[21]

Jude's New Testament namesake denounced bogus Christians: 'their mouth speaketh great swelling words, having men's persons in admiration because of advantage', i.e. being, unlike God, 'respecters of persons' for their own convenience, or self-interested snobs. Such were the Christminster authorities – especially the Master of Biblioll, whose great swelling name, Tetuphenay, meant in Greek nothing more Christian than 'to have beaten', the traditional occupation of bad schoolmasters. 'These are they', says St Jude, 'who separate themselves, sensual, not having the Spirit.' 'Sue, Sue', pleaded Jude, 'we are acting by the letter; and "the letter killeth"'. The text he quoted (also used as the novel's epigraph, continues: 'but the spirit giveth life.' Like Arnold's *Literature and Dogma*, the novel protested against taking the Bible too literally; and for Jude, as he implied when parting from Sue in the cemetery, the spirit of Christianity was contained in Paul's definition of *agape*, charity or loving-kindness.[22]

As that spirit's representative, Jude was once associated with Paul, repeatedly with Jesus. I doubt if the auctioned pigeons were meant to recall 'the Spirit like a dove descending' at Jesus's baptism, but the words then heard from heaven were certainly adapted for Jude's self-dedication: 'Christminster shall be my Alma Mater; and I'll be her beloved son, in whom she shall be well pleased.' In the serial, His first Christminster lodgings were in 'Capernaum', where Jesus started teaching. After reciting the creed in a pub, Jude sat down by the Marygreen well, remembering 'Jacob's well', and 'thinking ... what a poor Christ he made.' Matrimonially, he was more like the 'woman of Samaria'. He then planned to 'begin his ministry', like Jesus, 'at the age of thirty'. Threatened by 'the chief priests and the Pharisees', Jesus 'walked no more openly among the Jews, but went thence unto a country near to the wilderness'. Sacked by a vicar and churchwarden, Jude and Sue 'walked no more in ... Aldbrickham', but started touring the country. 'Crucify me, if you will!' Jude told Sue long-sufferingly; and having 'come up to Jerusalem to see the festival', 'perhaps to die there' ('like coming from Caiaphas to Pilate!', said Sue) he continued to parallel the Crucifixion story, right up to the penultimate words, 'I thirst'.[23]

Following Jude's Epistle, Revelation ends the New Testament with a vision of 'the holy city, new Jerusalem, coming down from God out of heaven, prepared as a bride adorned for her husband.' The city is 'adorned' with twelve jewels, including topaz, sapphire, and amethyst. Young Jude thought of Christminster as 'The heavenly Jerusalem', and first glimpsed it between 'bars of slaty cloud' as 'points of light like topaz'; but it was soon replaced as his 'bride' by Arabella. With her the jewels reappeared, when he saw her behind a bar, backed by 'bottles of topaz, sapphire, ruby, and amethyst' – the last meaning in Greek 'not drunk', though it was where he had once got drunk enough to recite the Creed in Latin.[24]

The novel's literary origins went back as usual to Homer and Greek tragedy. Arabella was a Circe, who diverted the hero from his course. Circe turned her lovers into pigs: Arabella used a pig's penis to make Jude her lover. Sue felt that 'a tragic doom overhung' the Fawleys, 'as it did the house of Atreus', and Jude's response to the hangings was to quote from the *Agamemnon*: 'Things are as they are, and will be brought to their destined issue.' There Aeschylus, like Sue presently, was interpreting human slaughter as divine vengeance for adultery.[25]

'My eyes are so swollen', Sue had said, 'that I can scarcely see; and yet little more than a year ago I called myself happy.' 'Call no man happy', warned the chorus after the blinding of Oedipus, 'until he reaches the end of his life without pain'. Little Jude had simply implemented the Sophoclean dictum, implicit throughout the novel: 'It is best not to be born, but the second best is to go back where you came from as quickly as possible.' In hanging himself he also imitated Sophocles' Jocasta; and his 'preternatural oldness' was possibly suggested by the literal meaning of the Greek word *presbuteron*, (older), which Hardy had quoted from the *Oedipus* in 1889: ' "*ei de ti presbuteron* etc. . . . and if there be a woe surpassing woes it hath become the portion of Oedipus" . . . Cf. Tennyson: "a deeper deep" '. He certainly remembered those words when he made Jude think 'of that previous abyss into which he had fallen . . . the deepest deep he had supposed then, but it was not so deep as this.'[26]

In comparing Hardy to Euripides, Swinburne doubtless recalled two Euripidean models for the child-killing: the first where Herakles recovers from a fit of madness, to see that he has just killed his *tekna trigona* (thrice-born children) – a phrase translated by Browning as 'triple woe', hence 'the triplet of little corpses'. The second was where Jason comes home to find his children murdered by Medea, and pleads with her over their corpses, almost as Sue pleaded with Jude over their children's grave. Their subsequent parting there was pictured in terms of Virgil's Hell: 'they proceeded through the fog like Acherontic shades', or like Aeneas and the Sibyl, when '*ibant obscuri sola sub nocte per umbram* (they walked, obscure, through the shadows in the solitary night . . .)' – a passage also recalled by the novel's title. Horace's '*Carmen Saeculare*, a hymn meant to be sung by 'virgins and chaste youths', added irony to Jude's 'polytheistic' prayer by the roadside, shortly before having sex with someone who was clearly 'no vestal'. And Ovid's account of Pyramus and Thisbe supplied, not only an epigraph, but a hint for Jude and Sue's cohabitation with an invisible wall between them.[27]

The novel's debt to later literature can only be summarized briefly. Spenser provided an apt nickname for a prostitute in a pub, 'Bower o' Bliss'; and perhaps, by his tale of Grill, suggested Jude's fear of 'turning back to his wallowing in the mire'. Jude's lifelong pilgrimage to Christminster grimly parodied the *Pilgrim's Progress* to the Celestial City, complete with Apollyon, and a 'brass band from the river' while Jude was dying, to match the 'trumpets' that 'sounded for him on the other side.' *Rasselas* gave the novel its structural pattern: a cumulative series of disillusionments. Fielding's type of slapstick marked Jude's parting 'scuffle' with Arabella, and the 'scuffle' between Phillotson's supporters and detractors. Gibbon not only helped Swinburne to make Sue briefly a sceptic, but also made her imitate Julian's nocturnal worship of pagan deities, wish that sexual reproduction could be replaced by 'some harmless mode of vegetation', and generally emulate the African virgins who 'permitted priests and deacons to share their bed, and gloried amid the flames in their unsullied purity.'[28]

Schopenhauer was partly responsible for little Jude's suicide, diagnosed by the doctor as a symptom of 'the coming universal wish not to live.' Shelley contributed arguments against marriage; Sue's imprisonment (like Emilia Viviani's) in 'a species of nunnery'; the 'trembling' of her spirit 'through her limbs'; and Jude's encounter, like the Magus Zoroaster's, with his 'own image': 'Sitting in his only arm-chair he saw a slim and fragile being masquerading as himself on a Sunday'.[29]

Tennyson's *In Memoriam* gave a model for Jude's ambition: the 'gifted man', born on a 'simple village green' who 'grapples with his evil star' (as Jude tried to 'battle' with his), to get to the top. Christminster, glimpsed by young Jude between clouds, was virtually Camelot, glimpsed by Gareth through mist. *Jude*, like the *Idylls*, represented 'the dream of man coming into practical life and ruined by one sin' (or at least one failing, Jude's 'weakness for womankind'). It also represented 'the world-wide war of Sense and Soul, typified in individuals', or as the Preface put it, 'a deadly war waged between flesh and spirit'. Even the 'cry of a rabbit caught in a gin' and awaiting 'the trapper', which partly symbolized Sue's feeling about her husband, had already been used by Tennyson to express Enid's fear of her lecherous captor.[30]

The 'optimistic' Browning was often conscripted as a pessimist, for instance when Sue took his sarcasm literally: 'The world and its ways have a certain worth'. Ruskin's revaluation of manual work gave Jude the 'true illumination, instantly lost', that a stone yard was as worthy a 'centre of effort' as a college. In Clough's *Adam and Eve*, (republished 1888), Eve jumped out of Adam's arms in the middle of the night, 'screaming "Guilt!"' Having failed to argue her out of her 'religious crotchet', Adam then found her 'kneeling on the turf', almost as Jude found Sue in St Silas'. Matthew Arnold not only inspired Jude's Christminster dream by his famous apostrophe to Oxford as the 'Adorable dreamer', but also anticipated, in his 'Gipsy Child by the Sea-Shore', the expression of the 'aged'-looking boy when 'his face took a back view over some great Atlantic of time'. And the boy's guilt about 'troubling' parents made tragedy of Samuel Butler's comic satire in *Erewhon*. There every child had to confess that 'he did with malice aforethought' set himself to plague and pester two unfortunate people who had never wronged him . . . for they say of people with large families that they have suffered terrible injuries from the unborn'.[31]

The plot, wrote Hardy, was 'almost geometrically constructed'. Like 'The History of the Hardcomes', it was a square dance performed by two couples. There the men swapped partners, before rejoining their original ones. Here Jude danced first with Arabella, then with Sue, and then again with Arabella. Phillotson danced first with Sue, then, less symmetrically, by himself (apart from two talks with Arabella) and then with Sue again. But symmetry was partly restored by other correspondences. Jude shared with Phillotson his Christminster dream and its failure. Arabella's religious phase, triggered by Cartlett's death, parodied Sue's when the children were killed. And Sue's lapse from bold scepticism into slavish superstition was matched by Phillotson's, from humane independence into self-seeking orthodoxy.[32]

In geometry parallel lines never meet. The plot structure implied the same rule in sexual relations. Initially, Jude and Arabella 'walked in parallel lines' on opposite sides of a stream, converging at a 'small plank bridge'; but despite their two marriages, there was no meeting of minds. In 'the broad street' Jude and Sue first 'converged towards the cross-mark'; but when she shied off that emblem of religious martyrdom, they 'walked on in parallel lines', before 'closing in'. But they never really met either: they just intersected. Jude crossed over to adopt her humanism, Sue, to adopt and fatally exaggerate his religious creed.[33]

Through this quadrangular tale of 'two bad marriages' ran the line of Jude's life, a series of oblique rises followed by vertical falls of progressively greater depth. Its pattern was pictured as a failed quest for light. Since the motto of Oxford University is '*Dominus Illuminatio Mea*', Jude first conceived Christminster as 'a city of light', and first saw it as 'points of light'. Vilbert seemed a possible source of 'intellectual light' – until he failed to bring the grammars. Arabella brought light only when 'he was illuminated with the sense that all was over between them.' The 'true illumination' that stonework might be as good as scholarship came only to go again. And it was in the 'lantern' of the (Sheldonian) 'theatre' that he finally 'awoke from his dream' of the University. Sue then took over the role of illuminator. Walking with her, he felt 'as if he carried a bright light': but she, he would recall, 'was once a woman whose intellect was to mine as a star to a benzoline lamp . . . Then her intellect broke, and she veered round to darkness.'[34]

The novel's tragic effect was darkened, not lightened, by laughter. Arabella was first heard among 'sounds of voices and laughter'. She and Anny usually 'laughed before talking; the world seemed funny to them without saying it.' She thought it 'Funny, rather!' to make Jude marry her again, and 'was suddenly seized by a fit of loud laughter'. When Jude was dying, she shook 'with suppressed laughter' at seeing the quack drink his own love-philtre; and when Jude was dead, 'she could have laughed heartily at the horse-play' if the memory of his face had not 'sobered her a little'. The authorial comment was written on the face of 'Arabella's boy': 'All laughing comes from misapprehension. Rightly looked at there is no laughable thing under the sun.'[35]

For the novel was primarily an indictment, not of marriage or the educational system, but of natural law. The first charge, variously enforced by the bird-scaring, the pig-killing, the rabbit-snaring, and the pigeon-selling episodes, concerned the treatment of animals. 'Nature's logic', Jude found, was that 'mercy towards one set of creatures was cruelty towards another'. Arabella could only see one side of the problem: 'Poor folks must live.' But Sue, like Jude, saw both, even when poor enough to sell the pigeons: 'O why should Nature's law be mutual butchery?' She found the same law in sexual relationships. Asked by Phillotson who was to blame for her physical horror of him, she replied, 'The universe, I suppose – things in general, because they are so horrid and cruel!' Phillotson himself suffered from the law's social results. Trying to be kind to Sue, as she to the pigeons, and Jude to the birds and pig, he too was victimized by society.

'Yes', he said, 'Cruelty is the law pervading all nature and society, and we can't get out of it if we would!'[36]

But the novel implied that one sometimes could, and should. Hardy feared that *Jude* was 'too much a book of moral teaching – the inculcation of *Mercy*, to youths and girls who have made a bad marriage, & to animals who have to be butchered.' Perhaps it was rather too didactic; but his points about education and marriage needed making then, as his point about animals does now. Nor did the moral teaching stop him producing in Sue his most interesting and arguably his most immoral heroine.[37]

19

The Well-Beloved

Hardy's last novel had been been 'sketched' when he was 'comparatively a young man, and interested in the Platonic Idea'. In his mid-thirties he had begun to read Volume One of Jowett's *Dialogues of Plato*. There the *Phaedrus* described how the true artist or lover reacted with shuddering awe to the sight of beautiful faces or bodies: remembering the 'Idea' of beauty once seen in Heaven, his soul grew wings again. Hardy's sculptor-hero was equally susceptible to ideal beauty; and Walter Paget's headpiece to the 1892 serial, *The Pursuit of the Well-Beloved*, showed the pursuer duly sprouting wings. A similar pursuit figured in the concluding dialogue, the *Symposium*, where the chopped-off half of the original human being was 'always looking for his other half'.[1]

The novel's plot was suggested by 'the remark of a sculptor that he had often pursued a beautiful ear, nose, chin, &c, about London in omnibuses & on foot'. That must have been Hardy's friend Thomas Woolner, with whom, in December 1879, he had discussed faces in 'the art of the future'. Then Woolner sent Hardy his poem, *Pygmalion* (1881). Here 'His Hebe come to life!' was no miracle. It simply meant that Pygmalion found in 'the maid Ianthe' exactly the right model to 'quicken Hebe's eyes' (i.e. realize his conception for a statue of Hebe) – and for him to fall in love with. Hardy's sculptor would keep finding girls like that to match his Idea of a Beloved. Woolner claimed to have interpreted the myth 'as an artist understands it', Hardy, to have illustrated 'the genuine artistic temperament'. Three of Woolner's sculptures came close to the novel: a marble statuette of 'Love', a bas-relief of Shelley's *Alastor* (who 'pursues' until he dies a woman seen in a dream), and a life-size bronze statue finished just before his death in 1892: 'The Housemaid' – caught wringing out a dirty cloth into a pail. This exactly pre-figured the charm of Avice II, first as a laundress, and then as Jocelyn's housemaid.[2]

After settling in Dorchester (1883) Hardy naturally spent more time with his family at Bockhampton, which perhaps caused friction with his wife. That would explain his note of March 1884: 'Write a novel entitled "Time against Two", in which the antagonism of the parents of a Romeo and Juliet *does* succeed in separating a couple and stamping out their love, – alas, a more probable development than the other!' As Jocelyn would point out, he and Marcia were 'split' like that. In 1889 Hardy thought of writing a 'novel or poem' about 'a face which goes through three generations or more'. He wrote both: the *Well-Beloved* and 'Heredity'. The same year he thought of calling his current novel 'Too late, Beloved!'. That novel became *Tess*, but the Shelleyan words possibly suggested another meaning, when the 'Young Man of Sixty' found his Well-Beloved in a girl of twenty.[3]

By 1890, when Hardy signed the contract for the serial, he had evidently decided to locate it in Portland. Nearby Weymouth was associated with former girl-friends like Tryphena, whose death in March had inspired these words by 'sympathetic telepathy': 'Not a line of her writing have I, / Not a thread of her hair . . .'. The serial began with Jocelyn burning letters from ex-girl-friends, and hearing 'a little fizzle' from '*her* hair'. At Easter he took a friend to Portland: 'Lunched at the Mermaid' – close to what is now labelled 'Avice's Cottage'. In August he visited Weymouth with Emma and one of his illustrators; and in September, when already 'writing, or planning the tale', he revisited Portland with Gosse. While still busy on the novel, he told Harpers (February 1892) that he meant it 'entirely' for 'serial publication', so might not let it appear as a book until he had rewritten it; and when serialization ended that December, he left the work on hold for nearly four years.[4]

When in 1896 he rewrote the beginning and end of the serial *Pursuit of the Well-Beloved*, and otherwise transformed it into the book-version *Well-Beloved*, he was feeling deeply depressed. That seems clear from the poems he was then writing – 'The Dead Man Walking', 'Wessex Heights' and 'In Tenebris II' and 'III'. His depression was partly caused by reactions to *Jude*. He found himself 'excommunicated by the press', treated 'peculiarly' by some of his 'country friends', told by his old friend Gosse over 'the lunch-table at the Savile that Jude was the most indecent novel ever written', charged by Mrs Henniker with advocating 'free love', and openly condemned by Emma for publishing such a novel without consulting her. 'Theatre-managers' followed suit. Plans for a London production of his '*Tess* play' suddenly fell through – though it would prove a 'success' when produced in New York the following year.[5]

In the spring of 1896 both Hardys were ill, Emma with eczema or possibly shingles, and 'severe bronchitis', Hardy with a 'chill, or whatever it was' and rheumatism. They tried, first Emma alone then both together, to recuperate at Brighton, but 'bicycling' may have done more for them. Emma was already quite good at it, so Hardy took up the 'arduous study' too, 'to keep her company'; but initially they repeated the 1870 procedure, with her in the saddle, and him on foot. Thus in August they went 'idling about Shakespeare's country', and in September made another tour of 'the Netherlands,' 'my wife on her bicycle,' as Hardy remembered, '& I walking frantically to overtake her'.[6]

'I rode my pretty mare Fanny and he walked by my side'. Were they consciously trying to recapture their feelings at St Juliot? Certainly at Brussels they 'put up for association's sake at the same hotel they had patronized twenty years before, but found it had altered for the worse since those bright days.' So, sadly, had their relationship. Emma's compensation was not having to trudge this time all over the 'Field of Waterloo': Hardy's, not having to share that field of research with any 'living creatures' but 'Shepherds with their flocks and dogs, men ploughing, two cats . . .' His year ended with an equally 'negative Christmas' – 'of the dull kind which contents so-called "pessimists" like me – in its freedom from positive sorrows.'[7]

That Christmas had been the deadline for getting his new 'Well Beloved to the printers', and he had been 'hard-pressed' to meet it, while also writing short stories 'in fulfilment of standing engagements'. When the book came out, as Volume 17 of the Wessex Novels, there was one exception to the generally friendly tone of the reviews. The *World*, with a stock response to the Latin meaning of 'Caro' (flesh), and a feeble pun on 'Wes*sex*, called Hardy a a sex-maniac. It was exasperating, for he had obviously taken great care to make Jocelyn's passion seem almost purely Platonic. 'After such misrepresentation', he told Mary Jeune, 'I feel inclined to say I will never write another line.'[8]

Paget's illustrations for the *Pursuit* made Jocelyn look rather like 'MR. THOMAS HARDY THE NOVELIST' in the full-page portrait preceding the first instalment. The resemblance was more than visual. Like Jocelyn, Hardy had had 'a long, long row' of beloveds, including a girl on horseback who 'smiled at' him. The latest was a married woman of thirty-three called Agnes Grove. Was she 'Mrs A.G –', the 'more seductive' of two 'beauties' between whom he sat at a lunch-party in 1891? Certainly in 1895 he danced with her in the moonlight and, according to the late poem, 'Concerning Agnes', sat 'apart in the shade' with her, holding her hand. She then succeeded Mrs Henniker as literary protegée. Hardy was fifty-two when he called the serial-Jocelyn 'A Young Man of Fifty-Nine', fifty-six when the book-Jocelyn became 'A Young man of Sixty'; and Jocelyn's prolonged youth merely exaggerated Hardy's view of himself: 'He was . . . a young man till he was nearly fifty.'[9]

Jocelyn touched his author's life at several other points. When ill in Rome, 'he had wished each night that he might never wake again': Hardy 'for many weeks and months' had 'gone to bed wishing never to see daylight again.' Remembering his own father's death in 1892, Hardy added 'self-reproach' to his 1896 hero's recollection that he had not visited his father for nearly four years. The sunlight that 'flashed' in 1886 from the coffin of Hardy's poet-friend William Barnes became the 'flashing lights from the sea', seen from a similar distance 'around and beneath' Avice I's coffin, just after a remark that Lycidas was 'blest with a poet as a friend'. Meeting Ellen Terry in 1891, Hardy had compared her to 'a machine in which, if you press a spring, all the works fly open'. He recycled the witticism, with some loss of brevity, to describe 'a leading actress' met by Jocelyn at a dinner-party.[10]

Marcia first appeared 'squarer' than Avis I, with a 'commanding, imperious face'; and Jocelyn had to walk fast to overtake her (though not on a horse or bicycle). She turned out bossy, bad-tempered, and highly critical of her husband – for in the serial they actually got married, and had a 'Continental' honeymoon). The serial ended with Jocelyn laughing hysterically to see how Marcia had aged. Hardy cannot conceivably have meant to caricature his wife, but his unconscious seems almost to have done so. In a photograph of 1895–6 Emma looks eminently square, with that 'rectilinear sternness of countenance' that the book-Marcia showed when angry, even a hint of Queen Victoria to match the serial-Marcia's label: 'queenly – far too queenly'.[11]

Consciously, Hardy was satirizing not Emma, but marriage, drawing material from his own experience of it. Thus Marcia's father, like Emma's, thought his daughter had married beneath her. And Marcia's life, like Emma's, 'began to be rather dull' when her husband's 'profession occupied him to the exclusion of domestic affairs'. In the book, the serial's crude finale was replaced by a subtler parody of Hardy's current prognosis for his own marriage: the aged couple achieved a loveless but friendly cohabitation, at the cost of the artist's creativity.[12]

Among the Beloved's various reincarnations were several from past literature. Avice II, with her 'shapely pink arms', 'spreading white linen upon the pebbly strand', was Homer's 'white-armed Nausikaa', about to meet Odysseus – though this time it was not the young girl but the older man who fell in love. Jocelyn sometimes 'dreamt' that his Well-Beloved was really the 'wile-weaving daughter of high Zeus' (*pai Dios doloploke*) in Sappho's ode to Aphrodite. Marcia was a reincarnation of Virgil's Juno, especially in her anger, 'her *quos egos* and high-handed rulings'. Hardy must have forgotten that '*quos ego*' (i.e. 'whom I shall punish severely') was actually spoken by Neptune, when cross about the unauthorized storm that Juno had created. But the threat was quite in character for Juno too. She then devised the cave-trick to get Dido seduced by Aeneas; so Jocelyn's seduction by Marcia began when they sheltered from the rain in the nearest cave-substitute, an upturned 'lerret'. When Avice I with 'impulsive innocence' ran up to Jocelyn and kissed him, she reincarnated Chloe as she 'jumped up and kissed' Daphnis, whose passionate response showed up the coldness of Jocelyn's.[13]

His Well-Beloved had also been Donne's in 'Aire and Angels': 'Twice or thrice had I loved thee, / Before I knew thy face or name . . . Still when, to where thou wert, I came, / Some lovely glorious nothing did I see.' She had then become 'She' in Crashaw's 'Lines to his Supposed Mistresse', which had been 'familiar to' Hardy since at least 1883, though not used for an epigraph to Part First until 1896. As Jocelyn's maid, Avice II had been Richardson's *Pamela* – but Jocelyn was so 'scrupulously fearful' of behaving like Mr B. that he never entered the kitchen without 'some culinary excuse'. As a beauty transformed into a 'wrinkled crone', Marcia had been Voltaire's Cunégonde. Now, to 'cultivate his garden', her Candide started replacing 'moss-grown' cottages by 'new ones . . . full of ventilators.'[14]

In the next century, the 'idol' of Jocelyn's 'fancy' had two Shelleyan avatars, the 'veilèd maid' pursued by the 'Poet' in *Alastor*, and the visionary 'Being . . . oft / Met' by the writer of *Epipsychidion*: 'In many mortal forms I rashly sought / The shadow of that idol of my thought'. But the *Alastor* 'Poet' influenced Jocelyn most. The 'skiff' into which the serial hero 'jumped . . . without an oar' was obviously the 'shallop' commandeered by the Poet 'To meet lone Death on the drear Ocean's waste'. Both suicide attempts failed. On the point of being dashed against some cliffs, the Poet was swept into a quiet underground stream. Jocelyn was duly dashed against the light-ship, only to be rescued by its crew.[15]

Confronted by signs of aging in the 'looking-glass', he relived Shelley's Poet's experience at the 'liquid mirror' of the well, where 'His eyes beheld / Their own wan light through the reflected lines / Of his thin hair'. Admittedly, this mirror-motif had personal as well as Shelleyan associations. 'I look in the glass', noted Hardy in October 1892. 'Am conscious of the humiliating sorriness of my earthly tabernacle . . .' Jocelyn's encounter with his reflection, though not published till December, had probably been written by the previous March, when the whole serial had been due at the printer's.[16]

'I saw my face in that mirror', wrote Newman in his *Apologia*, 'and I was Monophysite.' The mirror in question was the history of a fifth-century heresy, where he found nineteenth-century 'Christendom . . . reflected.' Was that curious passage behind Jocelyn's anachronistic allusion to Newman's title, when confessing his promiscuity to Somers? The irreverent comparison was apt enough anyway: Newman's *Apologia pro Vita Sua* described a series of flirtations with different 'Religious Opinions', ending with the desertion of his own 'dear Church' and of 'so much I love', to embrace the Church of Rome.[17]

The first Victorian pursuit of a well-beloved had been in *The Angel in the House* (1854): 'I never went to Ball, or Fete, / Or Show, but in pursuit express / Of my predestinated mate'. Patmore's hero then listed 'Supposititious Presentments' to match Jocelyn's 'Isabella, Florence, Winifred, Lucy' etc.: 'At Berlin three, one at St Cloud, / at Chatteris, near Cambridge, one, / At Ely four . . .' A more cryptic version of the theme was the 'quest' of Browning's 'Nympholeptos' (1876), which possibly made Gosse call the novel: 'The Tragedy of a Nympholept'. In *She* (1887) by Hardy's friend Rider Haggard, Lover and Beloved had changed places: 'The loveliest . . . woman the world has ever seen' waited 'some six and sixty generations' for the reincarnation of her beloved Kallikrates. When he finally turned up as Leo Vincy, she started to look her age: two minutes later 'she lay still before us . . . no larger than a monkey, and hideous – ah, too hideous for words.' Marcia's loss of looks was nothing to it.[18]

According to Hardy's Preface, *The Well-Beloved* differed from 'all or most' of his other novels 'in that the interest aimed at [was] of an ideal or subjective nature, and frankly imaginative', so he had paid less attention to 'verisimilitude in the sequence of events'. He later called it a 'fantastic tale of a subjective idea', and compared its 'theory' to that of the 'poem bearing the same name, written about this time'. The theory, which psychologists have now made too familiar to need such spelling out, was that what one loves in another person is a projection of oneself.[19]

Hardy called the work 'half-allegorical', and so were its names. The *World* was quite right to translate the surname Caro as 'flesh', though wrong to take it in a sexual sense. Hardy must have been joking when he claimed to have chosen it because it resembled 'the Italian for "dear"'; since 'incarnation', a key-word in the novel, is simply *in* + *caro, carnis*, 'embodiment in flesh'. The forename 'Avis or Avice' was 'borrowed' from a seventeenth-century daughter of the Talbots of Talbothays, but the first spelling shows why. Each Avice was a 'migratory' bird (*avis* in Latin) that 'flitted', in the sense both of flying and of 'moving house', from 'human shell to human shell', leaving behind each time 'the nest of some beautiful bird from which its inhabitant has departed and left it to fill with snow'. She was also, like Tess, as vulnerable as a bird. In the serial, Avice III cried out in anguish to her young lover, 'like a wounded bird'; and the image served further to unite her with her native 'island', shaped 'like the head of a bird'.[20]

For that purpose Jocelyn's surname, originally Pearston, became Pierston. This doubly suggested (by 'Piers' as a form of 'Peter', or *Petros*, as well as the final 'ston') his ties, through his family's trade and his own form of art, with the 'single block of limestone four miles long'. The womanizer in *The Woodlanders* had possibly been called Fitz*piers* for his stony indifference to women's feelings. Here the stone-flesh imagery recurrent in Tennyson's *Maud* ('O heart of stone, are you flesh, and caught / With that you swore to withstand?') had probably suggested a different meaning. Jocelyn was fairly sensitive to women's feelings, but would end in stony indifference to both beauty and art. And why 'Jocelyn'? Obsessed with history, his own, his family's, and his island's, he seemed to his last Beloved 'a strange fossilized relic in human form'. What better namesake could he have than the author of the Chronicle used to represent the past in Carlyle's *Past and Present*?[21]

Three other names are worth noticing. Marcia duly practised the martial arts of the sex-war. Leverre (the glass) was 'a transparency, a soul so slightly veiled that the outer shaped itself to the inner like a tissue.' And 'Red-King Castle' was more than an apt translation of 'Rufus Castle'. In Carroll's *Through the Looking-Glass* (1872) the Red King was found dreaming of Alice, who thus became 'only a sort of thing in his dream'. If he woke up, she was told, she would 'go out – bang! – just like a candle!'

Every 'Supposititious Presentment' of Jocelyn's Well-Beloved had at first suffered that fate: the moment she ceased to be the woman of his 'dream', she turned 'from flame to ashes, from a radiant vitality to a relic'. But eventually his feelings grew 'maturer': 'Once the individual had been nothing more to him than the temporary abiding-place of the typical or ideal; now his heart showed its bent to be a growing fidelity to the specimen, with all her pathetic flaws of detail; which flaws . . . increased his tenderness.' In the serial this crumbling of his old subjectivity was confirmed symbolically: the next paragraph 'revealed to him . . . the ruins of Red King Castle'.[22]

The book-version was generally more realistic and less obviously allegorical than the serial; but the final work remains a cross between a novel and a poetic fantasy. This does not make it any less attractive reading, but it does demand some flexibility in the reader's response. One must take characters sometimes as human beings, sometimes as moving parts in the machinery of a romantic poem. Leverre, for instance, is a Keats-stereotype inserted simply to trigger off Jocelyn's 'Magnanimous Thing'. The three Avices function surprisingly well in a composite love-affair which the third rightly finds rather absurd: 'And were you my great-grandmother's [young man] too?' But they are not very interesting people. As for Jocelyn himself, he is real enough to make us sometimes feel ashamed of him, especially when he urges Avice II, 'for old times' sake', to make her daughter marry him. But he is often less like a person than a figure in a day-dream or tall story.[23]

What seems most real is the island itself, its stone homes, its anthropology, and its history stretching back through Roman times to the Jurassic period. Conscious that its fossil-rich 'oolite' was 'eggstone' in Greek, Hardy started his story, (unlike Horace's Homer) *ab ovo* (from the egg), thus setting it against the background of all life on earth. The poetry of that setting, which still hangs about Portland a century later, is the best thing about his last novel.[24]

1 Hardy's birthplace, Bockhampton, © Thomas Hardy Memorial Collection, The Dorset County Museum, Dorchester.

2 Portrait of Jemima Hardy by Mary Hardy, © Thomas Hardy Memorial Collection.

3 Portrait by Mary Hardy of Thomas Hardy Senior, aged 66 years (1877), copied from a photograph, © Thomas Hardy Memorial Collection.

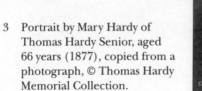

4   Thomas Hardy's First School, Lower Bockhampton, © Thomas Hardy
     Memorial Collection.

5   Thomas Hardy's birthplace, copied by Emma Hardy from a drawing by
     H. J. Moule, © Thomas Hardy Memorial Collection.

6 Thomas Hardy, aged 16, photograph
Pouncy, © Thomas Hardy Memorial
Collection.

View from my window
16. W. P. V.
June 22.-66.
I spent I in evening.

7 Drawing by Thomas Hardy, 'View From My Window – 16 Westbourne
Park Villas, 22 June 1866', © Thomas Hardy Memorial Collection.

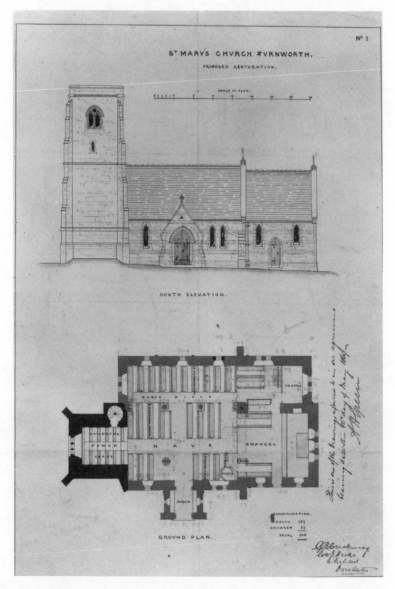

8   Turnworth Church 'Proposed Restoration' plans, © Thomas Hardy
    Memorial Collection.

9 St. Juliot Church before restoration in 1872 – interior, © Thomas
   Hardy Memorial Collection.

10 Sketch of Emma 'Searching for the Glass' by Thomas Hardy (19 August 1870),
    © Thomas Hardy Memorial Collection.

Thomas Hardy, by Emma Gifford (Mrs. Thomas Hardy)

11 Sketch of Thomas Hardy, by Emma Gifford (18 August 1870), © Thomas Hardy Memorial Collection.

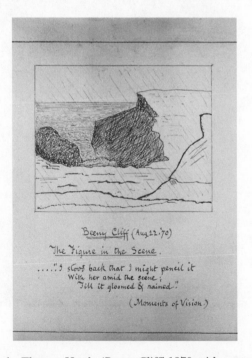

12 Drawing by Thomas Hardy, 'Beeny Cliff' 1870, with quotation from 'Figure in the Scene', © Thomas Hardy Memorial Collection.

13 Max Gate (built 1885), 1923, © Thomas Hardy Memorial Collection.

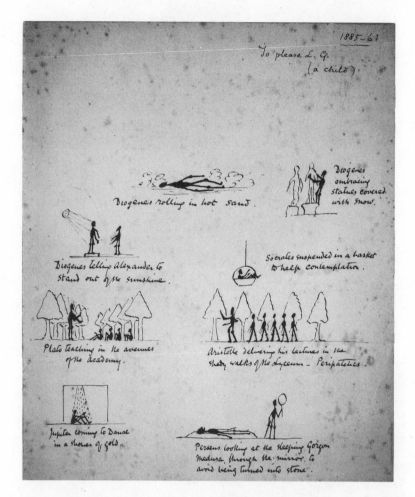

14 Scenes from the classics: pen and ink sketches by Thomas Hardy inscribed
'To Please L. G. (a child)', © Thomas Hardy Memorial Collection.

15 Thomas Hardy with Moss, his dog at Max Gate, 10 September 1890,
© Thomas Hardy Memorial Collection.

16 Thomas Hardy, *c*1890,
photograph Downey, © Mary
Evans Picture Library.

17 Emma Lavinia (Gifford) Hardy,
from *The Tatler*, 25 May 1904,
© Mary Evans Picture Library.

18 Thomas Hardy and Florence Dugdale on beach at Aldeburgh, August 1909,
© Thomas Hardy Memorial Collection.

19 Florence Hardy with Wessex, © Thomas Hardy Memorial Collection.

20 Florence Hardy at window of Max Gate, © Thomas Hardy Memorial Collection.

21 Thomas Hardy 'writer (and cyclist)'
at Max Gate, 1920s, © Mary Evans
Picture Library.

22 Cartoon by Max Beerbohm:
'Thomas Hardy composing a
lyric', © Thomas Hardy
Memorial Collection.

23 Thomas Hardy in academic
dress – Hon. Fellow Queen's
College, Oxford, 1923, © Thomas
Hardy Memorial Collection.

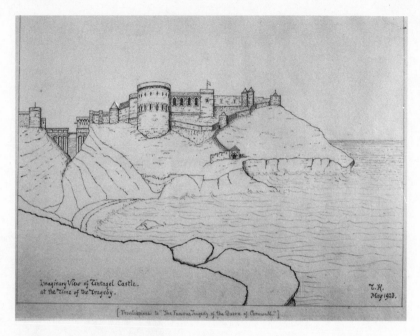

24 Pen and ink drawing by Thomas Hardy, 'Tintagel Castle', © Thomas Hardy Memorial Collection.

25 Thomas Hardy at Max Gate discussing the production of *Tess* with Miss Ffrangcon Davies, © Thomas Hardy Memorial Collection.

26 The burial of Thomas Hardy's heart at Stinsford, 16 January 1928,
© Thomas Hardy Memorial Collection.

27 J. M. W. Turner, *The Angel Standing in the Sun*, © The Tate Gallery,
London.

28 William Holman Hunt, *The Light of the World*, by permission of the
Warden and Fellows of Keble College, Oxford.

20

Wessex Poems

The *World*'s 'ferocious attack' on Hardy's fifteenth novel made Hardy 'inclined to say I will never write another line', and he never did write another novel – he wrote twelve volumes of poetry instead. Though the review may have tipped the balance, he had been considering a return to poetry since at least Christmas 1890, when the idea of 'resuming "the viewless wings of poesy"' had seemed to make 'new horizons . . . open . . . and worrying pettinesses . . . disappear.' Keats's metaphor for rising above ordinary life had for Hardy an almost literal meaning, soon expressed in a poem of 1896, 'Wessex Heights'. To feel free, to feel himself, he needed altitude as well as solitude: 'mind-chains do not clank where one's next neighbour is the sky . . . Down there I seem to be false to myself, my simple self that was . . .' With poetry in mind, he naturally chose Switzerland for their next trip abroad (June 1897). Hence his disappointment at the low clouds in Berne: 'up to the present the statement that there are mountains in Switzerland seems a groundless tradition'. No doubt he felt better when they went up the Riffel-Alp to an 'Hotel grandly situated', as Emma put it, 'as high as opposite Matterhorn'.[1]

'Perhaps', he had thought in October 1896, I can express more fully in verse ideas and emotions which run counter to the inert crystallized opinion . . . If Galileo had said in verse that the world moved, the Inquisition might have let him alone.' As a poet he could at least stop writing to deadlines. Two years later he told a literary agent: 'I have made up my mind not to sell anything till it is in existence.' But poetry offered much more than freedom for self-expression or escape from the pressures and problems of novel-writing. It would also let him exploit his passion for music – perhaps more profitably than by fiddling folk-tunes for a potential stage-Tess to dance to, as he did in January 1896.[2]

To the artist and the architect in him, too, poetry promised greater scope. He had 'discovered . . . a close and curious parallel' between architecture and poetry, whereas the novel 'was gradually losing artistic form, with a beginning, middle, and end, and becoming a spasmodic inventory of items, which has nothing to do with art.' By 'art' he meant much more than technique. In January 1897 he recalled Plato's phrase in the *Ion*, '*theion kai me technicon* (divine, and not technical)'. 'Inspiration not technicality' seemed to him a closer translation than Jowett's 'inspiration, and not art', since 'art' was 'too comprehensive in English to use here'. He had apparently forgotten the immediate context, where the phrase was applied, not directly to poetry, but to the Rhapsode's knowledge of Homer. Actually, a 'comprehensive' word was needed to allow for Socrates' ironic punning. Still, the note clearly reflected Hardy's current feeling that poetry was more 'divine' than the nuts and bolts of novel-production.[3]

Could he afford, though, to 'abandon at once a form of literary art he had long intended to abandon at some indefinite time'? People bought his novels: would they buy his poems? How long could he depend on his present royalties? It would be quite a gamble – but perhaps he remembered the compulsive gambler he had met at a Casino in September 1896, who suddenly abandoned his 'system', backed a number that 'came into his head as he was walking down the street . . . and won.'[4]

By February 1897 he was evidently close to a decision, for he jotted down a possible title for a volume: 'Wessex Poems: With Sketches of their Scenes by the Author'. The preparation of that volume, which he kept a secret even from close friends, gave him 'a good deal' of pleasure, especially the illustrations, which had for him an 'illegitimate interest . . . from their being a novel amusement, & a wholly gratuitous performance which could not profit me anything, & probably would do me harm.' The pleasure was slightly diminished by a sash-window that 'came down upon' his thumb and finger, making writing and drawing 'awkward' for some time. But he was so absorbed in the project that the New York production of his 'Tess-play' in March 1897 came as a a tiresome distraction: 'I had secretly hoped Tess was going to fall through altogether, as I have been, & am, more interested in other labours.'[5]

These were facilitated by release from 'mindchains', first in the Swiss Alps, and then, from the autumn of 1897, on his 'loveliest "Byke"', a £20 Rover Cob, window-shopped in February 1896, and subsequently bought and broken in. He soon found that 'the advantage of cycling for literary people is that you can go out a long distance without coming in contact with another mind, – not even a horse's – & dissipating any little mental energy that has arisen in the course of a morning's application.' In other words, you could escape from the novelist's prison, his study, and compose poems in open country.[6]

On 'that useful wheel' he travelled, in the summer of 1898, to Bristol, Gloucester, Cheltenham, Sherborne, Poole, Weymouth, and many other places', sometimes with his brother Henry, and 'sometimes with Mrs Hardy'.

Such mute companionship was probably best for both of them just then. Emma, too, had her literary projects, and her private thoughts. That year she published a perceptive article on cats, and how inconsiderately 'cottagers' treated them. Her bitterest thoughts were going into a diary-account, since destroyed, of how badly she was treated by her (ex-cottager) husband.[7]

The gist of its contents can be guessed from her letter of August 1899 to Mrs Kenneth Grahame. There she warned the young wife that husbands were naturally promiscuous, especially after fifty; apt to side with their families, whose 'interference' often caused 'estrangement'; and generally incapable of 'love proper, and enduring'. One should expect from them 'neither gratitude, nor attentions, love, nor *justice*', least of all 'adoration'. Of course, marriage *could* be a 'happy state' – if '*both*' were Christians. But Hardy, despite nostalgia for the church of his youth, was now a confirmed agnostic. His nearest approach to Emma's beliefs was to toy with an idea from J.S. Mill's 'Theism': 'Write a prayer, or hymn, to One not Omnipotent, but hampered; striving for our good, but unable to achieve it except occasionally.'[8]

Emma had now taken over the two new attic rooms at Max Gate, and was otherwise following her own advice to Mrs Grahame: 'Keeping separate a good deal is a wise plan in crises – and being both free'. So Hardy used his freedom to get on with his book. In September 1898 he signed an agreement for it with Harpers, offering 'to take on his own shoulders the risk of producing the volume, so that if nobody bought it they should not be out of pocket.' But they were 'kind enough', or perhaps far-sighted enough, to risk it themselves. The same month he contradicted newspaper reports that he was about to publish a 'long novel', and told Mrs Henniker what his 'mysterious occupation' had really been. In October he was correcting proofs, and the secret of the illustrations had been leaked to the press. By mid-November the book was off his hands, but 'waiting for the American issue'; and in mid-December 1898 *Wessex Poems and Other Verses* was published in London, Harpers prudently limiting the edition to five hundred copies.[9]

Only two years earlier Hardy had written: 'I find the Saturday Review brighter in its literary criticisms . . . than any other weekly that I come across just now.' It was not very bright about *Wessex Poems*, which it called a 'curious and wearisome volume . . . It is impossible to understand why the bulk of this volume was published at all – why he did not himself burn the verse . . .' Other reviews were more respectful, and E.K. Chambers, in the *Athenaeum*, recognized 'a small cluster of really remarkable poems'. But most reviewers assumed that Hardy was a natural 'proseman', who had late in life made the 'dubious experiment' of trying to write poetry, without having 'had time to master the mere *technique* of verse'. Annoyingly, their mistake contained a grain of truth: when he had first started writing poems again, he had found, 'with some consternation . . . an awkwardness in getting back to an easy expression in numbers after abandoning it for so many years'. And in February 1899 he confessed regret that he had not given 'due time to the removing of some of the too obvious defects of form in the verses.' But he had not expected 'a particularly gracious reception', and was not unduly discouraged. He had at least pleased himself, if no one else. 'He had written his poems entirely because he liked doing them, without any ulterior thought.'[10]

Browning had described his poetry as 'always dramatic in principle, and so many utterances of so many imaginary persons, not mine'. Hardy was less plausible when he called *Wessex Poems* 'in a large degree dramatic or personative in conception; and this even when they are not obviously so.' The first piece ('the Temporary the All') neatly fitted his present feeling that novel-writing had been a 'temporary' expedient 'never transcended' until now. The second, 'Amabel', written 1865, clearly expressed his reaction to the 'altered' appearance of Mrs Martin in 1863. In the seventh, the 'Friend in Trouble' was Horace Moule. 'She' of the sonnet-sequence, 'She to Him', was probably Eliza Nicholls: the tower in his illustration to Sonnet I has been identified as Clavel Tower, Kimmeridge Bay, just above Eliza's first home.[11]

Emma spotted much else in the volume that did not seem 'personative'. She doubtless felt targeted both as the stopgap 'maiden' in 'The Temporary the All', and as the lethally possessive 'Ivy-Wife' – a poem she found particularly hard to 'admire'. Seeing Tryphena promoted, in 'Thoughts of Ph ——', to Hardy's 'lost prize', she was naturally hurt that 'Ditty' (1870) was the only tribute to herself in the collection (though one reviewer thought it good enough to 'justify' the whole book). It was cold comfort that Tryphena, qua pub-keeper's wife, could have felt targeted too, as the hostess of 'The famed Lions-Three', with 'liquor-fired face' and 'thick accents / In naming her fee'.' If it is true that Hardy visited Tryphena's grave at Topsham near Exeter in or after 1890, that pilgrimage must have suggested the one in 'My Cicely'. Cicely's supposed grave was in 'the city / Where Exe scents the sea' and, according to the illustration, close to Exeter Cathedral. Did Emma also realize that 'At an Inn' described what had happened when her husband took Mrs Henniker to lunch at the George Inn, Winchester in August 1893?[12]

The poems touched Hardy's life at other points. 'The Dance at the Phoenix' featured dance-tunes that he had played in those early 'adventures with the fiddle'; and its fifty-nine-year-old addict of dancing was himself, in all but her sex and heart-failure. His own country-dancing with Agnes Grove at fifty-five had merely 'left him stiff in the knees for some succeeding days.' 'Heiress and Architect', written in Blomfield's office (1867) grew directly from his work there. 'The Impercipient', illustrated by a sketch of Salisbury Cathedral, recalled the services he had attended there with Emma in August 1897. It originally included the protest, 'But ah, they love me not, although / I treat them tenderly', and implicitly asked her (and people like the late bishop who had incinerated *Jude*) to be more tolerant of his agnosticism. 'In a Eweleaze near Weatherbury' evidently expressed his own sense of being too old to interest a pretty girl; and the final poem, 'I look into my glass', fused that feeling with an experience of October 1892: 'Hurt my tooth at breakfast-time. I look in the glass. Am conscious of the humiliating sorriness of my earthly tabernacle, and of the sad fact that the best of parents could do no better for me.'[13]

'There is no new poetry', wrote Hardy 'somewhere' about this time, 'but the new poet . . . comes with a new note.' It was partly by resonating to ancient poetry that his own new note was sounded. 'I have not read anything lately but old books', he reported to Mrs Henniker in April 1897. In August 1895 he had told her: 'I have made myself a present of Wharton's *Sappho* – a delightful book. How I love her . . . !' His interest in Sappho and her stanza had probably been started by Swinburne's 'Anactoria' and 'Sapphics' in *Poems and Ballads* (1866), and he now told Swinburne (1 April 1897) that he had been trying to improve on 'several English translations of a well-known fragment of Sappho'. Among Wharton's 'Selected Renderings' were some in English Sapphics, which doubtless encouraged him to use that stanza for the first of his *Wessex Poems*. There Sappho's fragment about the concealment of the stars by the rising of the full moon possibly contributed to the picture of the 'damsel' that would do 'till *arise* my forefelt / Wonder of women.' In the final version she became: 'unformed to be all-eclipsing'.[14]

Hardy later 'presented himself' with the 1911 edition of Mackail's *Select Epigrams from the Greek Anthology*. If, as seems likely, he had 'dipped into' the book, among 'a good many' others, when it first came out in 1890, he would have found an epigram, ascribed to Plato, spoken by an aging beauty. She dedicated her mirror to Aphrodite – 'because I don't want to see myself as I am now, and can't, as I used to be.' Mackail mentioned three other epigrams in the same genre, to which 'I Look Into My Glass' obviously belongs.[15]

But the 'equanimity' of that poem was Horatian: '*aequam memento rebus in arduis / servare mentem* (when things are difficult, preserve your equanimity'), and the *Odes* were more important models for Hardy's lyrics. In 1865, just before he started writing verse 'constantly', he had 'Read some Horace' and written 'Amabel', evidently named from the lady whom Horace had wrongly thought '*semper amabilem* (always to be loved'). The beginning of that *Ode*, '*Quis multa gracilis . . .* (What youth is making love to her now?)', was simply generalized: 'Who sings the strain / I sang ere warmth did wane? / Who thinks its numbers spell / His Amabel?' In 1890, the year he first considered 'resuming' poetry, Hardy transferred the theme of Horace's '*Vixi puellis nuper idoneus* (until lately I was suitable for girls)' to 'A Eweleaze near Weatherbury', replacing the 'arrogant' Chloe with the young 'Beauty' who would 'scorn my brave endeavour'.[16]

Of English poets, Chaucer set the pattern for 'The Fire at Tranter Sweatley's'. Its later ascription to 'A Wessex Tradition' need be taken no more literally than 'A Tradition of 1804', which Hardy confessed to having 'invented'. The January–May–Damian fabliau of 'The Marchantes Tale' was only slightly bowdlerized. If Tim did not instantly 'pullen up smok', as Damian did when he met May up a pear-tree, his 'soul like a lion 'ithin en outsprung' when he found Barbree 'half-naked' under 'a codlin-tree', and the Chaucerian consummation was not long postponed.[17]

Some other early poems were predictably influenced by Shakespeare. 'She at his Funeral' (1873) reworded Hamlet's contrast between 'suits of solemn black' and real mourning; and his listing of 'contumely' with 'disprized love' among the 'whips and scorns of time' doubtless suggested Hardy's statement that 'losing love' 'cuts like contumely'. Those words came in a sonnet expressing a 'Revulsion' against 'junctive law' like Shakespeare's against 'lust in action'; and Hardy's 'Confession' to an 'unseemly instinct' of self-preservation, matched Shakespeare's to a 'sin of self-love'.[18]

Gray's 'Elegy in a Country Churchyard', which Hardy knew by heart (except for 'the order of the verses'), was the model, not only for 'Friends Beyond', but for the whole volume's graveyard theme. So that poem's illustration, a view of Stinsford Churchyard, was used as frontispiece, with a quotation from Hardy's second stanza ('At mothy curfew-tide') plainly derived from Gray's first line, 'The curfew tolls the knell of parting day.'[19]

Crabbe, in whose poetry Hardy had noted (17 October 1896) 'a novel, good, microscopic touch', probably suggested the structure of 'My Cicely'. In 'The Lover's Journey' Orlando rode off 'gaily' to visit his Laura, 'And all he saw was pleasing in his sight.' Finding her away from home, he rode after her, hating every feature of the landscape. Cicely's lover rode off 'sadly' to visit her grave. Finding another woman buried there, he too saw the scenery transformed: 'And grasses and grove shone in garments / Of glory to me.' But his 'joyance' was brief: Cicely, though alive, had apparently become the coarse creature he had seen at a pub – like the gipsy slut seen by Orlando, whose 'bloodshot eyes on her unheeding mate / Were wrathful turn'd'. Crabbe's tale began with the dictum: 'It is the soul that sees; the outward eyes / Present the object, but the mind descries'. So Cicely's lover, instead of rushing off to meet her, decided to believe not eyes but soul: 'Far better / To dream than to own the debasement / Of sweet Cicely.'[20]

Wordsworth was not actually 'lonely as a cloud' but with his sister Dorothy when he saw the daffodils: 'A poet could not but be gay / In such a jocund company'. 'Middle-Age Enthusiasms', addressed to Hardy's sister Mary, debunked such fancies: 'We passed where flag and flower / Signalled a jocund throng . . . And, kindling, laughed at life and care, / Although we knew no laugh lay there.' Byron's romanticism was similiarly undercut in 'San Sebastian'. Rescuing a young girl from 'two villainous Cossacques' in the storming of Ismail, Don Juan was 'gazed on' by her 'large eyes . . . transfix'd with infant terrors'. Hardy's Sergeant played the 'Cossacque' himself, and was haunted by 'those eyes' ever after. He thus had better reason than Keats's 'knight-at-arms' for being found 'alone and palely loitering', and the poem's anti-romanticism was stressed by the burlesque of the 'Belle Dame' opening: 'Why, Sergeant, stray on the Ivel Way / As though at home there were spectres rife?'[21]

Shelley was the man Hardy most wanted to 'meet in the Elysian fields', for his 'genuineness, earnestness, & enthusiasms on behalf of the oppressed', and the *Alastor* Poet's enquiries into such things as 'the red volcano . . . fields of snow and pinnacles of ice' clearly encouraged 'A Sign-Seeker' to include 'abysmal fires and snow-cones' in his equally extensive research-project. Like Shelley in his 'Hymn to Intellectual Beauty', he had also tried to make contact with the dead; and the first line of 'Her Initials', 'Upon a poet's page I wrote', sounds like a reminiscence of Shelley's 'On a poet's lips I slept'. It soon becomes clear, though, that the main source was *In Memoriam*, where Tennyson pictured Arthur Hallam's 'marble' in the moonlight: 'As slowly steals a silver flame / Along the letters of thy name . . . The mystic glory swims away . . .' So here, 'from the letters of her name / The radiance has died away.'[22]

'A great artist', wrote Hardy of Tennyson in November 1897, 'but a mere Philistine of a thinker.' Thus, while prepared to borrow rhymes from *Maud* ('I felt that I could creep / To some housetop, and weep'), and the theme of 'Home they brought her warrior dead' for 'The Slow Nature', he parodied the moral of 'The Palace of Art' in 'Heiress and Architect', and in two other poems explicitly contradicted the ideas of *In Memoriam*. In 'The Sign-Seeker', for which he adopted the *In Memoriam* rhyme-scheme, 'Not the end!' was the answer invited by Tennyson's repeated question: 'Is this the end?'; and the people 'rapt to heights of trancelike trust' meant Tennyson, when 'whirled' in a 'trance' 'About empyreal heights of thought'. The 'All's Well' never 'breathed' to 'The Impercipient' had been 'whispered' in Tennyson's hearing by 'a sentinel . . . to the worlds of space'.[23]

In retrospect, Hardy thought he had spoiled his chances for this volume 'by not being imitative . . . There were Wordsworth, Tennyson, Browning: he had only to copy one of them to win commendation'. As for Browning, he was neither copied nor parodied. But 'A Meeting with Despair' resembled 'Childe Roland' in its use of a nightmare landscape; and 'The Burghers', in the metre of 'The Statue and the Bust', also shared that poem's moral ambiguity: was the husband's motive 'Charity' or revenge, by inflicting a chronic sense of guilt?[24]

In *Wessex Poems* Hardy was free to practise three arts denied him as a novelist: visual, in the pen-and-ink drawings; architectural or constructive, in designing both the whole collection, and the individual poems; and musical, in the verse. The best illustrations were emblematic or atmospheric. The sundial (which materialized on the wall of Max Gate after Hardy's death) epitomized 'The Temporary the All' with its image of an ineffectually circling shadow. The hourglass and butterflies, for 'Amabel', translated the notion of ephemeral beauty into a shape recalling a fashionable wasp-waist. The tower-capped hill against a sunset represented 'Life's sunless hill' in 'She to Him' with an outline suggesting a woman's breast; while a pair of such outlines (one identified topographically as Monte Urgull) symbolized the rape at 'San Sebastian'. The sinister atmosphere of 'The Burghers' was visualized as a sunset-backed figure in Dorchester High West Street, like 'The Angel standing in the sun'. The fiddler playing outside the lighted windows of the Ship Inn showed the Armageddon of 'Leipsig' distilled into a march-tune to amuse the next generation. 'The Dance at the Phoenix' began with the unrolling violin-score of a dance-tune called 'The Soldier's Joy', and ended with that joy's ending – a cortège-like column of soldiers marching away into the distance, their blackness against the white road, like the 'black night' into which the Trumpet-Major marched, hinting at death in battle. The neatest emblem of all was the pair of spectacles through which the 'The Eweleaze' appeared: sheep still clearly visible, but 'Love's fitful ecstasies' blotted out by presbyopia.[25]

How to give 'artistic form' to the volume as a whole was a problem incompletely solved. 'Well', he told Gosse (27 December 1898), 'the poems were lying about, & I did not quite know what to do with them.' What he finally did was to lump together poems written over more than thirty years, including personal ones from the 1860s, Napoleonic ballads presumably meant to go into the composite 'Iliad of Europe' planned in 1875, and recent expressions of agnosticism. The result, as the Preface warned, was a 'miscellaneous collection'. Apart from the impression of unity given by the illustrations, the volume was unified solely by its recurring themes: death, graves, guilt (in five out of fifty-one poems), and general dissatisfaction with 'A world conditioned thus'. Of individual pieces, the long ballad 'Leipsig' seems rather formless too, despite its framing device. Only the shorter lyrics, such as 'Unknowing' or 'I Look Into My Glass', were notably well-constructed.[26]

In using established verse-forms and inventing new ones, Hardy showed technical skill and versatility, though there was, as the *Athenaeum* complained, some 'woodenness of rhythm'. Nor was this excused, except in 'The Temporary the All', by the inherent difficulty of Anglicizing a Greek metre. One cause was the mixed character of the diction. Hardy cheerfully accepted Archer's comment that he seemed to see 'all the words of the dictionary on one plane . . . as equally available and appropriate for any and every literary purpose'. Why should not a poet do so? Only, perhaps, because a scientific and legal word like 'stillicide', for instance, however euphonious in itself, can interrupt the sense of flowing verse.[27]

Of course, not all the volume's verse was meant to flow. The Sapphics and sonnets, for instance, were probably meant to stand, like Horace's *Odes*, as if engraved in bronze. But the anapaestic rhythms in 'Thoughts of Phena' appear to mimic the hurrying beat of the train on which the poem was started; the smoothly regular movement of 'The Dance at the Phoenix' was as obviously 'tune-led' as Jenny's feet; and the verse-form of 'Valenciennes' sounds as if written to fit the six-eight melody of that name in Hardy's book of folk-dances. With anacrusis in line one of each stanza, and a slighter shift of accent in line three than that prescribed for 'Valencieën', the poem can easily be sung to the dance-tune.[28]

Despite his concern with art and music, Hardy felt he was challenging the fashionable view of 'poetry as the art of saying nothing with mellifluous preciosity', by producing poems on the 'principle of regarding form as second to content'. He had written them 'because he wanted to say the things they contained and would contain – mainly the philosophy of life afterwards developed in *The Dynasts*'. The essence of that philosophy, the idea of a universe governed by something unconscious, was only one of the hypotheses thrown out in 'Nature's Questioning': 'Or come we of an Automaton / Unconscious of our pains? . . .' But almost everything in the volume implied the conviction behind such questioning: that life was much too cruel to have been created by a benevolent God; and that death *was* 'the end'.[29]

The message is bleak, but Hardy's first collection of poems remains an attractive, almost an exhilarating book. What comes across is not only his deep sadness, but also his sense of new freedom to say what he felt, and do what he enjoyed doing. Though it gave few signs of his ultimate power in poetry, *Wessex Poems* already suggested a second flowering of his imagination, a personal renaissance.

21

Poems of the Past and the Present

When Hardy's next book appeared in 1901, its title was topical. At the end of every era past and present are inevitably compared. Now the Victorian age had ended, almost simultaneously with the nineteenth century. The most confident period of British imperialism had also ended in the Boer War – though in that case past and present looked almost indistinguishable. 'It seems a justification of the extremest pessimism', wrote Hardy in September 1899, 'that at the end of the 19th Centy we settle an argument by the Sword, just as they wd have done in the 19th centy B.C.' For him, though, past and present had just been strikingly contrasted, when he met the Jeunes at Stonehenge 'with their motor-car', and was then driven home 'at tremendous speed'. That year Marconi had established cross-Channel radio-contact, and in February 1901 Hardy was asked by William Archer if the age-old belief in ghosts might not be explained by the human brain's being 'a more powerful transmitter and a more sensitive receiver than any invented by Marconi'.[1]

But past-present contrasts in his own life meant more to Hardy then than new technology: 'my pleasures are all past, I fear!', he told Florence Henniker on New Year's Day, 1899. 'Who said a few weeks ago', he wrote to his friend Clodd in July, 'that he was not 60 and I was?' That jocular birthday greeting probably concealed some dismay that his own middle age was over. There were other endings. 'The sudden death of Sir Arthur Blomfield ... snapped a friendship which had extended over thirty-six years'; and the death of Emma's sister in December 1900 must have seemed to push those happy days at St Juliot even further back into the past. In November 1898 he had started a nostalgic poem about them: 'Show me again the time / When in the Junetide's prime / We flew by meads and mountains northerly!' 'A Second Attempt', written 'About 1900' according to the manuscript, implies that he had then tried, 'thirty years after', to revive his old relationship with Emma, only to find that 'Twice-over cannot be!'[2]

So they remained semi-detached. His occasional letters to her showed affection and concern for her health, especially around the time when her sister died: 'I am dreadfully afraid you will break down'. But they had ceased to think alike. Having bitterly mentioned to a friend their 'silver wedding' in 1899, Emma gave him a Bible for his birthday, but he remained unconverted. She then bought herself or was given Mary Wollstonecraft's *Vindication of the Rights of Woman*, but he showed no interest in feminism either – except to congratulate his 'pupil' Agnes Grove' on her 'forcible . . . rhetoric' in refuting 'Objections to Woman Suffrage'. Did Emma resent not being one of his literary pupils too – or had she refused such help? She certainly needed some: her 'Spring Song', published in 1900 by one of her husband's editors, was touching in sentiment but very messy in form. Struggling to assert herself in what evidently seemed a man's world, and her husband's in particular, she struck one visitor in March 1900 as 'a great bore, but at the same time so kind and good-hearted'.[3]

Hardy, meanwhile, kept writing poems 'from pleasure in them', and publishing some in periodicals. Most of these were about the war, on which his feelings were mixed: 'How horrible it all is', he wrote of the crucial Paaredeberg victory, picturing the Boer general attacked in 'that river bed' with 'his wife and other women' as well as 'his unfortunate army; & the mangled animals too, who must have terror added to their physical sufferings.'[4]

'I take a keen pleasure', he continued, 'in war strategy and tactics, following it as it were a game of chess; but all the while I am obliged to blind myself to the human side of the matter'. Either way, his 'thoughts' were 'all Kahki colour' just then. He watched 'our Battery of Artillery' leaving Dorchester Barracks 'amid rain and wind' for South Africa, asked Florence for a photograph of Major Henniker, 'In uniform preferred', and wrote him a letter of good wishes, calling him 'the most perfect type of the practical soldier that I know'. He then cycled to Southampton, and 'saw off 5000 altogether' of the troops being sent to the front. He later recalled 'the *excitement* of sending off the army to the Cape'; for while 'constantly deploring' war as 'the old and barbarous' method of settling disputes, he confessed: 'when I feel that it must be, few persons are more martial than I, or like better to write of war in prose & rhyme.'[5]

Thus stimulated as well as saddened by the war, and by 'a general sense of the unknown lying round us' in a new reign and century, he wrote quite cheerful letters, despite a catalogue of ailments – flu, 'a rheum' in the eye, 'dreadful languor', the loss of an 'absolutely' flawless front tooth, toothache, 'neuralgia in the teeth', 'a miserable sick headache 'almost chronic' for a month, and a right thumb cut in carpentering. What distressed him more was animal suffering, as in the 'dreadful' story told by a man invalided home, 'of being *compelled* to drive his horse to death on

the forced march, & of having to abandon others not quite dead.' Then
there were the victims of hunting (an 'immoral and unmanly' sport) and
shooting: he admired a vegetarian neighbour who had 'renounced shooting after being convinced by the arguments of his wife that it was wrong.
The animals are so tame round their house that the squirrels run up their
shoulders when they go outside.' A contrasting 'gloom' was thrown over
his own home in April 1901 'by the tragic death of a favourite cat – *my* cat
– the first I have ever had for "my very own"'. It was 'mutilated by the
mail-train' on a line a quarter of a mile off, and he blamed himself for not
having shut it in that night as he normally did. 'The violent death of dumb
creature[s] always makes me revile the contingencies of a world in which
animals are in the best of cases pitiable for their limitations.'[6]

It seemed a bad world for human beings too, and to try and make sense
of it he had been reading 'various philosophic systems', including
Hartmann's *Philosophy of the Unconscious.* On the last day of 1901 he passed
his verdict on their 'contradictions and futilities': '*Let every man make a
philosophy for himself out of his own experience.* He will not be able to avoid
using terms and phraseology from earlier philosophers, but let him avoid
adopting their theories if he values his own mental life.' *His* 'practical
philosophy', he had told William Archer in February 1901, excluded the
supernatural, but was 'distinctly meliorist.' The term, previously used by
George Eliot, implied that things were bad, but could, and probably would,
be made better by human effort. As for his abstract philosophy, he noted
in June: 'non-rationality seems, so far as one can perceive, to be the principle of the Universe. By which I do not mean foolishness, but rather a
principle for which there is no exact name, lying at the indifference-point
between rationality and irrationality', i.e. where those two forces cancelled
each other out. Such were the general ideas behind *Poems of the Past and
the Present.*[7]

In July, 'oppressed by the heat', he was 'hunting up the poems . . . &
trying to decide which to print & which destroy.' Having sent off his MS
in August, he began to regret having done so: 'one exposes oneself to
all sort of arrows by printing anything written in hours of impulse.'
But when the book came out in mid-November 1901 (dated 1902), the
critics' arrows drew no blood. Forced to admit that Hardy was 'a poet, and
a profoundly interesting one', even the *Saturday Review* could only complain
that despite metrical virtuosity he had no 'singing voice'. *The Times* found
his verse 'crabbed' and 'stiff'. A future Oxford Professor of Poetry, while
recognizing Hardy's 'music' and his scholarship, repeated the old cry that
poetry was 'not his proper medium'. Still, most of the reviews were good,
and sales were fast enough to require a second edition in January.[8]

Hardy's preface again played down the personal element in his poems
('much is dramatic or impersonative even when not explicitly so'), while
admitting that a 'portion' of the subject-matter, 'feelings and fancies written
down in widely differing moods and circumstances', might be 'regarded

as individual'. Such, clearly, were the 'War Poems'. 'The Embarcation' described the 'most impressive scene' that rewarded his cycle-ride to Southampton, and paraphrased his remark in a letter about the primitive 'way of settling disputes' still used by 'civilized' nations. 'The Going of the Battery', he said, 'was almost an exact report of the scene & expressions I overheard.' As for 'fancies', he had not 'witnessed' the scene 'At the War Office, London', but had found it easy to 'imagine with painful realism'. The setting of 'The Souls of the Slain' was drawn from memory, for he had not been to Portland Bill 'for years'. Major Henniker surely inspired 'The Colonel's Soliloquy', though he he was not made a Colonel until he got to South Africa. And 'The Sick Battle-God' expressed Hardy's real belief. 'Oh yes,' he had told William Archer, 'war is doomed . . . Not today, nor to-morrow, but in the fullness of time, war will come to an end, not for moral reasons, but because of its absurdity.'[9]

Equally 'individual' were 'Poems of Pilgrimage', all but the last dating from Hardy's trips with Emma, to Italy in 1887 and to Switzerland in 1897. Most of these described incidents and feelings recorded (sometimes more pointedly) in his *Life* or correspondence. Thus the thought of 'Rome: Building a New Street in the Ancient Quarter' appeared like this in a letter: 'For my part if I were going to erect a mere shed I shd say Is it worth while?' 'Shelley's Skylark', written near Leghorn, drew poignancy from the Bockhampton fieldfare: 'then, one day, fell – / A little ball of feather and bone'. 'The Bridge of Lodi' grew from Hardy's two frustrated searches there: for 'an old French tune of his father's', and for local knowledge of the battle. It is still frustrating to find that the tune is not with his father's music-collection at the Dorset County Museum; but it was probably the one still called 'The Bridge of Lodi', a hornpipe converted into a march. This is lively enough to have come 'capering' to the poet, and its 'straight 2/4 drum beat' may well have suggested his own 'forward-footing', four-trochee line. Collectively, 'Poems of Pilgrimage' brought out one aspect of the volume's title, as when the Strauss waltz heard in 'Caesar's house . . . blended pulsing life with lives long done, / Till Time seemed fiction, Past and Present one.'[10]

Hardy's own past and present were contrasted in the concluding section, 'Retrospect', especially in 'Memory and I', while 'Miscellaneous Poems' gave glimpses of specific experiences: illness in early childhood and in 1880, dancing as a small boy to his father's fiddle at Bockhampton, working late at night in his study at Max Gate. His feeling for animal life showed in several poems about birds, most movingly in 'The Puzzled Game-Birds': 'At a *battue* the other day', he had noted in 1877, 'lots of the birds ran into the keeper's *house* for protection.' His pessimistic 'meliorism' was also implied as a philosophy for one 'Who holds that if way to the Better there be, it exacts a full look at the Worst'.[11]

Philosophically, the most interesting poems in the book were those sketching an alternative theology. The first piece pictured Queen Victoria lying 'in the All-One's thought'. The use of Hartmann's term for the unconscious creative power was early evidence of his influence on Hardy's myth-making. This pictured creators with varying degrees of unconsciousness. 'The Bedridden Peasant' praises 'the mercies' of an 'Unknowing God'. 'The Sleep-Worker' will not know until she wakes up what a shameful mess she has made. In 'The Mother Mourns' 'Nature' already realizes her own inefficiency, and regrets having carelessly produced human beings bright enough to spot it. The poem thus dramatized a note of 1883: 'We have reached a degree of intelligence which Nature never contemplated when framing her laws.'[12]

In 'The Lacking Sense' she is blind, but remorseful for her unmeant 'crimes upon her creatures'. Human 'meliorism' is the only hope: 'And while she plods dead-reckoning on, in darkness of affliction, / Assist her where thy creaturely dependence can or may'. In 'Doom and She' the poor lady is disturbed to hear 'a groan, / Or multitudinous moan' from her creation; but Doom, being 'Vacant of Feeling', cannot tell her what is going on. A note of 1889 had deplored the 'woeful fact – that the human race is too extremely developed for its corporeal conditions, the nerves being evolved to an activity abnormal in such an environment. Even the higher animals are in excess in this respect.' Thus 'Nature, or what we call Nature' had gone too far: an unfeeling natural process had produced organisms sensitive to pain.[13]

The haunting image of the blind but kindly goddess, which fused Hardy's old idea of the 'Unfulfilled Intention' with his recent concept of 'One not Omnipotent . . . striving for our good', had possibly grown from his own picture of Mrs d'Urberville, blindly fondling her pet birds, and ultimately responsible for Tess's sufferings. Behind the image, too, were probably Keats's two *Hyperions*. 'Doom and She' first appeared as 'a mighty pair – / Slow, statuesque'. So did Hyperion and Thea, he 'quiet as a stone . . . list'ning to the Earth, / His ancient mother', 'she a 'Goddess of the infant world', with face as 'large as that of Memphian sphinx, but 'unlike marble' in its beauty and sorrow. *The Fall of Hyperion* prefigured in 'sad Moneta' the blind benevolence of Hardy's 'mildly' worried 'Matron': 'her eyes . . . with a benignant light' seemed 'visionless entire' of 'all external things . . . like the mild moon . . . who knows not/ What eyes are upward cast.'[14]

'Do your thing', urged Emerson in 'Self-Reliance', when Hardy was one year old. As a full-time poet at sixty he was finally doing so, writing what 'had always been more instinctive with him', and so relying less on previous literature. In May 1901 he noted a remark of Leslie Stephen: 'We cannot write living poetry on the ancient model. The gods and heroes are too dead . . .' But while creating new gods, Hardy still drew perceptibly on ancient poetry, though now too well assimilated to seem extraneous.[15]

'O friend', the sun warns 'The Tenant-for-Life', 'Bethink ye, I have shined / On nobler ones than you, and they / Are dead men out of mind!' Friend', Homer's Achilles told a man who begged for mercy, 'you too must die. Even Patroclus died, who was far better than you.' The souls of the suitors killed in the *Odyssey* went off 'past the streams of Ocean, and the rock of Leucas' (an island once a peninsular, like Portland) to Hades, 'squeaking' like night-birds or bats (*nukterides*) flying round a 'terrible cave'. 'The Souls of the Slain' were 'dim-discerned' from the 'Many-caverned' 'Isle' of Portland, with a 'whirr' of wings as of 'night-moths'; and those whose 'record' was not 'lovely and true . . . plunged' into an 'engulphing, ghast, sinister place', to join the 'myriads forgot.' The link between Hades and being forgotten, not explicit in Homer, was emphasized in the Fragment' translated from Sappho. Euripides' Heracles woke from madness to find he had slaughtered his children: the 'Mother' in 'The Sleep-Worker' might 'wake and see' what havoc she had inflicted on hers. 'To an Unborn Pauper Child' adapted Plato's Myth of Er, in which the unborn were offered a choice of lives, to fit Sophocles' dictum: 'Not to be born is best'.[16]

Like Sophocles, Virgil and Horace still made their presence felt behind the poems. In 'Embarcation', the troops were 'Yellow as autumn leaves'. This recalled the simile in the *Aeneid*, where a 'crowd' of dead people, 'many as the leaves that fall in the woods at the first autumn frost', rushed to embark in Charon's boat – for these 'hosts', too, might soon be dead. As 'Wives, sisters, parents, wave white hands and smile', the scene melts into Virgil's picture of death and bereavement: 'Mothers and men, bodies of dead heroes, boys and unmarried girls, and young men cremated before their parents' eyes.' 'The Tenant-for-Life' got much the same *memento mori* from the sun as Postumus got from Horace: 'Not one of these trees that you are growing will follow its short-lived owner': 'These flowers and plants I parch up hot – / Who'll water them that day?' Even the 'livier' image, though so relevant to Hardy's father, had its equivalent in that *Ode*: 'you must leave your land and home . . . a worthier heir will drink up your Caecuban wine and spill it on your floor . . .'[17]

When in 1890 Hardy 'dipped into . . . Lucian, "the Voltaire of Paganism"', he probably read the *Icaromenippus*, where Menippus flies up to heaven to interview Zeus, and the *Charon*, where Hermes and Charon survey human life from a great height, and find it very funny. In 'God-Forgotten', 'I towered far, and lo! I stood within / The presence of the Lord Most high, / Sent thither by the sons of earth, to win / Some answer to their cry.' Menippus found Zeus busy trying to answer contradictory prayers heard through a purpose-made hole in the floor. Hardy found God so busy dealing with 'voicings' from 'other orbs' that he had quite forgotten the earth, from which he no longer heard prayers. Charon was amused to see a man killed by a falling tile, just after accepting a dinner-invitation: 'It made me laugh, because I didn't see how he was going to keep his appointment.' In 'The King's Experiment', Doom was equally tickled by 'the comedy of things', the 'humour' of reversing Hodge's mood by killing off his fiancée. The mood-change theme doubtless came from Crabbe's 'Lover's Journey'; but the sadistic humour was Lucianic, and Charon and Hermes would soon reappear as the Spirits Sinister and Ironic of *The Dynasts*.[18]

In its verse, thought, and thematic coherence Hardy's second book of poems was much more interesting than his first. The aptness and variety of the verse-forms made nonsense of the charge that he lacked poetic technique. The lilting rhythms and internal rhymes, in 'The Going of the Battery' for instance, refuted the notion that he had no 'singing voice'. In 'The Respectable Burgher' the alleged 'proseman' had linked thirty-six lines on end with a single rhyme. Nor had he apparently found any difficulty with the triolet, a two-rhyme, eight-line verse-form 'in which the first line is repeated as the fourth and seventh, and the second as the eighth'. And such pieces showed more than technique. The Burgher's multiple rhymes with 'decl*are*' implied that all cherished beliefs were reduced by the Higher Criticism to much the same thing – hot air. In the triolets, the repeated lines were made to carry subtle changes of feeling, most powerfully in 'The Puzzled Game-Birds', where the words, 'They are not those who used to feed us', express (in that order) worried surprise, panic-stricken bewilderment, and incredulous horror.[19]

More ingenious examples of expressive prosody occurred in 'The Sick Battle-God':

> But new light spread. That god's gold nimb
> And blazon have waned dimmer and more dim;
> Even his flushed form begins to fade,
> Till but a shade is left of him.

The gradual reduction of stress on the rhyme-words 'nimb', 'dim', 'him' translated the visual effect into sound, while the parallel diminuendo from 'fade' to its internal rhyme, 'shade', suggested the dying echo of a loud noise. Elsewhere alliterative doublets ('heart and hand', 'rape and raid', 'rune and rhyme') recalled *Beowulf* as typifying a primitive view of war; and an intricate pattern of rhyme, alliteration and assonance simulated the complexity of influences leading to the contemporary view:

> That *m*odern *m*editation broke
> His *spe*ll, that *p*enmen's *p*leadings dea*l*t a *st*roke,
> Say So*m*e, and *so*me that *cri*mes too *d*ire
> *Di*d *m*uch to *m*ire his *cri*mson *c*loak.[20]

'The Battle-God is god no more.' Such demotion of divinity, in the transition from Past to Present, was a major feature of the volume's thought; nor was this the only 'deity of heretofore' presented as almost pathetic, for Hardy was replacing the suffering god of Christianity by suffering gods of agnosticism. Thus the 'Mother' of 'The Lacking Sense' suffered from a chronic sense of guilt, for 'unwittingly' creating a world 'whereat', in words borrowed from St Paul, 'all creation groans.' How seriously, one wonders, did Hardy take his new theology? Did it give him some kind of outlet for his obviously strong religious instinct? Sue Bridehead's neo-paganism makes that seem a possibility. Probably though, he was just trying out poetic images to convey his current thinking about life in general. He had lived long enough to know that 'wounding where one loves', like the 'Unfulfilled Intention', was an inevitable part of human experience; and such knowledge could best be symbolized by an anthropomorphic figure summing up human inadequacy: 'For thou art of her clay.'[21]

Poems of the Past and the Present lacked the visual charm of the illustrated *Wessex Poems*, but there were aesthetic compensations in the book's overall design. Opening with an obituary for Queen Victoria, which traced her 'purposed Life' to a fiat in 'backward Time', it closed with a 'Retrospect' of Hardy's own life and beliefs. Within this frame 'War Poems' dealt with the national Present, 'Poems of Pilgrimage' with the poet's and Europe's Past, and 'Imitations, etc.' with Past poetry. That inner frame enclosed the large central section of poems ostensibly 'Miscellaneous', but actually unified by shared or related themes. Thus all assumed the misery of life, but they explained it in different ways, and offered various suggestions for coping with it.[22]

The quasi-theological explanations have already been discussed. The methods of coping included deliberate self-deception. 'On a Fine Morning' prescribed as a source of 'Solace', not seeing facts and 'noting Life's conditions, but 'cleaving to the dream'. 'Song of Hope' sought solace that way. But 'The Well-Beloved' implied that 'the Dream' of love, at least, was essentially destructive. 'Thou lovest what thou dreamest her', Venus tells the lover, 'I am thy very dream' – and her effect is to make the human bride look 'pinched and thin'. 'The Dream-Follower' gave a similar warning, and in 'Her Reproach' the 'dream' of Fame was equally destructive of human love. As for the dream of religion, it led in 'The Church-Builder' to suicide. Yet that dream was attractive enough to be lovingly celebrated in the 'Mediaeval Legend' of 'The Lost Pyx', miraculously found encircled by kneeling animals.[23]

Here the animal theme had a special relevance to the religious one. In 'The Mother Mourns' human beings had lost their reverence for 'Nature' through developing beyond their animal origins. So religious belief became associated with an animal stage of development. The game-birds were puzzled by the sudden cruelty of their apparently kind keepers: 'For did we then cry, they would heed us'. The 'Bedridden Peasant' was equally puzzled to find that 'no cry can' catch the attention of his creator. As 'crumb-outcaster' Hardy himself played Providence to the 'Birds at Winter Nightfall', but failed to manifest himself when most needed. 'The Darkling Thrush' resembled a religious believer in cherishing against all the evidence 'some blessed Hope, whereof he knew / And I was unaware'. 'The Bullfinches', though surprised that 'the Mother' showed so little interest in them, still had hopes of an afterlife:

Come then, brethren, let us sing,
From the dawn till evening! –

> For we know not that we go not
> When the day's pale pinions fold
> Where those be that sang of old.'[24]

There was Sophoclean irony in the ambiguous expression: 'For we know not that we go not'. To the speakers it meant they had no reason to rule out such a possibility. To the sceptical reader, that their cheerful hymns showed their ignorance of the facts. Either way, not-knowing, whether as agnosticism or more generally as what I have called *agnosia*, was the theme that most held the volume together. The first poem emphasized that we could not yet know which 'deed' of Queen Victoria's would prove 'most bright in eyes to be'. The last was addressed to the 'Unknown God' of the Acts. 'Whom therefore ye ignorantly worship', Paul told the Athenians, 'him declare I unto you.' The god declared by Hardy was more ignorant than his worshippers: not just unknown, but 'labouring all-unknowingly'. And yet, like his own 'aged thrush', the poet had his 'Hope' – that the Almighty would eventually get to know what it was doing, and make things a bit better.[25]

Between those prefatory and concluding poems *agnosia* took too many forms to list them all here. But, besides the ignorance of the future inevitable in wartime, Drummer Hodge 'never knew' why 'Strange Stars' shone over 'his mound'; the Pauper Child insisted on making its 'ignorant entry' into the world; Shelley's Skylark 'knew not its immortality'; at Lodi 'not anybody / Seems to know' of the famous battle there; Hardy 'knew not' the 'earth-secrets' familiar to his insect-guests, nor 'the name or race . . . of man so commonplace' as his own past self; Lizbie Browne would never know his name either; the 'Dame of Athelhall' did not know that the husband she felt guilty to leave was anxious to get rid of her; the 'Last Chrysanthemum' did not know the right time to flower; and even in the comic 'Levelled Churchyard' each 'late-lamented' exclaimed, 'I know not which I am!'[26]

The most concentrated study of *agnosia*, and of the Past-Present theme, was 'The Self-Unseeing':

> Childlike, I danced in a dream;
> Blessings emblazoned that day;
> Everything glowed with a gleam;
> Yet we were looking away!

That present happiness is not known until it is past, would become after 1912 the keynote of Hardy's poetry. Meanwhile this poem's rich brevity foreshadowed the best of his later work. But his next production would be on a rather larger scale.[27]

22

The Dynasts Part First

Hardy was not feeling his best when he started writing his *magnum opus*. Overcome by 'physical inertness' in February 1902, he was still 'the reverse of vigorous' a year later, after being 'invalided by rheumatism', and 'troubled by neuralgia, which takes all poetry out of one.' He was also worried about royalties from past publications. 'All my investments have depreciated, and I am not going to write for money at my time of life.' But the take-over of his English publishers by Harpers, who then went bankrupt and reorganized under new management, had left him in the slightly precarious 'position of having only a subsidiary branch of an American house as [his] English publishers.' He felt he was 'getting old', and such publishing problems bored him, though he finally solved them by going back to his old publishers, Macmillan.[1]

Meanwhile the macrocosm looked even worse than his own little bit of it. The world-view of 'the Church', with its 'Theological lumber' and 'doctrines of the supernatural', seemed incredible. But the world revealed by science?

> The more we know of the laws & nature of the Universe, the more ghastly a business we perceive it all to be – & the non-necessity of it. As some philosopher [Hartmann] says, if nothing at all existed, it would be a completely natural thing; but that the world exists is a fact absolutely logicless & senseless.

Writing poetry in such a world seemed equally unnecessary. In May 1902 he told another poet: 'A growing sense that there is nobody to address, no public that knows, takes away my zest for production.' But about a month later he seems to have started describing that senseless world in a massive 'production' called *The Dynasts*. It 'grew up', he told Frederic Harrison, almost without my intending it.'[2]

It had been growing since his childhood, when his grandmother told him about the French Revolution, and how his grandfather had volunteered to fight against Napoleon. At eight he read an illustrated magazine-history of the war, at nine met some real soldiers at a harvest-supper, and around twenty-three heard Palmerston, who had been War Secretary during the Napoleonic war, speak in the House of Commons. In 1868 he outlined a poem on the Battle of the Nile, and perhaps first heard about Hartmann, whose *Philosophy of the Unconscious* appeared that year in German. In 1875 he talked to survivors of Waterloo at Chelsea Hospital, and thought of writing 'an Iliad of Europe from 1789 to 1815'. In 1876 (when Hartmann was being discussed in the *Westminster Review*) he 'explored the field of Waterloo', and again talked to Chelsea Pensioners who had fought there. In 1877 he told himself: 'Consider a grand drama, based on the wars with Napoleon'; and in 1879 he saw Napoleon's nephew, which helped him to imagine what 'Boney' had looked like.[3]

Having 'touched the fringe' of that 'vast international tragedy' in *The Trumpet-Major* (1880) and then retired to bed for many months, he 'projected as he lay', first a 'Great Modern Drama', then a 'Homeric Ballad, in which Napoleon is a sort of Achilles', and finally a new 'Mode' of 'historical Drama': 'Action mostly automatic, reflex movement, etc. Not the result of what is called *motive*, though always ostensibly so, even to the actor's own consciousness.' In 1882 he thought of handling the same idea in a different form: 'Write a history of human automatism, or impulsion'. Happily, he wrote that history as a drama; less happily, 'impulsion' lost its prefix in the curious language of the 'Fore Scene': 'You cannot swerve the pulsion of the Byss'.[4]

Around 1886 Hardy was still puzzling over 'the question of *The Dynasts*' at the British Museum, making notes from 'L'Homme Automate' and Coupland's translation of Hartmann (1884), and wondering how to dramatize the idea of automatism in a novel: 'Why not by rendering as visible essences, spectres, &c. the abstract thoughts of the analytic school?' He elaborated the notion in another note that day: 'The human race to be shown as one great network or tissue which quivers in every part when one point is shaken, like a spider's web if touched. Abstract realisms to be in the form of Spirits, Spectral figures, &c.' The 'spectres' would become the 'Phantom Intelligences' of *The Dynasts*, where the 'web', or 'Will-webs' of human destiny would be revealed by 'a penetrating light', 'exhibiting as one organism the anatomy of life and movement in all humanity and vitalized matter'.[5]

It was, Hardy thought, at Milan in 1887 that he 'conceived' the scene about Napoleon's coronation there, and that November he also conceived a luckily still-born plan to have Napoleon 'haunted by an Evil Genius or Familiar'. Next month he felt assured by Aristotle, Addison, and Coleridge that he need not try to make his long projected poem 'poetical all through.'

Some of its best bits would actually be in prose. A note of 1888 labelled God neuter: 'the Prime Cause would be ashamed and sorry if *it* knew'; and in 1890 'It' became ruler-designate of the poem's universe: 'View the Prime Cause or Invariable Antecedent as "It" and recount its doings.' Meanwhile in 1889, when the idea of staging a dramatized *Woodlanders*, even, seemed impossible, Hardy gave up any idea of writing his great drama for the theatre: 'I feel continually that I need a larger canvas . . . A spectral tone must be adopted . . . Royal ghosts . . . Title: "A Drama of Kings" '.[6]

In 1891 he thought of presenting his action as watched, if not yet from the Overworld, at least from above: 'A Bird's-Eye View of Europe at the beginning of the nineteenth century.' The Fore Scene would present a view of Europe 'disclosed' through the 'nether sky'; and 'A bird's-eye view of the sea' would introduce the battle of Trafalgar. In 1892 he again 'Considered methods for the Napoleon drama. Forces, emotions, tendencies. The characters do not act under the influence of reason'. While considering 'methods', he probably remembered seeing a 'Phantasmagoria', an 'exhibition of optical illusions produced . . . by a magic lantern', in which 'figures were made rapidly to increase and decrease in size, to advance and retreat, dissolve, vanish, and pass into each other.' Napoleon, on the surrender of the Austrian army, would seem 'Moved like a figure on a lantern slide' by the operator of a 'phantasmagoric show.'[7]

1895 brought a new dramatic medium to suggest other 'methods'. That December the first public film-show was put on by the Lumière brothers in Paris. In America Edison's film-strips (1893–6) had included a historical one, 'The Execution of Mary Queen of Scots'. From 1896 Georges Meliès was shooting films of conjuring tricks, and in 1902 made one about a trip to the moon. Then the 'School of Brighton' film-makers started experimenting with the effect of a moving camera. Hardy could have read or heard of these developments, when he visited Brighton (May 1896) and Paris (July 1897). As he sometimes went to London music halls, where short Brighton films where being shown from about 1898, he may well have seen one for himself. *Part First* would be full of cinematic tricks like zooming and panning. He may also have heard, perhaps when he dined with his surgeon friend Sir Henry Thompson in 1898, about the invention of X-rays (1895), the obvious model for the 'new and penetrating light' turned by the Spirit of the Years on the human 'organism'. After revisiting Waterloo in 1896, Hardy jotted down in Brussels possible characters for a drama in three five-act 'Parts', entitled 'Europe in Throes'; and 'about six years back' from 1903, i.e. 1897, he 'outlined' 'with fair completeness', the plan of *The Dynasts*. In 'the latter part' of 1902 he started writing it up.[8]

It was hard at first to get going. The work would take years to finish. Meanwhile he had neither the carrot of imminent publication nor the stick of a publisher's deadline. Emma was 'ailing' and increasingly unsympathetic, and he got no encouragement from friends because he kept the project largely to himself. As he told Clodd later, 'to be engaged in a

desultory way on a MS. which may be finished in 5 years . . . does not lead
one to say much about it.'[9]

His other activities at this time conspired to depress him. 'I have the
cheerful duty', he wrote to the same friend, 'at next Wedny's Assizes of
helping to find a true bill against two murderers.' He thought capital
punishment unrivalled as a deterrent, but apparently questioned 'the moral
right of a community to inflict' it. Revisiting Bath with Emma, where they
had been so happy together in 1873, he skidded and fell off his 'bran-new
free wheel bicycle' into some mud. Rubbed down with a sack by a 'kindly
coal-heaver', he looked so under-privileged that an equally kind shop-
keeper let him have an old book for sixpence. It was a first edition of
Hobbes's *Leviathan*, which told him that human life was 'solitary, poore,
nasty, brutish and short.'[10]

He pushed through his own solitary task to the end of Part First by
September 1903, and then decided to publish that much separately. As
he explained to Clodd, 'I had a sudden feeling that I should never carry
the thing any further, so off it went.' Besides weariness, he probably felt
a need for some feedback. To keep his options open, but not 'suggest
incompleteness too forcibly to the would-be purchaser', he got Macmillans
to put an ambiguous 'single star' on the book's spine, instead of 'Part
First'. Proof-reading was a lonelier job than usual, for Emma had gone off
to Calais 'for a change of air', leaving Hardy in charge of '4 cats'. Extrapolating from them to their larger relatives, he thought it 'unfortunate' that
'*our* race acquired the upper hand, and & not a more kindly one, in the
development of species. If, say, lions had, they wd have been less cruel by
this time.' After some delay caused by the American printers, *Part First* was
finally published in England on 13 January 1904.[11]

Hardy described its reception as generally 'invidious', often 'facetious'.
There were still the old complaints that he should have stuck to what he
was good at, prose, novels, and Wessex peasants. The *Times Literary Supplement* objected to the idea of a drama not meant for the theatre, an objec-
tion refuted by Hardy in 'A Rejoinder'. But several reviews were more
thoughtful and appreciative. In the *Saturday Review* Max Beerbohm made
fun of the the Nelson death-scene, comparing it to a peep-show at Brighton;
but he recognized the work as a 'noble' attempt at an 'impossible task',
a 'really great book', 'imperfect' but 'inevitably imperfect'. John Buchan
in the *Spectator* found fault with the 'misty philosophy and awkward rhythms',
yet at least acknowledged 'a certain epic grandeur in the conception'.
Hardy's initial disappointment at the reviews made him tell Gosse: 'It is
most unlikely that I shall carry the drama any further'. A week later he
admitted that the critics had been 'fairly respectful', and *The Dynasts* was
spared the advice given to the Unborn Pauper Child: 'cease silently'.[12]

The world of *The Dynasts* was created by an impersonal 'It', but much of
Hardy's personality went into the creation of *Part First*. While claiming
'tolerable fidelity to the facts' recorded in 'the abundant pages of the
historian, the biographer, and the journalist, English and Foreign', he

spiced European history with traces of his own life. In church as a child, he had started 'imagining that the vicar was preaching mockingly, and . . . trying to trace a humorous twitch in the corners of Mr S ——— 's mouth, as if he could hardly keep a serious countenance.' The Spirit Sinister says the same of the Archbishop who crowns Napoleon: 'Do not the prelate's accents falter thin, / His lips with inheld laughter grow deformed . . . ?' As a schoolboy Hardy was attracted by the sight of fighting cocks being 'let out into the street' from a Dorchester cellar. So Pitt's 'Great Alliance . . . claps a muffler round this Cock's steel spur . . .' The Stinsfield choir joined the cast as 'the zingers up in gallery' who told the young beacon-keeper that the world was round. Hardy's recent eye-trouble made King George's seem worth mentioning (with a Sophoclean hint of mental blindness too). Hardy's present home prompted a reference to 'the lantern at Max Turnpike'; and perhaps his five foot six and a half inches gave him extra empathy with his two short heroes, Nelson and Napoleon.[13]

In more important ways, history served as a vehicle for Hardy's personal feelings. His world-weariness was dramatized in the suicide of Villeneuve. His nostalgia for 'a local cult called Christianity', and his horror at the cruelty of life were voiced by the Spirit of the Pities, commenting on Napoleon's coronation, and Nelson's slow death. His feeling for animals as typical victims of cruelty came out in the cluster of bird-images round the slaughter at Trafalgar, culminating in the death of the man who 'in simplicity and sheer good faith' had shot Nelson: 'he fell / Like an old rook, smack from his perch, stone dead.'[14]

As an author of fiction and drama, Hardy was represented by the Spirit Sinister: 'Ay; begin small, and so lead up to the greater. It is a sound dramatic principle. I always aim to follow it in my pestilences, fires, famines, and other comedies.' In his general mode of creation, he was even the model for 'It'. All his books, he claimed in December 1902, had 'come to pass by chance . . . & I have often fancied that there is something automatic in the way . . . a story will insist upon shaping itself as its author did not originally wish or intend it to do.' Thus 'It' works unconsciously . . . eternal artistries in Circumstance', whose 'patterns' are 'wrought by rapt aesthetic rote'.[15]

Like *Jude, Part First* made satirical use of the Bible and Prayer Book. The Recording Angels sang their version of Hansard antiphonally, to stress by contrast their amoral attitude to history. The conversation between Jesus and the woman of Samaria was explicitly parodied when the Spirit of Rumour conversed with a Paris prostitute. In a travesty of the Incarnation four Phantom Intelligences, representing ineffectual pity, cold indifference, idle curiosity, and sadistic malice, decided to 'put on and suffer for the nonce / The feverish fleshings of Humanity'.[16]

Though epic in scope, and first conceived as an 'Iliad of Europe', the drama owed nothing to Homer but hints for its 'celestial machinery'. Homer's Olympian gods take sides in the Trojan War and have their human favourites, but are generally indifferent to human welfare. The Overworld 'Intelligences' are even more so. The Spirit of the Years is a scientific historian, voicing the 'passionless Insight of the Ages'. The Spirits Sinister and Ironic positively enjoy human suffering. The Spirit of Pities embodies, in Schlegel's phrase, 'the Universal Sympathy of human nature', but is quite powerless. Athene pulls Achilles' hair, and stops him murdering Agamemnon, but the Spirit of the Pities' whisper does not deter Napoleon. Zeus has his long-term 'plan', but 'Its designs' seem merely pattern-making. Still, the Overworld resembles Olympus in its use of Iris-like 'Spirit-Messengers', and of human disguises – though the chief disguised messenger, 'The Spirit of Rumour', came from Virgil, not Homer. Disguised as a 'Personage of Fashion' he spread the news of Napoleon's coronation, just as Virgil's 'foul goddess' *Fama* publicized Dido's affair with Aeneas.[17]

Sophocles, Plato, and Lucian also contributed. 'Not to be born is best' was paraphrased by the Shade of the Earth, and the Spirit of the Pities praised the protest in the *Trachiniae* against divine injustice (*agnomosune*, a form of not-knowing) which Hardy had once thought of turning into a lyric. Plato's cave simile, where only 'shadows' of the real 'Ideas' were visible to mortals, evidently suggested Hardy's note of 1886: 'The Realities to be the true realities of life, hitherto called abstractions. The old material realities to be placed behind the former, as shadowy accessories.' Such was the relationship between the Overworld and the human one. Lucian's *Charon* saw human beings hanging on threads spun by the Fates: The Spirit of the Pities saw them similarly controlled by 'retracting threads like gossamers'.[18]

Of English poets, Blake, Shelley and Newman probably did most for the drama. Blake's *French Revolution* pictured Europe, France, and its 'mountains' as 'Sick, sick', with a symbolic glimpse of a starved man lying in chains, 'his strong bones scarce cover'd with sinews'. *The First Book of Urizen* showed another 'inchain'd' figure: 'a vast Spine writh'd in torment / Upon the winds, shooting pain'd / Ribs...' Hardy's Europe 'was disclosed as a prone and emaciated figure, the Alps shaping like a backbone, and the branching mountain-chains like ribs...' Shelley's *Prometheus Unbound* was cited by Hardy as a precedent for an 'unactable', 'panoramic' drama 'intended for the study only'. Its 'Spirit of the Earth', combined with Earth's speech about 'The shadows of all forms that think and live', doubtless suggested Hardy's character, 'The Shade of the Earth', and its Demogorgon partly anticipated the conception of 'It': 'I see a mighty darkness / Filling the seat of power... Ungazed upon and shapeless; neither limb, / Nor form, nor outline'. Newman's *Dream of Gerontius*, another study-drama, probably inherited its mocking 'Demons' from the 'fiends' that tortured Prometheus, and then passed on their genes to the 'Spirits Ironic and Sinister'.[19]

Newman's sermon on 'Explicit and Implicit Reason' (1840) had first introduced the Victorians to the idea of unconscious thought; and Matthew Arnold's 'The Buried Life' (1852) adapted the concept for poetry. But the main source for such notions in *The Dynasts* was Hartmann's *Philosophy of the Unconscious*. Having shown evidence of 'unconscious ideas and unconscious will' in physiology, and in animal and human psychology, Hartmann described 'the principle of the Unconscious' as the '*nucleus*' round which the 'world *crystallises*', the *all-unity*' which 'embraces the Cosmos', and the 'core of all great philosophies, the Substance of Spinoza, the Absolute Ego of Fichte, Schelling's Absolute Subject-Object, the Absolute Idea of Plato and Hegel, Schopenhauer's Will, &c.' As such it replaced the '*Providence*' of Christianity, and the 'God of Theism'.[20]

Impersonal, amoral, and unconscious, this 'immanent God' 'in one's own breast' was unaffected by prayer, but directed human destiny with 'absolute wisdom' by a kind of unerring 'instinct'. It was 'at once unconscious and *super*-conscious': an 'unconscious clairvoyant intelligence', 'all-knowing and all-wise', 'which teleologically determined the *content* of creation and the world-process.' In history it operated by 'implanting an instinctive impulse in the masses' and producing 'men of genius as finger-posts and pioneers'. But neither the masses nor the men of genius understood the real object of their actions. Thus wars of conquest like those of Alexander, Caesar, and Napoleon left 'fields strewed with the corpses of . . . heroes duped by the Unconscious', but their purpose and result was 'a fertile marriage of different national civilisations'. Indeed, this supremely '*rational intelligence*' had created, in Leibniz's phrase, 'the best of all possible worlds'.[21]

But the operative word was 'possible'. Life in this world was not worth living. No sensible person would choose, at death, to go all through his life again; for as 'the greatest minds of all ages' had realized, happiness was an illusion, pain was inevitable, and 'non-being' preferable to 'being'. Most people, though, were still unconscious of this; so the 'only possible goal of the world-process' was for all mankind to become fully conscious, and for their consciousness to be '*penetrated* by the folly of volition [i.e. the will to live] and the misery of existence'. Then the 'negative part of volition in humanity', the human death-wish, would 'outweigh' and 'annihilate' the positive volition 'objectifying itself in the organic and inorganic world', 'and cause the whole kosmos to disappear at a stroke, by withdrawal of the volition, which alone gives it existence.'[22]

Hardy had too much humour to take his German namesake literally; but Hartmann's pessimism and concern with the unconscious were congenial, and his ontology was at least more in line with modern thought than Homer's. Yet in devising 'celestial machinery' to fit *The Philosophy of the Unconscious*, Hardy had been faced by formidable problems: how to present a 'Prime Mover' who, instead of going to sleep on only one important occasion, like Homer's Zeus, was never really awake; how to get dramatic conflict, when there was nobody to oppose the 'All-One'; how to give human interest to an impersonal Overworld; how to replace the comedy of the bickerings on Homer's Olympus; and how to find a distinctive language for Overworlders to speak.[23]

The problems had been tackled resourcefully, if not wholly solved. 'It' became a baffling off-stage presence, felt only through the comments of allegorical Phantoms. Conflict and comedy were reserved for the human plane, the former found chiefly in the war itself, the latter in Wessex reactions to it. The human interest of the 'machinery' was mainly supplied by the Spirit of the Pities' illogical resistance to the realism, sadism, or aesthetic detachment expressed by other Intelligences. The Overworld language was made preternaturally stiff, abstract, and opaque. Hardy admitted to Gosse that, 'owing perhaps to the evil example set by scientists & philosophers', the Spirits seemed 'to prefer words from the Greek to simpler ones', and he was 'appalled at some of the oversights in this direction.' Thus the first page confronted the reader with 'Byss' (from the Greek for the 'bottom of the sea') a technical term used by the mystical philosopher Boehme for 'the Being of all Beings'. But the alien diction contrasted strikingly with that of the Wessex stage-coach passengers, thus pointing the difference between the Overworldly and the worldly view of things, a difference underlined by the stage-direction: 'Their voices after the foregoing sound small and commonplace, as from another medium.'[24]

Such stage-directions were essential to the drama, and among its greatest attractions. They marked constant shifts of perspective, between the superhuman and the human angle, as here, but also between aerial and ground-level views, between distant views and close-ups, between geographical, national, or class viewpoints. Thus Hardy expressed his adaptation of Hartmann's philosophy, while solving, by shots of key incidents in the war, the basic problem of dramatizing a ten-year period of European history. Cinematic as this technique now seems, it was also theatrical. Mist, rain, smoke, or nightfall were explicitly used as curtains; and action-components too extensive to be dramatized in detail were often presented in 'DUMB SHOW' – a stage convention which also served to dwarf human activity against the cosmic backdrop.

Described on the title-page as *Part First* of a '*Drama*', the book was also a kind of epic poem, which Hardy hoped would be found 'as readable as a novel'. Dramatically, it succeeds most in the Trafalgar battle-scenes. Poetically, it achieves more by its imaginative scope than by its versification. The blank verse spoken by epic heroes like Napoleon, Nelson, Pitt, and Villeneuve, and by 'upper coteries' of society ('humblest hearts' speak in livelier prose) is fluent but rather monotonous. There is much prosodic invention in the lyrics, as in the almost unrhymed dactylic stanzas used by the Recording Angels; and some pleasant patterning of consonants and vowels where Nelson's corpse

> may be sodden: churned in Biscay swirls;
> Or blown to polar bears by boreal gales;
> Or sleeping amorously in some calm cave
> On the Canaries' or Atlantis' shore
> Upon the bosom of his Dido dear . . .

But these are just frills on the surface of a grandly austere conception. The prose of the stage-directions carries much of the work's poetry, and is indeed 'as readable as a novel'.[25]

23

The Dynasts Part Second

September 1904 found Hardy 'doing the battle of Jena', but work on *Part Second* was slowed down by 'distractions of a more or less sombre kind'. These included the deaths of three old friends, Horace Moule's brother Henry, Leslie Stephen (to whose biography Hardy contributed), and Mary Jeune's husband Francis; of Emma's brother Walter, of her uncle, who had married them in 1874, and of Snowdove, one more cat killed on the railway line. Hardy borrowed a special chisel from a sculptor friend to engrave a tombstone for her. But the most traumatic loss was the death of his mother at ninety (3 April 1904), leaving a 'gap ... wide, & not to be filled.' The best he could say of it in a poem was: 'Our well-beloved is prisoner in the cell / Of Time no more ... she has escaped the Wrongers all'. One of the 'wretches in the cellar' near Astorga would say much the same of the woman who died in his arms: 'my doxy is the only one of us who is safe and sound!'[1]

Commenting on photographs of his mother's portrait, Hardy added: 'My own [photographs] have rather a new expression, which I have not quite grown accustomed to, but no doubt it is there.' It expressed not merely grief, but anger at the human situation. This new mood, which would prompt the horrific war-reporting of *Part Second*, was like Swift's '*saeva indignatio*'. Condemning the 'barbarism' of 'sports that consist in the pleasure of watching a fellow-creature in its struggles to escape the death-agony', he made his own Modest Proposal:

> In the present state of affairs there would appear to be no reason why the children, say, of overcrowded families should not be used for sporting purposes. There would be no difference in principle: moreover these children would often escape lives intrinsically less happy than those of wild birds & animals.[2]

Children were much in his mind just then. Of the 'gap' left by his mother he wrote: 'I suppose if one had a family of children one would be less sensible of it.' In that case, he probably thought, relations with Emma might have been better too. Congratulating a young actress on the birth of a child in January 1904, he remarked: 'We here are interested in babies – I suppose because we have none!' Since his brother and sisters were unmarried, this meant that his death would extinguish the Bockhampton line of Hardys, a thought that clearly depressed him. In *Part Second* a similar 'worm' would be shown 'gnawing' Napoleon: Josephine's failure to produce a baby, and the 'the question of my dynasty'.[3]

Though here *The Dynasts* gave scope for empathy, the second instalment by no means wrote itself. It must have been hard to forget the poor reviews and sales of the first. 'I published it', he told Arthur Symons in June 1904, 'with much misgiving, & . . . I am not sure I shall carry the work any further, though I am hunting up a few records, &c., *as if* I meant to finish it.' But perhaps what made writing most difficult was a general sense, expressed in the 1904 poem, 'Shut Out that Moon', that the romance of life was over, leaving nothing but dreariness: 'Let dingy details crudely loom, 'Mechanic speech be wrought . . .' With Emma, especially, love had failed to prove 'All it was said to be'; and with Mrs Henniker, too, his 'fancy' that she was in Ireland made him think sadly of his first feelings towards her: 'Your being over there will remind me of old times – very romantic ones – when I was younger than I am now'. Such nostalgia for earlier loves was debunked in 'The Revisitation', a poem 'romantic in its particulars', but 'of general application to life'. There the blissful return of a beloved ended in bathos, with her loss of looks, and the lover's loss of drive: 'Love is lame at fifty years.'[4]

Even war had lost its old 'enthusiasm and romance'. To recapture them one had to visit the Queen's Hall and hear that 'impetuous march-piece' in Tchaikovsky's 'Pathetic Symphony . . . the only music he knew that was able to make him feel exactly as if he were in a battle.' Otherwise you had to make do with cycling to Glastonbury, 'and spending a romantic day or two there among the ruins'; or better still, with being given 'the honorary degree of LL.D.' at Aberdeen University (April 1905), an experience 'of a most pleasant and unexpected kind', which 'remained with him like a romantic dream.' When a more stimulating type of romance first presented itself in August 1905, it went unrecognized: asked for an interview by an unknown journalist called Florence Dugdale, he replied guardedly: 'Dear Madam, As you are not going to print anything about your visit, I shall be happy to be at home to you some afternoon during this month . . .' When she actually came is unknown. But on 'Jan 2 1906' he wrote thanking her for a 'box of sweet flowers' she had sent him, adding: 'I do not think you stayed at all too long, & hope you will come again some other time.'[5]

Meanwhile (28 September 1905) he had finished *Part Second*. 'Would it were the Third!' he told Frederick Macmillan, when sending off the manuscript. He felt 'pumped dry', for he had done it largely by will-power. 'I fear I must go on with the Dynasts', he had told an editor in April, 'if I am ever going to finish it.' In July he was warned by his publishers that 'the next part of The Dynasts ought to be ready, or the first part will be forgotten'; and he wanted anyway to cash in on the publicity for the Napoleonic wars created by the Nelson centenary of 1905. That month he must have been encouraged to defy the critics by 'a long chat' with a 'cheerful and boyish' Swinburne', who quoted a dour newspaper comment on the Aberdeen doctorate: 'Swinburne planted, & Hardy watered, & Satan giveth the increase.'[6]

With the book off his hands, Hardy became almost cheerful too. It was a 'mistake', he told Gosse in November, to think pessimists 'incurably melancholy . . . The very fact of their having touched bottom gives them a substantial cheerfulness in the consciousness that they have nothing to lose.' But he was soon 'oppressed' by the 'practical gloom' of proof-reading: 'I know it will be abused right & left, both for badnesses which deserve severity, & undeservedly [because] the author's views are not palateable to the smug & conventional.' One such view, in a Christmas-cardy letter' to Mrs Henniker, challenged the tradition 'of killing a host of harmless animals to eat gluttonously of . . . by way of upholding the truth of Christianity.' However, he managed to have what he called 'a nice dull' Christmas with Emma; and though Macmillans were not too keen to risk a repetition of *Part First*'s commercial failure, they bravely brought out *Part Second* on 9 February 1906.[7]

Both publisher's and author's fears proved, in Clough's phrase, liars. 'I cannot complain of the reviews of this Second Part', wrote Hardy in March, 'though some of them were rough enough on the first. I suppose, like Disraeli, I am educating my party.' The critics' swing from contempt to congratulation was one more case of *agnosia*: 'The business of *knowing* is mostly carried on in the papers by those who don't know – and for the matter of that, everywhere.' The thought encouraged him to ignore outside opinion. 'I do not myself know at all how it looks to other people', he told Arthur Symons, 'or what it is worth. I shall simply go on with it & finish it now, if I can.'[8]

Like the first, the second instalment of *The Dynasts* owed something to Hardy's history as well as Europe's. 'Dead! Stop a minute: he's alive enough, sure!' Jemima's 'monthly nurse' had 'exclaimed to the surgeon'. 'Doctor, the child's alive!' cried 'Skilled Madame Blaise the nurse' about Napoleon's precious heir, who proved like Hardy 'a feeble brat from the first.' The tactual memory of the starved fieldfare in Hardy's hand was used to suggest George III's feeling for his dead daughter: 'He has quite often named / The late Princess, as gently as a child / A little bird found starved.' The Second Deserter's longing to be 'a-leaning against old Bristol Bridge' recalled Hardy's homesickness for Dorchester (he had celebrated New Year's Eve 1904 'quite alone on a bridge'), and his remark three months earlier that war had lost its 'romance' was echoed by the Ironic Spirit's comment on the misery in the cellar: 'Quaint poesy, and real romance of war!'[9]

But the most obviously personal element in his version of history was the emphasis on animal suffering, chiefly of horses and birds, to epitomize the world's cruelty. The battle of Vimiero began with the 'shrieks of horses'. Between Benavente and Astorga the French 'counted eighteen hundred odd' horses 'pistoled' or left dying by the retreating English and Spanish; and the 'dreadful' story of the man '*compelled* to drive his horse to death' in the Boer War developed into the picture of the 'rearmost' Englishman 'bestriding a shoeless foundered creature whose neck is vertebrae and mane only. While passing it falls from exhaustion.' Birds were used symbolically. Before Albuera 'The birds in the wood, unaware that this day is to be different from every other day they have known, are heard singing their overtures with their usual serenity.' The 'girlish' Maria Louisa, on the point of being sacrificed by her father to appease Napoleon, reports the sudden disappearance of 'five poor little birds . . . I sought a trace / Of scattered feathers, which I dread to find!'[10]

How far, one may ask, did Hardy identify with Napoleon in his ruthless treatment of Josephine? Perhaps, in terms of 'Confession to a Friend in Trouble', Napoleon served as a 'lawless figure' to exorcize an 'unseemly instinct', by acting it out in imagination. Even if the thought of replacing Emma by a more fertile wife never crossed Hardy's conscious mind, he may at some level have blamed her for their childlessness, and he evidently showed no lack of interest in potential Maria Louisas. But Napoleon's coarse inhumanity ('My friend, you are forty-three / This very year in the world') was probably accentuated in the play by Hardy's own 'staunchness' towards Emma; and what Josephine said to Napoleon in this context was doubtless what Hardy had often told himself, when trying to accept his childlessness:

> Will you not purge your soul to value best
> That high heredity from brain to brain
> Which supersedes mere sequences of blood![11]

To this *Part* literature and the Bible contributed rather less than usual with Hardy. The Queen of Prussia had 'gone through an Iliad of woes', but there was only a vague resemblance between her situation and Hecuba's, or between the 'fluttering group of ladies' reading war-bulletins from a window in Berlin, and the women who watched the fighting from the walls of Troy. Yet in calling Napoleon and his brother Joseph '*par nobile fratrum!* (a famous pair of brothers)' for 'Cutting up Europe like a plum-pudding', Hardy doubtless remembered how Horace's 'twins in wickedness and folly . . . breakfasted on nightingales'. Napoleon himself was allowed to borrow an image from Browning. Having fallen out of love, the speaker of 'Two in the Campagna' asks his ex-beloved: 'Must I go / Still like the thistle-ball, no bar, / Onward, whenever light winds blow . . . ?' Dismissing Josephine, Napoleon explains: 'We are but thistle-globes on Heaven's high gales, / And whither blown, or when, or how, or why, / Can choose us not at all!'[12]

The Bible figured most dramatically when the Spirit of the Years gatecrashed the Prince Regent's party, 'like the gentleman with the Hand at Belshazzar's Feast', to predict that within five years 'the rawest Dynast of the group concerned' would 'down-topple to the dust like soldier Saul'. The *Dynasts* of the title, incidentally, came from Hardy's Greek Testament, not, as one might guess, from Aeschylus' *Agamemnon*: 'I was thinking', he wrote, 'rather of where the word *dunastas* occurs in the *Magnificat* – "He hath cast down the dynasts from their thrones" . . . in our translation, "the mighty from their seat"'.[13]

But neither past literature nor the Bible affected *Part Second* so obviously as Hartmann's *Philosophy*. In a chapter on 'The Unconscious in History', Hartmann had stated that 'a particular phase of the IDEA is actualised in a certain period', e.g. in 'the European revolutions evoked by Napoleon', by 'implanting an instinctive impulse in the masses', and by producing an individual 'genius' to serve as 'finger-post and pioneer'. The first point was illustrated by the war-fever in 'The Streets of Berlin', on which the Spirit of the Years commented: 'So doth the Will objectify itself / In likeness of a sturdy people's wrath . . . Uncertainly, by fits, the Will doth work / In Brunswick's blood, their chief, as in themselves'. As for the pioneering genius, Napoleon told the Prussian Queen: 'Some force within me, baffling mine intent, / Harries me onward, whether I will or no . . . It is unswervable!' The last word (which I am tempted to derive from Hardy's early problems on his bicycle) recalled the opening of *The Dynasts*: 'You cannot swerve the pulsion of the Byss'. Hartmann's mass-instinct was illustrated again by the 'swelling zeal for war' in the café in Vienna, and his 'finger-post' image possibly led, by lateral thinking, to another image for 'The mutative, unmotived, dominant Thing': 'So the Will . . . moulds the times, / With mortals for Its fingers!'[14]

But Hardy had not swallowed Hartmann's philosophy whole. He had just used it for his own purposes. 'It suggested to me', he told William Archer, 'what seems almost like a workable theory of the great problem of the origin of evil – though this, of course, is not Hartmann's own theory – namely, that there may be a consciousness, infinitely far off, at the other end of the chain of phenomena, always striving to express itself, and always baffled and blundering . . .' That notion was certainly not Hartmann's. Far from baffled or blundering, his Unconscious was a 'supremely rational intelligence', 'clairvoyant', 'all-knowing and all-wise', which had produced, by infallible 'instinct', the 'best of all possible worlds'.[15]

In 1914 Hardy would claim that his 'view of the unconscious force as gradually *becoming* conscious: i.e. that consciousness is creeping further and further back towards the origin of force, had never (so far as I know) been advanced before *The Dynasts* appeared.' That claim may seem surprising, since Hartmann explicitly predicted the 'outweighing' of the world's unconsciousness by the developed consciousness of humanity. But again Hardy's 'view' was not Hartmann's. To Hartmann the 'goal of the world-process' was for humanity to realize consciously the 'misery of existence', and so annihilate the 'kosmos'. Hardy's 'meliorism' toyed, however irrationally, with the fantasy that the creative force Itself grew conscious, and learnt to improve the kosmos. Such was the implication of the Part's final chorus:

> Yet It may wake and understand
> Ere Earth unshape, know all things and
> With knowledge use a painless hand,
>   A painless hand![16]

Historically, *Part Second* continued the story of the Napoleonic wars from 1805 to 1811, largely concentrating on the struggle in Spain. It also illustrated the central theme of *The Dynasts*, partly by Napoleon's efforts to produce an heir to his dynasty, but more generally by the contrast between the essential triviality of dynastic ambition, and the amount of human misery it caused. Thus before the battle of Albuera, in which a quarter of the 'victorious' allied forces were killed, the Spirit of the Pities saw 'men – unnatured and mechanic-drawn – / Mixt nationalities in row and row, / Wheeling them to and fro / In moves dissociate from their souls' demand, / For dynasts' ends that few even understand!'[17]

So the horrors of dynastic wars were constantly emphasized. Sir John Moore's shoulder was 'knocked to a bag of splinters' by a canon-ball. After a 'frightful massacre' Ebersberg was burnt down, 'vast heaps of dead and wounded being consumed, / So that the streets stink strong with frizzled flesh.' At Albuera, where the combatants fire 'grape and canister at speaking distance', and discharge 'musketry in each other's faces', 'Hot corpses . . . accumulate on the slopes', amid a litter of 'knapsacks, firelocks, hats, stocks . . . red and blue rags of clothing, gaiters, epaulettes, limbs and viscera.' Nor are such horrors confined to the battlefield. Threatened by her obstetrician with what even Napoleon calls 'those cursed sugar-tongs', Marie Louise screams, 'Why should I be tortured even if I am but a means to an end!' And one of the dynasts themselves, George III, is similarly tortured by his medical advisers. Constant bleeding, enforced by a strait-jacket, fails to satisfy the Apothecary: 'You should take twenty ounces, doctor, if a drop – indeed go on bleeding till he's unconscious . . . And the watering-pot would do good again – not less than six feet above his head.'[18]

Examples like these of cruelty caused by 'The mutative, unmotived, dominant Thing' in charge of the universe hardly make enjoyable reading, but there are compensations elsewhere in *Part Second*. For those hoping to 'find the drama as readable as a novel' there is the 'sensational' opening scene of the mysterious 'foreigner' who offers to assassinate Napoleon, and the pleasant melodrama of the English spies at the summit meeting between Napoleon and Alexander I: 'Somebody must ride like hell to let our Cabinet know!' There is light comedy when the womanizing Godoy systematically saves his mistresses from an angry mob, and is then saved himself by his ill-used wife. 'You have saved your real wives', she tells him. 'What can it matter what happens to your titular one?' There is also a lyric on Napoleon's wedding, sung by Ironic Spirits in the style of a Savoy Opera:

> She'll bring him a baby,
> As quickly as maybe,
> And that's what he wants her to do,
> Hoo-hoo!
> And that's what he wants her to do![19]

But most of the humour is more grimly satirical. 'Providence', says Napoleon, 'has flung my good friend Sultan Selim from his throne, / Leaving me free' – to carve up the Turkish Empire. Having forced Josephine to accept a divorce, he warns her: 'You are a willing party – do you hear?' The soldiers conscripted to kill one another at Talavera drink from the same stream, and 'grasp hands across the rill'. Marie Louise mistakes her fiancé for a highwayman – which in effect he is. Dying in iatrogenic agony, George III is informed that he has 'won a battle'. Told that his father is dead, the Prince Regent exclaims: 'Dead? Then my fête is spoilt, by God!'[20]

Despite the pungency of such local effects, the pleasure of reading *Part Second* is slightly spoilt by the oddness of the diction. This ranges disconcertingly from the flat colloquial ('Ha-ha! It never rains unless it pours') to the grandiose obscure:

> Tiptoed Assassination haunting round
> In unthought thoroughfares, the near success
> Of Staps the madman, argue to forbid
> The riskful blood of my previsioned line
> And potence for dynastic empery
> To linger vialled in my veins alone.

Here Napoleon's inflated language was possibly meant to emphasize his lapse from a democrat into a dynast; but sometimes the wording of the blank-verse dialogue seems merely careless, as in the Empress-Mother's protest against Napoleon's jilting of Alexander's sister: 'But I do feel a rare belittlement / And loud laconic brow-beating therein!'[21]

The blank verse itself was fluent enough to keep the drama moving, but prosodic invention was confined to the lyrical forms employed by various Spirits – the iambic-anapaestic triplets used by the Ironic ones, the octameter stanzas in the same rhythm, where the Years and Pities comment on the Tilsit summit, the use of 'Albuera' as a refrain (much as Tennyson used 'Oriana') for the Pities' lament over that battle, the Sapphic stanza in which they described the first night at Talavera:

> Worn-out lines lie down where they late stood staunchly –
> Cloaks around them rolled – by the bivouac embers:
> There at dawn to stake in the dynasts' death-game
> 　　All, till the ending!

The last metre, associated with Sappho's love poems, seems surprising in the context. Perhaps it was meant to recall the second of Horace's *Odes*, also in Sapphics, which called on the latest dynast, Caesar Octavian, to end the bloodshed of 'battles which thinned out the youth' of the next generation.[22]

But the most striking effects of *Part Second* were not in verse, but in prose. Notable among them were those produced by movements in various planes of the dramatic eye. At night, from 'on high over the Straits of Dover', the diplomatic exchanges between England and France are seen as 'couriers shooting shuttlewise' between one 'little swarm of lights surrounded by a halo' and another. As the English forces head for Spain, 'from high aloft, in . . . July weather, the vision sweeps over the ocean and its coastlines from Cork Harbour on the extreme left, to Mondego Bay, Portugal, on the extreme right', with 'Four groups of moth-like transport and war ships . . . silently skimming this wide liquid plain.' The fortifications at Torrès Védras are seen being built by 'innumerable human figures . . . busying themselves like cheese-mites', and the English army arrives as 'three reddish-grey streams of marching men', whose motion looks 'peristaltic and vermicular, like that of three caterpillars.'[23]

Such perspectives vividly enforced the sense of human insignificance against the impersonal forces controlling human behaviour. Other stage-directions showed history almost as a kind of nightmare. Thus the Walcheren disaster was pictured surrealistically:

> The horizontal rays from the west lie in yellow sheaves across the vapours that the day's heat has drawn from the sweating soil. Sour grasses grow in places, and strange fishy smells, now warm, now cold, pass along. Brass-hued and opalescent bubbles, compounded of many gases, rise where passing feet have trodden the damper spots.

Against that background appeared 'skeletoned' soldiers on parade, 'some flushed, some shivering . . . kept moving because it it is dangerous to stay still. Every now and then one falls down, and is carried away to a hospital with no roof . . . In the distance soldiers are digging graves' for funerals delayed until after dark, 'that the sight of so many may not drive the living melancholy-mad.' Napoleon's switch of matrimonial alliance from Russia to Austria was similarly marked by a dance recalling the dance of death in Tennyson's 'Vision of Sin':

> The maskers surge into the foreground of the scene, and their motions become more and more fantastic. A strange gloom begins and intensifies, until only the high lights of their grinning figures are visible. These also, with the whole ball-room, gradually darken, and the music softens to silence.[24]

'Death is king, and Vivat Rex! / Tread a measure on the stones, / Madam – if I know your sex, / From the fashion of your bones.' Thus Tennyson's 'gray and gap-toothed man as lean as death' reduced sexual love, with all other positives in human life, to matter for sour ridicule. Nor did God's final 'rose of dawn' give a satisfactory answer to the question: 'Is there any hope?' *Part Second* ends with an equally vague and unhelpful suggestion from the Chorus of the Pities that 'It may wake and understand' how to make things a bit better. So for all the brilliance shown in the execution of Hardy's vast project, the reader is left with a largely negative impression.[25]

That is not just to say that the work is depressing. The real problem is inherent in its philosophy. Drama, like fiction, needs to make its characters seem important and interesting. But where, for instance, a general exodus from Vienna looks like 'a file of ants crawling along a strip of garden-matting', a 'puny concatenation of specks'; where the main character, Napoleon, is a mere dupe of the Unconscious, no member of the huge cast is likely to make much impact on the reader's imagination. Searching *Part Second* for anyone nearly as memorable as Tess or the Mayor, the nearest I can find is poor Josephine with her bleak axiom, so reminiscent of Jemima: 'Yet all joy is but sorrow waived awhile.'[26]

24

The Dynasts Part Third

'I hope you will come again some other time', wrote Hardy in January 1906 to the young journalist, Florence Dugdale. About three years later, in 'After the Visit', he invited her rather more warmly to 'Come again', with her 'large luminous living eyes', into the 'dark corridors' of his home. Meanwhile, as he told Gosse in November 1907, he had been 'mentally travelling in regions of inspissated gloom'. But by then those eyes had done something to lighten his darkness, and help him to finish *The Dynasts*.[1]

This second Florence in Hardy's life (who, true to her name, had just sent him 'a box of sweet flowers') was the daughter of a church school headmaster at Enfield. Born there on 12 January 1879, she had left school at fifteen, and after two years as a pupil teacher of girls, and four years' probationary teaching of boys, had passed her qualifying examination in 1906, with special credit in English Literature. Literature was her passion; but teaching in an overcrowded National School was hardly an ideal job for her, as she was always getting colds, flu, or laryngitis. So she soon started trying to become a 'literary woman' instead, by reading a paper on Tennyson's king Arthur to the Enfield Literary Union (1901). Helped by an impoverished and tubercular freelance writer called Alfred Hyatt ('the only person', she thought later, 'who ever loved me'), she had recently begun to contribute pieces for children to the *Enfield Observer*. Thus Hyatt had initiated her into the techniques of journalism and literary research; and it was probably his plan to edit a Hardy anthology that prompted her to ask Hardy for an interview in August 1905.[2]

The gloom into which this luminous young creature penetrated (at nearly 27 to Hardy's 65) was 'inspissated' by several factors. 'I want to get on with the third part', he told Mrs Henniker just before Christmas 1905, 'but I feel rather gloomy about it, and indeed about most things; and do little.' Writer's block was exacerbated by general ill-health. Flu 'in its most violent form' was followed by 'a cold which has settled in my face in the form of neuralgia, or rheumatism, or whatever may be the scientific name for a ceaseless ache about jaws. teeth, &c'. That kept him 'prisoner for a week', with a 'woollen comforter' wound round his head, 'which adds considerably to my appearance.' Other features of his appearance noted by Blanche, who painted his portrait in June 1906, were 'a gouty hand, white, puffy and limp . . . hollow cheeks . . . drooping moustaches' and a 'corpse-like green' complexion.[3]

In London that summer he felt 'limp with the heat & the people & the noise', 'too limp for any kind of writing'. The next spring found him still 'feeling dreadfully tired & disinclined to do anything.' Emma had been ill too, and in May 1906 had a 'strange fainting fit' while gardening at Max Gate: 'My heart seemed to stop', she confided to her diary – but not, it seems, to her husband. They had long ceased to confide in one another, and her submerged resentment occasionally surfaced in criticisms hardly muted by the presence of other people. He responded privately with thoughts of past romance. Reminding Agnes Grove of their moonlight dance together, he confessed 'a strong temptation to grow "romantical"' though 'long past all such sentiments'. He felt 'quite romantical', too, about his 'best illustrator', Helen Paterson. But for 'a stupid blunder of God Almighty', he told Gosse that July, he would have married Helen instead of Emma in 1874.[4]

Feeling like that about his marriage, he was ungratefully sarcastic about a 'handsome invitation' from the Pittsburgh Institute to attend an opening ceremony, 'with wife or daughter, free of expense to us'; and 'romantical' sentiments doubtless increased his haste to enrol Florence Dugdale as his latest literary protegée. He wrote references for her to Macmillans and the *Daily Mail*, helped her to make one of her short stories publishable, and used his influence to get it accepted by the *Cornhill Magazine*. But it would be wrong to vulgarize his motives. In a poem written soon afterwards he saw her as 'A wee white spot of muslin fluff' disappearing down a 'Departure Platform'; but he was not just looking for a bit of fluff. Florence had a real if minor talent for writing, with much courage and determination. She was trying to do what Hardy himself had found so difficult: to leap, across the barriers of poverty and inadequate education, from a safe profession into the risky trade of authorship. Temperamentally pessimistic, her experience of clergymen in church schools had turned her into an agnostic. She also had two grandparents who came from Dorset. All these things made Hardy keen to encourage her.[5]

As for Florence, she genuinely admired Hardy's writing; and if she wanted his help to further her literary ambitions, she wanted to help him, too. She got a Reader's Ticket at the British Museum (December 1906), and was soon acting as his research assistant there. In April 1907 Hardy thanked her for 'going so carefully through the files of The Times', and asked her to meet him 'by the Trajan column' at the South Kensington Museum.

The closer relationship that developed from such meetings supplied the stimulus he needed to finish *Part Third*; but the pleasure of Florence's company was probably reduced by frustration and guilt. His advanced views on marriage in the abstract seem to have given him little sense of freedom in his own. Though increasingly fed up with Emma, he still felt loyal to her.[6]

Meanwhile his despair of things in general was confirmed and focused by thoughts about animals. In June 1906 he asked the RSPCA to investigate the treatment by Alhambra Theatre conjurors of 'rabbits, pigeons, barn-fowls, ducks, &c . . . possibly . . . drugged or blinded to make them passive'. In March 1907 a friend called Perkins died, whom he admired for 'his staunch support of the principle of justice to animals'. But the facts of life, he knew, were against any such principle. In October 1906 he had told Frederic Harrison:

> I, too, call myself a 'meliorist', but then, I find myself unable to be in such good spirits as you are at the prospect. In regard to Sport [i.e. blood sports], for instance, will ever the great body of human beings . . . see its immorality? Worse than that, supposing they do, when will the still more numerous terrestrial animals – our kin, having the same ancestry – learn to be merciful? The fact is that when you get to the bottom of things . . . nature is *un*moral – & our puny efforts are those of people who try to keep their leaky house dry by wiping off the waterdrops from the ceiling.[7]

'The question', he went on, 'of the treatment of animals is a tremendous one.' So long as people had accepted the theological view that 'the non-human animal was . . . a creature distinct from man, there was a consistency in treating "brutes" brutally.' But with that view 'exploded, a tremendous responsibility is thrust upon us – an impossibility almost, of doing right according to our new lights, & this, as I say, prevents my taking such a hopeful view forward as you do.'[8]

'Work without hope', as Coleridge said, 'draws nectar in a sieve', but Hardy kept on working. In July 1906 he was 'trying to enter into Part III'. In October he was 'distractedly trying to give something like a clear picture of that maelstrom of confusion, the Battle of Leipsig' (Act III). On 'the Eve of Good Friday' 1907 he recorded: '11.30 p.m. Finished draft of Part III of "The Dynasts."' But that July he was still 'settling down to the somewhat mechanical work of omitting superfluous matter . . . as I don't want it to b over-long'. Late in September he told Mrs Henniker: 'I have broken the back of "The Dynasts" at last, but have not quite finished it'. Only on 10 October did he send off to Macmillan 'what I believe to be the longest English drama in existence, though I have tried my utmost to keep it as short as possible.' By New Year's Eve he had almost got through the proofs. It had been a long haul, and he was too tired for any sense of achievement. Signing himself Mrs Henniker's 'rather gloomy friend', he finally escaped from his *magnum opus*, as Byron's 'Prisoner of Chillon' from his dungeon, with a sigh: 'It is a good thing to have nearly got rid of it, though I shall miss the work.'[9]

When it finally came out (11 February 1908), the sigh of weariness must have turned to one of satisfaction. Nearly all the reviews were enthusiastic. Hailed in a front-page article by the *Times Literary Supplement* as 'a great work of art' comparable to Shakespeare's history plays, by the *Edinburgh Review* as a work of 'undoubted genius', *The Dynasts* was forgiven such small faults as 'monotonous' propaganda for 'negative ideas' and 'extremely bad verse'. Here Hardy, for once, was his own harshest critic: 'Well, there it is', he told Arthur Symons (11 March 1908), 'some pages done carefully, some galloped over, & now staring me accusingly in the face. I wonder if I shall ever be able to revise them.'[10]

The first bit of Hardy's recent life to enter *Part Third* was his martyrdom to colds and flu. Before the battle of Borodino Napoleon caught the germ that had kept his author 'dripping' in May 1906, and developed similar symptoms: cough, 'rheumy throat', 'husky accents', 'red eyes, raw nose, rheumatic manner when he moves, and thick voice in giving orders.' Hardy's interest in architecture, music, and dancing figured too. Moscow was 'a jumble of architectural styles, the Asiatic prevailing over the European.' The battle of Leipsig was heard as 'a loud droning, uninterrupted and breve-like, as from the pedal of an organ kept continuously down' – doubtless the organ of St Paul's Cathedral, 'where I go', Hardy had confessed in July 1904, 'to hear the very fine pedal notes of the organ'. Before Waterloo the dance-music was silenced by a military drum-beat, given in musical notation. This symbolic effect echoed Hardy's earliest reaction to dancing and to dance-tunes, some of which 'always moved the child to tears'; – for the dancing at Brussels also ended in tears, when the partner of an officer called 'to instant war' begged 'one dance more', before she was left to 'Wait, wait, and weep'.[11]

Hardy's youthful 'adventures with the fiddle', his 'merry minstrellings' at 'village weddings', were grimly parodied by the 'camp-follower . . . playing a fiddle' at the Women's Camp' near the battlefield, where women were in labour, and wounded men faced surgeons armed with 'bone-saws, knives, probes, tweezers, and other surgical instruments', but without anaesthetics. The day that Horace Moule cut his throat with a razor had found Hardy 'walking to Woodbury-Hill Fair.' What he saw there must have acquired in retrospect 'surgical' associations: the morning of Waterloo found the French troops wheeling 'into their fighting-positions . . . their arms glittering like a display of cutlery at a hill-side fair.'[12]

At several other points Hardy's life can be glimpsed behind his text. The burning of Napoleon's effigy at Durnover (i.e. Fordington, Dorchester) drew vividness from memories of 1850, when the poet, 'still a small boy', saw the Pope and Cardinal Wiseman similarly dealt with. 'The sight was most lurid, and he never forgot it'. Sergeant Thomas Young, who survived Waterloo to die in 1853, spoke nostalgically in *Part Third* about his native

'Stourcastle'. That was how Hardy now felt about his 'Sturminster Newton idyll'. Another Young, William, the ex-postilion who drove Hardy and Emma to Badbury Rings in 1881 had a right leg 'discoloured . . . where the carriage-pole used to rub for so many years'; so one of the postilions who drove Napoleon to exile in Elba had 'a running pole-wound'. The French soldiers dying of cold in Lithuania have 'icicles dangling from their hair that clink like lustres as they walk'. At Wimborne in 1882 Hardy had heard of some people being driven through freezing rain in an open cart: 'the men's beards and hair were hung with icicles. Getting one of the men into the house was like bringing in a chandelier of lustres.'[13]

But perhaps the most personal element in *Part Third* was Hardy's vestigial faith in Providence. Rationally he had long assumed that religious belief was absurd, and *The Dynasts* presented the Napoleonic Wars as 'but one flimsy riband of Its web', a web 'Inutile all – so far as reasonings tell.' Yet he ended his great work in the spirit, and almost in the language of *In Memoriam*. There Tennyson had 'faintly trusted the larger hope' that 'all is well' in the universe, that 'all, as in some piece of art, / Is toil cooperant to an end', and that his dead friend is part of that artistic beauty: 'Thou standest in the rising sun, / And in the setting thou art fair.' The final chorus of *The Dynasts* expressed faint trust in an equally irrational hope: 'That the rages / Of the ages / Shall be cancelled, and deliverance offered from the darts that were, / Consciousness the Will informing, till It fashion all things fair!'[14]

The unresolved conflict between such faith and the facts was occasionally sharpened by a sardonic use of the Bible. The French army wandering in the 'wild waste' of Russia was compared to the Israelites in the wilderness. The snow that buried their corpses was manna from heaven: 'behold, upon the face of the wilderness there lay a small round thing, as small as the hoar frost on the ground' – 'and thus it nears Smolensko's walls, / And, stayed its hunger, starts anew its crawls, / Till floats down one white morsel, which appals.' Napoleon, here a Moses, soon becomes a Jesus: his consultation with his generals at Leipsig 'Savours of a sad Last-Supper talk / 'Twixt his disciples and this Christ of war'. Judas was played by the Austrian Emperor, Napoleon's father-in-law, 'primed' by rather more than thirty pieces of silver from England: 'Bull's gross pay'.[15]

Part Third showed similar sarcasm in the use of Homer's *Iliad*. Marie Louise, 'visioning a future' with another man, refuses to join her husband on Elba. But she first plays Hector's loyal wife Andromache, in a travesty of the Homeric conversation between them. The spoilt King of Rome plays Astyanax ('King of the City'); and Napoleon, who has saved his own skin by leaving the rest of his army to die in Russia, feebly apes the fatalism of Troy's devoted defender. 'Don't grieve too much in your heart about me', said Hector to Andromache, 'for nobody is going to send me to Hades, unless that is my fate, and nobody, I think, has ever escaped his fate.' 'Dismiss such fears', says Napoleon', 'You may as well as not. / As things are doomed to be they will be, dear.' The faithful Mameluke, shocked

that the Emperor does not commit suicide when forced to abdicate, para-
phrases Helen's comment on Paris, when found fiddling with his armour
in his bedroom: 'If only I were married to a better man, who could feel
people's angry reproaches!' 'Would that I had served a more sensitive
master!' sighs Roustan. 'He sleeps there quite indifferent to the dishonour
of remaining alive!' Even comic relief in the *Iliad* turned sour in the 'Iliad
of Europe'. Homer's Aphrodite panics at the loss of a little 'ichor' on the
battlefield. The Spirit Sinister is amused to find shells blowing 'tunefully
through' his 'ichor' at Waterloo: 'It's merry so; / What damage mortal
flesh must undergo!'[16]

The Ironic Spirit's penultimate comment on the 'idle show' staged by
'the dreaming, dark, dumb Thing' was to question its reality: 'As once a
Greek asked, I would fain ask too, / Who knows if all the spectacle be
true, / Or an illusion of the gods (the Will, / To wit) some hocus-pocus
to fulfil?' The Greek was Aeschylus in the *Agamemnon*. There the immediate doubt was whether Troy had really fallen. But the context of the line
quoted came closer than that to the thought of *The Dynasts*, for it questioned the whole ethos of war, and the moral status of 'many-killing' 'city-
sackers' like Agamemnon (or Napoleon), who won fame by sending back
to countless loving wives 'a little scraping of dust instead of a man, for
them to mourn bitterly and put neatly away in an urn'. Another 'Greek' to
hold that view was Lucian, who observed that 'those famous militarists,
the Myrmidons, were originally ants', and vividly compared a human community, as seen from a great height, to 'an ant-hill . . . with lots of ants
crawling round it'. On the morning of Waterloo, the English and French
soldiers 'hurry to an fro like ants on an ant-hill. The tens of thousands of
moving specks are largely of a brick-red colour, but the foreign contin-
gent is darker.'[17]

After questioning the world's reality, the Ironic Spirit posed 'Last as first
the question' of its purpose: why the Will 'Ever urges on and measures out
the droning tune of Things.' Here he paraphrased Horace; '*quid velit et
possit rerum concordia discors* (what is the purpose and result of the disson-
ant harmony of things).' Even the Third Servant in the Empress's household took comfort from the Horatian tag that tall pines are the likeliest
to be blown down: 'No allies are going to tickle our skins . . . The storm
which roots the pine spares the p--s--b--d [i.e. pissabed or dandelion]'[18].

Hardy had known Horace well since the age of sixteen; but a stronger
Roman influence dated from that book his mother gave him when he was
eight, 'Dryden's *Virgil*'. On the night that Troy was sacked, Aeneas dreamt
he saw Hector, 'black with bloody dust . . . his pierced feet swollen . . . his
beard and hair stiff with blood'. At Waterloo Napoleon starts up from
momentary sleep: 'A horrible dream has gripped me – horrible! / I saw
before me Lannes – just as he looked / That day at Aspern: mutilated,
bleeding!' Perhaps it was Virgil, too, who suggested the wording of an
unforgettable stage-direction. In the *Aeneid*, among pictures of eternal
torment in Hell, was that of Theseus, fixed for ever to a rock that he had

wearily sat down on: '*sedet aeternumque sedebit / Infelix Theseus* (unhappy Theseus sits and will sit eternally).' Juvenal adapted the phrase as a metaphor for senile impotence. Hardy seems to have made it epitomize the hell of the Russian campaign, when a group of French 'officers and privates . . . their noses and ears . . . frostbitten, and pus . . . oozing from their eyes', huddled together for warmth round a dying fire: 'The fire sinks and goes out; but the Frenchmen do not move. The day dawns, and still they sit on.'[19]

Reminiscences of English poets were probably less conscious, as when at Salamanca Wellington echoes Lady Macbeth ('Well, what's done can't be undone'); or when, after vomiting the poison he had taken, Napoleon exclaims, 'God – here how difficult it is to die', thus contradicting the last words of Byron's Manfred ('Old man! 'tis not so difficult to die') but also, less forgettably, of Horace Moule in 1873 ('Easy to die'). No doubt Hardy realized his basic debt to Byron when handling the 'revelry by night' in 'Belgium's capital' before Waterloo; but he cannot have meant to be quite so Tennysonian in his transition from the Peninsular War to the campaign in Russia:

> Marmont's Aide, then, like a swallow
> Let us follow, follow, follow,
> Over hill and over hollow,
> Past the plains of Teute and Pole!

In *The Princess* the lover dashed South at the call of a 'Voice' in the wind: 'Follow, follow, thou shalt win.' The effect became even more incongruous with the faint echo of Tennyson's 'The Brook': 'I come from haunts of coot and hern . . .'[20]

With Napoleon's escape from Elba, and the need to defeat him a second time, history offered Hardy a ready-made climax to his drama, full of surprise and suspense. But he made *Part Third* still more climactic by gradually stepping up the horrors of war, so that Waterloo became not just a famous victory, but a culminating example of senseless cruelty. Borodino was heard as a 'roar – / A mash of men's crazed cries entreating mates / To run them through and end their agony'. of 'horses maimed in myriads, tearing round / In maddening pangs'. From a bridge over the Beresina 'eighteen thousand' French 'fugitives' were plunged into the icy river, with 'women . . . limply bearing their infants between wizened white arms stretching above'. At Leipsig 'Each cannon-blaze / Makes the air thick with human limbs'. At Waterloo the French cavalry's 'horses' hoofs squash out our poor fellows' bowels as they lie', while other horses are seen 'wandering about without riders, or crying as they lie with entrails trailing or limbs broken.' And when the 'heroic' French Old Guard are finally beaten, 'The English systematically 'proceed with their massacre' of that 'devoted band'.[21]

Thus *Part Third* became the peroration of a pacifist manifesto, demonstrating the barbarous injustice of war. Waterloo was a crowning example of 'Warfare mere / Plied by the Managed for the Managers;/ To wit; by frenzied folks who profit nought / For those who profit all!' Even more unjust was the suffering inflicted on animals, which served here, as so often in Hardy's writing, to typify all that was wrong in the world. On the night that the Kremlin is set on fire, 'Cocks crow, thinking it sunrise, ere they are burnt to death.' When the snow starts falling at Smolensko, nothing is heard but 'the incessant flogging of the wind-broken and lacerated horses'. Napoleon's return to power was celebrated by loud laughter from 'the soldiery' at the sight of 'a howling dog, with a white cockade tied to its tail.' The eve of Waterloo was marked by a lyric, which struck Hardy in retrospect as 'the most original' thing in the book, describing the terror of the local wildlife – rabbits, swallows, moles, larks, hedgehogs, snails, worms, and butterflies.[22]

One form of suffering shared by animals and men was lack of sleep. Retreating from Leipsig, 'The marching remnants drowse amid their talk, / And worn and harrowed horses slumber as they walk.' From the window of the Brussels ballroom 'long lines of British infantry' are seen sleeping on the pavements. They will have to march 'eighteen miles beneath the heat, / And then to fight a battle ere they rest.' When they 'bivouac' after the battle of Quatre Bras, they will 'have been on foot since one o'clock the previous morning'. Napoleon has the same problem. He drops off while dictating orders both at Leipsig, and at Charleroi, and during the battle of Waterloo 'nods in momentary sleep', to be woken by that 'horrible dream'.[23]

The sleep theme was not just a part of Hardy's case against war. It also reinforced the idea of Napoleon as a somnambulist, hypnotized by the 'dreaming, dark, dumb Thing' that, 'like a knitter drowsed', was unconsciously weaving this particular 'riband of its web', to realize a 'horrible dream' of its own. That Napoleon was just a puppet of the Will was similarly implied by a passing image when, at the start of the Russian campaign, the 'figure of NAPOLÉON' was 'diminished' by distance 'to the aspect of a doll'. His puppet-status was also made explicit in his own thoughts: 'History makes use of me to weave her web'. His gradual 'diminishing' was a central motif of *Part Third*, from the ominous fall from his horse on the bank of the Niemen, to his concluding self-assessment in the Wood of Bossu: 'I have ever known / That such a will I passively obeyed . . . But for all this and this / I shall be nothing.' Thus, the crescendo of horror that led up to Waterloo, was accompanied by the pathetic diminuendo of Napoleon's decline and fall.[24]

He was shown declining in character as well as power. From an inspired leader and strategist he sank to a sulky paranoiac, with 'a gloomy resentful countenance' and 'a dismayed scowl'. The egotism that dismissed the loss of six hundred thousand lives as 'quite ridiculous' made him blame everyone but himself for his own failures: 'May Heaven curse the author of this war – Ay him, that Russian minister, self-sold / To England, who fomented it. – 'Twas he / Dragged Alexander into it, and me!' As

Emperor, he now descended to cynical PR tricks, posing with Marie Louise as the 'type and model of domestic bliss', and gilding 'the dome of the Invalides / In best gold leaf', to give 'the good folk of Paris . . . something to think about.' As general, after deserting his troops in Russia, he got his new ones to 'toil for a chimaera trustfully' at Waterloo, by pretending that their Prussian enemies were French reinforcements.[25]

Despite all this, Napoleon ends up thinking himself a great man who has, to borrow Othello's phrase, done the world 'some service': 'Great men are meteors that consume themselves / To light the earth. This is my burnt-out hour.' But as a tragic hero he is here Othello's opposite, having lost, as the Spirit of Rumour says, 'his last chance of dying well.' And the Spirit of the Years sums him up, not as 'great of heart', but as one of those men who

> Are in the elemental ages' chart
> Like meanest insects on obscurest leaves
> But incidents and grooves of Earth's unfolding'.

In making such an insect his hero, and tracing so reductively the process of its disintegration and 'extinction', Hardy abandoned the ancient form of tragedy, to create a new form of his own, where the tragic hero represented, not the greatness of the human spirit, but its insignificance.[26]

That is perhaps one reason for dissatisfaction with *The Dynasts*. Another is its diction, which often in *Part Third* seems to be turning into a private language. Under pressure, for instance, of prosody and alliteration, *defend* and *defence* tend to lose their first syllables, with odd results. 'You fend your lives, your land, your liberty' is at least intelligible (even without spotting the echo of a passage in Aeschylus' *Persae*); but what, at first reading, is Death's 'fendless tap'? 'It formulates our fence' is the shortest but hardly the most lucid method of saying that French tactics before Waterloo dictate English ones; and in the review of the troops on the battlefield one can only guess what is meant by 'Rylandt's brigade, set forward fencelessly'. A growing addiction to the same handy but ambiguous suffix obscures Napoleon's warning to his generals at Leipsig of a 'now voidless battle'; and this comment on the bloodshed at Waterloo is one of many passages where the poet was evidently too tired or impatient to use any but the first words that came into his head: 'Why should men's many-valued motions take / So barbarous a groove!'[27]

But in a drama of 'Nineteen Acts, and One Hundred and Thirty Scenes' some pages might well be 'galloped over', as Hardy said they were. And by galloping over them ourselves we can best appreciate the whole work's finest features: its integration of countless facts and insights into one compelling, if depressing, world-view; its translation of that view into visual and auditory terms on a scale ranging from the astronomic to the microscopic; its extraction of human drama from history without serious infidelity to the historical records; and its highly original literary form.[28]

Covering at speed the extensive landscape of *Part Third*, we can still get pleasure from passing details of versification, like the semblance of a triple drumbeat that dominates the rhythm of the 'aerial music' before the battle of Salamanca ('The skies fling flame'), or the similar hint of 'sprung rhythm' in the 'smart *Clink! Clink!*' among the anapaests of 'Budmouth Dears'. We can also enjoy such incidental felicities as the sphincter imagery describing the struggle round Leipsig. This may also serve to represent the whole work's perspective on human war – grand strategy seen in terms of individual suffering:

> Now triple battle beats about the town,
> And now contracts the huge elastic ring
> Of fighting flesh, as those within go down,
> Or spreads, as those without show faltering![29]

25

Time's Laughingstocks

'Now that The Dynasts is finished', wrote Hardy in March 1908, 'I am quite in a whirl of small drudgeries that have been postponed.' The first of them was sorting out problems of text and copyright for a selection from Barnes's poems that the Oxford University Press had asked him to prepare. It did not help that letters from the Press might 'go to Dorchester, Oxon' instead of Dorchester, Dorset. Another bit of drudgery was giving architectural advice on repairs to Stinsford Church, though at least this gave him a chance to suggest reconstructing the 'old west gallery'.[1]

More tiresome was the job of supervising improvements at Max Gate, which included the addition of a dormer window to Emma's attic bedroom, while she was on holiday in Calais. This meant a large hole in the roof, to be covered by brother Henry with a tarpaulin 'if he can fix it' – so of course the work was delayed by 'incessant' rain. When the rain gave place to a heatwave, and the roof was opened, new problems arose: 'though it was hot last week', Hardy reported to Emma, 'the plaster does not dry in your upstairs room, though the first coat is on, but the glass of the window is not yet in, in order to have a draught to dry the walls.' With 'hammering all day', 'the front door closed up' to enlarge the porch, and 'a general messiness outside', Max Gate was not a good place for writing poetry.[2]

The chaos was increased by the cats. Marky caused 'a great fright' and a midnight search of the garden with lanterns by 'absolutely' disappearing, only to reappear 'calmly' next morning from the stable loft. To accommodate her kittens, Kitsy shredded a maid's 'Sunday hat' which had 'cost 4/11d'. Hardy gave the maid five shillings, and then had to drown the kittens, the last 'such a pretty one – white, with black streaks on its back.' The need to do so doubtless confirmed his gloomiest 'conclusions about the universe'. Nor was it cheering to be told by Clodd about a 'theory of consciousness in plants'. 'I have always known it intuitively', he replied, '& hate maiming trees on that account.'[3]

One more drudgery was house-hunting in London. At the last moment Emma turned down a 'pretty house' in St John's Wood that Hardy 'very much wanted', so he had to 'flit up and down' and be 'squeezed' in a crowded hotel. 'The fact is', Emma explained to some friends, 'my strength and SIGHT are fast failing & two houses are too much for me now.' 'As to our coming to Town', her husband told an editor, 'I am in great doubt, for my wife has grown to dislike housekeeping in London, & I dislike going to an hotel or lodgings.' It was not the only difference between them. They now disagreed, not only about religion, but also about votes for women. Emma actively supported the Women's Suffrage movement (except when 'the *Suffragettes*' threw stones and tried to 'assassinate the Prime Minister'). But Hardy thought 'the action of men therein should be permissive only – not cooperative', and refused to let his name appear even as 'a possible contributor' to a projected suffragist newspaper.[4]

It was now quite a name to conjure with. *The Dynasts* was actually proving a commercial success, the Society of Authors made him its president, as the acknowledged 'head of our profession', and in November 1908 Asquith, the Prime Minister hated by the Suffragettes, offered him a knighthood (which he asked for a year to think over). But the public's high opinion of him was not shared by his wife. 'My Eminent partner', she told some friends, 'will have a softening of brain if he goes on as he does and the rest of the world does.' When she started criticizing him like that in front of guests, joint entertaining became awkward. Hesitating to accept an invitation to stay with his friend Clodd, he wrote vaguely of 'my domestic circumstances which, between ourselves, make it embarrassing for me to return hospitalities received'.[5]

He did, though, visit Clodd at Aldeburgh in July 1909. On the train coming back he told his friend more about those 'domestic circumstances', and also confided the secret of his relationship with Florence Dugdale. Clodd was sympathetic, and discreetly helpful. Nine days later Hardy took Emma to Covent Garden for the first night of a *Tess* opera, in which they heard his 'Wessex dairymaid singing in choice Italian', and saw her go off stage to commit suicide. Clodd had arranged to take Florence separately. 'I will call round on you in your seats between the acts if I possibly can', wrote Hardy gratefully, '& at the end of the performance.' Clodd then gave what struck Hardy as a 'charming' and 'timely hint' that he might bring his 'young friend and assistant' to Aldeburgh. That visit took place in August, and they seem to have enjoyed their first holiday together, to judge from the touching if faintly pathetic photograph of the pair sitting side by side on the beach. The only 'mishap' was when their boat got stuck in the mud of the River Alde, and they had to be rescued in a punt. Hardy was anxious, perhaps because Florence was with him, that the paragraph about it in the local paper should not 'get into any London print'.[6]

After the contrived meeting at the opera Hardy told Mrs Henniker that he was 'very much depressed with London, &., alas, with life generally – which I should not be particularly sorry to take my leave of.' Perhaps he felt slightly better after their Aldeburgh holiday. How much Emma knew about Florence at this stage is not clear, but in October Hardy and Florence started touring cathedrals together – first Chichester by themselves and then, with Henry Hardy, York, Durham, and Edinburgh. Yet these brief interludes probably reminded him of Shelley's 'green isles' in the 'deep wide sea of Misery'. They were samples of a situation that could never become permanent; and even at the time they must have seemed spoiled by their surreptitious character. Hardy's next volume would make Gosse hope his friend was not quite as unhappy as his poetry. But he probably was.[7]

He had been collecting the new poems since before January 1909, when he told Frederick Macmillan: 'I was intending, in fear and trembling, to ask you some time this year to print them.' In May he had suggested the title, 'Time's Laughingstocks, and other verses'; and by 7 September, his 'strength' as well as 'appetite . . . increased by 'the Aldeburgh air', he had sent off the complete MS, 'to be printed', he told Clodd, 'for a public which does not desire a line of it.' But when the volume came out (3 December 1909), it sold so well that within three weeks it needed reprinting. Hardy disguised his satisfaction as bibliographical zeal: 'It will be well to make the most of that unusual event in the history of new verse; & to so mark the titlepage, or the back of it, that dealers in old books do not hereafter sell the second for the first impression'.[8]

Again his Preface followed the Browning formula: 'those lyrics penned in the first person . . . are to be regarded, in the main, as dramatic monologues by different characters.' But it was no persona that expressed love for Florence Dugdale in 'On the Departure Platform', gratitude to his grandmother in 'One We Knew', or grief at his mother's death in 'After the Last Breath'. 'George Meredith' celebrated the poet's friendship with the publisher's reader who had advised him about his first novel 'forty years back'. 'Aberdeen' expressed his feelings when he took his honorary doctorate there, and the motives misinterpreted by a pretty girl in 'The Dear' must have been his own too, for he said that the poem was 'made on a real incident that seemed worth recording for its own sake'.[9]

How about the other first-person poems? In 'The Revisitation', which opened the volume, romantic memories of an alienated girl-friend ended in bathos, because she had lost her looks, and he his libido. The theme had already been handled in 'The Well-Beloved, but was relevant enough to Hardy's current situation to make him assure Florence Dugdale that the poem's conclusion, 'Love is lame at fifty years', was not true. In 'The Curate's Kindness: A Workhouse Irony', segregation of the sexes promised a husband the one thing he wanted – to 'get free of this forty years' chain', his marriage. That, too, had some relevance to Hardy's feelings; and the best solution to his emotional problems must often have seemed that of 'He Abjures Love', a poem written in 1883 but even apter to his present circumstances. The same can be said of 'The Dead Man Walking', though dated 1896. Emma's recent displays of antagonism had given new meaning to the words: 'And when my Love's heart kindled / In hate of me, / Wherefore I knew not, died I / One more degree.'[10]

Most such connections between the poet and his lyric voices can only be guessed at; but in other ways he certainly drew on his own and his family's experience. The fieldfare of his childhood returned as the 'starving bird' of 'The Reminder', and the sparrows above his Bockhampton bedroom, described in a letter to Gosse (23 February 1903), were made to 'flit / From the riddled thatch' on 'The Night of the Dance'. His juvenile 'adventures with the fiddle' supplied a novel perspective in 'The Fiddler', his pleasant visits to London dance-halls in 1862–3 grew melancholy in 'Reminiscences of a Dancing Man', and his theatre-going around then prompted the melodrama of 'The Two Rosalinds', where the actress who had roused his 'ardour' in 'eighteen sixty-three' became a 'hag' 'hawking' the text outside the box-office. Melodramatic too was an image used both in a letter of 1908 and in the grim little saga of 'John and Jane'. Stung by a statement in the *Daily News* that his life's journey had 'ended in despair', Hardy had accused 'professional optimists' of wearing 'too much the strained look of the smile on a skull': the once optimistic parents of a 'worthless son' now 'rate the world as a gruesome place, / Where fair looks fade to a skull's grimace'.[11]

Some better poems were based on Hardy's family history. 'A Church Romance' celebrated the love between his parents. 'The Dead Quire' fantasized about the church-music played by his grandfather, uncle, and father. The husband of 'the Rash Bride' was named after Hardy's maternal grandmother, Betty Swetman, and the psalm sung at the Bride's grave was that sung in 1892 at the funeral of Hardy's father, who had often played it himself at Stinsford funerals. Betty Swetman came from Melbury Osmond, where an 'incident' in the Ilchesters' park inspired 'Autumn in King's Hintock Park'.[12]

The theme of that poem, with its refrain, 'Raking up leaves', perhaps owed something to Millais' *Autumn Leaves* (1856). There the young girls' faces seem to express 'sighs at life's russet hue', like those of Hardy's 'old woman' at the sight of young 'Lords' ladies'. To her, autumn leaves suggested 'grey ghosts' of people she had known. Shelley had seen them as 'ghosts from an enchanter fleeing', Virgil as the shades of the dead in hell; but all three poets' original source was the *Iliad*: 'As the generations of leaves, so are those of men. Some leaves the wind blows to the ground, others the forest grows, when it flourishes in spring' – or, as Hardy put it, 'New leaves will dance on high / – Earth never grieves! / Will not, when missed am I / Raking up leaves.'[13]

In Sophocles' *Trachiniae* (which Hardy had once thought of exploiting for 'a lyric'), a wife awaits her husband's return from a war, only to find that he has brought another woman with him. 'A Wife and Another' opens with the same situation; but instead of giving her husband a supposed love-charm which makes him die in agony, Hardy's Deianira treats hers with the utmost kindness – which may, to judge from 'The Burghers', prove as agonizing as Heracles' poisoned shirt, and 'carry wounds that none can cicatrize.' Plato's 'Myth of Er' was the ultimate source of 'The Unborn'. 'It was pathetic, absurd, and astonishing', said Socrates, 'to see how each soul chose its life.' Hardy's deluded 'shapes' were more pathetic still, for they had no choice – 'Driven forward like a rabble rout / Into the world they had so desired, / By the all-immanent will.'[14]

The volume showed further traces of Hardy's classical reading. In the series, 'At Casterbridge Fair', Theocritus' refrain, 'Begin, dear Muses, the bucolic song', was adapted for 'The Ballad-Singer' as 'Rhyme, Ballad-rhymer, start a country song'. An epigram to a flower-seller in the *Greek Anthology* probably suggested a love-story for 'The Market-Girl'; and the section called 'More Love Lyrics' concluded in 'He Abjures Love' with a theme rehandled from a Horace *Ode*. But Victorian poets left their mark too, most amusingly where Rossetti rubbed shoulders with Bunyan in 'One Ralph Blossom Soliloquizes'. This multiple seducer's seventh conquest heard nothing of the trumpets that had sounded for Mr Valiant-for-Truth 'on the other side': 'These trumpets here in Heaven are dumb to me / With you away.' Thus the Blessed Damozel was recast as a fallen woman. The seven stars in her hair became seven feathers in Ralph's cap, Caroline, Jane, Cicely, Rosa, Lizzy, Patience, and Anne, whose names, if not quite such 'sweet symphonies' as those of the Lady Mary's handmaidens, 'Cecily, Gertrude, Magdalen, / Margaret and Rosalys', at least echoed two of them.[15]

Blossom's soliloquy about his seven loves recalls the 'Soliloquy of the Spanish Cloister' about a monk's obsessive hatred; but Browning contributed more to the volume than the form of the dramatic monologue. In 'Panthera' a Roman centurion witnessed the crucifixion of a son he had casually fathered on a pretty girl near Nazareth 'some thirty years' before. It was a type of poem pioneered by Browning in 'Karshish', presenting the gospel story from a contemporary pagan angle. 'The Flirt's Tragedy', where the speaker hires 'a needy Adonis' to seduce and jilt his 'jilter', seems to have derived its unlikely plot from 'A Light Woman', where a man seduces his friend's probable jilter simply to get him out of her clutches. 'Porphyria's Lover' strangles her to make sure she is never unfaithful, then tentatively assumes divine approval: 'And yet God has not said a word!' Hardy's 'Wife' acts with contrasting generosity towards her unfaithful husband and 'Another' woman, then concludes: 'I held I had not stirred God wrathfully.'[16]

'The Revisitation' parodied the theme and setting of 'Love among the Ruins', where a girl and boy 'rush' madly into each other's arms amidst a landscape full of historical relics. So Hardy's speaker was 'a swain of fifty', soon to become a relic himself; and the 'girl with eager eyes and yellow hair' was replaced by a grizzled and 'wasted figure' incongruously called 'Agnette', i.e. Lamb. The name also burlesqued Browning's words about 'our sheep / Half-asleep' – for these pastoral lovers celebrate their reunion after twenty years by slumping down hand in hand on an 'ancient people's stone', and nodding off. No wonder Browning's envoi, 'Love is best!', was amended to 'Love is lame...'[17]

Confessing to Newbolt in January 1909 his poor opinion of *In Memoriam*, Hardy added: 'though I did my duty in adoring it in years past.' His old admiration for Tennyson's poetry was still obvious in this volume. Where the 'great Hall' once stood, read the peroration to 'Aylmer's Field', 'the mole has made his run'. So, too, with 'The House of Hospitalities': 'Where we sang, the mole now labours, / And spiders knit.' The dance of death in 'The Vision of Sin' offered an apt conclusion to 'Reminiscences of a Dancing Man: 'Whither have danced those damsels now! / Is Death the partner who doth moue [i.e. grimace at] / Their wormy chaps and bare? / Do their spectres spin like sparks within / The smoky halls of the Prince of Sin...?' 'In the Mind's Eye' described a female 'phantom / Borne within my brain', which 'abides with me.' It strongly resembled the 'abiding phantom', the 'blot upon the brain' that haunted the lover in *Maud*; and the pacifist moral of 'The Man He Killed' was enforced by the echo of 'Their's not to reason why' in 'The Charge of the Light Brigade': 'He thought he'd 'list, perhaps / Off-hand like – just as I / Was out of work – had sold his traps – / No other reason why.'[18]

But the book's chief debt to Tennyson was for its title and organizing principle. This came from a tirade in *The Princess* against backsliding students of the women's college. 'No wiser than their mothers', they would live mere

> laughing-stocks of Time,
> Whose brains are in their hands and in their heels,
> But fit to flaunt, to dress, to dance, to thrum,
> To tramp, to scream, to burnish, and to scour,
> For ever slaves at home and fools abroad.

The Prince of that poem believed in men's 'aiding' the 'woman's cause'; Hardy, we have seen, did not. According to Emma in 1894, 'His interest in the Suffrage Cause is nil in spite of "Tess"'. So he ignored the feminist meaning of 'laughing-stocks of Time'. Once, indeed, he almost contradicted it. Though the advice followed by 'The Orphaned Old Maid' came from a self-interested male, it had a distinct flavour of women's lib: 'If you care for your freedom you'll listen to me, / Make a spouse in your pocket, and let the men be.' Its effect was to leave her 'lonely and poor' in old age.[19]

Elsewhere Hardy drew broader meanings from Tennyson's feminist phrase, and structured his collection around them. One was that Time made laughing-stocks of women anyway, whether or not their brains were confined to their hands and heels, by destroying their physical beauty.

Such aging women figured frequently in the volume, from Agnette in the first piece to the girl progressively stripped of her charms in 'God's Education', near the end of the book. There God pooh-poohs the notion that (as in a poem by Hopkins) He 'hoards' the transient elements of female beauty for 'some glad day' in the future: 'Oh no, / They charm not me; I bid Time throw / Them carelessly away.'[20]

Another aspect of the title-theme was expressed in three 'Tragedies', where Time made fools of men as well as women by revealing too late the consequences of their actions. The 'Trampwoman' would not have 'teased' the man she loved, if she had known he would murder his supposed rival, and be hanged for it. The speaker of 'A Sunday Morning Tragedy' would not have given her daughter 'physic for untimely fruit', if she had known the physic would kill her, and that the 'fruit' would have been legitimate after all. The man responsible for 'The Flirt's Tragedy' would not have hired the 'needy Adonis', had he known it would lead to murder, suicide, and his own lifelong 'suffering' from 'mighty remorse'.[21]

One more meaning apparently extracted by Hardy from his Tennysonian title was the way things change in retrospect: Time mocks human beings by making their past look different from how it looked when it was their present. That had been the subject of 'The Self-Unseeing' in Hardy's previous volume, but in this one the idea was specially associated with bereavement. In a small group of poems spoken by widows, 'The Farm-Woman's Winter' reminds her how her 'frail' husband used to work 'Long hours in gripping gusts'. Now that 'his ploughshare rusts', her worries about him then look futile. 'She Hears the Storm' approaches the same thought from another angle: 'I should have been distressed by fears / At such a night as this.' But the reason for her present immunity to storms gives even that past distress a tinge of happiness. The speaker of 'Bereft' remembers 'black winter mornings' when she was woken at five a.m. by a light 'struck near [her] eyes'. It cannot have been pleasant at the time, but now, like all the routine of her married life, it has come, as in 'The Self-Unseeing', to 'glow with a gleam'. In that sense Hardy himself would soon become one of Time's laughing-stocks, when Emma died.[22]

Unconscious of the impending link between his life and poetry, he epitomized his book's burden in a poem which seems consciously self-dramatizing, 'The Dead Man Walking'. There 'Time's enchantments' gradually revealed themselves as forms of ridicule, and finally left their victim 'smiling' – 'the smile on a skull'. All these variations on the title-theme tended to offset the 'lack of concord' admitted in the Preface, between 'pieces written at widely severed dates, and in contrasting moods and circumstances'. Thus his 'miscellany' contrives to give quite a strong impression of unity.[23]

As to the pieces themselves, Hardy was told, and apparently came to believe that 'The Trampwoman's Tragedy' was 'upon the whole, his most successful poem' – a curious notion best explained by his lifelong fondness for the ballad form, and his annoyance when the poem was rejected by the *Cornhill* in 1903, for 'impropriety'. He had similar reasons to over-value 'A Sunday Morning Tragedy'. When first asked to be President of the Society of Authors, he had warned them of his determination 'to exhibit what I feel ought to be exhibited about life to show that what we call immorality, irreligion, &c, are often true morality, true religion &c, quite freely to the end.' But much that needed exhibiting then has since become conventional wisdom, so the subversive elements in the volume have lost their impact, while narrative verse, in an age of novels, films, and television drama, has lost its general appeal.[24]

More attractive now than the ballads are what might be called the lyrical epigrams. Of these, three are philosophical fantasies, ironically dramatizing thoughts familiar from *The Dynasts*. 'Before Life and After' blames consciousness for the world's misery. 'New Year's Eve' makes grim fun of the paradox that products of unconscious evolution can learn to 'ask for reasons why' such a process should ever have started; and 'God's Education' plays further with Feuerbach's idea that 'God is the product of man' – so 'divine benevolence' is just a sign of human civilization. The same type of oblique humour was used to convey Hardy's passionate feelings about animals. 'Wagtail and Baby', superficially a mere display of rhyming technique, implicitly repeated his remark about vivisection in 1903 that no other species, not even lions, had they become dominant, would have showed such *'general* cruelty ... to the "lower" animals' as human beings did.[25]

But the finest things in *Time's Laughingstocks* were two short lyrics confronting unacceptable aspects of the human condition. The cruelty of aging was starkly brought out by 'Autumn in King's Hintock Park', where an ancient symbol drawn from nature, art, and literature, set in a satisfying pattern of imagined sight and verbal sound, was made to simulate individual experience. The essence of bereavement was 'exhibited' in an extract from Hardy's own feelings when his mother died, 'After the Last Breath'. Both poems include the consolations by which people try to convince each other and themselves that such things are acceptable. The old woman tells herself she is part of the natural cycle; the son makes the most of 'a numb relief' that his mother is no longer in pain. But each poem makes it clear that such consolations are about as much help as the medicine bottles by the deathbed: 'Each palliative its silly face presents / As useless gear.'[26]

26

A Changed Man and Other Tales

Hardy was a changed man himself when he published these tales in October 1913. Outwardly he had changed from a literary *enfant terrible*, 'determined to exhibit' what the public wished to hide, into a Grand Old Man; inwardly, from an unhappy husband recommending easier divorce ('marriage should not thwart nature'), into an inconsolable widower. A scholarly joke made by a character in one of the 'other tales' had proved for their author a bitter truth. Marriage, said the rector in 'The Waiting Supper' (1887) was a 'Tragedy . . . It is full of crises and catastrophes, and ends with the death of one of the actors.' Hardy's own marriage had just ended that way; and Florence Dugdale (apparently dating its decline from 1893) had called it a 'tragedy of twenty years'.[1]

The change in Hardy's literary reputation was shown in many ways: a collected edition of his works; more translations of them, not only into foreign languages, but also into Braille; stage-versions of his novels performed by Dorchester amateurs, but attracting London critics; a London production of *The Three Wayfarers*; and a film of *Tess*, on which he commented: 'It was a curious production, & I was interested in it as a scientific toy; but I can say nothing as to its relation to, or rendering of, the story.' The Dorset County Museum wanted copies of all his books, and Sydney Cockerell, Director of the Fitzwilliam Museum at Cambridge, suggested and arranged the distribution of Hardy's original manuscripts to important museums and libraries. 'The cupboard which contained the MSS is now agreeably empty', Hardy reported in October 1911, '& my responsibility all gone.'[2]

Formal tributes to his achievement began with an Order of Merit from George V in July 1910, which involved having his portrait done by William

Strang, to hang in Windsor Castle. That November he was made a Free-
man of Dorchester. Unable for once to avoid making a speech, he used
it to urge the conservation of Dorchester's 'ancient features', if only for
the benefit of American tourists – mostly brought there by his own novels.
In June 1913 he was given an 'honorary degree of Litt.D.' at Cambridge,
where he had once hoped to take 'a pass-degree' *en route* for a curacy 'in
a country village'. His subsequent switch from architecture to authorship
had also been symbolically celebrated, when the RIBA's silver medal of
1863 was capped in 1912 by a gold one from the Royal Society of Literature. It was presented on his seventy-second birthday, after lunch at Max
Gate on a table shared with two cats, by two poets, Newbolt and Yeats.[3]

The sad thing about this crowning honour was Hardy's insistence that
Emma should leave the room before the presentation. She had recently
tended to exaggerate her own contribution to his novels. Denouncing 'the
pride of the male' in a published letter to the *Nation*, she had claimed that
'a good deal that is carried out as original and finished work has been
suggested, and often completely thought out, by a woman, though never
so acknowledged.' Hardy reacted with what Emma called 'an *obsession* that
I must be kept out of [his affairs] lest the dimmest ray should alight upon
me of his supreme story'. Hence, presumably, his mean behaviour now
towards one of the earliest encouragers and inspirers of his writing, who
had fair-copied so many of his manuscripts, and been so largely responsible for getting the *Laodicean* finished.[4]

It showed just how bad things had got between them. Meanwhile,
unknown to Emma, Hardy had been seeing more of Florence Dugdale.
Around 1910, the triangle came into sharper focus. Emma and Florence
had somehow met one another, perhaps at the Lyceum Club to which
they both belonged, and struck up a kind of friendship. Florence was
invited to some of Emma's London parties, and also to visit Max Gate, as
a friend who could do Emma's typing, and otherwise help with her writing. This now included poems, religious essays, and her *Recollections*, which
ended with a nostalgic account of her time at St Juliot with Hardy, and
'that lovely day' of their wedding.[5]

Florence found both 'comedy' and pathos in 'the Max Gate menage'.
'Mrs Hardy is good to me, beyond words', she told Clodd, 'and instead of
cooling towards me she grows more & more affectionate. I am *intensely*
sorry for her, sorry indeed for both.' But on Christmas Day 1910 she
became the *casus belli* for 'a violent quarrel' between husband and wife
('oh dear oh dear *what* a scene'), over whether she should be taken to
Bockhampton or not. After that she kept well away from Max Gate, though
in 1911 she spent 'a delightful fortnight' with Emma alone at Worthing.
Did Emma realize how Hardy felt about Florence? Probably, to judge from
a 'queer' question she once put to her: had Florence noticed Hardy's
strong resemblance to Crippen – the man who had recently murdered his
wife, with the suspected connivance of his mistress? 'She added darkly',

wrote Florence, 'that she would not be surprised to find herself in the cellar one morning. All this in deadly seriousness.' But Emma had her own brand of humour – and of magnanimity.[6]

When the *Titanic* went down in April 1912, with 'two acquaintances' of Hardy's among the fifteen hundred drowned, he wrote a poem 'for a matinée in aid of the bereaved', on the unforeseen 'Convergence of the Twain', i.e. the ship and the iceberg: 'Alien they seemed to be: / No mortal eye could see / The intimate welding of their later history, / Or sign that they were bent / By paths coincident, / On being anon twin halves of one august event.' Working up to ten hours a day on the proofs of the Wessex Edition, Hardy was equally unconscious of impending bereavement – that he and his alienated wife were converging towards a disaster which would bring her closer to his heart than she had been for nearly forty years, and make her almost a twin half of his poetic personality.[7]

That August Emma's health deteriorated. She had eczema, angina, gall-stones, and chronic pain in her back. According to Dolly Gale, the fourteen-year-old maid who looked after her, she 'habitually lived, and had her meals' in her attic bedroom, only coming downstairs in the evening for dinner. On 24 November she was 'distinctly unwell', but refused to see a doctor, for fear of an operation: 'she did not want to be cut up'. On the 26th she agreed to see one, who 'did not think her seriously ill, but weak from want of nourishment from indigestion.' That evening Hardy came back late from the dress rehearsal for a local stage-performance of *The Trumpet-Major*: 'all the house was in bed and he did not disturb her.' Next morning, Dolly reported sixty years later, she found her 'moaning and terribly ill', and 'rushed downstairs' to fetch Hardy from his study. He looked at her 'disdainfully' for 'several seconds', told her that her collar was crooked, 'remained seated and carefully and methodically arranged the things on his desk as though that was more important than directly going to his wife.' After 'a couple of minutes', though, he 'followed' Dolly upstairs. Then, 'shocked by his wife's appearance . . . he hurried to her bedside and said "Emm, Emm, do you know me, Emm" . . . Mrs Hardy was too far gone to answer him and until she died in less than five minutes she did not speak.' The death certificate ascribed it to impacted gallstones and heart failure.[8]

Dolly liked Emma 'very much' but 'despised' and was always 'afraid' of Hardy. Her parents had told her that he 'had a mistress in London, a woman named Florence Dugdale . . . It was these things that worried me most rather than his supercilious manner and crooked nose both of which I disliked.' But whatever allowance is made for Dolly's prejudice, Hardy's own memories of his behaviour that morning must have added unbearably to the load of guilt accumulated throughout his surreptitious meetings with Florence. Suddenly he realized that he had failed to show Emma even the 'ordinary loving-kindness' he believed in, even when she was dying. Absorbed in his own work and feelings, he had never even thought of her dying. In reply to letters of condolence, he kept repeating the gist of what he told Mrs Henniker (17 December 1912): 'Emma's death was absolutely unexpected by me, the doctor, & everybody, though not sudden, strictly speaking.' That was apparently true. But as her husband he felt he 'ought to have had more insight', which might have enabled him to 'prolong her life a little by assiduous attention.' Instead, he had 'imagined her quite sound, even robust' – an illusion doubtless fostered by Emma's solid appearance and habitual courage.[9]

His pain and remorse were increased by the discovery of her diaries, full of his own failings as a husband; but worse still was the 'vacancy', the 'blankness and silence', the 'great blank' left in his life: 'The saddest moments of all are when I go into the garden & to that long straight wall at the top ... where she used to walk every evening just before dusk, the cat trotting faithfully behind her; & at times when I almost expect to see her as usual coming in from the flower-beds with a little trowel in her hand.' Thus missing her visually, he developed a new respect for her as a personality, centring on 'her *courage* in the cause of animals, surpassing that of any woman I have known'. The 'differences' between them, the 'painful delusions she suffered from at times' ceased to matter, and his original love for her, submerged but never quite extinguished by years of bitterness, was rekindled and further fuelled by a 'very painful' pilgrimage to St Juliot in March 1913.[10]

This 'all but incredible *volte-face* in his attitude', as it has been called, was really a quite natural response to bereavement. Naturally, too, people rallied round to help him at Max Gate: 'My sister and Miss Dugdale attend to my wants excellently', he told Clodd, '& Mrs Hardy's niece, who has also been here, is coming to stay in a few days.' Florence Dugdale had 'moved in' too, with what struck Emma's maid as 'inordinate haste'. Dolly then moved out – doubtless to regale local gossips with her story of the 'two hairpins' found in Hardy's bed. But Florence saw her role differently: 'He wanted a housekeeper who could be a companion and read to him – etc. – so I came in.' The 'etc.' included sparing Hardy's eyes, weak from excessive proof-reading, by letting him dictate replies to all the letters of condolence. But her most vital service just then was probably affectionate counselling, which helped him to resist the assaults of grief and guilt, and get moving again: 'I have been quite inert for the last two months', he told Clodd in February 1913, '... the house is as much asleep as I. But it, & myself, must wake up'.[11]

The first thing he felt equal to publishing was a reprint of some old short stories, which he told a friend were 'mostly bad'; but he felt 'unhappily obliged' to include them in his collected works, 'because pirated editions of some, vilely printed, are in circulation in America, & imported into England by the curious.' Harpers had suggested the volume in January 1913. That April he wrote that it was still '*in nubibus* (in the clouds)', but by August he had decided on the book's contents, and on the 19th sent off 'a rather formidable bundle of copy' to Macmillan, with the title under which it was published on 24 October: *A Changed Man and Other*

Tales. He had expected 'the pleasure of listening to reviewers lamenting the feeblness to which I have declined (for they always assume everything published to have been written the preceding month)'. It was well enough received, though, for Macmillan to suggest reprinting 'An Indiscretion in the Life of an Heiress'. But Hardy was against it. He thought he might find the idea 'amusing in [his] old age' to reconstruct, from that 'modification, aided by memory, & a fragment still in existence', his first, unpublished, novel, *The Poor Man and the Lady.*[12]

Written between 1881 and 1900, the twelve stories were, of course, unrelated to Hardy's recent life, but several drew material from his childhood environment, and from certain features of his own personality and experience. Thus 'The Changed Man' described the cholera epidemic outside Dorchester when Hardy was fourteen, and Maumbry's heroic efforts for 'the relief of the suffering poor' were based on those of Horace Moule's father, the vicar of Fordington. The 'new parson' in that story who wanted 'to stop the band-playing' resembled the new vicar who stopped the music of the Stinsford Choir, which also suggested the musical setting of 'The Grave by the Handpost'. 'The Duke's Reappearance', Hardy told Clodd, was 'a tradition in my mother's family, who are mentioned in it under their real names.' The suspect archaeologist in 'A Tryst at an Ancient Earthwork' was sufficiently like a Dorsetshire antiquarian, called Edward Cunningham, for Hardy to fear it might be thought libellous, 'though it was meant for nobody in particular.'[13]

Hardy's lifelong interest in the poor man-lady theme, dating from his early 'passion' for the Bockhampton 'lady of the manor', appeared in both 'The Waiting Supper' and 'What the Shepherd Saw'. His sense of the contrast between romantic love and prosaic marriage was central to 'The Romantic Adventures of a Milkmaid'. There his own attacks of suicidal depression were caricatured in the Baron – whose 'hat that seemed as if it would open and shut like an accordion' oddly recalled the 'small accordion' or 'toy concertina' given to Hardy by his father at the age of four. Suicide was treated more seriously in 'The Grave by the Handpost', and two stories showed Hardy's old fondness for window-pictures. 'A Changed Man' was told from the angle of an 'invalid' watching the world through an 'oriel window' overlooking the 'Casterbridge' High Street, as Hardy must have longed to do, when flat on his back at Tooting, with no view but the bedroom wall. 'What the Shepherd Saw' was seen from the 'little circular window' of a lonely hut.[14]

Through this window he watched a drama played in front of a 'trilithon, consisting of three oblong stones in the form of a doorway', as if to simulate an ancient Greek theatre. As a solitary watcher by night, he was like the Watchman at the start of Aeschylus' *Agamemnon.* As a shepherd who witnessed a murder by a Duke, he was like the shepherd in Sophocles who saw King Oedipus kill his father'; and the story contained one fine example of Sophoclean irony. Oedipus promises to investigate the murder of

Laius as zealously 'as if he were my own father'. Hardy's Duchess, unaware
that her husband has killed and buried her lover, tells the murderer, 'He
may be lying very quiet because of you'. There was even what looks like
a reminiscence of Aristotle's brief history of Greek tragedy. 'Aeschylus',
wrote Aristotle, 'increased the number of actors from one to two . . .
Sophocles made it three'. In the tragedy watched by Hardy's shepherd, the
characters entered one by one. After the third 'individual' had disappeared,
'the boy remained in the hut, confronting the trilithon as if he expected
yet more actors on the scene, but nobody else appeared.' When referring
here to the 'scene' and the 'hut', Hardy must have remembered that the
Greek word *skene*, defined by Liddell and Scott as 'a wall at the back of the
stage, with columns and doors for entrance and exit', originally meant
'tent or hut'.[15]

A passage once quoted by Matthew Arnold to convict Lucretius of
undue 'depression and *ennui*' was adapted by the Byronic Baron to describe
depressives like himself: 'To escape themselves they travel, take picturesque houses, and engage in country sports.' In 'The Waiting Supper' the
frustrated lovers live on opposite banks of the river Froom – one more
implicit allusion to the dead on the banks of the Styx, in Virgil's musical
line: '*tendebantque manus ripae ulterioris amore* (and they stretched out their
hands in love of the farther bank)'. The 'gilded image' possibly pocketed
by the unscrupulous archaeologist was appropriately one of Mercury, celebrated in a Horace *Ode* as 'clever at concealing, in jocular theft, whatever
takes his fancy.' Chaucer's theme of a January-May marriage (soon to be
realized in Hardy's own life) became the basis for black comedy in 'A
Mere Interlude': 'That night she lay between the two men she had married – Heddegan on the one hand, and on the other through the parti-
tion against which the bed stood, Charles Stow', a drowned equivalent of
Chaucer's Damian. Shakespeare supplied two models for that 'melancholy,
emotional character', the Baron. He was 'the Jacques of this forest and
stream', and his power over the 'innocent' milkmaid was 'that of Prospero
over the gentle Ariel.'[16]

From Tennyson's *Enoch Arden*, the problem of a supposedly dead husband's reappearance was rehandled in both 'Enter a Dragoon', and 'A
Waiting Supper' – in the latter combined with the procrastinating-lovers
theme of 'The Statue and the Bust'. Browning was the chief influence,
too, on 'Alicia's Diary', though it began with a parody of Vaughan's 'They
are all gone into the world of light / And I alone sit lingring here': 'Caroline gone abroad, and I left here!' But the diarist's unconscious betrayal
of her own unpleasant character showed the technique of Browning's
dramatic monologues.[17]

In June 1912, while reading the proofs of his collected works, the poet
commented: 'the novels seem immature to me.' After the novels, he must
have found these short stories even less mature, except in their ingenuity
and neat construction. As 'criticism of life' few can be taken seriously. In
most of them real life is simply manipulated into a pattern apparently

designed to show how amusingly, symmetrically, or perversely things might
in theory work out. Blackmailed by a witness of her wedding on Monday,
the bride of 'A Mere Interlude' confesses her 'tragedy' to the man she
marries on Tuesday – that her first husband was drowned within hours of
the wedding. Her second husband then confesses his 'tragedy' too – 'four
strapping girls' by his first marriage, whose education is intended to be his
second wife's main job. In 'Master John Horsleigh, Knight', the clandes-
tine mistress turns out to be the legal wife, and the lady known as 'Dame
Horsleigh', the mother of his children, has knowingly committed bigamy.
'The Grave by the Handpost' is an elaborate demonstration of life's unfair-
ness. Urged by his father to join the army, Luke hates it so much that his
bitter reproaches drive his father to suicide. Full of remorse, he arranges
to have the body moved 'to a decent Christian churchyard', and goes off
to the 'war in Spain', hoping this time 'to be worthy of father'. Returning
to find his father still buried at the crossroads, he commits suicide himself, leaving a written request to be buried beside his father. 'But the paper
was accidentally swept to the floor, and overlooked until after his funeral,
which took place in the ordinary way in the churchyard.'[18]

Well aware that some of these stories were 'not particularly good', Hardy
was probably right in thinking that 'A Changed Man' was 'the best'. But
the most enjoyable was 'The Romantic Adventures of a Milkmaid'. A
satirical fairy tale, with supernatural overtones, and an obvious debt to
'Cinderella', it was also an allegory of sexual attraction as a threat to marriage. It ended with a parody of what Hardy had called 'the regulation
finish that "they married and were happy ever after"'. The heroine is last
seen as a contented wife and mother, but admits that she would never
'have the power to disobey', if the Baron suddenly turned up and said,
'Margery, come with me!' Though she takes it back next moment, her
recantation inspires little confidence: 'Yet no . . . It would be so unfair to
baby.' Her husband wisely puts more faith in his rival's conscience than
his wife's love.[19]

27

Satires of Circumstance

Like Creon in Euripides, when fetched by a maid to find his daughter
horribly killed, Hardy had gone up to Emma's bedroom that morning of
1912 'in ignorance (*agnosia*) of disaster'. That *agnosia* was paralleled in
1914. The Great War took him as much by surprise as Emma's death had
done: 'He had been completely at fault, as he often owned, on the coming
so soon of such a convulsion as the war'. And when he married Florence
Dugdale (10 February 1914), he seems to have known hardly more of her
inner feelings than he had known of Emma's – before he read her diaries.[1]

Some of Florence's feelings were confided in letters to Clodd and other
friends. By January 1913 she had got sick of hearing about Emma: 'I must
say that the good lady's virtues are beginning to weigh heavily on my
shoulders.' In March, having registered the 'depth' of Hardy's 'affection',
'goodness' and 'unselfishness', she added: 'All I trust is that I may not, for
the rest of his life, have to sit & listen humbly to an account of her virtues
& graces.' For an anniversary 'pilgrimage' to Emma's grave that November
he asked her to wear mourning: 'After wearing colours for some months
I suddenly had to go back into black – buying all new black things . . . I
think I can break out into colours again soon.' When he even suggested
that she 'should *aways* wear half mourning in future, as a mark of devotion
to *her* memory', Florence understandably wondered 'if there is something
in the air of Max Gate that makes us all a little crazy.'[2]

Bewildered by 'this extraordinary idealization of Mrs Hardy', and
humiliated by the snobbish rudeness of that 'Mrs Hardy in little', Lilian
Gifford ('I was never brought up to earn *my* living'), Florence firmly refused to marry Hardy if Lilian was to remain there '*permanently*, as one of
the family'. The ultimatum worked, but the subsequent wedding must have
depressed the thirty-five-year-old bride. Fearful of 'reporters and horrible

snap-shotters', Hardy 'seemed quite determined that *no one* outside the house should be asked'. So none of her family was there at Enfield Church, except her father and youngest sister. Their 'honeymoon – if it could be called such –', Hardy told Frederic Harrison, was 'taken in slices . . . between the prosiest of home doings in the way of seeing to repairs, the kitchen garden, getting in manure, & such like.'[3]

Absorbed in writing poems about the 'romance of S. Juliot', and embarrassed at having to inform the St Juliot Rector of what might sound like another romance, Hardy stressed how 'soberly, I may even say gravely' he had remarried, implying that his chief motive had been to avoid 'a rupture of continuity', since 'my wife was a great friend of my late wife'. He took the same line, though in less parsonical language, when breaking the news to his friends. 'We thought it the wisest thing to do', he explained to Cockerell, 'seeing what a right hand Florence has become to me, and there is a sort of continuity in it . . .' 'We came straight back here', he told Clodd, 'and I am going to put over my study door, "Business as usual during alterations"'. His least romantic, but perhaps most powerful motive for the 'alterations' was confessed to Mrs Henniker: 'such a course seeming an obvious one to me, being as I was so lonely and helpless.'[4]

Florence's motive, as explained to the Cockerells, was more altruistic: 'I did indeed marry him that I might have the right to express my devotion – & to endeavour to add to his comfort and happiness. Had I not married him, I realized that I should not be able to remain at Max Gate, & dreaded that, when the time came that he most needed my care, I should not be able to be with him.' She cannot have expected much romance, but must have been slightly hurt by his apparent wish to minimize that aspect of their relationship. Ten months later, recalling the death of her friend Hyatt, 'who was more to me than anything else in the world . . . the only person who ever loved me', she 'sometimes' felt 'that there is no one much in the world who cares whether I be happy or sad.'[5]

Nor did marrying a successful author promise to help her become one herself. In April 1914, to her 'great grief', she felt 'obliged to refuse' a publisher's request for 'a book about dogs', and even to put aside 'a pile of books' for review. 'I suppose that it is unfair to my husband to take up so much outside work.' By July she was actually wondering: 'Ought I – in fairness to my husband – to give up my scribbling?' Meanwhile marriage limited her freedom not only to write about dogs, but even to keep them. When a bitch of Mrs Henniker's had puppies, Florence was 'weak enough to feel' she wanted one of them, 'as a playmate for Wessex', the terrier puppy she had adopted as a watchdog when she first moved into Max Gate: 'But my husband objected – quite wisely I am sure.'[6]

Hardy's ignorance of his young bride's feelings was doubtless dispelled gradually; but his ignorance of 'the way the human race was going' (Arnold's phrase, betraying equal ignorance) ended traumatically in August, when war was declared on Germany. The sudden refutation of his belief that war, as in 'The Sick Battle-God', was on its way out, 'led him to despair of the world's history thenceforward.' There seemed nothing to do but 'sit still in an apathy, & watch the clock spinning backwards, with mild wonder if, when it gets back to the Dark Ages, & the sack of Rome, it will ever move forward again to a new Ranascence, & a new literature.' Such was his initial response. 'The horror of this', wrote Florence, 'is making a great change in him – I can see. He seems ten years older. The thought of it all obsesses him. That is why, I think, he writes no poem about it. He cannot about the things he feels most deeply.'[7]

Yet though 'a man of peace', he was no pacifist: 'events proved to me with startling rapidity that there was no other course for us but to fight.' Anxious to do what he could, at seventy-four, to support the war-effort, he attended a London meeting of authors 'called hurriedly' by the minister in charge of propaganda. Whatever he contributed to the discussion, his only memory of it was visual and atmospheric: 'the yellow September sun shone in from the dusty street with a tragic cast upon them as they sat round the large blue table'. He was rather more in his element when writing (and disclaiming copyright for) a 'soldiers' war-song . . . which won an enormous popularity'. But perhaps his best bit of war-work was allowing, and minimally helping, Granville-Barker to stage a potted patriotic version of *The Dynasts* which ran for 72 performances at the Kingsway Theatre in London. Though, unlike later historians, Hardy did see the war as a 'dynastic struggle', 'all wrought by the madness of one man', the Kaiser, he recognized the absurdity of turning his anti-war drama into war-propaganda, by expurgating its subversive philosophy: 'It is, indeed, rather a comical result of the good Barker's abridgement that I am made to appear thereby as orthodox as a churchwarden'. Still, it was probably good for sales, to which his marriage had given extra importance. 'It struck me', he told his publisher, 'that such a production might send people to the book.'[8]

Meanwhile he had been busy on another book. After making Cockerell his literary executor, he had explained to him in August: 'What I care most about just now is that the poems entitled, "Satires of Circumstance" . . . should be brought out by the Macmillans at some time or other.' And what he cared most about in that volume was the section called 'Poems of 1912–13'. He had told Mrs Henniker why:

> Some of them I rather shrink from printing – those I wrote just after Emma died, when I looked back at her as she had originally been, & when I felt miserable lest I had not treated her considerately in her latter life. However I shall publish them as the only amends I can make, if it were so.[9]

He had sent off 'the MS. of "Satires of Circumstance"' as soon as the war started, not expecting them to be published immediately, but at 'any favourable time – say, when people get tired of the war – if they do!' The whole volume was named after a series of eleven poems first published in the *Fortnightly Review* (April 1911); and when it came out (17 November

1914) as *Satires of Circumstance: Lyrics and Reveries with Miscellaneous Pieces*, reviewers naturally assumed the relatively inferior section called 'Satires of Circumstance' to be the heart of the book, and concentrated on that. To a friend who found the Satires 'too strong' Hardy explained: 'I did not like them – particularly in the same volume with those written at a later date when my thoughts had been set on quite another track by painful events.' But as they had already appeared 'in a prominent periodical', so were likely to be 'raked up' anyway, he had decided to include them, and his publisher had then called the whole volume after them.[10]

Already uneasy about 'the harsh contrasts which the accidents of [his] life during the past few years had forced into the poems', Hardy cannot have relished the terms in which young Lytton Strachey chose to praise them. They were, he suggested, 'modern as no other poems are', simply because they were commonplace, prosaic, unmusical, 'incorrect', 'fumbling', 'drab', and 'clumsy': 'the flat undistinguished poetry of Mr. Hardy has found out the secret of touching our marrow-bones.'[11]

The harshest contrast in the volume was between the voices of personal experience and of fictional melodrama, in 'Poems of 1912–13' and 'Satires of Circumstance' respectively. The former section, 'the only amends' that Hardy could make to his first wife, expressed, like Sergeant Troy's flowers, what Byron called 'the late remorse of love'. It stemmed directly from Hardy's reactions to Emma's death. In 'The Going' he relived that dreadful morning of 27 November 1912; in 'Your Last Drive', the 'damp dark afternoon' of the 22nd, when 'she motored to pay a visit six miles off', and – 'I drove not with you . . .'; in 'The Walk', all the walks he had taken without her, because she was 'weak and lame . . . and I did not mind, / Not thinking of you as left behind.' 'I found her out there' opened a series of poems about their first love-affair at St Juliot. Others recalled special things about her: her dislike of getting wet and her lifelong love of daisies ('Rain on a Grave'); her habit of abrupt disappearances, like her sudden dash to Calais in 1908 ('Without Ceremony'); her delight in entertaining, especially at Max Gate garden-parties ('The Lament'); her confident riding ('The Phantom Horsewoman'). But the most powerful expression of Hardy's new feelings about Emma was 'The Voice': 'Woman much missed, how you call to me, call to me . . .'[12]

Yet the personal element in the volume was not confined to 'Poems of 1912–13'. The opening section, 'Lyrics and Reveries', surveyed more generally Hardy's current state of mind, placing Emma in the context of his whole love-life. Thus 'In Front of the Landscape' and 'The Ghost of the Past' expressed a new sense of living only partially in the present; and 'When I Set Out for Lyonnesse', celebrating his first love for Emma, was set alongside 'A Thunderstorm in Town', about Mrs Henniker, 'The Torn Letter', about an unknown female fan for whom he felt a romantic 'ache', and two poems about Florence Dugdale, 'After the Visit', and 'To Meet or Otherwise'. By way of epilogue to these love-poems, 'After the Last Lamp' presented an archetypal image of love: a 'mysterious tragic pair' of lovers, 'blinded ... to time and place', and with faces that 'held in suspense a misery / At things which had been or might be', for ever 'Creeping slowly, creeping sadly' through rain and darkness.[13]

Compared with such products of genuine feeling, the 'Satires of Circumstance' seem cerebral and contrived. Even their title seems unsatisfactory. Is Circumstance the satirist or the target of satire? When first used in *The Hand of Ethelberta*, 'a satire of circumstance' evidently meant the former; but when later protesting against *Punch* parodies of the *Fortnightly* poems, Hardy implied the latter meaning: 'people supposed these mere imitations were clever satires of the poems, not perceiving, even with the title before their eyes, that the originals themselves were satires ... caustically humorous productions ... issued with a light heart before the war.' The reader is left swinging uncomfortably between the two interpretations'. The poems themselves read like melodramatic parables to show how badly people treat one another, and how badly life treats them; but the tone is is so sour, and the plots so far-fetched that one feels like dismissing the whole section as a symptom of paranoia.[14]

One of the 'Lyrics and Reveries' might conceivably attract the same criticism: 'Ah, Are You Digging on My Grave?' This too is 'caustically humorous', and deliberately structured to reach a climax of disillusionment: not even the faithful dog remembers its dead mistress. But there is something different here, perhaps because it arose from Hardy's visits to Emma's grave, and guilt about having so promptly proposed to Florence. Whatever the reason, this poem makes more than cerebral satire of the *agnosia* theme which it shares with the 'Satires of Circumstance', and gives that impression of genuine feeling which characterizes Hardy's best poetry.[15]

Though so much of importance in the volume came from bitter experience, material from literature was also interestingly used. According to Plato's *Symposium*, human beings were originally spherical, until they were chopped in two – since when each half has longed to be reunited with its other half. This comic theory of affinity evidently underlay 'The Convergence of the Twain', where the *Titanic* and its 'sinister mate', the iceberg, are 'twin halves of one august event'. When 'consummation comes', it 'jars two hemispheres' – a punning phrase with a literal and a figurative meaning: both sides of the Atlantic, and also both parts of the original whole. In Lucretius Nature dissuades mortals from wishing to live any longer, because '*eadem sunt omnia semper* (all things are always the same)'. In 'Channel Firing' God tells the dead: 'The world is as it used to be'. '*Caelum non animum mutant qui trans mare currunt* ('By dashing across the sea people change their sky, not their state of mind', wrote Horace. The 'Starlings on the Roof' say much the same about people who move house: 'They look for a new life, rich and strange; / They do not know that, let them range, / Wherever they may, / They will get no change.'[16]

'Poems of 1912–13' have an epigraph from Virgil: '*Veteris vestigia flammae*'. Translated simply as 'Vestiges of an old flame', the words were apt enough;

but their original context was relevant too. Dido was recognizing her passion for Aeneas by its likeness to what she had felt about her dead husband, Sychaeus. Was Hardy hoping to make this section more acceptable to Florence, by hinting that, like Dido's love for her husband, his 'old' love for his first wife had been wholly superseded by a new passion?[17]

Other vestiges of Hardy's old love of classical and English literature can be spotted throughout the collection, with Lucian, Donne, Milton, Wordsworth, Tennyson, Browning, Rossetti, and Swinburne betraying their continued presence in his mind. Nor were such traces confined to the less personal poems. Of course 'The Going' needed no prompting from Patmore's rather similar poem, 'The Departure': here Hardy's traumatic experience found its own expression. But even 'The Voice' ('Woman much missed, how you call to me, call to me') initially echoes the rhythm of Browning's 'Lost Leader' ('Just for a handful of silver he left us'), however brilliantly adapted as the final lines shorten and fade into silence:

> Thus I; faltering forward,
> Leaves around me falling,
> Wind oozing thin through the thorn from norward,
> And the woman calling.

One may even suspect those 'leaves' of descending from the same tree as 'the autumn fall of leaves' that the Blessed Damozel's lover mistook for her hair.[18]

As an artistic whole, the collection certainly suffered from the split between the 'rather brutal' 'Satires', constructed 'from notes made some twenty years ago', and the 'Poems' forced out of Hardy by more recent trauma. But the crack was occasionally papered over by a common theme. The last 'Satire of Circumstance', for instance, written in 1910, though not printed in the *Fortnightly*, was strangely concordant with Hardy's feelings after November 1912. In it a 'lonely workman' stood by 'her grave', yearning to 'raise her phantom', yet – 'she was the woman I did not love, / Whom all the others were ranked above, / Whom during her life I thought nothing of.'[19]

More generally, the two groups of poems were linked by the concept of *agnosia*, constantly stressed in the 'Satires': 'The happy young housewife does not know . . .', 'How little he thinks . . .', 'But their folks don't know . . .', 'What I really am you have never gleaned . . .', 'O but you don't know!', 'But you did not perceive me', 'his body had not been known.' The same concept pervaded the poems about Emma: 'O you could not know / that such swift fleeing / No soul foreseeing – / Not even I – would undo me so!' Even if Hardy had been with her on her 'Last Drive', he 'would not have seen' any 'last-time look' on her face. She will 'not know' how often he visits her grave, or what his thoughts are. She is 'powerless to know' that she might have been giving a garden- or dinner-party today. As 'The Haunter', she cannot 'let him know' that, wherever he goes, she goes too. The fashion-house that sends her an advertising 'Circular' does not know that she has long been 'costumed in a shroud.' Her 'voiceless ghost' leads him back to St Juliot – 'Where you will next be there's no knowing', and the birds and seals remain 'Ignorant of what there is flitting here to see'. In 'Beeny Cliff', 'the woman . . . whom the ambling pony bore . . . nor knows nor cares for Beeny'; and the implicit burden of all these 'Poems' was 'if only I had known!'[20]

Despite such unifying factors, the volume remains a 'miscellany', less valuable for its overall effect than for one of its sections, 'Poems of 1912–13', and some fine single pieces. The section gives from one man's experience a picture of bereavement which any bereaved person will recognize as authentic – even to the disproportionate irritation at junk mail still arriving for the deceased. The finest of the other pieces is 'Exeunt Omnes', written on Hardy's seventy-third birthday. It describes with equal force and accuracy a by-product of bereavement: the feelings of an ageing person who does not believe in an after-life, as his or her nearest and dearest die off. Here Hardy used the end of a Dorchester fair to dramatize, far more strikingly than the island-image in Matthew Arnold's 'Isolation', the ultimate fact that 'We mortal millions live *alone*':

> Folk all fade. And whither,
> As I wait alone where the fair was?
> Into the clammy and numbing night-fog
> Whence they entered hither.
> Soon one more goes thither![21]

28

Moments of Vision

'We are quite dormant at present', Hardy told Clodd in February 1915, 'but mean to wake up in the spring'. 'T. is like a dormouse', added Florence in a postscript to his letter, '& loves to be curled up in his study waiting for the spring. We have been married a year & a day, & *really & truly* (I am not joking now) it has been a year of *great* happiness.' The hibernation-image was superficially apt, and Florence doubtless meant what she said. But far from dozing in his study, Hardy was working towards his largest collection of poems; and the happiness had been patchy.[1]

His dormouse-aspect reflected a new reluctance induced by the war, the death of his closest sibling, Mary Hardy, and a sense of 'increasing age', to tangle with the outside world. After Mary's funeral in November 1915 Florence reported: 'Tom – to my great dismay – says he feels that he never wants to go anywhere or to see anyone again. He wants to live on here, quite quietly, shut up in his study.' Eighteen months later he confessed to Mrs Henniker: 'The war has taken all enterprise out of me (I should add that it is partly because of the practical difficulties of getting about), and I have almost registered a vow that I will not see London till the butchery is over.' In June 1917, though quite fit at seventy-seven, he refused an invitation from John Buchan to visit the front in France: 'I remember that I am not so young as I was, & am compelled to give up almost all enterprises nowadays that comprise travelling more than a few miles'. Apart from brief pilgrimages to Sturminster Newton, St Juliot, Plymouth, and Tintagel, he scarcely exaggerated when he told Clodd: 'We go nowhere . . . except in the immediate neighbourhood, the war cloud & the railway difficulties keeping us at home.' While thus becoming, in Florence's words, 'more and more of a recluse', he turned out increasingly introverted poetry. *Moments of Vision*, as defined in the opening poem, were produced by a mysterious process which 'throws our mind back on us, and our heart, / Until we start'.[2]

As for Florence's year of 'great happiness', it had ended in 'horrible pain' at reading *Satires of Circumstance*, not just because of the 'Poems' about Emma, but because 'it seems to me that I am an utter failure if my husband can publish such a *sad sad* book'. In theory, as her sympathetic confidante, Lady Hoare, told her, 'one must not make the man responsible for what the poet writes'. But in real life Florence's reaction to the volume was inevitable. So was Hardy's need to publish it. For this, and for other causes of Florence's unhappiness, it would be silly to blame either party. Any marriage between depressives with an age-difference of nearly forty years was bound to have its problems; and the Hardys' 'modest hope' that 'the union of two rather melancholy temperaments may result in cheerfulness, as the junction of two negatives forms a positive', was realized quite as fully as could have been expected.[3]

But Florence was also unhappy about things she could not have foreseen, like the 'attendant horrors' of Mary's death: 'They kept on worrying and worrying us to go up to see her, even to the last moment', and 'to keep on kissing her'. At Plymouth she found Hardy's researches into the 'wretched decayed houses' and neglected graves of Emma's parents and grandparents intensely 'dismal'. She herself had various ailments: 'a touch of sciatica'; 'tiresome nasal catarrh', for which she underwent a minor operation; chronic pharyngitis, for which she was given two courses of 'inoculations'; and eye-trouble, which reduced her to wearing, at only thirty-eight, 'a tremendous pair of horn spectacles'. Thus handicapped, she read aloud to Hardy every night 'until 10.30', after working so hard all day on his correspondence that she had little 'energy & time' left for her own 'literary work'. Nor can she have enjoyed typing out Hardy's humorous apologies for writing 'by machinery nowadays' – as though the typist, too, was a machine.[4]

Meanwhile for Hardy the war cast 'a shade over everything.' He thought it would end in a German victory, or at best 'an indecisive issue, Germany preponderating'. With its 'huge cavalry camp', Dorchester was sometimes 'a surging mass of soldiers.' There was also a POW camp, and when German submarines threatened food-shortages, German prisoners of war were sent to 'enlarge the kitchen garden' at Max Gate. Zeppelins bombed the outskirts of London while Florence was still in a London nursing-home. One of her sisters married a pilot in the Royal Flying Corps during his ten days' leave from the front. Hardy called them 'rather thoughtless young people', Florence, 'Poor pathetic children!' But the war came closest to Max Gate when a 'very dear cousin' of Hardy's, Frank George, was killed at Gallipoli. He was 'almost the only, if not the only, blood relative of the next generation' in whom Hardy had 'taken any interest'. He had liked him enough to think of making him his heir and, for 'a man of peace', was surprisingly proud to relate how Frank, in 'rushing a Turkish trench', had 'bayonetted some 8 or 10 Turks'.[5]

Conscious of his age, Hardy was anxious to maximize posthumous royalties for Florence's benefit. So he finalized arrangements for making Cockerel and Florence his literary executors, published a book of *Selected Poems* (3 October 1916), to boost sales of his next volume, impressed on two book-length critics of his works that the poems mattered more than the novels, and sorted out a muddle about film rights. Had he foreseen the market for Hardy films in the 1990s, he might not have told Florence in May 1915: 'I wish I had never agreed to let the novels be used for cinema purposes; it is a perfect worry.'[6]

He was even more worried about his posthumous reputation. On a fictionalized life of Gissing he had commented: 'The power of telling lies about people through that channel after they are dead, by stirring in a few truths, is a horror to contemplate.' He had already suffered from newspaper reports of his private life, based on incidents in his novels, or Dorchester gossip, and from a biographical chapter in a French book about him. Now, in January 1916, wrote Florence, he was 'horrified at learning that one of his friends [was] going to publish a volume of reminiscences'. It was Clodd, to whom they had both confided potentially damaging secrets; and Florence 'had to write a very decided letter' warning him not to publish 'anything about [her] husband'. Clodd's *Memories* proved harmless; but two other friends were keeping diaries, and Hardy began to feel surrounded by snoopers collecting material for future books about him. 'He has such a dread', Florence told one of her own less reliable confidantes, 'of the person who comes here & goes away to write down things'. How right he turns out to have been![7]

One way of minimizing the 'lies' that could be told about him was to reduce the number of truths that could be 'stirred in' to make the lies plausible. So Hardy was busy going through his private papers, burning what seemed not to be needed for a fair account of his life. But who was to write that account? Obviously Florence, and the first plan was simply to feed her the information, oral and documentary, that she would require for the purpose. 'I have been taking notes', she told Cockerell in July 1917, 'but find them very difficult to do without constantly appealing to T.H. for verification, and he is now almost at the end of his present job – revising his note-books (they are practically diaries) – and we are going to work together.' But such collaboration is never easy. Predictably, since he knew the facts and was also the more experienced author, Hardy eventually produced the text as well. Thus he started writing his autobiography in the third person singular, to be published as a biography by his widow after his death. That was the private meaning of the remark in *The Later Years*: 'Hardy's mind seems to have been running on himself at this time [1915–17] to a degree quite unusual with him'.[8]

Meanwhile he was collecting poems which were also autobiographical, for their 'moments of vision' were new insights into aspects of his own past. But he was alive to the present state of the poetry market, and after sending off his 'parcel' of manuscript to Macmillans (21 August 1917), he shrewdly suggested that the first impression should be 'quite small . . . so as to set collectors advertising for it as soon as a second impression is announced, and thus drawing attention to the book.' He was more alive, too, this time to Florence's probable reactions. Before *Moments of Vision* came out on 30 November 1917, he gave her a copy inscribed: 'From Thomas Hardy, this first copy of the first edition, to the first of women Florence Hardy'. It was just as well, for the first woman she would come across in the text was the poet's first wife.[9]

In *The Well-Beloved* Pierston suddenly caught sight of himself in a mirror, looking far older than he felt. 'Moments of Vision' were like that, only in retrospect and in depth: sudden, disconcerting glimpses of oneself at specific moments in one's past, in 'that mirror / That makes of men a transparency', forcing them to see *through* their past selves. Thus the poet, recalling how bored and irritated he had felt with Emma, that wet day at Bournemouth in 1875, was forced to recognize his ignorance on that occasion: he 'did not know' what he was missing in her personality, what a gift of life he was 'wasting'. The same pattern of belated realization appeared in most of the other poems about Emma. 'Near Lanivet, 1872' recorded his failure to take seriously enough the prophetic image of Emma's 'crucifixion'. Of three poems resulting from a visit to Riverside Villa in June 1916, 'On Sturminster Foot-Bridge' implied his unawareness that, like the swallows on the roof above her, Emma would soon be migrating from the 'dark world' in which she now represented a solitary 'latticegleam'. 'Overlooking the River Stour', as at Bournemouth, he gazed out of the window into the rain, but never turned his head 'To see the more behind [his] back'; 'mindless' as 'The Musical Box', he 'did not hear', 'did not see', that he had to 'make the most of what is nigh': such welcomes home were not to last 'lifelong'.[10]

   Not all the 'moments', though, related to Emma. 'The Oxen' reflected Hardy's childhood response to a tradition probably recalled in youth when, working with Hicks on Rampisham Church, he saw a carving of 'a kneeling bovine'. 'Afternoon Service at Mellstock' contrasted his 'mindless' but happy 'psalming' at ten with the 'subtle thoughts' that had made him a gloomy agnostic. 'Apostrophe to an Old Psalm Tune' compared the various stages of his life at which he had heard it, the last in August 1916; and 'Quid Hic Agis?' did the same with the lesson about the 'still small voice', heard first at Stinsford, then (among other places) at Kilburn in 1862, and then read by himself in St Juliot church around 1870. 'To My Father's Violin' celebrated not only his father's playing, but those shared 'adventures with the fiddle'. 'The Last Signal' 'mirrored by the coffin' also mirrored Hardy's feelings in 1886, at the death of the poet-scholar he had first consulted about Greek grammar in 1856; and 'Logs on the Hearth' pictured the literal or symbolic cremation of the tree he had climbed with his dead sister Mary, 'almost [his] only companion in childhood.'[11]

These fragments of autobiography were set in a context of general thought about time, often imaged by forms of clock. Thus the dead were called from their graves at Wimborne Minster by the 'jack-o' clock' that mechanically sounded the quarters there. The moon, as the clock of the months, interrogated in a seven-line stanza suggestive of weeks, summed up human history 'In [her] time' as a 'show / God ought surely to shut up soon'. The calendar, as the clock of the years, surreptitiously created 'drought' for Hardy and Emma: 'the Kalendar / Moved on, and Time / Devoured our prime.' Changes observed on 'An Anniversary', at the 'like minute' of the same 'date-day', showed Time's destructiveness more clearly. In accordance with Dorset folklore, the pointing 'shade' of a sun-dial predicted Mary Hardy's death; and making 'the clock of the years go backward', to save a dead 'her' from extinction, only reduced her to pre-natal 'nought at all', extinguishing even the 'memory of her'.[12]

For poetry so subjective and personal, Hardy needed no help from literature, but the volume still contained traces of reading that had deeply affected him. Plato's *Phaedrus* and 'Myth of Er' can be sensed behind the thought of the 'journeying boy' in the train: 'Knows your soul a sphere . . . Our rude realms far above, / Whence with spacious vision you mark and mete / This region of sin that you find you in, / But are not of?' The 'Nether Glooms' and 'Mournful Meads' where Hardy's father might need his violin, were Virgil's *infernae tenebrae* and *lugentes campi* (lower darkness and mourning fields), where Anchises' 'sad ghost' was seen to 'liven at the sound', not of his fiddle's 'string' but of his son's voice.[13]

Horace's Lalage was a young girl who would soon be 'pursuing' her lover; 'Timing Her' pictured her 'rushing' across country towards him, her euphonious Greek name made a dactyl for her rapid approach, but climactically reverting on arrival to its original anapaest: 'Lalage's coming . . . Here's Lalage!' Another surprisingly cheerful poem, 'Great Things', listing Hardy's favourite pleasures in life, ended with a paraphrase of Horace's rule: make sure, when you come to die, you can at least say '*Vixi* (I have really lived)!' More typical in mood was an adaptation of Horace's '*post equitem sedet atra cura* (Black Care sits behind the horse-man): 'The Interloper' describes a sinister fourth figure, later identified by Hardy as 'Madness', who 'sits' unnoticed with 'three folk driving in a quaint old chaise'. Thus the Horatian image was made to hint that Emma had shared the Gifford tendency to insanity.[14]

Seeing for himself 'The Upper Birch-Leaves' 'jig as in glee / To this very last', Hardy need not have remembered Coleridge's 'one red leaf, the last of its clan, / That dances as often as dance it can, / Hanging so light and hanging so high, / On the topmost twig that looks up at the sky'. But he had never actually 'journeyed from [his] native spot / Across the south sea shine', and the marginal glosses demonstrate that 'His Country' was consciously modelled on 'The Ancient Mariner', including its moral, 'He prayeth well who loveth well / Both man and bird and beast'. This was sarcastically extended to include, not only 'slimy things' that 'crawl with legs / Upon the slimy sea', but even 'Foreigners – not like us . . . Stretch country-love beyond the seas? / Too Christian!'[15]

More faintly, Tennyson's 'Brook' can be heard behind the start of 'The Wind's Prophecy' ('I travel on by barren farms'), his 'Talking Oak' behind 'The Tree and the Lady', and such tortuous melodrama as Browning's 'A Forgiveness' behind 'The Statue of Liberty'. In Browning's dramatic monologue, the monk who hears the husband confess to murdering his wife turns out to have been her lover. In Hardy's, the man found washing the statue proves to be no libertarian, but the father of the girl who modelled for it; and the casual questioner is the man who carved it – but he does not inform the father that his daughter, 'held so saintly', died in 'dens of vice'. In a less absurd allegory of his own life, 'The Something that Saved Him', Hardy escaped from another sort of den: 'I . . . looked back at den, ditch and river, / And sang.' Reading Mackail's *Life of William Morris* in February 1917, he could not understand how a man who could write 'real poetry' could 'care about tapestries and carpets'. Was he now remembering the best moment in Morris's *Sigurd the Volsung*? There Gunnar, thrown into a snake-pit, 'woke' his 'fainting harp' and burst into 'song': 'And I fought and was glad in the morning, and I sing in the night and the end'.[16]

With Hardy's mind 'running on himself' in early youth, when the Bible had meant so much to him, two of his favourite passages in it also affected the volume. The story of Elijah and the 'still small voice' was used not only to mark critical stages of Hardy's past life, but to express his conflicting feelings in the present: a sense of deep discouragement that made further writing seem pointless, but also of obligation to go on writing. Having found his real voice as a poet, he felt bound to use it, and having got people to read him, to 'prophesy in the land'. This meant, among other things, contributing to war-propaganda, though well aware that he had no gift for it. In the 'soldiers' war-song', 'Men Who March Away', phrases like 'purblind prank' and 'dolorous sigh' seem ridiculously remote from a Tommy's normal vocabulary, and the poet's obvious 'doubt' if 'Victory crowns the just' can only have disheartened anyone in his 'heart of hearts believing' that it did. As for 'A Call to National Service', its rhetoric was fatally undermined by the admission that the caller's own days of 'serving with never a slack' were over.[17]

So the title-question of 'Quid Hic Agis?' was given a non-Biblical implication: '(Though, as in old wise, / I might still arise, / Go forth, and stand / And prophesy in the land), / I feel the shake / Of wind and earthquake, / And consuming fire / Nigher and nigher, / And the voice catch clear, / What doest thou here?' The original question meant: 'Why aren't you prophesying in the land?' Here it sounds more like, 'Why, with death so close, are you still in the land of the living?'[18]

The second Biblical passage was adapted to prophesying on a more congenial subject than the war. In 'The Blinded Bird' St Paul's definition of Charity (which Jude told Sue would 'stand fast when all the rest that you call religion has passed away!') was used to expose a particularly revolting form of cruelty to animals. Singing as a physiological response to having the eyes put out with a red-hot needle was described, with an odd blend of pathos and sarcasm, as a type of true Christianity: 'Who hath charity? This bird. / Who suffereth long and is kind . . . Who thinketh no evil, but sings?'[19]

Again the song-pain image of 'The Something That Saved Him'. Whether or not derived from Morris, it evidently held a personal meaning for Hardy then. To his young poet-friend Siegfried Sassoon, recovering from war-wounds in hospital, he wrote in April 1917: 'I don't know how I should stand the suspense of this evil time if it were not for the sustaining power of poetry.' In linking these two poems, the image was one of several factors that held the collection together. 'Well: the poems are of a very mixed sort', Hardy told Gosse when they were published. 'To arrange them was beyond me.' They partly arranged themselves, though, around certain shared themes: a general concern with the dead, often lightened, as in 'Jubilate', by the thought that they were well 'out of it all'; concern with an inner world of memory and imagination more vivid than the 'real' one ('The House of Silence', for instance, implicitly describing Max Gate); and concern with aspects of kinship between all living things. These included family ties and traits ('Heredity'), linguistic bonds between Germans and Dorset people ('The Pity of It'), 'fellowship' between humans, animals, and plants ('The Wind Blew Words'), and 'Transformations' of the buried dead into trees, grasses, and flowers – 'A ruddy human life / Now turned to a green shoot.'[20]

There was also a unifying tendency in the recurrent echoes of Bockhampton music-making. An effort at cheerfulness came out as 'I will get a new string to my fiddle'; its failure, as a 'hollow wind, like a bassoon'. 'At Madame Tussaud's' celebrated the 'first fiddler' of the 'orchéstra' (the right accent for the Greek word) who had gone on playing 'staunchly' for 'four decades'. Hardy's grandfather, uncle, and father had played at Stinsford Church for a period 'covering inclusively just under forty years.' Among the 'Old Furniture' was a 'viol' evoking visions of a dead fiddler, perhaps Hardy's father: 'The tip of a bow receding, advancing / In airy quivers, as if it would cut / The plaintive gut.' More recent grief was expressed in 'The Last Performance', recalling how, shortly before her death, Emma 'suddenly sat down to the piano and played a long series of her favourite old tunes, saying at the end she would never play any more.'[21]

One form of 'arrangement' that must have been deliberate was repeating elsewhere in the volume the 'mirror'-image of the title-poem, 'Moments of Vision'. In 'The Pedigree' Hardy sees his ancestors, all doubles of himself, reflected in his 'uncurtained' bedroom window, made a 'mirror' by the darkness outside; and thinks that his 'I' is merely a reflection of them: 'I am merest mimicker and counterfeit!' 'Old Furniture' similarly shows him 'hands of the generations':

Hands behind hands, growing paler and paler,
    As in a mirror a candle-flame
Shows images of itself, each frailer
    As it recedes, though the eye may frame
        Its shape the same.

Even the broken mirror of 'Honeymoon Time at an Inn', though expressing a rather immature despair of 'wedlock' and 'the lot of all', had a structural excuse for being there: the mirror-fragments hastily collected by the
bride exactly suited the volume's central metaphor, which presented the
poems as a random collection of 'reflected' *Moments* in the poet's life.[22]

Externally the poems gave a new impression of lightness and ease. They
were mostly short, in purpose-built stanzas that rhythmically read themselves. Ballads were happily banished, and prosodic skill was shown, not by
metrical experiment but by pointed and apparently spontaneous expression, as in the lyrical epigram, 'In Time of "The Breaking of Nations"'.
There the effect of spontaneity had taken forty-five years to achieve:
an 'agricultural incident in Cornwall' during the Franco-Prussian war,
'recalled to him by a still bloodier' one, together with 'the feeling that
moved [him] in 1870', was finally versified in 1915.[23]

In March 1916 (two years before the first edition of Hopkins's poetry)
Hardy doubted whether 'the sequence of vowels' in Yeats's 'Innisfree'
'had much to do with its beauty, or whether any great poet ever thought
much about such sequences – except perhaps Gray & Tennyson.' So the
repeated *o*-sounds in 'The Last Performance' were presumably unintentional: 'I am playing my *o*ldest tunes, declared she, / All the *o*ldest tunes
I kn*o*w, – / Th*o*se I learnt ever s*o* long ag*o*.' / Why she should think just
then she'd play them / Silence cl*o*aks like sn*o*w.' He was annoyed, though,
that an Australian critic failed to register, in 'On Sturminster Foot-Bridge',
the 'onomatopoeia' of rhythms 'intended to convey . . . the impression of
a clucking of ripples into riverside holes when blown upon by an up-
stream wind': 'Reticulations creep upon the slack stream's face / When
the wind skims irritably past . . .' He therefore added '(*Onomatopoeic*)' to
the poem's title.[24]

But he seems to have cared less now for such verbal effects than for the
larger potential of certain images: a blind giant led by a dwarf, a caged
bird left on a grave, a small boy sitting alone in a railway-carriage, a man
climbing a dark tower to wind a clock, the remains of a sunshade found
in a seaside rock, a pencil dropped into a cranny of an ancient building.
However, these images were not used with equal success. Nothing came of
the giant and dwarf but the feeble comment, 'I have thought it the sorriest
of pantomimes, / If once, a hundred times!' The caged bird on the grave
was explained in the first draft by a trite love-story, far less convincing than
the tale of the caged goldfinch in *The Mayor of Casterbridge*. Printed here
without any explanation, it had a stronger impact, but did not quite add
up to a poem. The 'journeying boy', realistically accounted for in *Jude*, was

somewhat over-interpreted in 'Midnight on the Great Western'. 'The Clock-winder', climbing nightly to 'the trackway of Time', would have been more suggestive without the last sixteen lines, added in proof to reveal his hopeless love. The 'skeleton' of the sunshade was rather too explicitly connected with that of its owner.[25]

Only in the last of these images was the best balance struck between telling the reader too much and too little. After picturing the ghosts of the famous dead buried near him, the architectural student unconsciously prefigured the time when he himself would be buried – and forgotten:

> They waste to fog as I stir and stand,
> And move from the arched recess,
> And pick up the drawing that slipped from my hand,
> And feel for the pencil I dropped in the cranny
> In a moment's forgetfulness.[26]

Moments of Vision was another 'sad sad book'; but it contained much of Hardy's best poetry, and was not quite without comic relief. Baptism and burial were allowed their small ration of laughter. Rather than 'disappoint' 'The Royal Sponsors', their godchild's cot-death was kept a secret from them, so the christening went ahead, and they duly 'answered' for the future good behaviour of 'a corpse'. The 'Choirmaster's Burial', like that of Hardy's grandfather, disappointed his hopes of a musical send-off; not, as in 1837, because 'the remaining players' were 'the chief mourners', but simply to save time:

> 'I think', said the vicar,
> A read service quicker
> Than viols out of doors
> In these frosts and hoars.
> That old-fashioned way
> Requires a fine day,
> And it seems to me
> It had better not be.'
> Hence, that afternoon,
> Though never knew he
> That his wish could not be,
> To get it through faster,
> They buried the master
> Without any tune.[27]

29

Late Lyrics and Earlier

'We feel very depressed about the war', wrote Florence in February 1918, '– although of course T.H. is wonderful – with that inner radiance of his: a true sunshine-giver.' Surprising, but evidently true: the 'magic light' that he bore in his breast 'In the Seventies', was again transmuting gloom into poetry, and making the poet 'most cheerful'. In December 1920 she reported: 'He is now – this afternoon – writing a poem with great spirit: always a sign of well-being with him. Needless to say it is an intensely dismal poem.' Had she noticed the parallel with her younger sister Eva, when taken to the theatre at eight years old? Eva had burst into tears for Sydney Carton, then 'mopping her eyes said "Oh how lovely! I *am* enjoying myself." '[1]

Paradoxical, too, was Hardy's attitude towards the 'notes' he was writing about his own life. Florence warned Cockerell *'on no account'* to 'mention the word "autobiography" or call them "autobiographical". If they are regarded as being of that nature . . . they will be promptly destroyed . . . T.H. declares that he would never write an autobiography the mere idea – or suggestion – annoys him.' To his mind, perhaps, the Greek prefix *auto*-implied that *'self*-importance' which *Moments of Vision* had tended to 'mortify . . . by showing, or suggesting that human beings are of no matter or appreciable value in this nonchalant universe.' It was quite different to write a detached, third-person biography of someone in whom he 'took no interest . . . as a personage', but on whose life-history he was the greatest living authority. So he went on writing 'notes' for Florence to type up and pass back to him for correction and constant revision. In August 1922 she told Cockerell it was 'finished, so far as is possible'.[2]

Among the papers sifted through for these 'notes' were piles of old reviews. Their wrong-headedness over the years, combined with the 'lack of grasp' shown even in the generally 'kind' notices of his last book, made Hardy impatient to put newspaper critics right, once and for all. That feat would be attempted in the 'Apology' which prefaced his next volume. Meanwhile he listed their mistakes: 'quizzing' the author instead of the book, as though it were a 'deep-laid scheme of his', rather than something for which he is 'almost irresponsible'; judging poetry by its 'theological and political propriety' (now 'political correctness'); resisting originality ('It is *the unwilling mind* that stultifies the contemporary criticism of poetry'); assuming that poets should be 'impractical' and preferably die young, on the principle that 'the mean age for the best *literary* work is thirty-seven'; thinking 'literary form of more importance to poetry than vision'; and regarding 'situations described in verse' or in prose-fiction as 'actual transcripts of the writer's personal experience'.[3]

Outwardly, he now had few personal experiences worth transcribing. His last 'War-work' was 'to adjudicate at the Police Court on several food-profiteering cases', convict a fellow-magistrate of overcharging for whisky, and fine Florence's grocer for the same crime over rice. After the Armistice (11 November 1918) he designed a war-memorial tablet for employees of the Dorchester Post Office, and opened a war-memorial 'club-room' in Bockhampton 'close to his first school'. He helped in stage productions from his novels by the Dorchester Debating and Dramatic Society (better known as the Hardy Players), and upset Florence by seeming 'quite crazy' about their attractive young leading lady, Gertrude Bugler. He also had the 'odd experience' of 'talking to the Mayor, Mrs Henchard, Eliz. Jane, & the rest, in the flesh', when scenes from the *Mayor of Casterbridge* were being filmed in Dorchester. Otherwise, around this time, he was 'not doing much', and 'hardly going anywhere'. 'I am as stationary as a tree,' he told Mrs Henniker late in 1920, '& don't feel any the worse for it, though whatever moss I may gather is taken away by the tax-collector.'[4]

If old age reduced what he called his 'powers of locomotion', it also tickled his sense of humour. For his seventy-ninth birthday (2 June 1919), he was given a volume of manuscript poems by forty-three younger poets. One jumped the gun by producing a dirge, as if for Hardy's death. 'The verses are very striking', he told the author, '& they will keep.' As reported in the papers, the 'Poets' Tribute' was inscribed: 'On this birthday of your eightieth year'. Congratulated, in consequence, on being eighty, Hardy replied: 'though I have been 80 in America for several years, & am now called 80 in England, I shall not be really 80 till the middle of next year, when people will doubtless begin to say: "How many more times is that Hardy going to be fourscore!"' With four months still to go, he was fêted at Oxford with an OUDS production of *The Dynasts*, and an honorary D.Litt.; and when it finally came, his eightieth birthday was marked by a deputation from the Society of Authors, and congratulations from the King, the Prime Minister, the Lord Mayor of London, and the Vice-Chancellor of Cambridge University. Finding 'what friends there were about me up & down the world', Hardy told a Cambridge friend, he had temporarily 'suspended' his 'judgement against the desirability of being so long upon earth.'[5]

One effect of his age was to make startling changes in that world around him. A mid-Victorian of rather inflexible habits, he let Florence drag him gradually into the Twenties: 'we have a telephone in this house', he told Gosse, '. . . we are 43 Dorchester . . . I personally am uncallable, not being able to hear what is said'. Electricity had not yet reached Max Gate: 'We are still in the Dark Ages here, so to speak, using lamps and candles.' What made him feel that civilization had '*retrograded*' into a more serious form of 'Dark Age' was the use of new technology for the 'scientific slaughter of hundreds of thousands', and a 'far from satisfactory' peace, calling up 'visions ahead' of 'ignorance overruling intelligence', with 'great danger' to 'art & literature'. Among signs of encroaching ignorance were the 1921 coal strike, Labour Party policy ('this illiterate section of the party overpowering by their numbers the thoughtful ones'), and the 'craze' for spiritualism: 'Our ancestors used to burn these mediums – or witches as they were then called; but we reward them – a more humane, though more mischievous treatment.'[6]

The modern developments that most interested him were in poetry. He told Amy Lowell he was too 'old-fashioned' to believe in 'polyphonic prose . . . Though of course in divine poesy there is no such thing as old fashion or new. What made poetry 2000 years ago makes poetry now.' He did not believe in 'vers libre' either, but he thought twenty-three lines of T.S. Eliot's *Prufrock* worth copying out, although by 'a poet of the vers-libre school'. They included an image rather less up to date than the X-ray one in *The Dynasts*: 'as if a magic lantern threw the nerves in patterns on a screen.' He 'refrained from criticizing' poems sent him by Ezra Pound: 'As I am old-fashioned, and think lucidity a virtue in poetry, as in prose, I am at a disadvantage in criticizing recent poets who apparently aim at obscurity. I do not mean that *you* do, but at least I gather that you do not care whether the many understand you or not.' There was one young poet, though, that he found particularly congenial, in life as well as on paper. In January 1922 Florence heard her husband saying aloud to himself: 'I wrote my poems for men like Siegfried Sassoon.'[7]

He was then seriously ill, with what two doctors diagnosed as cancer. But by February he was up again, and 'hard at work on a preface' for his next volume of poems. The production of these had gone on through a series of lesser ailments: coughs, colds, diarrhoea, bilious attacks, recurrences of the Tooting 'bladder inflammation', and a 'complaint of the eyes which made it painful . . . to look at writing paper for more than a minute or two.' He had also had to proof-read *The Dynasts* and seven previous volumes of poetry for the Mellstock Edition, while fighting the effects of old age on memory, speed of thought, and energy.[8]

He had managed all this by accepting almost as much practical help from Florence as he had from Emma at Tooting, and by a ruthless working routine, which Florence described in May 1920: 'He allows nothing to interfere with his morning's work ... and by lunch time he is always tired and unfit for conversation, but after a rest in the afternoon he is generally quite fresh again, & glad to see friends then.' He never went out to lunch, which he found 'disorganise[d] ... the whole day'. For her it was 'a frightfully disappointing rule', but it served its purpose. In November 1921 he was able to tell his publisher that enough poems had 'accumulated' since 1917 to fill, with some others 'on hand', a volume 'quite as thick as Moments of Vision'. It came out on 23 May 1922 as *Late Lyrics and Earlier*. Only the *Spectator* exemplified the 'impotent or mischievous criticism' denounced in the Apology, by dismissing 'almost all' the pieces as mere 'raw materials of poetry', and complaining of Hardy's 'extraordinary ineptitudes'. He responded, aptly enough, by telling Macmillans not to waste any more review-copies on the *Spectator*.[9]

The life-component of this work appeared first in the Apology. Here, with a bitterness partly due to the serious illness during which Florence had heard him 'talking to himself ... about critics', he expressed a life-time's exasperation with reviewers, culminating in February 1920, when his old friend, Frederic Harrison, had found in *Moments of Vision* a 'monotony of gloom'. The Apology also publicized his private fear of 'a new Dark Age', replacing Darwinism by Spiritualism; and his continuing devotion to the Church of England, despite its failure to apply 'the principle of evolution to [its] own faith', join 'hands with modern science', and so gather 'millions of agnostics into its fold'. He even presented it, with its ancient associations, 'scope for transmutability', and 'architectural spell', as the best hope for stopping the decline of national 'morality'. This showed the side of himself that he called 'churchy; not in an intellectual sense, but in so far as instincts and emotions ruled' – which explained his otherwise surprising remark to a friend in 1922: 'I believe in going to church. It is a moral drill, and people must have something.'[10]

Replying for her husband in October 1919 to an 'inquiry if "Jude the Obscure" is autobiographical', Florence wrote: 'Speaking generally, there is more autobiography in a hundred lines of Mr Hardy's poetry than in all the novels.' *Late Lyrics* were certainly full of such autobiography, though she herself figured in very few of them. 'I sometimes think' directly acknowledged her vital support, and the 'Jog-Trot Pair', who were 'happier than the cleverest, smartest, rarest', was perhaps a backhanded compliment to his second wife. Soon after the wedding she had told Clodd: 'T & I have settled down into a very humdrum married couple.' 'The Two Houses' reads almost like a satire on Florence's efforts to modernize Max Gate. In January 1919 Hardy was glad to report that he had no 'frozen ... water-pipes, because' he had hardly any to freeze. In 1920, among other improvements to the plumbing, Florence had got an upstairs bathroom installed. The 'right' house of the poem boasted that 'water-pipes thread all my chambers through', only to be snubbed by the 'left' for its lack of 'character' and human history.[11]

There was a hint of mockery, too, in one poem about Emma. 'The Old Gown' recalled, among other things she had worn on various occasions, her grand clothes and manner when in 1907 she had been driven in a carriage to a royal garden party at Windsor Castle, leaving Hardy to walk up on foot: 'And once or twice she has cast me / As she pomped along the street / Court-clad, ere quite she had passed me, / A glance from her chariot-seat.' Elsewhere, more seriously, her image dominated the book, whether clearly identified or vaguely sensed behind generalized versions of what she meant to Hardy. In the first class, 'A Duettist to her Pianoforte (E.L.H. – H.C.H)' evidently referred, not to the duets that Emma 'sang' with her sister in 1870', but to piano-duets for four hands that they played together ('our fingers . . . strike to her stroke . . . the fellow twain of hands'). In the second class of poems, 'Penance' turned her piano into a harpsichord, and Hardy's feelings about her into a faintly surrealist picture of a 'pale thin man' sitting in a room 'cold as a tomb', and gazing remorsefully at 'the chill old keys, / Like a skull's brown teeth / Loose in their sheath'. Many poems of both classes implicitly shared the theme used as a title for one of them: 'If you had known'.[12]

Other women in Hardy's life were also exploited for poetic material. Helen Paterson, the lady he once thought he ought to have married, was invited, as an 'Opportunity' missed, to share a volume with the two ladies he *had* married. A Piccadilly prostitute, who 'held a long-stemmed narcissus to [his] nose' in 1891, proved in 'The Woman I Met' to have spent the rest of her life 'sighing' for him. Louisa Harding, to whom he had been 'attached' for 'a year or longer' around 1856, suffered much the same fate in 'The Passer-By'; but such dreams of himself as an *homme fatal* concluded in 'The Rake-Hell Muses' with a comment that suited him better: 'That she lives best without me, / Who would live well.'[13]

More impressive than these fictions of love were two poems inspired by filial affection. The 'One Who Lived and Died Where He Was Born' was obviously Hardy's father (1811–1892). He had indeed 'died . . . in the house in which he was born', though the poet adjusted his age to 'eighty years', and changed his death-month from July to the more rhythmical and symbolic 'November'. The crippling rheumatism attributed to his father's heavy work as a builder (though with Henry's help he had still built Max Gate) doubtless suggested the 'old mason', 'proud' to have 'fixed . . . firm' the 'quoin' of a 'mansion-front', though he 'got crookt' and started his 'life's ache' doing it.[14]

Hardy's father had been a fiddler in the Stinsford Choir, Emma a singer and pianist, and the poet himself played the violin; so vocal, string, and keyboard music figured prominently in the volume. It opened with two vocalists: the 'little brown nightingale' and Miss March, 'the sweetest of singers – thrush-like in the descending scale, and lark-like in the ascending', whom Hardy and Emma had heard at a concert in 1878, just before leaving Sturminster Newton. The eighth poem introduced the strings, with 'Barthélémon . . . first-fiddler at Vauxhall Gardens' composing a hymn-tune which 'spread to galleried naves and mighty quires', as well as to less mighty ones at Stinsford, and at St Peter's Church Dorchester, where Hardy had heard it sung in July 1921. The twelfth poem was the first of many to be subtitled 'Song', or given a musical description. This one, 'The Curtains are now drawn', was originally marked 'Major' (for Emma's happy singing at St Juliot in the first stanza) and 'Minor' (for those 'notes' of hers, remembered in the second beside 'her stone'). In 'The Strange House (Max Gate, A.D. 2000)' she was still heard playing the piano, 'Just as a ghost might play'. Then, travelling back in time to '185–', her keyboard became a manual with 'pedals' for 'The Chapel-Organist', whose 'life-love' had been 'music', and who chose to do what Emma did involuntarily in 'The Last Performance' – die after her 'last playing'.[15]

In 1918 Hardy's own instrument had still meant enough to him to ask a Dorchester girl, who had just 'studied piano playing and the violin' for three years at the Royal Academy of Music, to 'accompany him on the piano while he played old dance tunes on his fiddle' – the one he had saved up money to buy in 1862, and then used to practise 'pieces from . . . romantic Italian operas' with a pianist fellow-lodger. She agreed to do so, and 'it was the first of many such interludes', which 'gave him much pleasure.' She rated him 'a good player' and, as they 'mainly' played 'dance tunes of his young days', felt that 'his mind was clearly back in his days of childhood'. Important to him at so many stages of his life, the 'viol' was a special feature of this late collection. The first, and among the last, to speak in 'Haunting Fingers: A Phantasy in a Museum of Musical Instruments', it accompanied 'Two Serenades' *pizzicato* ('I skimmed the strings'); was 'fancy-fiddled' 'In the Small Hours'; used hubristically ('Too gay!') 'to fiddle in front of the party', instead of behind it, in 'The Country Wedding (A Fiddler's Story)', thus inviting its conversion into a double funeral; and then, with touching irony, played by a 'pitying child' to a 'man in . . . handcuffs' on his way to prison ('At the Railway Station, Upway').[16]

The child could not have been Hardy himself (though he had cousins living at Upway, and others who worked as prison-warders on Portland), for there had been 'no railway further than Dorchester' when his father took him to Weymouth at thirteen. But he *had* been able 'to tune a violin when of quite tender years' and, like 'music' to the 'Chapel-Organist', the violin had been his 'life-love'. As such it fitted well into the volume's overall theme: a retrospect of his life. Vividly allegorized in 'He Follows Himself' and 'The Seven Times', epitomized in 'Epitaph', increasingly self-critical in 'After Reading Psalms XXIX., XL. Etc.', this retrospect ended in 'Surview' with sad self-condemnation: for failing, in what he did and in what he 'taught', to live up to advice from St Paul that he believed in: to concentrate on 'whatsoever things are 'true . . . just . . . pure . . . lovely', and on the 'greatest' of Christian virtues, 'charity'.[17]

Thus the Bible (which he had been 'looking into' in March 1919) had the last word in the book, as a standard of morality. It had almost the first word too, in the Apology, as a precedent for Hardy's so-called 'pessimism'. He called it just realism – 'the exploration of reality . . . with an eye to the best consummation possible: briefly, evolutionary meliorism.' Far from being a 'pernicious new thing', it was 'so old as to underlie the Gospel scheme'. To ignore the facts was a 'Levitical passing-by', as unchristian as the conduct of the Levite in the parable of the Good Samaritan. By another neat use of the Bible the 'churchy' poet compared himself, as an innovator, with St Paul preaching at Athens, but charged his own critics with 'a yearning the reverse of that of the Athenian inquirers on Mars Hill', which was 'to hear some new thing'. The poem on the Armistice, ' "And there was a Great Calm" ', used the Bible more subversively. The title referred to Jesus's miraculous stilling of the storm, the 'peace on earth' to the Christmas story of the shepherds and the angels. But the allusions served to clinch Hardy's thesis that the war had been 'an absolute negation of Christianity'. Here it was presented as a meaningless disaster, delightful to the Spirits Sinister and Ironic, bewildering to the Spirit of Pity, and presumably just dreamt up by 'It'.[18]

Literary as well as biblical influences appeared early in the volume. The 'preface' mentioned by Florence, probably first conceived as a poetic manifesto like 'Wordsworth's famous preface to Lyrical Ballads', which had 'influenced [Hardy] much' in 1867, had become an 'Apology', because he thought that title 'more piquant'. Its piquancy lay in the word's Greek meaning ('speech by the defendant'), recalling Plato's *Apology of Socrates*. There the maligned moralist, on trial for his life, had refuted among others the charge of atheism. Socrates' counter-claim to have been 'helping' and 'serving the god' at Delphi was amusingly paralleled by Hardy's expression of zeal for the reform of the Anglican Church.[19]

As ancient precedents for 'pessimism' he had mentioned not only the Gospels but also 'Greek drama', and the title of one poem, 'Where Three Roads Joined', took its tragic resonance from Sophocles. Literally, the spot was Tresparrett Posts, near St Juliot, where Hardy had once been 'in bliss' with Emma. Symbolically, it was also the 'triple highways (*triplai hamaxitai*) in Phocis, where Oedipus killed his father, thus starting his sequence of sorrows. The key-phrase occurred twice in the *Oedipus Tyrannus*, and Jebb translated it: 'where three highways meet'. At the opposite pole of Hardy's classical reading, Horace's *Odes* and '*Carpe diem*' philosophy had clearly inspired one of the *Earlier* lyrics, 'A Young Man's Exhortation' (1867). In July 1865 he had noted: 'Read some Horace'. 'Through this winter' he kept on noting 'continually': 'Read some more Horace'; and he was deeply impressed by 'the Horatian exhortation . . . to keep his compositions back till the ninth year'. He kept this poem till the fifty-fifth.[20]

In such products of 1865–67 Hardy saw 'qualities . . . curiously resembling Donne', and in 1922 claimed 'a certain kinship with Donne' in his 'view of the world, the grave, etc.' The verbal and thematic kinship between 'Drawing Details in an Old Church' and a passage in Donne's *Devotions*, was certainly close enough to suggest unconscious reminiscence, understandable at Hardy's age: 'never send to know for whom the *bell* tolls; it tolls for *thee.*' 'I ask not whom it tolls for ... So, some morrow, when those knolls ... sound out for me ...' Elsewhere in the volume Shelley, Tennyson, Browning, and Rossetti left similar but more predictable traces; and the Chapel-Organist's problems with puritanical 'deacons' would probably not have been treated so theatrically, if Hardy's playwright friend H.A. Jones had not handled a similar situation in his cross between melodrama and the theatre of ideas, *Saints and Sinners* (1884).[21]

Hardy had always been tolerant of melodrama: a surprising pattern of events mattered more to him in narrative than probability, as in 'A Woman's Fancy', where the woman gets herself buried with her double's husband, though she has never met either of them. In this collection such pure fantasy worked best when stripped of a story-line altogether. Thus 'On Stinsford Hill at midnight' recorded a fantastic but true incident unspoilt by its explanation – that the woman 'Sing-songing airily / Against the moon' 'belonged to the Salvation Army'. Hardy was perhaps groping towards this kind of narrative-free fantasy in 'The Sailor's Mother', which focused only on the last scene of his short story, 'To Please his Wife'; perhaps also in 'She Who Saw Not', where the image of a man sitting in a house 'With eyes on the sun' retained some of its mystery, though set in a transparent allegory (about failure to see the essence of people until they are dead). But he certainly produced one image of this free-standing kind in the richly suggestive 'Fallow Deer at the Lonely House'.[22]

What *Late Lyrics* added, though, to Hardy's existing achievement was chiefly verbal music and relevance to real life. To register the musical advance since *Wessex Poems*, we need only compare the opening pieces of the two volumes: for the stiff Sapphics of 'The Temporary the All' we now have the dancing rhythms of 'Weathers', where even drenching rain is made to sound delightful:

> And meadow rivulets overflow,
> And drops on gate-bars hang in a row,
> And rooks in families homewards go,
>   And so do I.

So, too, throughout the book: 'Voices from Things Growing in a Churchyard' is typical in extracting cheering music from a melancholy theme.[23]

As for relevance, Hardy had already achieved definitive expression in poetry for one of life's built-in tragedies, bereavement. In this volume he did the same for at least two aspects of another, old age. The first was the frustrating knowledge that the people who gave meaning to one's life have gone, or are going, into a subjective underworld of painful memories, where nothing can be done about them. Thus 'I was the Midmost' puts the pertinent question: when youthful egotism has long been anachronistic, and the central object of my altruism has disappeared, 'Where now is midmost in my world?' The rickety, overcrowded 'Garden Seat' compresses into twelve sadly humorous lines the mounting sense of a depopulation explosion:

> At night when reddest flowers are black
> Those who once sat thereon come back;
> Quite a row of them sitting there,
> Quite a row of them sitting there.

The second aspect of old age was the sense of becoming an anachronism oneself, of being crowded out by 'hungry generations'. True to Horace's advice, to 'dilute bitter things with slow laughter', 'An Ancient to Ancients' prepared for a graceful exit, after another 'apology', addressed to the next generation: though 'Sophocles, Plato, Socrates / Gentlemen / Pythagoras, Thucydides, / Herodotus and Homer . . .' 'Burnt brightlier towards their setting-day', we shall not trouble you long.

> Much it there waits you we have missed,
> Much lore we leave you worth the knowing,
> Much, much has lain outside our ken;
> Nay, rush not: time serves: we are going,
>   Gentlemen.[24]

30

The Queen of Cornwall

In a letter of condolence dated 6 October 1922 Hardy wrote: 'Your being so sadly interested in the dead past of your sister, now that such interest can avail nothing, is, of course, the experience of most of us, and the penalty we pay for not dying early.' Hence his own search for Emma's father's grave in 1913, and his publication this month of a poem written sixty years before by Horace Moule. He was paying that 'penalty' constantly these days. 'So friends & acquaintances thin out', he had told his least replaceable friend Mrs Henniker in March, '& we who remain have to "close up"'. Even she would die in April 1923, and he would exclaim in his notebook: 'After a friendship of 30 years!' But already he was living largely in his own 'dead past', especially on 27 November 1922, when he noted: 'E's death-day, ten years ago. Went with F. and tidied her tomb, & carried flowers for hers and the other two tombs.' It was then, perhaps, that he decided to complete a tribute to Emma which might 'avail' slightly more than flowers or a tidy grave: *The Famous Tragedy of the Queen of Cornwall.*[1]

He had first thought of writing it in August 1870 when, during three 'most happy' weeks at St Juliot, he went with Emma to see Tintagel Castle. After going there again with Florence in 1916 he told Cockerell, 'Alas, I fear your hopes of a poem on Iseult . . . will be disappointed. I visited the place 44 years ago with an Iseult of my own, and of course she was mixed in the vision of the other.' Though he did, it seems, start writing the *Queen* that autumn, he soon gave it up. Perhaps the associations were too painful, or the 'mixture' of visions too confusing. But in 1923, with the Hardy Players wanting him to write something specially for them, with Gertrude Bugler capable of acting the Queen, and his own writing capacity unlikely to last much longer, he tried again. By the end of April he had finished a rough draft.[2]

Meanwhile he had been paying other penalties for not dying early. Physically, he told a friend, he was ' "in a manner of spaiking" – as they say here – quite well; nevertheless I feel an increasing burden in little things which have intrinsically no weight at all, and my eyes are often very weak'. He also had reason to suspect that 'diseases transmute themselves, but don't ever take an absolute departure', though he had failed to interest any doctor in writing 'a book on these transmutations for the use of ordinary people.' Then there were the penalties of fame: requests to write for good causes, autograph books, give interviews to thesis-writers, approve scholarly works about him. Most good causes he evaded by pleading his age and bad eyesight, but he did write a message of 'hearty support' to a meeting on 'slaughterhouse reform', demanding for every 'victim' a 'quick exit, with the minimum of suffering (mental & physical)', and 'less painful than the animal's natural death from age or infirmity – which is the only justification for killing such fellow-creatures at all.'[3]

'Unknown people' who 'pestered' him with 'large parcels' of his own books to inscribe, were made to donate half a guinea per autograph to the Dorset County Hospital. A 'young woman' was refused an interview (though recommended by Agnes Grove), since 'personal details' were 'quite unnecessary for writing a "thesis", that should be based on published works alone of course.' Frank Hedgecock, whose French doctoral thesis had annoyed Hardy in 1909 by its 'erroneous biographical passages', was with difficulty dissuaded from having his work translated into English. Two American professors found Hardy a stern examiner of their books about him. A lecturer in Jersey who described Hardy as coming 'from a line of unmixed peasants . . . a rural peasant with a rural mind', was treated more gently, perhaps because he had once been a curate at Dorchester: 'The personal details you give have amused us as being rather imaginative . . . It would have interested your audience if they could have been told that my forebears came from the very isle you were lecturing in.' But the thirst for 'personal details', seemed to be unquenchable: 'a dear friend who was, as I thought, dying, sent off my epistles to a dealer immediately they came.'[4]

Such things, Hardy admitted, had their 'amusing side', but they were also tiresome and time-consuming. Royal recognition fell into both categories. Choosing twelve of his poems for the library of the Queen's doll's house was probably quite fun: his first choice was 'The Oxen' and, had his eyesight been better, he would clearly have liked to transcribe them all in miniature handwriting himself. But having the Prince of Wales to lunch at Max Gate (20 July 1923) was different. It was a headache, all too literally, for Florence: where, for instance, in a house so inadequately modernized, could the Prince 'wash his hands – etc.'? It also meant a 'police cordon' round the house. If Hardy's last surviving sister Kate wanted to watch the arrival and departure from 'the bedroom behind the jessamine', she would need a 'police pass – or one from us', unless she got there 'before 12'. Even for Hardy the honour proved unflattering, to judge from this specimen of the Prince's small talk: 'My mother tells me you have written a book called *Tess of the d'Urbervilles*. I must try to read it some time.'[5]

More literary-minded guests at Max Gate included the novelist E.M. Forster, who had once edited a verse translation of the *Aeneid*, and 'Lawrence of Arabia', who would follow up *Seven Pillars of Wisdom* with a lively prose translation of the *Odyssey*; and a pleasanter form of honour was an Honorary Fellowship at Queen's College, Oxford. 'It came,' Hardy wrote, 'as a romantic surprise to me (Oxford being the romantic University as Cambridge is the intellectual).' Invited to visit the College, and painlessly transported there in a friend's car, he and Florence 'enjoyed . . . very much' their two-night stay in Queen's (25–26 June 1923). The thirty-one-year-old Fellow who showed them round was impressed by the visitor's 'charming youthfulness' at eighty-four, and thought he looked far less 'bookish' than most of 'his new colleagues'.[6]

Though 'apparently unwearied' when sightseeing at Oxford that June, he had given a different impression in November 1922: 'It is as much as I can do nowadays to find energy to put out a small poem once in a while'. Yet in the interval he had finalized *The Queen of Cornwall* and illustrated it with a drawing, made 'with infinite care, an imaginary view of Tintagel Castle.' At the end of August he wrote to Frederick Macmillan: 'I am about to startle you by sending up . . . a short MS. of a one-act play – quite a different production from anything I have sent before.' Explaining that 'a local dramatic society' was 'going to act it in the middle of November', he suggested that it 'might be worth while to print the play as a thin volume', and thus take advantage of the 'attention' that the performances were likely to attract, 'although only by amateurs.' He must have set his heart on getting it published separately, as a final memorial to Emma; for he piled up arguments to make such a very slim volume sound commercially viable. The 'illustrations' might be 'some help' (he had now done a second, of the castle interior); 'Collectors' might buy copies; and so, he implied, might amateur dramatic societies, since the play had one novel feature: 'though for acting, it announces itself as requiring no theatre or scenery' – a thing no 'modern author' had ever done before.[7]

Macmillan agreed, and publication was planned to synchronize with the Dorchester production. Hardy had adopted several suggestions about staging from Granville Barker, and was actively concerned in rehearsals (although Mrs Bugler was prevented by pregnancy from acting the Queen). To ensure at least one sensible review, he had explained the theory of the piece to his friend Harold Child of *The Times*, e.g. that the 'unities' were 'strictly preserved', and that he had tried to strike a balance between 'turning the rude personages of, say, the fifth century, into respectable Victorians, as was done by Tennyson, Swinburne, Arnold, &c.', and the 'impossible' opposite extreme: 'to present them as they really were, with their barbaric manners and surroundings.'[8]

He finally decided 'that the book should antedate the acting', if only by a few days, so a 3,000-copy edition of *The Famous History of the Queen of*

Cornwall appeared on 15 November 1923, and the production started on the 28th. He was in the audience on the 30th (when according to Florence 'they were all so much better' than on the first night), and was 'loudly cheered' on being recognized during the interval. John Drinkwater was 'moved . . . to tears' by Tristram's second song, sung by a local doctor. But though the 'performance, and particularly the rehearsals, gave Hardy considerable pleasure', 'naturally a poetic drama did not make a wide appeal.' The BBC's plan to broadcast the first night was called off in favour of Mendelssohn's music for *A Midsummer Night's Dream*, and a repeat performance in London during February 1924 'was not altogether a success', partly because they could not find a building with a suitable stage, and had to make do with a 'rather small concert platform'. The book was not a big hit either. Even Alfred Noyes, whom Hardy thanked for his 'dispatch' in getting a friendly review into the London *Evening News* on the day of publication, did not much like the verse. But on the whole Hardy thought the press had been 'very civil to the play – indeed eulogistic', and it had to be reprinted twice that month.[9]

'T.H.' reported Florence, 'actually went in to the evening performance on Friday, although it was the anniversary of the funeral of E.L.H.' 'Because' would have been a better conjunction, for he obviously saw the performance as a kind of memorial service for that 'Iseult of my own', eleven years after her funeral, 53 years after their happy visit to Tintagel. That was the chief personal element in the work. But the legend fitted his personal history rather too neatly. As a violinist he shared Tristram's 'minstrel character' and his skill on 'tinkling strings'; as a poet with a name for pessimism, he almost shared the suggestions of Tristrams's name (from *tristis*, Latin for 'sad'). Malory's Tristram was 'the sorrowful born child', because his mother died at his birth; Hardy's 'had been near death's door in bringing him forth' and been 'very much hurt' when he told her as a child 'of his conclusions on existence': that 'he did not wish to grow up'. Soon after Emma's tenth 'death-day' (which was probably when he resolved to complete the *Queen*), he told Florence 'he had never felt so despondent in his life.'[10]

Tristram's love-life, though, presented more embarrassing parallels. His two Iseults threatened to recall Hardy's two Florences (Henniker and Dugdale) and, still more awkwardly, his two wives. It was the Cornish Iseult that Tristram really loved; the one from Brittany was just a wife whose lie, in the most famous version of the story, caused his death. Thus Hardy had been faced with the problem: how to handle the legend, without seeming to downgrade his own Iseult of Enfield? According to Malory, Tristram's marriage was never consummated: 'when they were abed' the thought of the first Iseult made him all dismayed, and other cheer made he none but with clipping and kissing; as for other fleshly lusts Sir Tristram never thought nor had ado with her'. Hardy's second marriage was evidently not like that. Two months before the play was published, Florence had told

Marie Stopes, the campaigner for birth control: 'the idea of my having a child at his age fills him with terror . . . He said he would have welcomed a child when we married first, ten years ago, but now it would kill him with anxiety to have to father one.' The context shows that the last verb was used, not in its first dictionary meaning, 'beget', but in its second: 'behave as a father towards' – in 1918 she had described him as 'genuinely afraid of babies'. But any personal application of the legend was liable to raise speculation in this very private area.[11]

He had had another problem, too: ideally, the *Famous History* should be dedicated to his own 'queen of Cornwall', Emma (though none of his previous books had been dedicated to anyone); but how would Florence feel about that? He tried to solve this problem by making Emma the first and Florence the last of four initialled dedicatees, the other two being Emma's sister and brother-in-law, who had accompanied the lovers to Tintagel in 1870. But this dedication was slightly spoilt by its conclusion: 'who have now all passed away save one.' Florence had been witty about a 'grave fault' in *Late Lyrics* – that its poem to a cat was not balanced by one to her own dog, Wessex: 'T.H. says he could write one if Wessie were *dead* – but why should the poor little animal have to *die* before a poem is written to him? . . . Other people's dogs are dying all round . . . but Wessex flourishes, although a poem awaits him if he only had the thoughtfulness to pop off.' The sole reference to her in Hardy's latest book must have made her feel rather like Wessie.[12]

Nor can she have enjoyed being implicitly cast as the wrong Iseult. Admittedly this character was made quite appealing, and absolved from actually causing her husband's death by her lie about the colour of the sail. But Florence must have noticed that the most touching speeches assigned to Iseult the Whitehanded were borrowed from Elfride in *A Pair of Blue Eyes*, a character inspired by Emma.[13]

Taking his story mainly from Malory, Hardy naturally made the most of 'the little brachet . . . that Sir Tristram gave [the queen] the first time that ever she came into Cornwall, and never would that brachet depart from her but if Sir Tristram was nigh'. He also got a bit of window-dressing from Thomas of Britain's *Romance of Tristram and Ysolt*, sent to him by its American translator, Roger Loomis. Loomis had interpolated 'a French couplet supplied by Gottfried [von Strassburg], which doubtless he had taken over from Thomas': 'Ysolt ma drue, Ysolt m'amie, / En vous ma mort, en vous ma vie!' Hardy quoted the lines on the title-page of his first edition, but subsequently removed them, perhaps regretting such a display of spurious erudition. From the Tristram poems of Tennyson, Arnold, and Swinburne he apparently got nothing but a warning not to Victorianize. He even made fun of his old idol Swinburne's plan, 'in that romance of irreconcileable discrepancies', '"to adhere sternly to Fact & Reality"'.[14]

Other English authors were occasionally drawn upon. The Queen stole Mark Antony's image in *Julius Caesar* to describe Tristram's stab-wound:

'this mute red mouth / You've gored in my Belovéd, bids me act'. Merlin's Prologue rephrased Browning's lines in *The Ring and the Book*: 'How title I the dead alive once more? . . . Let this old woe step on the stage again! / Act itself o'er anew for men to judge'; and his Epilogue to 'Our shadowy and phantasmal show' of 'throes and themes . . . now dead as dreams' echoed Prospero's famous speech in *The Tempest*, 'Our revels now are ended . . .' In 'The Eve of St Agnes' the drunken orgies of 'hot-blooded lords' serve as auditory background to the love story, until 'the hall door shuts again, and all the noise is gone.' The effect was almost replicated by King Mark and his drinking companions: '*Noise of cups, trenchers, drunken voices, songs, etc., resumed till the door shuts, when it is heard in subdued tones.*' The 'litle hound her friend' that shared the Queen's death-leap was obviously inspired by the example of Bill Sikes's 'white shaggy dog' in *Oliver Twist.*[15]

Making Iseult of Cornwall jump 'Over the blind rock' into 'the Atlantic', after killing King Mark with his own bloodstained dagger, was a refreshing innovation of Hardy's own. She usually dies more passively, of a broken heart. Her prompt revenge was in the spirit of Tess, and her death recalled a passage about Tintagel in Emma's *Recollections*: 'In the winter the storms were magnificent and the wind dangerous to contend with on the cliffs. I was nearly blown into the Atlantic ocean and clung to the rocks frightened.' Hardy must also have been thinking of Sappho's legendary suicide, by jumping off a cliff into the Mediterranean. His early reading of Ovid had probably included her love-letter in the *Heroides*, and her theatrical exit had already figured in his elegy for Swinburne: 'she, the music-mother . . . who leapt, love-anguished, from the Leucadian steep / Into the rambling world-encircling deep.'[16]

But Hardy's most conscious model had been Greek Tragedy. Having often used it for novelistic purposes, he had finally attempted a quasi-Greek tragedy of his own, complete with Aristotelian 'Unities'. He justified the liberties he had taken with the legend by the example of 'the Greek dramatists . . . notably Euripides.' He introduced 'Chanters' to 'play the part of a Greek chorus.' Though he could not 'for the moment recall' any precedent 'in a Greek play' for a chorus of 'ghosts', there were plenty of individual ghosts for him to have cited: Darius in Aeschylus' *Persae*, Clytaemnestra in the *Eumenides*, or even the phantom-Helen that caused all the trouble in the *Helen* of Euripides. How close his imitation was meant to be, emerged from his statement in January 1924: 'I have always meant to revise it a little, to bring it roughly to the average length of Greek Plays' – though at only '800 lines', by his own estimate, it would need quite a lot of revising. The *Oedipus Tyrannus* was nearly twice as long.[17]

Certainly the compressed opacity of the play's dialogue comes dangerously close to A.E. Housman's hilarious 'Fragment of a Greek Tragedy' (1893). This, for instance, is how Tristram tells the Queen he was told that the sail was black: 'Know I was duped by her who dons your name; /

She swore the bellied sheeting of your ship / Blotted the wind-wafts like a sable swan.' Parodying the Greek dramatists' obsession with nautical metaphor, Housman's Chorus asked the 'head of a traveler' how he had got there: 'Sailing on horseback, or with feet for oars?' In rather too similar terms the Queen reproached her lover for gratuitously adding to their problems: 'Yet, Tristram, would my husband were but all! / Had you not wedded her my namesake, Oh, / We could have steered around this other rock'. The Chanters also reproduced the occasional vapidity of real Greek choruses, as when sympathizing with Tristram's wife: 'Fluttering with fear, / Out-tasked her strength has she! / Loss of her dear / Threatening too clear, / Gone to this length has she! / Strain too severe!'[18]

Several features of Hardy's mediaeval plot had convenient parallels in the *Trachiniae* of Sophocles: the well-meant gift (by Brangwain and Deianira) of a love-philtre that proved lethal; death by being 'hurled' from a height into the sea (the Queen by her own despair and Lichas by Heracles); the heroine's exit to commit suicide; and the hero's dying speech about his past exploits. It was probably Heracles' list of his 'Labours' for Eurystheus that suggested Tristram's dramatically ineffective account of services rendered to his murderer – for Mark is hardly the type to be moved by such reproaches, although he '*drops his head in silence*', as if repentant.[19]

Perhaps in *The Queen of Cornwall* Hardy had tried to do too many incompatible things at once: to celebrate a fifty-three-year-old love-affair of his own, while dramatizing a twelfth-century legend; to make a classical Greek tragedy out of a mediaeval romance; to write a verse-script, actable by amateurs more used to acting prose-versions of Victorian novels, yet describable as 'A Play for Mummers'. Since Mummers wore masks and traditional costume, and made no attempt at realistic acting, this last model might seem not too remote from that of Greek tragedy, and Hardy took it equally seriously. Discussing, in the Preface to *The Dynasts*, how 'plays of poesy and dream' might be produced, he had offered a 'practicable compromise' between purely 'mental performance' and the ordinary theatre,

> taking the shape of a monotonic delivery of speeches, with dreamy conventional gestures, something in the manner traditionally maintained by the old Christmas mummers, the curiously hypnotizing impressiveness of whose automatic style – that of persons who spoke by no will of their own – may be remembered by all who ever experienced it.[20]

For the rest of us, unfortunately, it is hard to imagine being impressed at all by the kind of mumming described in *The Return of the Native*; and the extracts given there from 'Saint George's play' suggest that its example was largely to blame for the *Famous Tragedy*'s most disappointing feature, the flatness of its verse. But there are compensations. Since the words are so unmemorable, one is left to enjoy undisturbed, in retrospective 'mental performance', the dramatic impact of the admirably tight construction, especially the climactic stabbings and leap over the parapet. Here

Horace's veto against on-stage violence, and the messenger-convention of Greek tragedy were both happily ignored. Only a 'Watchman' turned up (presumably from the *Agamemnon*) to emulate the wisdom of a Greek chorus:

> She's glode off like a ghost, with deathly mien:
> It seems toward the sea, – yes, – she – the Queen.[21]

31

Human Shows

'Well, if I look like that', said Hardy, seeing a newspaper photograph of his portrait by Augustus John (1923), 'the sooner I am under ground the better.' But he stayed obstinately above it, struggling through a 'thicket of infinitesimal affairs', caused chiefly by unwanted correspondence. The most prickly part of the thicket was a request from Ernest Brennecke in America to authorize a *Life of Thomas Hardy* which, 'though quite eulogistic', turned out to be full of 'quizzing impertinence', and 'personal details' which Florence called 'mostly fictitious': 'He describes the manner in which T.H. smokes a cigarette – T.H. has been a non-smoker all his life, & detests the cigarette habit, & so forth.' Hardy's refusal to authorize, sent by cable as well as surface mail, failed to stop publication in New York, and a letter to *The Times* was required to warn English publishers that the biography was unauthorized. More deliberately exasperating was a book by 'that ludicrous blackguard' George Moore, whose series of snide remarks about Hardy published from 1886 onwards now culminated in a diagnosis of 'brain-paralysis'. At this Middleton Murry, who had been so quick off the mark in lamenting Hardy's death, was equally prompt in springing to his defence, with a counter-charge of 'senile indecency'.[1]

There was also something more serious to worry about. In September 1924 Florence was advised to have a potentially cancerous lump removed from her neck, which was done in a London nursing-home. She preferred to 'go up by herself', in case Hardy fell ill, as he usually did if he went to London; so he stayed behind, feeling he could be 'of more service ... in an active state' at Max Gate than with her 'if incapacitated'. Of course, as he told Cockerell, it was 'a very depressing time' and he had 'all sorts of imaginings'. His secretary remembered being 'shocked to see the change in his appearance. Suspense was taking a heavy toll on him'; but on

30 September he recorded: 'Telegrams saying operation had been "quite satisfactory" & "growth completely removed: patient doing well"'. In October he got his brother Henry to bring her home in his car, thoughtfully equipped, as Hardy told her, with 'the black fur rug, the brown, and the plaid, & 2 cushions . . . and an empty hot water bottle wh. I dare say they wd fill at the Home.' Even so he urged her to 'keep the wind from the wound', as the car was 'not an absolutely closed one'. How anxious he had been throughout her absence was clear from his poem about her return, 'Nobody Comes.'[2]

His own physical ailments were not too troublesome: 'inflammation of one eye and rheumatism in the neck and head', a short bout of flu, 'growing hardness of hearing', and occasional 'lumbago'. Psychologically, though, he had developed the old person's tendency to fuss about minor problems. 'People little know', Florence told Cockerell, 'when they see how bright and vigorous he is to outsiders, what a state of frenzy he works himself into when alone here with me. The only remedy is to remain quiet and say nothing, and he calms down after a while.'[3]

Meanwhile new deaths and old memories battered away at his morale. He went to the funeral of his surgeon-friend, Frederick Treves, once his sister Mary's schoolfellow, whose father had sold him the writing-desk he still kept in his study: 'Sad procession to the cemetery', he noted. 'Casket in a little white grave.' Then Wessex correctly predicted the sudden death of another Dorchester friend, within an hour of his last visit to Max Gate, by greeting him most untypically with 'a piteous whine', and at intervals touching 'his coat solicitously with his paw, which he always withdrew giving a sharp cry of distress.' Anniversaries were now for Hardy 'the saddest days of the year'. Living 'close to the spot of [his] childish memories', he 'very often revive[d] them' by visiting Stinsford churchyard, 'finding no pain in so doing'; but when he revisited after seventy years the barn where as a child he had 'heard the village young women sing the ballads', and 'looked around at the dusty rafters and the débris', Florence felt he wished he had never tried to 'revive a scene from the distant past.'[4]

He was cheered, though, and revitalized by two bits of what he called 'footlightery'. The first was when he co-operated with Rutland Boughton, a composer who had just had a big success with an opera called 'The Immortal Hour', over an operatic version of *The Queen of Cornwall*. According to Florence, Hardy 'said he liked Boughton better than anyone he had ever met', in spite of his communism, which he thought he could he could soon talk him out of. Florence felt no urge to do so; having recently become a local magistrate, she had 'amazed' the chairman of a meeting by declaring herself 'Labour'. But Hardy liked the music as well as the composer, and welcomed his 'glorification' of the play. Though he missed the first night of the opera at Glastonbury, he did go to a matinée on 28 August 1924. Writing to a 'globe-trotting' friend three days before, instead of his usual 'I hardly ever go anywhere', he concluded briskly: 'You will excuse a hasty note; I have to rush off to Glastonbury.'[5]

In the other bit of 'footlightery' he was more personally involved. When the Hardy Players asked for something to perform in the winter of 1924, 'to save himself trouble' he 'exhumed' and gave them the *Tess*-play he had written in 1894–5. But in November he told Masefield: 'Instead of trouble being saved I find myself insensibly drawn into the details of production, which I must say is, for a change, very entertaining.' When the play opened in Dorchester (26 November 1924), with Gertrude Bugler as Tess, its 'unexpected success' led to a London production, with Tess played by Gwen Ffrangçon-Davies (the star of Boughton's *Immortal Hour*). After opening at Barnes, this ran for a hundred performances at the Garrick Theatre, closing on 12 December 1925. That August Florence had told Cockerell: 'T.H. is very pleased about "Tess" being produced by professionals at last. It is long since I have seen him so happy about anything'.[6]

For her the whole episode had been most unhappy. Within eight days of coming home from her operation, feeling 'unexpectedly weak, & as if I could hardly crawl about the house', she had rehearsals going on in her drawing-room. As her parlour-maid remembered, 'Mr. Hardy seemed to come out of his shell when talking to younger women as if a light was suddenly breaking through and he could see them in one of his books. Myself, I do not think he thought of them as women, but just shadowy figures fitting into a space like a jig-saw.' Since he saw Gertrude Bugler as 'the very incarnation' of his Tess, the 'light' in her case (or 'irradiation', the equivalent term in the novel) must have appeared to be dazzling, and Florence assumed that he was simply in love.[7]

In her weakened physical state she possibly overreacted. Determined to save her husband from an 'unnatural excitement' that could not be good for him 'at his age', and from publicly making a fool of himself, she went all out to eliminate the apparent threat to her marriage. Through letters, a telegram, and an 'agitated' personal visit unknown to her husband, she persuaded Gertrude to spoil her prospects of a stage career, by refusing an offer to play Tess in a series of matinées at the Haymarket Theatre. But she did try to make up for it after Hardy's death, when she invited Gertrude to play the part again in a revival of the play by a professional company at the Duke of York's Theatre (August 1929). So Gertrude had her moments of glory after all – though not on the night she reached the theatre late and 'exhausted', after getting 'lost . . . on Waterloo station'.[8]

Back in 1925, by what Hardy called a 'curious coincidence', the *Tess*-opera, the *Tess*-play, and a new serialization of the novel in *John o' London's Weekly* synchronized to create advance publicity for his next book. His 'excitement' about Gertrude may also have helped him to write it, if there was any truth in the extract from the *Times Literary Supplement* that he noted down in May 1924: 'It is always the lover who writes poetry, whether the object be the absolute, or his mistress: its subject is always that expansion towards some external thing.' Though he told Cockerell in February 1925 that he had 'nearly given up writing verses', he already had plenty of poems 'on hand'. By July he had 'accumulated' enough pieces 'published of late years in periodicals' to fill a volume the size of *Late Lyrics*, and he sent them off to George Macmillan under the provisional title, 'Poems Imaginative & Incidental, with Songs and Trifles'. In August he came up with one equally cumbrous, but rather less dull, and 'easier for readers and booksellers to remember, as in the shops the book will be called merely "Human Shows"'. So it came out (20 November 1925) as *Human Shows, Far Phantasies, Songs, and Trifles*. Though the first edition was larger than that of the previous volume (5,000 copies instead of 3,250) it was practically sold out before it was published.[9]

In June 1924 Hardy had told J.C. Squire: 'A short time ago I was inveigled into setting up Wireless, & did not know what was going to happen.' What happened first was that on his 84th birthday he heard Squire broadcasting an 'Appreciation of the Life and Work of Thomas Hardy', to which Wessex 'listened attentively.' Then, at eighty-five and a half, he heard the New Year in with Florence 'on the wireless . . . dancing at the Albert Hall, Big Ben striking twelve, singing Auld Lang Syne, God Save the King, Marseillaise, hurrahing.' For him, if not for her, it had been a good year, and he had something to hurrah about.[10]

Human Shows, the last book of poems that Hardy was able to arrange himself, began and ended with pieces about his own old age. In the first, he and a star are 'Waiting Both' for extinction, or, in Job's words, 'till [their] change come', words which in their original context make non-survival an argument against suicide: 'If a man die, shall he live again? all the days of my appointed time will I wait, until my change come.' The last piece, 'Why Do I?', arose from a feeling expressed in a letter Hardy wrote to Cockerell, after sending off the final proofs of the volume: 'I don't expect much from it: indeed I am weary of my own writing, & imagine other people are too by this time.' The only reason he can give in the poem for going on 'doing these things', for continuing all the 'mechanic repetitions' involved in the process of writing, publishing, and even living is that Florence is still alive. 'I must proudly point out', she boasted in a joint letter to Siegfried Sassoon, 'that one of the poems is written to me: "Why do I go on doing these things." I was very surprised when T.H. told me & cannot resist telling all my friends. 'The "popular personage"', she concluded', 'is now listening with absorbed interest to his lovely broadcasting, or he would send a greeting – i.e. a growl.' That was another boast: that even her obstreperous dog, a confirmed radio-addict, had at last got a poem written to him too – without having to die for it.[11]

Florence figured implicitly in several other poems. The addressee of 'When Dead' was presumably left a blank because it could be the wife of any aged husband who knew he was a burden to her; but it reads most convincingly as an apology to Florence for the kind of 'querulousness . . . strivings and stress' that she had described as a 'state of frenzy' when he was alone with her. 'Tragedian to Tragedienne' suggests a feeling that his own second marriage was 'a tragedy', not just because it would end 'with the death of one of the actors', but because Florence would be a widow unfairly soon, and would then have to face her own death without him: 'I not there to succour you.' The 'Dog' of the preceding poem who wonders 'Why She Moved House', sounds in that context like Florence's Wessie; and the date, '9 October 1924', identified Florence's return from the London hursing-home as the subject of 'Nobody Comes'.[12]

Emma was similarly identified by the date of 'Ten Years Since' ('Nov. 1922') as the owner of the symbolic funeral urn suggested (in the manner of Herbert's 'Easter-Wings') by the shape of the poem's text. Her death was still a recurrent theme of Hardy's poetry, often mixed, as here, with selfcriticism: 'light note I took / Of what shut like a book / Those ten years since!' The simile had special significance: it was chiefly his books that had made him shut his eyes to her uniqueness, as a book he could read only once. 'The Monument-Maker' was dated 1916, the year he inspected a memorial tablet to Emma 'erected to his own design' in the church at St Juliot. In the poem the 'memorial' was 'scorned almost, / By her sweet ghost', and its maker mocked: 'you . . . carve there your devotion; But you felt none, my dear!'. 'Every Artemisia' implicitly satirized Hardy's efforts to commemorate Emma in poetry; for Artemisia was the queen who built the Mausoleum as a tomb for her husband, and here an objective questioner points out her irrationality: 'You plod to pile a monument / So madly that your breath is spent.' She can only reply that she does it to 'ease' the 'scalding fires' of remorse, for being such a bad wife: 'I was the woman who slighted him'. Hardy, it seems, was still trying to make Emma 'the only amends' he could for being a bad husband.[13]

But non-wives also generated poems: his girl-friend in adolescence, Louisa Harding; an 'equestrienne' who fell when jumping through a hoop at a circus in 1884, making Hardy 'deeply interested in her recovery'; Mrs Channing, whose execution (1705) in Maumbury Ring, Dorchester, for poisoning her husband (a crime 'not proven' of which she claimed to be innocent), had long horrified him by its 'atrocity'; another woman convicted of husband-murder and hanged in 1923 ('wicked', he agreed, but still demanding sympathy); and, in that rather mixed company, Mrs Henniker, as a vague threat to his first marriage in 1893.[14]

From Hardy's recent life, overshadowed by losses of friends and his own increasing age, the chief input into the volume was a natural concern with death. Contemptuous of spiritualism and religious doctrines of an afterlife, he felt faintly reassured by science. In June 1921 Florence had reported: [he] ponders Einstein's Theory of Relativity in the night'. From a *Quarterly* article on the subject he had copied down these extracts: 'Events do not happen, they are just there & we come across them in the voyage of life . . . Time is not a particular direction but depends on the motion of the observer . . . Physics is not interested in it [the distinction of past & future]. For physics, past is − t, & future is + t, just as left is − x, & right is + x.' Hence his note of June 1923: 'Relativity. That things and events always were, are, and will be (e.g. Emma, Mother and Father are living still in the past).'[15]

That was the gist of 'The Absolute Explains': that 'Time is a mock' – a notion made vivid by the image of the individual 'Plodding by lantern-light' along a 'dark highway' between 'Future and Past', both equally part of 'Being's length'. But the real comfort for death remained, as in 'The Six Boards', insentience:

> Those boards and I – how much
> In common we, of feel and touch
> Shall share thence on, – earth's far core-quakings
> Hill-shocks, tide-shakings –
>
> Yea, hid where none will note,
> The once live tree and man, remote
> From mundane hurt as if on Venus, Mars,
> Or furthest stars.[16]

There Hardy illustrated half of his statement that Virgil and Lucretius had 'arrested [him] in times past perhaps more than any others of "the Ancients"'; for he was paraphrasing part of Lucretius' argument against the fear of death: 'once we are dead, nothing whatever can happen to us or make us feel anything, not even if the land is mixed with the sea, and the sea with the sky.' Virgil's comparison of the dead approaching judgement and punishment in the Underworld to fallen autumn leaves was briefly adapted for 'Last Week in October': 'A spider's web has caught one while downcoming, / That stays there dangling when the rest pass on; / Like a suspended criminal hangs he'. In 'Genitrix Laesa' ('The Injured Mother'), Horace helped to mock Nature's 'fancy' that her creation was harmonious, that 'Life that rhythmic chime is holding . . . (This "concordia discors"!)'.[17]

Of the Greek 'Ancients', Aeschylus was ingeniously persuaded to support the RSPCA. In the *Agamemnon* the king and his brother were seen as a pair of eagles cruelly killing a pregnant hare 'litter and all', and thus inviting retribution. 'Cry *ailinon, ailinon* (woe! woe!)', says the Chorus, 'but let the good prevail!' In 'Compassion: An Ode' to mark the RSPCA centenary, 'Mild creatures, despot-doomed' continue to suffer 'hideous' cruelty, 'But here, in battlings, patient, slow, / Much has been won – more, maybe, than we know – / And on we labour hopeful. "Ailinon!" / A mighty voice calls: "But may the good prevail!"'[18]

Nineteenth-century literature was occasionally drawn on too. Keats's 'Bright star' sonnet served as contrasting background to 'Waiting Both': Hardy's star was no more 'stedfast' than he was, and its eyelids, far from 'eternal', would one day close like his. Tennyson's 'Charge of the Light Brigade' had conspicuously ignored the sufferings of the horses, to con-centrate on the brave obedience of their riders: 'Their's not to reason

why'. Hardy's 'Horses Aboard' shifted attention to the more pitiable ignorance of the animals: 'Whither are they sailing? They do not know, / Nor
what for, nor how', 'unwitting' of their imminent conversion into 'war-
waste'. Unable to 'reason why', they are finally left just 'wondering why'.[19]

Matthew Arnold saw the Grande Chartreuse as 'a living tomb' because
he had been taught to trust 'the high, white star of Truth', which condemned such irrationality. In Hardy's 'Cathedral Façade at Midnight',
that star became the moon which 'blanched' (as he had seen it do in
August 1897) the 'pious figures' on the 'west front' of Salisbury Cathedral,
slowly moving along them like 'Reason's movement, making meaningless
/ The coded creeds of old-time godliness.' So, too, Arnold's 'East London', concluding that the efforts of a Bethnal Green 'preacher' were not
really 'lost toil', was clearly the model for Hardy's 'An East-End Curate',
which suggested a different conclusion: 'And the long pallid, devoted face
notes not, / But stoops along abstractedly, for good, or in vain, God wot!'[20]

'At a Fashionable Dinner' evidently took something from Meredith's
Modern Love (a title itself taken from Keats). There the estranged couple
keep up the conversation so well 'at dinner' that the guests 'see no ghost',
though really taking part in a game of 'HIDING THE SKELETON',
and seeing, not a 'golden . . . marriage-knot', but 'Love's corpse-light.' In
Hardy's weird verse-anecdote, 'Lavine' (Emma Lavinia?) sees what she
thinks is her 'own corpse', and predicts a 'new bride' for her husband.
The forgetfulness, 'years later', of the lover in another short narrative
poem, 'The Last Leaf', recalled the climax of W.S. Gilbert's tragicomedy
Sweethearts; and 'A Watering-Place Lady Inventoried', with its jaunty cynicism
and trisyllabic rhymes, reads strangely like a patter-song in a Savoy Opera.[21]

Such 'Trifles' represented a slight but deliberate shift towards comedy in
this volume. Reviewing its contents in the page proofs, Hardy calculated
its proportions: 'Tragedy or sadness 2/5 of the whole / Reflection, love,
or comedy 3/5.' The 'comedy' included 'At Wynyard's Gap', a miniplay
about a brief flirtation, probably meant as a curtain-raiser for the Hardy
Players; elsewhere it tended to be black, or savagely satirical. In the first
class, 'The Sexton at Longpuddle' overlooks the snag about his expanding
market: 'Thinks he'll not lack / Plenty such work in the long ensuing /
Futurity. / For people will always die, / And he will always be nigh / To
shape their cell.' 'Farmer Dunman' asks to be buried on a Sunday, so that
his mourners are free to get adequately drunk at his 'Funeral'. Even 'The
Six Boards' was comic about the lack of customer satisfaction: 'I shall not
know / How well my want they'll have supplied / when notified'; and the
deeply felt elegy for the surgeon, Frederick Treves, was built on a medical
and evolutionary joke – that he was back in the calcium of which his body
was partly composed, among limestone fossils of the earliest living organisms: 'This chalky bed? – I surely seem to have been here before?'[22]

In the second, satirical, class of 'comedy' the light-hearted mockery of
'Lady Vi' became caustic at the mention of animals. She finds travel 'most
thrilling' if 'joined to big-game killing', and at home likes nothing better

than tormenting a fox: 'When Reynard nears his time to die, / 'Tis glee to mark his figure flag, / And how his brush begins to drag, / Till, his earth reached by many a wend, / He finds it *stopped*, and meets his end.' In 'Bags of Meat' (the current term is now 'agricultural products'), Hardy made what as late as 1970 was described by a critic as 'a satirically humorous attack' on the ethos of a cattle-auction. But here Hardy's indignation expelled all humour: 'Each beast, when driven in, / Looks round at the ring of bidders there / With a much amazed reproachful stare, / As at unnatural kin . . .' Though he had signed an appeal for a memorial to Byron in Westminster Abbey, he felt far less passionate about that issue, so was able, in 'A Refusal' to make splendid fun (if with rather hard-earned rhymes) of the Dean: 'Twill next be expected / That I get erected / To Shelley a tablet / In some niche or gablet./ Then – what makes my skin burn, / Yea, forehead to chin burn – / That I ensconce Swinburne!'[23]

All such 'comedy' apart, *Human Shows* is an enjoyable, almost a cheerful book to read. The title implies that human life is a matter of appearances, not merely inadequate as in Platonism, but positively deceptive. Yet some of the appearances described are inspiriting ones, as in 'A Bird-Scene at a Rural Dwelling', where the birds' 'joy at being alive' feels quite infectious. The pain of consciousness is everywhere assumed; but pleasure can be found in the 'far phantasy' of 'The Aërolite', which brings to earth, not traces of life in Mars (as reported in 1996), but 'a germ of Consciousness' from a 'globe' of 'supreme delight', where 'this disease / Called sense' was an unmixed blessing. The not-knowing syndrome, epitomized in 'Known Had I', is still shown to be endemic in human life. Death, seen in 'Not Only I' as a cause of irretrievable 'loss to the world', and in 'An Inquiry' as a major flaw in the scheme of things, is still a recurrent theme. But in this collection the two depressing subjects are allowed to cancel each other out – *agnosia* being reckoned the only good thing about dying. Death's imminence means that 'Maybe now / Normal unwareness waits rebirth.'[24]

The key-note of the volume was struck by the cheery little 'Epitaph on a Pessimist'. Originating in the Greek Anthology, this actually came from a 'French rendering' where the tone was 'changed to humorous'. Thus sadness, inseparable from Hardy's thoughts about the past and the present, was often relieved by his continuing zest for life, expressed in 'Pessimist' humour. But his vitality came out more generally as a simple delight in the musical side of poetry:

> Any little old song
>   Will do for me . . .
> Newest themes I want not
>   On subtle strings,
> And for thrillings pant not
>   That new song brings:
> I only need the homeliest
>   Of heartstirrings.[25]

32

Winter Words

In February 1926 Hardy was invited to be a 'Patron of the Special Choir' at Westminster Abbey. Declining the honour with 'many regrets' on the 16th, he added: 'though I have never had anything to do with the Abbey music I have known the building with a certain intimacy for a good many years (ever since in fact, I was present at Lord Palmerston's funeral in 1865)'. Just two years after he wrote those words, the intimacy would become permanent: the funeral would be his own.[1]

Meanwhile he was working to a new type of deadline. As a serial novelist he had often struggled to meet an early publication date. As an aging poet he set himself a late one, which proved impossible to meet. Remembering that Sophocles, as he had once pointed out, wrote some of his best tragedies 'when nearly ninety', he now, according to Florence, 'hoped to bring out a new volume of poems on his 90th birthday'. That was the thought behind his 'Introductory Note' to *Winter Words*: 'So far as I am aware, I happen to be the only English poet who has brought out a new volume of his verse on his . . . birthday, whatever may have been the case with the ancient Greeks, for it must be remembered that poets did not die young in those days.' Like them, he would have considered it *hubris* to insert the ordinal number too soon.[2]

Physically, there seemed no reason why he should not make it, so long as he did not get overtired or overexcited. 'I have had such grave warnings', wrote Florence in March 1926, 'from more than one doctor about his heart and blood pressure, and the danger of excitement, that I dare not upset him or even argue with him. If he keeps quiet all is well.' His activities around then were suitably unexciting: advising the Vicar of Stinsford about the church bells; explaining to a puzzled 'Japanese gentleman' that in *Tess* 'To have green malt in floor' meant 'to have a daughter in childbed before she is married'; composing an Independence Day 'message of congratulation and friendship' from Weymouth Eng. To Weymouth Mass.; warning the doorkeeper at the County Museum not to give any 'personal particulars' about him to 'gossiping journalists'; and signing his name 825 times for limited editions of *Tess* and *The Dynasts*.[3]

More interesting things happened too. In June 1926 'the Balliol Players', a group of Oxford undergraduates who had staged the *Oresteia* on the Max Gate lawn in 1924, returned with Euripides' *Hippolytus*. At the end of July Leslie Stephen's daughter Virginia Woolf came with her husband to tea. Three years before, she had written in the *Times Literary Supplement*: 'Mr Hardy has long since withdrawn from the arena.' Since then he had published two more books, but by now her premature statement had apparently proved prophetic. He struck her as not caring much about his novels or his poems either. 'The whole thing – literature, novels &c – all seemed to him an amusement, far away, too, scarcely to be taken seriously. Yet he had sympathy & pity for those still engaged in it.' Seeming 'to be free of it all', he impressed her most by his 'ease, & vitality', by his cheerfulness, affability, and kindness: 'he is a very kind man, & sees anyone who wants to see him. But clearly he preferred solitude himself.'[4]

In September the London producers of *Tess* brought to Weymouth for a 'flying matinée' John Drinkwater's stage-version of the *Mayor*, which had opened at Barnes. Hardy went to see it and got 'a great ovation' both from the audience and from the 'enthusiastic crowd' outside the theatre. 'From balconies and windows people were seen waving handkerchiefs as he drove past.' He must have rather enjoyed it, despite his ungrateful note: 'Snapshotters for newspaper illustrations very pestering.' He responded more gracefully to another tiresome effect of his celebrity. Asked to confirm that he had met and presented some of his books to a 'Miss Rosine Indergand', when staying in an hotel at 'Amsteg, Switzerland, in the seventies or eighties', he replied: 'I have never in my life set foot in Amsteg . . . I have never known any lady of that attractive name, which is quite new to me. It is a pity to spoil the story, but I cannot help it'.[5]

1926 ended discouragingly. In October his doctor diagnosed a hernia and prescribed a truss (which Hardy refused to wear). Florence reported him 'pretty well, but of course the passing years take their toll of vigour. He still writes – poems only, of course, but he burns practically all that he writes, which is I believe the wiser plan.' In November he felt unjustly 'passed over' for the Nobel Prize for Literature in favour of George Bernard Shaw. Then T.E. Lawrence, now a 'most valued' friend, came to say goodbye before leaving for India, and Hardy was 'grieved' to have unintentionally missed the last sight of him as he left on his motor bike.[6]

December brought a sight so disturbing that Hardy drew it in pencil and thought of it 'for long after': rows of railway trucks taking bullocks and cows to Islington for slaughter, 'with animals' heads at every opening, looking out at the green countryside they were leaving for scenes of horror in a far-off city.' (What would he have thought of the lorries taking

calves to French veal-crates seventy years later?) Then came the deaths of
Agnes Grove, with whom he had danced under the moon in 1895, and,
two days after Christmas, of Wessex. The dog had been 'in a bad way'
since the end of November, when Hardy wrote: 'We don't like to put an
end to him; a neighbour did to hers when he was ill, & she has regretted
it ever since.' But as Hardy told the Granville Barkers, Wessex 'was in such
misery with swelling and paralysis that it was a relief when a kind breath
of chloroform administered in his sleep by 2 good-natured Doctors (not
vets) made his sleep an endless one.' In Florence's notable litotes, 'poor
Wessie' had not been 'a good dog always', but both Hardys were deeply
distressed. 'I hope no one will ask me about him', wrote Florence, 'or
mention his name'. It appeared on his tombstone in the Max Gate animal
cemetery as 'THE FAMOUS DOG WESSEX'. The night after his burial
Hardy made this note: 'Wx. sleeps outside the house the first time for
13 years'; and 'those among Hardy's friends who thought that his life was
definitely saddened by the loss of Wessex' were probably right.[7]

Grief must have 'taken its toll of vigour' too; and by his eighty-seventh
birthday, spent with the Granville Barkers in Devon (whose cat soon
'established itself on his knees') he had a different joke to make about
Augustus John's portrait: 'I don't know whether that is how I look or not
– but that is how I *feel*.' He had kept writing, though, and not only poems:
in January a note on 'The Ancient Cottages of England' supporting an
appeal for funds to preserve them, and in March a brief message of support in *The Times* for a meeting called at Taunton by the League for the
Prohibition of Cruel Sports. He had also gone on corresponding with his
publisher about future editions of his works, and arranged for an updated
and expanded version of *Selected Poems* (1916). In a letter of thanks for a
royalty cheque of £5,392.2s.6d he remarked: 'I suppose that though I can
hardly be called a "best-seller", I may be called a long-seller, seeing that
some of the books were published fifty years ago.' He might have said four
hundred and eleven years ago, if the fan from Kansas City who asked for
a signed copy of his *Utopia* was to be taken seriously.[8]

Hardy usually refused to make speeches, but he made one in July 1927,
when laying the foundation-stone of a new building for the Dorchester
Grammar School, of which he had just ceased to be a Governor. He spoke
chiefly about the school's Elizabethan founder, Thomas Hardy, whom he
regarded as a distant relative; but he must have been thinking of his own
three-mile walk to school when he called the new building, 'not so far
from the centre of the borough as to be beyond the walking powers of the
smallest boy.' He had recently told the Bishop of Salisbury: 'I have all my
life suffered from a weak throat, hindering all speech-making (a good
thing)'; yet though it was a windy day he managed to make himself heard
'on the outskirts of the crowd that collected to hear him.' But when he got
home, feeling 'very tired', he said it had been 'his last public appearance.'[9]

Three days later he had bounced back, and Florence reported him
'working tremendously hard' – possibly on the short 'Reminiscence' of

George Meredith that he had just agreed to write. But such things were no longer easy to produce, and it was not until October that he sent it off, saying: 'I am sorry the article is no better, but though I am well I am not very vigorous at writing nowadays.' Perhaps he was beginning to doubt if he could last out quite as long as Sophocles after all. That month, though, a quasi-Sophoclean theme arrived on his doorstep in the shape of a 'young Chinaman' claiming to have had an experience which sounded 'quite equal to a Greek tragedy in its events.' He said that when his sister was found to be 'in the same condition as "Tess"', he was ordered by the head of the family to murder her baby at birth, which he did by sitting on it. Her brothers then forced her to save the family honour by drinking a lethal dose of opium in wine. Hardy was so impressed that he introduced the tragic hero to a publisher-friend of his. Florence was more sceptical when the visitor asked for Hardy's autograph.[10]

Late in November she wrote: 'T.H. is fairly well, but he feels very tired today, for no reason apparently, which always rather worries me.' It was the first symptom of his last illness. On 5 December he felt too tired to go out, which was 'rather unusual with him', but seemed 'always very contented & cheerful.' On the 11th, for the first time in his life, he felt totally unable to work.' On Christmas Day he wrote to Gosse: 'I am in bed on my back, living on butter-broth and beef tea, the servants being much concerned at my not being able to eat any Christmas pudding, though I am rather relieved . . . I think my aches are diminishing.' They were, but only in the sense that his 'Wish for Unconsciousness' was in process of being fulfilled. It was a wretchedly slow process. While watching it 'during the last few days' Florence kept thinking of the words in *King Lear*: 'O, let him pass: he hates him / That would upon the rack of this tough world / Stretch him out longer.'[11]

In his agnostic love of the Bible, his indignation at the human condition, and his fighting spirit, he remained himself throughout. Thinking on Boxing Day about 'the Nativity' and the 'Massacre of the Innocents', he asked Florence to read him the gospel accounts, and 'remarked that there was not a grain of evidence that the gospel story was true in any detail.' After a 'strong rally' on 10 January, he asked next morning to be read a verse of Fitzgerald's *Omar Khayyám* which blamed the Creator no less than his creatures for what went wrong in the world: 'Oh, Thou who Man of baser Earth didst make, / And ev'n with Paradise devise the Snake: / For all the Sin wherewith the Face of Man / Is blacken'd – Man's forgiveness give – and take!'[12]

That afternoon, in a less forgiving mood, he composed and dictated retaliatory epitaphs on G.K. Chesterton, who had called him 'a village atheist brooding and blaspheming over the village idiot', and George Moore, who had described his novels as 'ill-constructed melodramas, feebly written in bad grammar'. For Moore Hardy modernized a Biblical Proverb, but reversed its meaning. By giving 'thine enemy' food and drink, said Solomon, 'thou shalt heap coals of fire upon his head'. 'Heap dustbins on him;', amended Hardy, 'they'll not meet / The apex of his self-conceit.'[13]

He died that evening 'shortly after nine' (11 January 1928). There are three versions of his last words: a cry of distress to Florence's sister Eva, who as a trained nurse was looking after him: 'Eva, what is this?'; 'a few broken sentences, one of them heartrending in its poignancy, [showing] that his mind had reverted to a sorrow of the past'; and the one syllable, 'Em'. The first was reported by Eva and confirmed by the parlour-maid. The second was in the original draft of Florence's conclusion to the 'biography'; the third came from one of her executors. There was probably some truth in all three versions – though the thoughts ascribed by the last two may have remained unspoken.[14]

Florence was left to cope with her grief, the funeral, the 'biography', and the last collection of poems. How she felt can be guessed from her letter of 28 January: 'It is all . . . like a dreadful nightmare . . . Life seems absolutely at an end for me – & I wish it actually we[re].' The funeral presented an apparently insoluble problem. In 1924 Hardy had told the Vicar of Stinsford: 'Yes; regard me as a Parishioner certainly. I hope to be still more one when I am in a supine position one day.' His will began: 'It is my wish that I may be buried in Stinsford Churchyard Dorset near to the Grave of my parents and if possible in my wife Emma's Grave or close to the foot thereof'. But Cockerell and Barrie decided that such a national figure should be buried in Westminster Abbey. Unlike Byron, Hardy was not banned by the Dean; and the Vicar, possibly remembering Solomon's solution to a problem of disputed maternity, came up with a similar idea, for which there were good historical precedents: why not bury the heart at Stinsford, and the rest in the Abbey?[15]

Cockerel was 'all for it', Barrie went along with him, and poor Florence was in no state then to resist their advice, though the partial realization of the poem, 'His Heart: A Woman's Dream', can only have intensified the widow's sense of nightmare. So the heart was duly excised, wrapped in a towel, and kept, as the parlour-maid recalled, 'in my biscuit-tin' until the 'heart-burial at Stinsford'. The rest of the body was cremated, and the ashes buried in Poet's Corner. On Monday 16 January three church-services were held for the late agnostic: a state-funeral in the Abbey, a 'rural' one at Stinsford (where the anti-blood sports protester was mourned by 'some Dorset gentry in their hunting kit'), and a 'memorial service' in St Peter's Church, Dorchester, attended by members of the local authority and people from 'the whole neighbourhood.'[16]

Then there was the 'biography' to be finished and published. Hardy's completed narrative stopped at the end of 1918, leaving Florence nine more years to cover. Although he had continued to feed her material until his last illness, writing it up in publishable form was a formidable as well as painful task to face immediately after bereavement; nor was it made any easier by the secrecy involved. No wonder she told Daniel Macmillan (8 February 1928): 'Whether I shall be able to write the concluding chapters

I do not know. At present it is difficult for me to write anything, but I may be able to do so later with some assistance.'[17]

She got rather more of that than she wanted, especially from Cockerell, whose style of assistance struck her as domineering. But Barrie (whom she once thought of marrying) helped her most in the process of editing Hardy's text. On his advice she made numerous alterations, and several more on her own initiative, which her husband's 'Private Memorandum: Information for Mrs Hardy in the preparation of a biography' had left her quite free to use. It is sad, but quite understandable, that she occasionally used it to delete references to Emma. She had got tired of hearing about Emma's 'virtues & graces' within weeks of her own wedding; and she had heard and read a lot more of them since then. Otherwise she did her awkward job well. It was purely a labour of love, for all she was likely to get out of it was a little reflected glory, soured by the hateful sense of being a fraud. But perhaps it slightly relieved the 'remorse, almost beyond expression', from which she suffered in March 1928, 'because I know I failed him at every turn. Indeed, had it not been that he left work for me to do, I would not have lived on.' 'Her' book came out in two independent instalments, as *The Early Life of Thomas Hardy 1840–1891* (2 November 1928) and *The Later Years of Thomas Hardy 1892–1928* (29 April 1930).[18]

But the first thing she had to edit when the funerals were over was an 'envelope' of manuscript poems for Hardy's last volume, which he had told her 'could go to press as they were, at a pinch'. It was not quite as easy as that, for some verses were only pencilled in, some works were altered in pencil, and apart from the poems at the beginning and end it was not clear how far their order had been finalized. But with, and sometimes probably against, Cockerell's advice she established a text, which was published on 2 October 1928 as *Winter Words in Various Moods and Metres*. Thus, having ghosted his wife's book, Hardy made his own 'last appearance on the literary stage', like the Chanters in *The Queen of Cornwall*, as a ghost.[19]

Once more Hardy began and ended the volume with poems about himself. 'For the last few months he grew very weary of life', wrote Florence later. 'He knew that he was nearing the end & I think he did not regret it.' In 'The New Dawn's Business' he was perfectly 'willing' for his own burial to be one of the 'odd jobs round here / That Time to-day must do'; and the 'He' of the final poem, 'He Resolves to Say No More', was the third-person subject of the 'biography'. His weariness of life came out in other pieces: 'A Wish for Unconsciousness'; 'To Louisa in the Lane', where he was impatient 'with flung-off flesh' to rejoin the dead girl friend of his adolescence; and 'A Forgotten Miniature' (doubtless the one of Emma reproduced in *The Early Life*) where 'Some wait for sleep' clearly referred to the poet.[20]

Elsewhere he made poetry out of self-images, not all predictable: an almost invisible man, melting into the environment ('I Am the One');

a bewilderingly complex personality ('So Various'); 'A Placid Man'; an unambitious 'Private Man'; a pessimist proved right ('He Never Expected Much'); and in 'Not Known' 'a phasm they name as me, / In whom I should not find / A Single self-held quality / Of body or mind.' A self-image was hinted, too, in 'The Aged Newspaper Soliloquizes'. Though written for the 135th birthday of the *Observer*, it was equally relevant to the poet himself, who had observed, if not the 'history of a hundred years', at least of eighty: 'And I beat on. Yes; yes; I am old.'[21]

Recent events inspired some poems. Agnes Grove was mourned in 'Concerning Agnes'; Wessex, more movingly, in 'Dead "Wessex" the Dog to the Household'. The death of Hardy's sculptor friend Hamo Thornycroft (December 1925) and his parting from Lawrence a year later lay behind 'We say we shall not meet', and many sad visits to the Bockhampton cottage, the last in November 1926, behind 'Silences' and 'Concerning his Old Home'. And perhaps that Chinaman, who killed his sister's bastard baby before her other brothers killed its mother, can also be blamed for 'The Brother', who 'hurled' his sister's lover (by then her husband) over a cliff for 'wantoning' with her.[22]

A traumatic event of many years before inspired two more interesting poems. The addressee of 'After the Death of a Friend', who 'died, and made but little of it', was probably Horace Moule, whose dying words in 1873 had been, 'Easy to die'; and 'Standing by the Mantelpiece (H.M.M. 1873)' alluded to his suicide in deliberately private terms. Though biographers and critics have had a field-day interpreting the poem, it is enough to assume that Hardy's first great friend was imagined predicting his own death to some woman who had turned against him, in circumstances which Hardy had no wish to publicize.[23]

Naturally, at his age, the poet had sometimes recycled old thoughts and feelings. There was nothing new, for instance, in 'A Philosophical Fantasy' (written 1920–26) except the delightfully chatty style of the interview with the Absolute:

'Such I ask you, Sir or Madam,
(I know no more than Adam,
Even vaguely, what your sex is, –
Though feminine I had thought you
Till seers as "Sire" besought you; –
And this my ignorance vexes
Some people not a little,
And, though not me one tittle,
It makes me sometimes choose me
Call you "It", if you'll excuse me?)'
Call me "It" with a good conscience,
And be sure it is all nonsense
That I mind a fault of manner
In a pigmy towards his planner.'

Hardy's feeling for animals was even older than his thoughts about 'It', and in this last volume he spoke up for them more powerfully than ever, first in the bitter satire of 'The Lady in the Furs', and then, most horribly, in 'The Mongrel', where a man deliberately drowns his dog by throwing a stick 'Into the midst of the ebbing tide'.[24]

'Concerning Agnes' recalled 'that old romance' with her at the moonlight dance, and pictured her lying in death 'bedraped / Like Kalupso'. The allusion was almost too apt, for Calypso's Greek name meant 'covered' or 'concealed', and she kept Odysseus away from his wife in the *Odyssey*, just as Hardy's concealed feelings about Agnes Grove must have helped to estrange him from Emma in 1895. But Homer did less for this volume than the Greek Anthology, which offered more concise material to a poet who could not do much reading. 'The Bad Example' surprisingly converted a defence of promiscuity by Meleager into advice to young girls not to let themselves be 'tumbled' (like Tess) before Mr Right came along; and 'Faithful Wilson' modernized and heterosexualized Strato's epigrammatic claim that one does not notice the beloved's gradual loss of looks if one is always with him. Why 'Wilson'? Perhaps to suggest an element of wishful thinking.[25]

Pausanias' ten-book *Description of Greece*, the original source of the mini-tragedy, 'Aristodemus the Messenian', seems an unlikely work for Hardy to have been browsing in just then. But he may have looked up the two relevant pages of Pausanias when writing *The Dynasts*, or leafing through it later, perhaps while autographing the limited edition in 1926; for it included a scene in 'London. The Opera-House', at a performance of 'the opera of "Aristodemo"' by Vincenzo Puccitta which actually took place at the King's Theatre, Haymarket on 9 June 1814. The story was unappealing: a father killed his daughter and 'ripped her up' (Hardy's literal translation of *anetemne* in Pausanias) to prove that she was not pregnant. 'I did not like [it]'. wrote Florence, when editing *Winter Words*, '& I am afraid I annoyed T.H. by saying so. He actually thought it was suitable for performance here', i.e. by the Hardy Players. One sees her point; but the piece is interesting for its hendecasyllabic metre, a favourite of Catullus, more recently used by Swinburne ('In the month of the long decline of roses', after Tennyson's much more Catullan 'O you chorus of indolent reviewers'.[26]

For the Victorians, like the Greeks, still affected Hardy's poetry in the Twenties. 'An Evening in Galilee' was the latest descendant of Browning's 'Karshish', and 'The Poet's Thought' continued the theme of Tennyson's 'The Poet' (1830) and 'The Flower' (1864). In the first, the poet's thought was a 'flower all gold', which 'multiplied' to make the world / Like one great garden'. In the second, the flower becomes so common that 'people / Call it but a weed.' The third poem (1928) carried Tennyson's disillusionment one stage further: 'It came back maimed and mangled. And the poet / when he beheld his offspring did not know it: / Yea, verily, since its birth Time's tongue had tossed to him / Such travesties that his old thought was lost to him.'[27]

But disillusionment is not the impression left by the volume as a whole. Its spirit is more like that of 'Squire Hooper', who determined that his death 'in six hours' should not 'spoil the sport' for his guests; or rather (since the eigheenth-century Squire's idea of sport was shooting game) of Farmer Dunman in the previous volume, determined that his neighbours should enjoy his funeral. Despite its bleak title, and the sadness of poems like 'Throwing a Tree', with its hints of human death, or 'Lying Awake', with its imagined prospect terminating in a graveyard, *Winter Words* is not a depressing book. It has almost the feeling of a memorial service hospitably designed by the deceased to create a party atmosphere. As a a party turn there is a wonderful cross-talk act by 'Liddell and Scott', congratulating each other on the completion of their massive Greek lexicon, and remembering how often they had despaired of ever reaching Omega. Their sense of achievement against enormous odds must have parodied Hardy's own, as he looked back on his career:

> O that first morning, smiling bland,
> With sheets of foolscap, quills in hand,
> To write *aáatos* and *aáges*,
> Followed by fifteen hundred pages,
>   What nerve was ours
>   So to back our powers,
> Assured that we should reach *oódes*
> Whiled there was breath left in our bodies!
> Liddell replied: 'Well, that's past now;
> The job's done, thank God, anyhow.'

Hardy had done a bigger job, single-handed. If there really was, as Florence thought, 'a radiant look of *triumph*' on his dead face (and 'triumphant' was the word used independently by both Cockerell and a journalist who got in without her 'knowledge or consent'), there was plenty to justify it.[28]

Notes

Notes to Introduction

1 Samuel Smiles, *Self-Help: With Illustrations of Character and Conduct*, London, 1859, p. 9.
2 W. Wordsworth, 'The Waggoner', iv, 210.
3 Matthew Arnold, 'The Function of Criticism', SUP iii 270.
4 'So Various', line 65, CP 871; 'R. Browning, 'A Grammarian's Funeral', lines 78, 125; J.B.S. Haldane, *Possible Worlds and Other Essays*, London, 1927.
5 LW 400.
6 Thucydides, *History of the Peloponnesian War*, viii, 66.
7 UGT 33; RN 34; W 25; MC 27; L 431.
8 LW 376–7.
9 M. Arnold, *Friendship's Garland*, SUP v 316; CL iii 231.

Notes to Chapter 1

1 M. Arnold, Preface, *Poems* (1853), SUP i 9; 'Domicilium', CP No 1; CPW i 279–80, 335.
2 'How I Built Myself a House', *Chambers's Journal*, 18 March 1865, pp. 161–4; P 293; M 15.
3 Sketch reproduced in *Hardy's Cottage*, National Trust pamphlet, opposite p. 12; 'Domicilium', line 13, CP 3.
4 LW 13–17, 27.
5 LW 19, 21.
6 M 12.
7 LW 23–4.
8 LW 20.

9 LW 501.
10 LW 19, 26; DFB 13; LW 479, 22.
11 Gl 45–6, M 49, 51–2.
12 C. Lacey, 'Memories of Thomas Hardy as a Schoolboy', MAT 2 102; LW 37, 29–30.
13 M 55; LW 32–5.
14 LW 36–7.
15 LW 37–8.
16 LW 8, CP No 1; A. Tennyson, 'Tears, idle tears', *The Princess* (1847), iv, 21–40.
17 LW 41; M 75–6.
18 LW 45, 476.
19 For Donne, see LW 51; Gl 120; LW 42.
20 LW 42–3; A.C. Swinburne, *Atalanta in Calydon*, 1865, p. 47; LW 158; CL ii 158.
21 PN 104–14; LW 53.
22 'Amabel', CP No 3; LW 43, 49, 52–3.
23 M 79–81; LW 46–7; M 87, *Thoughts of the Emperor Marcus Aurelius Antoninus*, tr. G. Long, London, 1862, p. 125; LW 183; W. Pater, *Marius the Epicurean*, 1885.
24 LW 49–50; *Chambers's Journal*, 18 March 1865, pp. 161–4; P 293.
25 D. Jerrold, 'Mrs Caudle's Curtain Lectures', *Punch*, 1845, viii, 85, 95; 'How I Built Myself a House', HBH 164.
26 HBH 161, 162, 163.
27 HBH 162–3 (my italics).

Notes to Chapter 2

1 LW 52; CL i 7; LW 55.
2 'She to Him' I–IV, CP Nos 14–17; LW 50–1.
3 LW 54, 57.
4 LW 56; 'Heiress and the Architect', CP No 49.
5 LW 58; WRR 118–19; P 275–6; 'An Indiscretion in the Life of an Heiress', *New Quarterly Magazine*, July 1978, pp. 315–78; P 274.
6 LW 57–8, 56.
7 L. Deacon and T. Coleman, *Providence and Mr Hardy*, London, 1966; M 105; MSS 93; CL i 7–8.
8 LW 59–60, 62–4; ILH 7–9; M 115.
9 E. Gosse, 'Thomas Hardy's Lost Novel', *Sunday Times*, 22 January 1928, WRR 115–20, ILH 11–13.
10 LW 43; ILH 16; M 80, ILH 7.
11 WRR 127; ILH 41, 30, 94; ILH 66, LW 50.
12 ILH 12.
13 A. Tennyson, *Maud*, I, 119; 'Aylmer's Field', line 569; M 109, ILH 122.
14 E. Barrett (E.B. Browning), 'Lady Geraldine's Courtship', lines 17, 15, 41, 5; ILH 108–9, 70.
15 R. Browning, 'The Flight of the Duchess', lines 174–5, 18–3, ILH 34; 'The Statue and the Bust', lines 138–41, ILH 72.
16 J. Dryden, *The Works of Virgil*, World's Classics edn, 1903, p. 123, Virgil, *Aeneid*, v, 439–42, 449; A. Tennyson, *The Princess*, Prologue lines 27–34; J. Froissart, *Chronicles*, tr. Lord Berners, 1901–3, Chapter 80; *Aeneid*, iv, 160–76, ILH 50.

17 WRR 120, ILH 13; 'A Poor Man and a Lady', endnote, CP 793; ILH 122–3; P.B. Shelley, *The Revolt of Islam*, lines 2605–6, 2658.

Notes to Chapter 3

1 LW 65–6; RG1 168–9; M 116.
2 RG1 169, FBP 86; LW 66; RG1 171, M 106; 'At Waking', CP No 174; 'The Dawn after the Dance', CP No 182.
3 LW 64, 66.
4 LW 66–7; P 4; SR 55; FBP 94.
5 CL iv 299; LW 77.
6 SR 4; DKR 12–13; SR 46, 53, 22.
7 SR 50–1, 55; C. Patmore, *The Angel in the House*, Book I, Canto ii, section 3; LW 77–8, cf SR 57.
8 LW 78–9; M 126–7; WRR 135.
9 M 123; SR 39.
10 P 4–5; PN 6–7; LW 85.
11 P 5; PN 6–7; *Spectator*, 22 April 1972, pp. 481–3; CH 3–5; LW 507.
12 DR 38; HC 383; DR 307, 309.
13 DR 21; DR 139, G1 172, DCC 28 October 1869; DR 15; LW 65; DR 17, 18, 164; PN 6–7, DR 23.
14 LW 20, DR 42–3.
15 WRR 146; HC 17; LW 135; M.E. Braddon, *Lady Audley's Secret*, 1862, pp. 91, 9, 69.
16 DR 52; D.G. Rossetti, 'The Blessed Damozel', lines 104–5.
17 M.E. Braddon, *Lady Audley's Secret*, pp. 107–8, 43, 110; DR 111–13.
18 DR 139, 315.
19 LW 61; Virgil, *Aeneid*, i, 1–8, J. Dryden, *Works of Virgil*, World's Classics edn, 1903, p. 1 (my italics); LW 21; *Aeneid*, i, 257, 657; iv, 120–8, DR 109–16.
20 DR 64–70; C. Dickens, *Great Expectations*, 1861; DR 321.
21 LW 87.
22 DR 204, 207, Virgil, *Aeneid*, vi, 307, 314; DR 43, J.M.W. Turner, *The Angel standing in the sun*, Revelation, 19: 17, 12:1, 5; LW 20; DR 115, 172.
23 LW 87; WRR 120, ILH 13; DR 46, 58, 110, 123–4; CL ii 87, J.S. Mill, *The Subjection of Women* (1869), Everyman edn, 1929, p. 241; DR 35–6.
24 PN 6–7, DR 313–14.
25 DR 280, 209–10, 319.

Notes to Chapter 4

1 CL i 11.
2 CL i 8; M 134.
3 LW 60; CL i 11; see p. 21.
4 *Saturday Review*, 30 September 1871, xxxii, 441–2, CH 6–8.
5 CL i 13; M, 135; CL i, 13; M 138.
6 CL i 13–14.
7 M 138–9; LW 89; LW 90.
8 CL i 15–16.

9 CL i 16n; M 141; LW 91; CL i 16; P 8.
10 CL i 17; *Saturday Review*, 28 September 1872, xxxiv, 417; CH 11–14; M 141–2; *Athenaeum*, 15 June 1872; *Pall Mall Gazette*, 5 July 1872; P 12.
11 UGT 37; LW 88, P 7; LW 14–17, M 14, HC 21.
12 UGT 64, 72, 71, 34, 112.
13 UGT 103, 166–7, 178–9.
14 W. Shakespeare, *As You Like It*, II, v, 37–56; Horace, *Odes*, I, v, 9–11, J. Milton, 'The Fifth Ode of Horace. Lib. I', 9–11.
15 LW 85; CH 11; J.P. Eckermann, *Gespräche mit Goethe*, 1837–48, see *Conversations with Goethe*, tr. John Oxenford, London, 1875, p. 529; Giles Barber, *Daphnis and Chloe: the markets and metamorphoses of an unknown bestseller*, London, 1988, p. 60; E.B. Browning, *Aurora Leigh*, i, 829.
16 DC 17, UGT title-page; W. Shakespeare, *Love's Labours Lost*, V, ii, 908; UGT 33; *Merchant of Venice*, III, ii, 63–72; DC 24, 26, UGT 156, 153, 109.
17 UGT 166–7, DC 86; UGT 143; UGT 164, DC 28; UGT 144, DC 72; UGT 204, DC 120.
18 DC 18; UGT 164–5.
19 UGT 70, 91, 89.
20 UGT 82, 114–17, 208.
21 UGT 34, 52, 54, 37, 112, 111–13, 106.
22 UGT 136; 160–1, 166; UGT 204; C.R. Darwin, *Origin of Species*, 1859, ed. J.W. Burrow, Penguin, 1968, pp. 459, 171–2; LW 377.
23 DR 52; A. Tennyson, 'Miller's Daughter', lines 75–88, 124; *Enoch Arden*, 738–66; UGT 55.
24 UGT 77, 100, 166.
25 'The Self-Unseeing', line 12, CP 167; 'In Front of the Landscape', lines 1–7; UGT 122–3.

Notes to Chapter 5

1 P 11; LW 92; CL i 17–18.
2 LW 92–3.
3 JOB 351; CP 436.
4 PBE 226–39; PN 11, PBE 169; PBE 165, LW 93, SR 42.
5 M 144, PBE 108–15; CL i 18; LW 94; P 12, CL i 20.
6 M 145, LW 94; P 16, M 147, LW 97–8.
7 LW 97–8; CL i 21; P 12.
8 LW 95–6; LW 507; M 150; *Spectator*, 28 June 1873, 831; CH xvi.
9 LW 76–7.
10 PBE 261, LW 48–9; PBE 143–4, 1 Kings xix, CP 441, FBP 107.
11 PBE 93, 158.
12 M 150–1; PN 14; PBE 286.
13 LW 85; PBE 92–3.
14 Longus, *Daphnis and Chloe*, i, 17, cf. DC 50; PBE 45, 245–6.
15 DC 30–1, 24–6.
16 PBE 166–7, 175–7.
17 PBE 37, Horace, *Epodes*, xvii, 36–7, v, 47–8; PBE 97, Virgil, *Aeneid*, i, 648; PBE 14, *Aeneid*, ii, 289f.
18 PBE 47, 272; PBE 108, *Aeneid*, i, 453–6.

19 LW 38; PBE 231f, Aeschylus, *Eumenides*, 117f; PBE 256–9, 270–1, Sophocles, *Oedipus Tyrannus*, 1056f; *Oedipus Tyrannus*, 105, 264, PBE 49.
20 PBE 308, Sophocles, *Antigone*, 1221–5, 891, 1206; W. Morris, 'The Love of Alcestis', *The Earthly Paradise*, Part ii; F. Leighton, *Hercules Wrestling with Death for the Body of Alcestis*, 1871; H. Moule, 'The Story of Alcestis', *Fraser's Magazine*, November 1871, pp. 575–85.
21 PBE 169, 303, 368; H. Moule, ibid., p. 579.
22 H. Moule, ibid., p. 580.
23 PBE 296; *English Plays of the Nineteenth Century*, ed. M.R. Booth, Oxford, 1973, iv, 229; PBE 302.
24 Euripides, *Alcestis*, 72–3, 1140–1; PBE 172, 248; PBE 14, 18, 59, 261, 192, 308.
25 PBE 169, 175, P 10; *Fraser's Magazine*, lxxxvi (OS), 6 (NS), pp, 645–61.
26 PBE 169, 171.
27 CL i 14, PBE 30, 53; PBE 253, 179.
28 PBE 131, 137, 44f, 249f, 197f, 207f, 308, 207.
29 W. Shakespeare, *Love's Labour's Lost*, V, ii, 713f.
30 PBE 286, Song of Solomon, 8:6, PBE 296, 59–60, 259.
31 CL i 22n; Sheridan, *The School for Scandal*, III, iii.

Notes to Chapter 6

1   CL i 27; BFP 114; LW 98, 95.
2   LW 96; Gl 257, M 154–5, FBP 112–13.
3   CP 11–12, P 97; *Saturday Review*, 2 August 1873, xxxvi, 158–9, CH 15–18, Gl 252–3.
4   T. Gray, 'Elegy in a Country Churchyard', line 108; LW 97; P 336; BFP 113.
5   P 16, M 156–7; LW 98–9, CL i 24–5.
6   CL i 22; FBP 114; CL i 23–5, 34.
7   M 157–9, BFP 114–15; CL i 26, vii 66.
8   P 338; CL i 20; CL i 28; P 339.
9   LW 100, 103; CL iii 218; *Spectator* 3 January 1874, 7 February 1874, P 16–17.
10 LW 103; PN 17; BFP 123.
11 PBE 92; LW 103; Emma Hardy, *Diaries*, ed. Richard H. Taylor, 1985, pp. 27, 49, 32; CL i 31; M 164–6, FBP 121–2, DKR 85–7, MSS 205–9.
12 Fran Chalfont, THJ, February 1993, ix, 1, p. 41; BFP 123.
13 Henry James, *Nation*, 24 December 1874; CH 27–31; LW 104.
14 FMC 344, 339, 286–7.
15 PBE 37, 63; LW 78, PBE 42.
16 CL iv 58, LW 21; LW 97; J.S. Mill, *The Subjection of Women*, Everyman edn, London, 1929, pp. 266–7; Mary Wollstonecraft, *Rights of Woman*, Everyman edn, London, 1929, p. 163.
17 FBP 20; CL i 17; FMC 93; SR 50–1; e.g. TD 197, 51.
18 FMC 24, 290; FMC 32, LW 95.
19 FMC 196f, 249f, 256f.
20 J. Milton, 'Lycidas', lines 165–7; FMC 51; FMC 53–4, DC 24–5; FMC 52, DC 33.
21 FMC 53; Virgil, *Eclogues*, vi, 43–4; FMC 54; Theocritus, *Idylls*, xiii, 36–60; Apollonius Rhodius, *Argonautica*, i, 1164, 1240–8.
22 Theocritus, *Idylls*, i; FMC 27–8.

23 Theocritus, *Idylls*, xi, 17f, FMC 45; *Idylls*, xi, 35–6, 47, 38, FMC 49; *Idylls*, vi, 9–11, FMC 46; *Idylls*, vi, 17, FMC 47–51; *Idylls*, vi, 34–8, FMC 29.

24 M 91; Auguste Comte, *A General View of Positivism*, tr. J.H. Bridges, 1865, p. 3, p. 219, pp. 228–8.

25 A. Comte, *A General View of Positivism*, p. 43, 26, 30; FMC 32, 36; Virgil, *Aeneid*, iv, 569; Comte, ibid., 243, 251, 236; FMC 339–40, Comte, ibid., pp. 256–7, p. 251.

26 C.H. Hazlewood, *Lady Audley's Secret, Nineteenth-Century Plays*, ed. G. Rowell, Oxford, 1953, p. 266; FMC 323, 262; *English Plays of the Nineteenth Century*, ed. Michael R. Booth, Oxford, 1869, i, 233; T.W. Robertson, *Six Plays*, ed. Michael R. Booth, Ashover, 1980, pp. 315, 322; FMC 324–5.

27 FMC 52, 238, 294, 34, 54

28 FMC 291, 140, 142.

29 CL i 28; CH 28.

30 FMC 60–3, 64–5, 83–4, 147–8, 148; 150, *Book of Common Prayer*, Communion service, Prayer of Consecration; FMC 152, 340, 343.

31 A. Comte, *A General View of Positivism*, p. 43; FMC 274; FMC 265, Exodus, 20:2; FMC 265.

32 A. Comte, ibid., p. 220; FMC 266; Matthew 25: 35–6, FMC 267.

Notes to Chapter 7

1 LW 105; M 169; LW 105.

2 LW 105; F.W. Maitland, *Life and Letters of Leslie Stephen*, London, 1907, p. 276; M 169; CL i 35; HE 51.

3 M 170; LW 110; LW 109; CL i 37, M 108–9.

4 LW 110; 'We sat at the window', line 9 in holograph, CPW ii 161.

5 CL i 39; LW 110; DKR 92–3, EHD 59, 65.

6 CL i 41; CP p. 429; LW 110.

7 CL i 42; LW 111; P 23; CH xix; P 23; DKR 59.

8 HE 1, 177–8, 178f, 316, 290f.

9 LW 28; HE 29, LW 28; HE 17, 19, 18; HE 17, 62.

10 HE 73, 83; M 15n., FBP 135; LW 111, M 149.

11 LW 105; HE 320, 72, 13, 58; 'The Fire at Tranter Sweatley's', *Gentleman's Magazine*, November 1875, pp. 552–5, CL ii 61, P 103, CP p. 71, CPW i 365, 390–3.

12 HE 124–6.

13 HE 84, 147, 150, J. Milton, *Paradise Lost*, i, 678f; HE 141, 184.

14 LW 107; CL i 28; HE 300, 111.

15 HE 2–4, 213–14, cf. PBE 296; HE 310; 'Destiny and a Blue Cloak', *New York Times*, Sunday, 4 October 1874, pp. 2–3, CSS 899.

16 HE 149; Lucretius, *De rerum natura*, iv, 1186, 1058–91.

17 HE 59, 13; LW 32; Homer, *Iliad*, i, 311; HE 319, 313, 319; Homer, *Odyssey*, xxii, 424, 462–73.

18 T. Carlyle, *French Revolution*, Everyman edn, ii, 37; R. Browning, *The Ring and the Book*, vi, lines 483–1151; HE 318.

19 A. Tennyson, 'The Lord of Burleigh', lines 7–8; HE 44; Tennyson, 'The Lord of Burleigh', lines 79–80, 76, 37; HE 317; Tennyson, lines 39–40.

20 HE xxiii, 5–6; Homer, *Iliad*, xii, 200–43; P.B. Shelley, *Revolt of Islam*, lines 190–252; Homer, *Odyssey*, xix, 535–581; DC 79–80.

21 HE 10, 5.

22 HE 180, 1, 181, 1, 179, 181.
23 HE 181, 180; Revelation 21: 2; HE 184, Zechariah, 9:9, Matthew, 21: 5–9; HE 253; HE 183–4, Matthew, 27: 74–5.
24 HE 183–4; LW 107; HE 157; HE xxiii, RG1 290, M 12.
25 MC 258; A. Comte, *A General View of Positivism,* tr. J.H. Bridges, 1865, i, 32; HE 322.
26 HE 317, 189; HE 319, 253, 309, 320.

Notes to Chapter 8

1 CL i 43; LN I, xxxii, xxxvii–viii.
2 CL i 45; LW 113, 114, 110; e.g. L 347–50; LW 113.
3 SR 48; EHD 83–4, 87; LW 114.
4 CL i 45; EHD 89, 90, 91.
5 HE 20; EHD 103; LW 114–15, 118–19.
6 EHD 103; LW 109, 116; G1 23; M 186; DKR 98; MSS 240.
7 F.B. Pinion, 'The Composition of "The Return of the Native"', *TLS,* 21 August 1970, p. 931; Hardy, in F.W. Maitland, *Life and Letters of Leslie Stephen,* London, 1906, pp. 276–7; S. Gatrell, *Hardy the Creator,* Oxford 1988, pp. 29–51; LW 120; M 188.
8 CL i 49; P 27; CL i 54, 57, 51; TH, 'The Thieves Who Couldn't Help Sneezing', *Father Christmas,* London, 1877, pp. 1–3.
9 RN 34, 324–36, 457 (Hardy's footnote of 1912).
10 'An Indiscretion in the Life of an Heiress', *New Quarterly Magazine,* July 1878, pp. 315–78, P 274–5; LW 121–3; Fran Chalfont, 'Hardy's Residences and Lodgings', THJ, February 1993, ix, 1, p. 44; CL i 57–8.
11 P 27; RN 364; *Athenaeum,* 23 November 1878, p. 654, CH 46; *Saturday Review,* 4 January 1879, xlvii, 23–4, CH 50; *Spectator,* 8 February 1879, pp. 181–2, CH 55; *Academy,* 30 November 1878, p. 517, CH 48; LW 127.
12 CL iv 212; RN 296–302, 170; LW 90.
13 RN 227, LW 122; RN 206, CL i 31; RG2 25; CL i 61, *Return of the Native,* ed. Simon Gatrell, World's Classics, Oxford, 1990, p. ix; Frontispiece 1st edn, P 24; M 199.
14 RN 242, LW 118; RN 302; RN 334, LW 121; RN 220–1, DFB 126, LW 112.
15 LW 113; RN 318, 322, 91, 149.
16 *Saturday Review,* xli (17 June 1876), 770; LN i, 47, 297 (No 463; A.C. Swinburne, 'Hymn to Proserpine', line 46 (article-writer's italics, not Swinburne's); RN 82, 406, 340, 167.
17 SUP iii 222, 229; RG2 19; J. Keats, *Endymion,* iv, lines 173–81; W. Pater, *The Renaissance: Studies in Art and Poetry,* ed. Louis Kronenberger, New York, 1959, p. 151.
18 RN 167, LW 355–6; RN 81–2; CL i 52.
19 John, 8: 12; Revelation, 3: 17–20; Ruskin, letter to *Times* (5 May 1854), quoted T. Hilton, *The Pre-Raphaelites,* London, 1970, p. 92; FMC 176, 178.
20 J. Ruskin, Letter to *Times,* quoted T. Hilton, *The Pre-Raphaecites,* p. 92; FMC 176, 178; RN 225, 263, 302, 321, 318, 330, 321.
21 Virgil, *Eclogues,* viii, 74–81; Theocritus, *Idylls,* ii, 28–9; RN 68, 80, 165, 125, 214.
22 M. Arnold, SUP iii, 216f, 230–1; LN i 47 (No 461); Aeschylus, *Prometheus Vinctus,* 1080–91, RN 320–1.

23 RN 39, 41; E. FitzGerald, *Agamemnon, A Tragedy Taken from Aeschylus*, London 1876; R. Browning, *The Agamemnon of Aeschylus, Transcribed*, London 1877; Aeschylus, *Agamemnon*, 281–311, RN 40, 98, 31, 77.
24 RN 34; Sophocles, *Oedipus Tyrannus*, ed. R.C. Jebb, 1885–1981, pp. 2, 4.
25 RN 281; Aristotle, *Poetics*, 11 (1452 a 29–33); RN 283, 356.
26 RN 293, 188, 296; Sophocles, *Oedipus Tyrannus*, 105, RN 286–7.
27 Aristotle, *Poetics*, vi (1449 b 27); RN 266.
28 Sophocles, *Oedipus Tyrannus*, 1–13, 1480; RN 356, 364–5.
29 RN 33, 38, 167, 364.

Notes to Chapter 9

1 LW 131; F. Chalfont, THJ February 1993 (iv, 1), p. 44; CL i 57; CL i 57, LW 135–6, CL i 62; LW 139–40, 125; FPP 188.
2 LW 128; CP p. 466; LW 151.
3 LW 127–8; W. Wordsworth, 'Ode: Intimations of Immortality', line 18.
4 'Fellow-Townsmen', *New Quarterly Magazine*, April 1880, reprinted in *Wessex Tales* (1888).
5 C. Dickens, *Martin Chuzzlewit*, Oxford Works of Charles Dickens, p. 99; LW 127–8; CL i 66, 77; 'Distracted Young Preacher', *New Quarterly Magazine*, April 1879, reprinted as 'The Distracted Preacher' in *Wessex Tales* (1888), P 59.
6 Cf. CL i 11; P 34; W. Shakespeare, *Hamlet*, II, ii, 427; RN 46, 41; CH 56–7; CL i 65.
7 M 206, MSS 253; P 28; LW 125.
8 P 32; CL i 73; LW 121; *New Quarterly Magazine*, October 1879, pp. 469–73, PW 94–5.
9 P 34; LW 128, 141, 140, 142; CL i 78, *Graphic*, 24 July 1880; LW 142–3, 145; M 215; MSS 253; P. 35.
10 *Athenaeum*, 20 November 1880, CH 72; SR 11.
11 LW 130–1.
12 TM 193, 103, 92, 155, 77, 146.
13 CL i 65; TM 164, 260–3; Romans 12:10 (my italics).
14 B. 12; TM 67; P.J. Bailey, *Festus*, 1839, 10th edn 1877; LW 21; M 18; TM (Preface) 24; LW 9, 18; Sir Thomas Masterman Hardy (1769–1839), 2nd son of Joseph Hardy, of Portisham, Dorset.
15 PN 117–86; PN 129–30, TM 113; TM 190, PN 122.
16 LW 110; Homer, *Iliad*, ii, 872–5, TM 49–50; Homer, *Iliad*, vi, 325–39, 521–5; LN i 56, Herodotus, *Histories*, vii, 44, PN 126, TM 100.
17 F. Rabelais, *Gargantua and Pantagruel*, tr. J.M. Cohen, Penguin Classics 1955, pp. 574–9 (Book iv, chs 59–60); TM 117–20; W. Pater, *The Renaissance: Studies in Art and Poetry*, 1873, ed. L. Kronenberger, New York, 1959, p. 157.
18 A. Tennyson, 'The Lord of Burleigh', lines 7–8, TM 27, 55; 'The Miller's Daughter', lines 105–27, TM 148; TM 262, *Enoch Arden*, lines 909, 754–66, 794, TM 199.
19 TM 200–1, 205, 208, 280.
20 TM 136; W. Shakespeare, *Hamlet*, I, ii, 180–1, TM 144–5; T.W. Robertson, *Ours*, II, ii (*Six Plays*, ed. M.R. Booth, 1980, p. 88), TM 280; illustration by John Collier, *Good Words*, December 1880, p. 801.

21 W. Shakespeare, *Hamlet*, ii, 429, 426; TM 276, 153, 198.
22 CL i 64; F.W. Maitland, *Life and Letters of Leslie Stephen*, 1906, p. 277; TM 142 (my italics); CL i 65; TM 280, 292–3.

Notes to Chapter 10

1 CL i 72; LW 150; PN 180–3; subtitle of 1st edn, P 36.
2 CL i 72; P 40; LW 149–50, 153; Winston Churchill, Speech, House of Commons 18 June 1940.
3 CL i 82; LW 152, 150; LW 151, W. Shakespeare, *Hamlet*, IV, v, 78–9; LW 152 (Carlyle died 5 February 1881, George Eliot died 22 December 1880); LW 150–1; LW 151, cf M. Arnold, 'The Literary Influence of Academies', SUP iii 245–50, 'Pagan and Mediaeval Religious Sentiment', SUP iii 230–1.
4 LW 150, 152; Eduard von Hartmann, *Die Philosophie des Unbewussten*, 1868, tr. W.C. Coupland, London, 1884; LW 153.
5 LW 153; T. Gray, 'Ode: On the Pleasure arising from Vicissitude', lines 49–56; LW 154.
6 LW 154; CL i 95; *Chambers's Encyclopaedia*, 1895, iii, 377; the surgeon urologist Sir Henry Thompson, G2 47.
7 LW 154–5, A. Marvell, 'The Garden', line 48; first published in America 25 November 1881, *A Laodicean* appeared in London the first week of December, P 40; letter of 28 September 1881 from editor, T.B. Aldritch, P 44.
8 W. Archer, *Real Conversations*, London, 1904, p. 4; LW 150; P 40; W. Archer, *Real Conversations* p. 33, L 1, 126, 2; L 100, M 79; L 42, LW 18–19; L 85, LW 20; L 87–9, LW 33–4; L 39–40, LW 49; L 40, LW 89; L 39; M 55, L 48–9.
9 LW 149–50; L 268; LW 151, L 219, L 223, 293, 299.
10 L 201–2.
11 Sir L. Woodward, *The Age of Reform: 1815–1870*, Oxford, 1962, pp. 246–7, Compact DNB, Oxford 1975, p. 1570 (David Pacifico).
12 LW 149–50; L 311, LW 114; L 250, LW 113; LW 113, L 324, 341.
13 LW 139 (chapter title); L 145, Virgil, *Aeneid*, iv, 160–6, L 154–6; L 321, cf. Horace, *Odes*, III, xxvi, II, iii.
14 L 168; Ovid *Metamorphoses*, xv, 453–9; A. Tennyson, 'Godiva', lines 66–9, L 195–8; Ovid, *Metamorphoses*, xv, 459, L 300.
15 M 87, L 285; DC 26, L 47; DC 25, L 104; DC 29–30, L, 86–9; L 278; DC 39, L 386–7, 396.
16 W. Shakespeare, *Love's Labour's Lost*, I, i, 37, L 185; W. Shakespeare, *Romeo and Juliet*, I, v, 97–111, L 255; *A Midsummer-Night's Dream*, III, ii, 290–8, L 46, 57; L 213; CL v 237; see T.H. Ward, ed. *The English Poets*, 1880, i, 424–30, and Edmund Gosse, ed. *Works of Thomas Lodge*, 1883; J. Milton, *Paradise Lost*, i, 600–1, L 256, 378–9.
17 L 176, Byron, *Don Juan*, XIV, xvii, 4–5.
18 R. Browning, *Christmas-Eve*, line 438' L 46; L 145–6, 155; T.H. Ward, *The English Poets*, 1880–1, iv, 589–607; A.H. Clough, *Amours de Voyage*, ii, 335; L 293f, 401f.
19 T.H. Ward, ed. *The English Poets*, iv, 600–1; L 369, 371; A.H. Clough, *Dipsychus*, xiv, 58–9, L 188, 390.
20 L 37, 125; A. Tennyson, 'Godiva', lines 69–72, L 395–7; *Maud*, I, 810–24, L 127, 175, 236, 242, 254.

21 L 65, 420–3; A. Tennyson, *Princess*, Prologue, line 205; L 52; *Princess*, Prologue, lines 225, 74, 77–8, L 109, 272, 275.
22 M. Arnold, 'The Forsaken Merman', lines 70–7, L 43–5; M Arnold, *St Paul and Protestantism*, SUP vi, 121–5; *Culture and Anarchy*, SUP v 165, L 87–9, 108, 65.
23 LW 34–5, 586; M. Arnold, 'Equality', SUP viii 296–7, 195, L 431–2.
24 A. Comte, *A General View of Positivism*, tr. J.H. Bridges, i, 230; L 436–7; M. Arnold, 'Pagan and Mediaeval Religious Sentiment', SUP iii 230; LW 137.
25 Tom Taylor and A.W. Dubourg, *New Men and Old Acres*, in *English Plays of the Nineteenth Century*, ed. M.R. Booth, iii, 289, 247, 249, 287, 265, 303, 297, 301–2, 285.
26 T.W. Robertson, *Progress*, in *Six Plays*, ed. M.R. Booth, 1980, pp. 182, 202, 200–1, L 119; L 64, *Progress*, p. 198.
27 L 163, 262; Sir J.T. Knowles, who designed Tennyson's last home, founded the Metaphysical Society (1869) and the *Nineteenth Century* (1877); L 228, 403, 380.
28 L 62–3, 47; Revelation 3:15, L 404, 408, 410, Revelation 1:20, L 411, 412, 414.
29 L 435–6; *Oxford Companion to the Theatre*, Oxford, 1983, p. 489; L 439.
30 L 434, 92; for a different interpretation of Paula's whisper see MSS 268–9.

Notes to Chapter 11

1 FMC 32; R.A. Proctor, *Essays on Astronomy*, Appendix C, p. 372f; CL i 97; Compact DNB 1267–9.
2 L 25.
3 PN 22; for photographs of Charborough Tower, see V. Jesty, *Hardy's Wessex Today*, 1990, pp. 62–3; CL i 96–7, 101–2; P 44.
4 CL i 99; P 28–9; M 226–7.
5 LW 158; M 227; LW 158; CL i 105.
6 TT 82, 13, 18; LW 157; P 44.
7 CL i 109; LW 160; CL i 114; P 44; *Saturday Review*, 18 November 1882, liv, 674–5; *Spectator*, 3 February 1883, p. 154; CH 97–103; CL i 114.
8 TT 207, M 15; TT 68, M 15; TT 10, cf 'One We Knew', CP 274–5; LW 43, TT 69; TT 211, LW 43.
9 TT 4, 28, 'We Sat at the Window', line 3, CP p. 428; TT 106, 116.
10 TT 48, 51; DFB 13–14, TT 181; M 55, TT 133; TT 9, 11; PN 6–7, TT 81, 213.
11 TT 200 (Sir John Frederick William Herschel, 1792–1871); R.A. Proctor, *Essays on Astronomy*, 1872, pp. 12–13, TT 32, 212; Proctor, *Essays on Astronomy* p. 5, TT 205; ibid., p. 24, TT 5.
12 LW 158; C. Darwin, *Origin of Species*, 1859, ed. J.W. Burrow, 1968, p. 221, TT 14; TT 173, cf. J.S. Mill, *Utilitarianism*, 1861.
13 T.H. Huxley, 'Literature and Culture', *Collected Essays*, 1893, x, 141, 153; LW 125; TT 110; P 41; M. Arnold, 'Literature and Science', SUP x 71, 67, 68, 69–70.
14 TT 199, 212.
15 TT 70, DC 82; TT 99, 101, *Paul and Virginia* (Hardy's copy), Edinburgh, 1849, pp. 1, 41, Bernardin de Saint-Pierre, *Paul et Virginie*, ed. J. van den Heuvel, Paris, 1984, pp. 155, 159.
16 S. Johnson, *Rasselas, Johnson: Prose and Poetry*, ed. Mona Wilson, London, 1950, pp. 465–6, TT 36, 45, 80.

17 LN i 372, No 1217n; CL ii 195; H. Fielding, *Tom Jones*, World's Classics edn,
ed. G.S. Haight, OUP, 1981, pp. 150–1, 525; *Eton Latin Grammar*, ed. T.W.C.
Edwards, 24th edn, 1850, p. 242; LW 27; HC 39; TT 46; Firmicus Maternus,
Mathesis, V ii 11, TT 21.

18 TT 32; TT 183–4 (my italics); Virgil, *Aeneid*, vi, 452–4; TT 206, Horace, *Odes*,
I, iv, 13–14.

19 LW 157; TT 32, 31, 3; TT 4, W. Shakespeare, *The Tempest*, I, I, 409–13; TT 9;
Shakespeare, *Twelfth Night*, II, iii, 145–83, TT 194; *Love's Labour's Lost*, IV, iii,
302–27; TT 72, *Sonnets*, xiv, 1–2, 9; *Venus and Adonis*, 380–1, TT 29, 35.

20 TT 186, J. Milton, 'On the Morning of Christ's Nativity', lines 229–31, 237;
G.G. Byron, 'Darkness', lines 2–5, *Don Juan*, I, cxxxvi–clxv (Hardy may have
known the similar scene in Mozart's *Figaro*), II, 148–51, 32.

21 LW 134–5; P.B. Shelley, *Prometheus Unbound*, IV, 425f, esp. 444–5; TT 103,
P.B. Shelley, *Revolt of Islam*, III, xiv, IV, i, iii; TT 86, 39.

22 TT 4, *Lemprière's Classical Dictionary* (1788), ed. F.A. Wright, London, 1963,
pp. 223, 204; TT 168, 32; J. Keats, *Endymion*, iv, 984–5, TT 4–5, 212, cf. 'loving-
kindness and mercy', *Psalms*, xxiii in *Book of Common Prayer*.

23 A. Tennyson: 'bee-like swarms/ Of suns', see note to 'The Palace of Art', 1832
edn, in *The Poems of Tennyson*, ed. C. Ricks, London, 1969, p. 412, 'globes that
flew in groups like swarms of bees', TT 203; MCN 188–9; A. Tennyson, 'The
Palace of Art', 1842 edn., line 291, TT 10, 99f, 190; R. Browning, *Red Cotton
Night-Cap Country or Turf and Towers* (1873); TT 121, D.G. Rossetti, 'The Blessed
Damozel', line 12.

24 TT 180, A.C. Swinburne, *Tristram of Lyonesse* (1882), London 1915, p. 40;
TT 79 (my italics), Swinburne, *Tristram*, pp. 40, 165.

25 Voltaire, *Candide*, tr. John Butt, Harmondsworth, 1947, p. 137; TT 213;
TT Preface, xxv; TT 24, 25–6; CL i 114.

26 TT 80, 90, 159, 176; T.J. Hogg, *Life of Percy Bysshe Shelley*, 1856, i, 69–70.
TT 164–5; TT 166–9, 172–4.

27 Preface, TT xxv; G.M. Hopkins, 'The Starlight Night' (1877), first published
in *Poets and Poetry of the Century*, ed. A.H. Miles, 1893, p. v; TT 22–3.

Notes to Chapter 12

1 CL i 105; F. Chalfont, 'Hardy's Residences and Lodgings', Part Two, THJ,
Feb 1993, No 1, pp. 47, 52; LW 167, DR 307, 309; M 239–40; the house off
Shire-Hall Lane, now Glyde Path Road, has been replaced by local govern-
ment buildings.

2 CL i 110; LW 167; DKR 115; M 234; LW 160; LW 163–4, 'Romantic Adventures of a Milkmaid', *Graphic*, Summer Number, 25 June 1883, P 47–9, CSS
813; cf. film, *Brief Encounter* (1945); 'He Abjures Love', lines 45–8, CP 237.

3 LW 168, M 241; 'Some Romano-British Relics Found at Max Gate, Dorchester',
PW 191–2; MC 274.

4 'The Three Strangers', *Longman's Magazine*, March 1883; P 58; CSS 7–27;
'The Dorsetshire Labourer', *Longman's Magazine*, July 1883, pp. 252–69, P 50;
CL i 119, PW 170–1; PW 174–5, MC 150.

5 'Our Exploits at West Poley', *The Household*, November 1892–April 1893;
P 301–3; CL i 123; TH, *Our Exploits at West Poley* ed. R.L. Purdy, Oxford
1978, pp. 3, 78, 74, 78.

6 MCN 237, 241, 239; CL i 111; Sylvaticus i.e. J.F. Pennie, *The Tale of a Modern
Genius*, London, 1827; Compact DNB ii 1632 (J.F. Pennie); LW 171.

7   LW 177, PN 25; M 256; CL i 217; LW 169, 170; F. Chalfont, 'Hardy's Residences', THJ February 1993, No i, pp. 53–4; LW 177, 181; DKR 116.
8   LW 177; Fanny Stevenson, quoted M 270; LW 178, 182–3.
9   P 51–3; *Saturday Review*, 29 May 1886, lxi, 757, CH 134–6; *Spectator*, 5 June 1886, 752–3, CH 136–9; LW 175.
10 See N.J. Atkins, 'The Country of "The Mayor of Casterbridge"', Tour Pamphlet No 7, Thomas Hardy Society, Dorchester, 1976; M 243; MC 183; LW 163; MC 34; MC 27, LW 114; MC 273.
11 MC 53, 197, 203, 86, 113, 180, 279, 286.
12 LW 9–11; LW 479, MC 281; G1 55, M 47n., MC 226; LW 32–3, MC 266–7; MC 79, PW 192.
13 LW 177; MC 86, 285, 109; MC 114, Genesis 30: 25–43, 27: 36.
14 MC 171, 1 Samuel 9: 18–24, cf. 28: 7–25; 1 Samuel 16: 14–23 (cf. R. Browning, 'Saul', 1855), MC 265, 69; MC 61–2; MC 120, Genesis 25: 3.
15 MC 157, 203, Luke 16: 8; MC 144, Matthew 26: 69–74; Matthew 26: 57, MC 235; Luke 23: 37, MC 284–5; MC 285–6, Matthew 4: 13–16.
16 MC 35, 54, 84; Homer, *Iliad*, xviii, 104, MC 239, 274.
17 MC 109, 105, 101–2; MC 274, *Iliad*, vi, 200–2.
18 Aeschylus, *Agamemnon*, 177, MC 123; M.C. Howatson, *Oxford Companion to Classical Literature*, Oxford, 1989, p. 533, LW 182; MC 63.
19 LW 37–8; MC 31, 268; *Oedipus Tyrannus*, 1449–54, *Oedipus Coloneus*, 1f., MC 208; MC 285, OT 1437.
20 *Oedipus Tyrannus*, ed. R.C. Jebb, Cambridge, 1883, lines 716, 730, MC 174; see Frederick Barry, *View of the Town Hall and Market Place during the Fair*. 1835, reproduced on cover of World's Classics edn of novel by D. Kramer, Oxford, 1987; cf. 'Where Three Roads Joined', CP 587–8.
21 Virgil, *Aeneid*, vi, 454, MC 210, cf. TT 206; MC 97, 117–18, *Aeneid*, iv, 160–5; MC 97, *Virgil*, ii, 201–31, 48.
22 MC 198–200, 239, 253, 258, Horace, *Satires*, II, iii, 31–42; Bede, *Ecclesiastical History*, ii, 13, A. Smith, *Edwin of Deira*, 1861, MC 32; MC 157, Dante, *Purgatorio*, xxx, 108–10: '*le rote magne / che drizzan ciascun seme ad alcun fine*' (the great wheels that direct each seed to some end); MC 156–8, P.B. Shelley, *Prometheus Unbound*, I, 192–9.
23 M. Arnold, *Empedocles on Etna*, II, 90–1; M 269, *Pall Mall Gazette*, 9 July 1886, p. 5.
24 LW 185, 182; MC 65, 278, 284, 147, 190 (my italics), 193, 280.
25 LW 180; MC 161, 163, 113, 208, 120, 95, 93, 261, 266, 114, 235, 281, 174, 185–7.
26 MC 187, 34, 208, 219, 271, 234, 251, 258.
27 MC 66–7.

Notes to Chapter 13

1   CL i 166; *The Mayor of Casterbridge*, 10 May 1886, *The Woodlanders* 15 March 1887; P 53, 57; D. Kramer's edn of *The Woodlanders*, Oxford, 1981, pp. 3–5, CL i 131–2; LW 182, 105; CL i 138, 156; G2 71; LW 192.
2   LW 183; CL i 156, 157; W 64, CL i 149.
3   LW 182; M 257; LW 192; CL i 151; LW 188; M 270.
4   CL i 166, M 272; LW 186, 184–5; CL i 150–2, M 274; LW 190; LW 191; J.B. Bullen, *The Expressive Eye*, pp. 181–2; LW 187.

5   LW 182, 185.

6   Alfred Fouillée, 'L'Homme Automate', *Revue des deux mondes*, lxxvi (1 August 1886), 548–71, LN i 184 (No 1438); LW 190, 192.

7   'The Rev. William Barnes, B.D.', *Athenaeum*, 16 October 1886, pp. 500–2, PW 10; CL i 151; P 57; LW 193.

8   M 283; *Spectator*, 26 March, 1887, pp. 419–20, CH 143–4; C. Patmore, *St James's Gazette*, 2 April 1887, CH 148; CL i 161; C.J. Weber, *Hardy of Wessex: His Life and Literary Career*, 1965, p. 154.

9   W 101, LW 193; W 176–7, LW 113; W 114–15, 130, LW 185; W 74, LW 182; W 188, LW 190–1; W 106, 97, PW 102 (my italics), 106.

10 W 345, CL i 163–4, HC 367–9, G2 72, M 9–13, 279.

11 W 111, 103; FBP 6; M 491; PW 188–9; W 174; PW 181 (my italics); W 106–7.

12 MC 193; W 243; LW 182; W 77.

13 *Spectator*, 26 March 1887, pp. 419–20; CH 142–3; LW 208; W 253; CL i 151; W 25, 323.

14 LW 183, W 155.

15 W 62; *Macmillan's Magazine*, November 1886, P 55; A. Fouillée, 'L'Homme Automate', *Revue des deux mondes*, lxxvi (1 August 1886), pp. 548–71); W 192, 193, 206, 216; W 196, A. Fouillée, 'L'Homme Automate', pp. 548–9.

16 LW 191, W 30, 137, 139, 141, 160, 258.

17 LW 190, W 64; LW 192; 'In a Wood', CP 64 (No 40); W 65; W 191–2, J.M.W. Turner, *The Visit to the Tomb*, 1850, reproduced John Rothenstein and Martin Butlin, *Turner*, London, 1964, No 127, Graham Reynolds, *Turner*, London, 1969, p. 205.

18 W 45 (i.e. Achilles dragged Hector round Troy: Homer, *Iliad*, xxii, 395–400, xxiv, 14–18); W 182; *Iliad*, xxiv, 509–12, W 234–5; *Odyssey*, xxiii, 89–93, W 321.

19 W 27; W 75, Sophocles, *Oedipus Coloneus*, 1225; Aristotle, *Poetics*, iv, 1449a 18–19, LW 192; W 322, Sophocles, *Antigone*, 543.

20 W 23, 312, Euripides, *Hippolytus*, 612; WRR 44.

21 LUC 152; Lucian, *Anabiountes E Halieus*, LUC 179–81, 166–7; 'Scenes from Classical History' reproduced opposite M 272; LW 185; W 65.

22 W 118; W 53, Plato, *Phaedrus*, 253 e 7–254 a 7; W 174–5, Virgil, *Eclogues*, i, 64–78; *Aeneid*, iv, 160–6, W 127, 268; W 237, Horace, *Satires*, II, iii, 271: '*insanire. . . . certa ratione modoque*'; W 265, Ovid, *Metamorphoses*, i, 475 (cf. W 94–5, 159), 481, 621.

23 W 300, Shakespeare, *Measure for Measure*, III, ii, 152–63; W 117, P.B. Shelley, *Revolt of Islam*, 865–73; E. Dowden, *Life of Percy Bysshe Shelley*, 1886: W 125–6, Shelley, *Alastor*, 151–87; W 190, Shelley, *Epipsychidion*, 149–59, 220–2, 160–1, W 194;

24 W 202, W. Shakespeare, *Hamlet*, III, ii, 71; W 191, 166, J. Keats, 'To Autumn', lines 21–2; W 305, R. Browning, 'The Statue and the Bust', line 246; A. Tennyson, *Maud*, I, 916–17, W 245.

25 LW 105; W 136; A. Tennyson, *The Promise of May*, in *Poems and Plays*, Oxford University Press, London, 1965, pp. 733, 730, 728, 726, 735, 726, 731; W. Pater, Conclusion to *Renaissance*, 1873, ed. L. Kronenberger, 1959, p. 158; Tennyson, p. 726, W 297; Pater, *Marius the Epicurean*, 1885, Everyman edn, 1934, pp. 236–7, W 132.

26 Dion Boucicault, *The Colleen Bawn*, Royal Adelphi Theatre, September 1860 (360 performances); *Nineteenth-Century Plays*, World's Classics, 1953, pp. 196, 222.

27 CL iv 212; W 146, 215, 289.

28   W 70, 309, 243, 312.
29   W 276, 267.
30   W 240, 251, 323.

Notes to Chapter 14

1   LW 212, 196; ED 144. 138.
2   'The Profitable Reading of Fiction', *Forum* (New York), March 1888, pp. 57–70, PW 111, 114; LW 198, Horace, *Satires*, I, ix; LW 197; CP Nos 68–71, pp. 102–5; LW 203, *Dynasts*, Part First, I, vi; 'Alicia's Diary', *Manchester Weekly Times*, 15, 22 October 1887, CL i 162, 163n, P 152, CSS 654–60.
3   LW 195, CL i 163, COD (1990) 800–1, WT 49.
4   LW 210, 207–8; letter to R.B.W. Noel, CL i 165; M 284; CL i 166.
5   CL i 168; PW 120–2, Aristotle, *Poetics*, 8, 1451a 30–4.
6   PW 117; CL i 168; *Chambers's Encyclopaedia*, 1895, i, 345; LW 211, 213.
7   M 288; CL i 171, 174–5.
8   P 59–60.
9   WT 1; WT 3, LW 28; WT 9, LW 33; HC 293, WT 12.
10   WT 14–15, Shakespeare, *Much Ado about Nothing*, III, iii, 64–5.
11   'The Three Strangers', *Longman's Magazine*, March 1883, P 58–9, 29; 'The Three Wayfarers' (1893), P 78–80; 'The Profitable Reading of Fiction', PW 120.
12   CL i 172, 168; LW 211; WT 62–3, LW 33.
13   WT ed. Kathryn R. King (World's Classics edn), Oxford 1991, p. 296; WT 64, HC 293.
14   WT 51, 44; CL i 172; LW 213; WT ed. K.R. King, p. 296.
15   'Fellow-Townsmen', *New Quarterly Magazine*, April 1880, CL i 72, P 30; LW 128, 100, 69; CL iii 151; WT 82, Virgil, *Aeneid*. i, 159–69; WT 81, *Aeneid*, i, 167–8.
16   WT 85, 86, Homer, *Odyssey*, 149–50, 196–7; WT 108,109.
17   W.S. Gilbert, *Sweethearts*, 1874; CL ii 33; WT 101, 107, 86, 102.
18   CL iv 164, WT 116; M 9–13, WT 129, 126–7; WT 119, M 12; WT 115, 113, M 15.
19   WT 129, 127, 131; CL i 125, *English Illustrated Magazine*, May 1884, P 59; WT 138.
20   WT 122; C.H. Hazlewood, *Lady Audley's Secret, Nineteenth-Century Plays*, ed. G. Rowell (World's Classics), Oxford, 1953, p. 248; WT 127.
21   WT 114, 138.
22   WT (Note) 188, cf WT (Preface) xiv; note 22 March 1871; WT 163, PN 8–9, WT 143–5; WT (Preface) xiii–iv, 176–7; CL i 204.
23   G.P.R. James, *The Smuggler: A Tale*, London, 1845, John Banim, *The Smuggler: A Tale*, London, 1831, PN 151; WT 172–3, 170; WT 157, 154, 171; Romans 2: 21, 5: 1, WT 181; 1 Corinthians, 7:1, 7:9, WT 148.
24   WT 185–6, for Stinsford sermon see p. 8, M 55; WT (Note) 188, 139, 185.

Notes to Chapter 15

1   LW 217–18, 222; 'The Melancholy Hussar', *Bristol Times and Mirror*, 4, 11 January, 1890, CL i 178, P 60; 'A Tragedy of Two Ambitions', *Universal Review*,

December 1888, CL i 178–9, P 81; 'The First Countess of Wessex', *Harper's New Monthly Magazine*, December 1889, P 62–3; GND 41.

2   CL i 239; LW 218.

3   LW 224, 234, 218; W. Pater, *Renaissance* (1873), ed. L. Kronenberger, 1959, p. 157.

4   P.H. Gosse died 23 August 1888, CL i 179; LW 221, 229, 219, 230.

5   LW 224; M 284; LW 226; CL i 188, P 72; CL i 200.

6   P 72; LW 232; 'Candour in English Fiction', *New Review*, January 1890, pp. 15–21, PW 132, 129, 128, 129, 126.

7   CL i 189; LW 236–7; P 65–6; S. Gatrell, *Hardy the Creator: A Textual Biography*, Oxford, 1988, pp. 81–96; P 66, 63, 67.

8   G. Boccaccio, *Il Decameron*, 1349–51; G. Chaucer, *The Canterbury Tales*, 1478; W. Morris, *The Earthly Paradise*, 1868–70; A.H. Clough, *Mari Magno or Tales on Board*, 1869; M 235, CL i 195, 185; *Graphic Christmas Number*, December 1890, p. 4, GND 42–3; M 244; GND 185–6, LW 207.

9   GND 77, 5, 179, 164; Alfred Parsons would illustrate 'The First Countess' in *Harper's New Monthly Magazine*, P 62–3; GND 47, 149.

10 GND 35, LW 229.

11 GND 65, 119–21, 124, 118.

12 PW 127–8; 'The First Countess of Wessex', GND 41; 'The Honourable Laura', GND 161, 179.

13 P 66–7; M 13n, 13; CL iii 190.

14 CL i 239; Preface (1896) GND xi; John Hutchins, *The History and Antiquities of the County of Dorset*, 3rd edn, 1861–73, iii, 298, GND 75; Hutchins iv, 269, GND 134, 136; Hutchins, iii, 329, GND 145; Hutchins on Peter Walter, iii, 671, GND 122, 123; Hutchins, ii, 679, GND 24, 42.

15 GND xi, 183–4.

16 Plato, *Symposium*, xvi (19D 6–7), GND 77–8; GND 82, C. Patmore, 'The Woodman's Daughter', J.E. Millais, *The Woodman's Daughter*, 1851; GND 88, 90, W. Shakespeare, *King Lear*, I, iv, 312–13.

17 Oscar Wilde, *The Picture of Dorian Gray, Lippincott's Monthly Magazine*, July 1890 (published June); GND MS sent to *Graphic* 9 May 1890, P 65; GND 55–6, C. Brontë, *Jame Eyre* (1847), Clarendon edn, London, 1969, p. 549, E.B. Browning, *Aurora Leigh* (1856), London, 1890, p. 364.

18 Juvenal, *Satires*, vi, 116–29, GND 68–9.

19 GND 69, 72, W. Shakespeare, *The Taming of the Shrew*, IV, i, 190–207; LW 220, GND 74.

20 P.B. Shelley, *Alastor*, lines 649–62, GND 116, 120, 118; GND 118, 117, 115, 113; Luke 7: 39, 47, GND 117, 119; John 20: 15–16, 113, 119.

21 'The Duchess of Hamptonshire', as 'The Impulsive Lady of Croome Castle', *Light*, 6, 13 April 1878, as 'Emmeline, or Passion versus Principle', *Independent* (New York), 7 February 1884, P 63–4; R. Browning, 'The Statue and the Bust' in *Men and Women*, 1855; GND 153–4, R. Browning, *The Ring and the Book*, 1868–9, vi, 702f; GND 161, C. Dickens, *Oliver Twist*, ed. H. House, London, 1949, pp. 370–1.

22 GND 155; A.H. Clough, 'The Questioning Spirit' and 'Duty – that's to say complying', in *Ambarvalia* (1849), *Poems of Arthur Hugh Clough*, ed. F.L. Mulhauser, Oxford, 1973, pp. 3–4, 27–8; GND 155, 130.

23 T.S. Eliot, *After Strange Gods*, London, 1934, pp. 57–8; S. Gatrell, *Hardy the Creator*, pp. 81–2.

Notes to Chapter 16

1 P 68, 71; DR 1–3, TD 175f; DR 322, CL i 200, P.B. Shelley, *Epipsychidion*, line 131, GND 120.
2 LW 117, 118, TD 34.
3 LW 118, 119, M 191, TD 109.
4 TD 268, MCN 267–8; LW 158; LW 158, TD 156.
5 CL i 143–4; Mary Jeune, 'Saving the Innocents', *Fortnightly Review*, September 1885, pp. 345, 346, TD 196, 190; M. Jeune, 'Saving the Innocents', p. 352, TD 159, 223; M. Jeune, 'Helping the Fallen', *Fortnightly Review*, November 1885, p. 680, TD 105, 107–8.
6 M. Jeune, 'Helping the Fallen', 672, 673, 682.
7 LW 209; 215, TD 313. 292; LW 215, 226–7, TD 132; CL i 194.
8 'A Tragedy of Two Ambitions', CL i 178; M 12, MCN 265, 400, TD 1, 35.
9 LW 220, 237, 225.
10 LW 222, TD 159; LW 192.
11 G2 84–7, but see M 294; LW 223–4.
12 LW 224, CL i 190, TD 47, 183; LW 224, TD 373.
13 CL i 200; LW 232; G2 98, DKR 135–6, M 224; LW 239.
14 P 68, 73; 1912 Preface, TD 26; *Athenaeum*, 9 January 1892, CH 183; *Saturday Review*, 16 January 1892, 73–4, CH 190; *Quarterly Review*, April 1892, clxxiv, 319–26, CH 220; LW 232; M 322.
15 M 15, 16, EL 18, LW 501; TD 210, PN 21–3; LW 10; TD 57, 67, 57, 69, 318.
16 TD 217, LW 23–5; LW 53, TD 128; TD 127, M 68, CL vii 40; TD 164; TD 208, 253, CL i 31; TD 252, LW 183; TD 252, note of 5 January 1888, LW 212; TD 79, 123, 129.
17 TD 100, 331, 41; LW 115–16, TD 214.
18 'The Dorsetshire Labourer', PW 186–7, 189, 178, TD 299, 309–11, 331–3, 339; PW 170, TD 130; TD 240–3.
19 PBE 276, TD 225; LW 192, 212; TD 243; HC 505, V. Jesty, *Hardy's Wessex Today*, Belper, 1990, pp. 10–13; LW 140.
20 LW 225; TD 33, 108–9, 148, 185.
21 LW 225; TD 202; LW 226; TD 321.
22 Matthew 17: 2; TD 84.
23 TD 85, 109, 118, 196, 200, 211, 227, 328.
24 Revelation 19: 17–18, TD 218; TD 227, 221, Jude 8, 12; TD 236, 1 Corinthians 13: 4–5.
25 TD 40, Job 7: 6; Exodus 13: 21, TD 328; TD 330, John 4: 17–18; TD 152, Ecclesiastes 3: 5, TD 236; TD 152, Genesis 29: 17–25, TD 260.
26 TD 267, Homer, *Odyssey*, v 481–7, vi, 115–22; TD 267–8, Aeschylus, *Prometheus Vinctus*, 124–5, 170, 1093, TD 373.
27 LW 231, TD 338, Aeschylus, *Agamemnon*, 1415–19; LW 230, Sophocles, *Oedipus Tyrannus*, 1365–6, ed. R.C. Jebb, 1887, pp. 178–9.
28 TD 362, Euripides, *Alcestis*, 1–8, 193–5, TD 245; TD 263, J. Milton, Sonnet xix, 1–2, 13–14.
29 TD 221, Horace, *Odes*, I, xxii, 1–2, TD 221; *Odes*, III, i, 40, TD, 265.
30 TD 113, DC 23, 77, TD 139, 155; Longus, *Daphnis and Chloe*, tr. Angel Day, ed. Joseph Jacobs, London, 1890.
31 TD 77, S. Richardson, *Pamela*, London, 1962, i. 47–9; TD 82–3, H. Fielding, *Tom Jones*, Everyman edn 1962, i, 126–7; TD 68–71, J. Austen, *Northanger*

Abbey, Everyman edn 1906, p. 45; TD 330, J. Milton, *Paradise Lost*, ix, 626–31, 634–42.

32 A Marvell, 'To his Coy Mistress', 11. 43–4, TD 181; W. Blake, 'Auguries of Innocence', 11. 56–62, TD 179; Notes on Reynolds, *Poety and Prose of William Blake*, ed. G. Keynes, 1948, p. 777, TD 323; TD 109, Genesis 3: 16, cf. 35: 18, J. Keats, *Endymion*, iv, 280–1; TD 109, Keats, 'To Autumn', line 27; TD 104, Keats, 'Ode to a Nightingale', lines 66–7.

33 TD 242; TD 247, R. Browning, *Pippa Passes*, i. 228–9; TD 247, Browning, 'By the Fire-side', lines 192, 181; 288.

34 A. Tennyson, *Maud*, ii, 316 etc., TD 59–61; *Maud*, ii, 239–40, 244, TD 241, 243; TD 193, TD 205, Tennyson, *Idylls of the King*, 'Lancelot and Elaine', lines 132–3; TD 205, 'The Boy and the Mantle', No 29 in F.J. Child's *English and Scottish Popular Ballads*, 1882–98; Tennyson, *Idylls*, 'Guinevere', lines 541–2, 592, 'Merlin and Vivien', line 162, TD 194, 228; 'Guinevere', line 421, TD 237; 'Guinevere', line 557, TD 247.

35 Brenda Tunks, *Whatever Happened to the Other Hardys?*, Canford Heath, Poole, Dorset, 1990, pp. 31–2; R. Crashaw, 'Hymn to the Name and Honor of the Admirable Saint Teresa', lines 19–22, 44, 23–4.

36 TD 197, 103, 317, 132, 134, 226, 227, 278, 315, 70, 265.

37 TD 318, TD ed. D. Skilton (Penguin), 1978, p. 519, TD 1st edn., London, 1891, iii, 148.

Notes to Chapter 17

1 LW 267, 241; J. Keats, 'Ode to a Nightingale', line 33; CL ii 7, P 78–80; P 92–5.

2 CL i 253, 264; LW 257.

3 CL i 271, 279, LW 262–3.

4 LW 264, M 13–14; LW 265, 453; LW 265, CL i 287, 269.

5 CL i 280; M 327; LW 268, 257, 270; 'Alike and Unlike', line 9, CP p. 789, P 242.

6 ORFW iii, xvi, cf. P.B. Shelley, 'Julian and Maddalo', lines 449–50.

7 ORFW 1f, CL ii 10f; 'The Spectre of the Real', *To-Day*, November 1894; CL ii 24, 33, 26, 23, 14, 17, 20; ORFW xxxii–iii; CL ii 31–2.

8 'A Thunderstorm in Town', CP No 255; P 161; CL ii 23, 29, 38; P 85, CL ii 51.

9 Prefatory Note, LLI 1, P 60, 85, LW 276.

10 CL ii 25, LLI 13, 1–2; CL ii 108; M 342; LLI 5, 12, 19–20; LLI 10, 'The Division', CP No 169, P 141, CPW i 383; LLI 17, CL ii 16, 23, 27, 29 etc.; LLI 20.

11 SR 48; LLI 33, LW 219, 28; M 8, 344; RG 1 55, M 47; LW 234, 'Thoughts of Phena', CP No 38.

12 P 60; LLI 184, 162; LLI 185, LW 24, 476.

13 LLI 129, W. Holman Hunt, *The Awakening Conscience*, see T. Hilton, *The Pre-Raphaelites*, 1970, pp. 91–2.

14 LLI 59, Matthew 27–29; LLI 71, 1 Kings 18: 44; LLI 58, 82, Hebrews 12: 2, 5–7.

15 Sophocles, *Antigone*, 891; LLI 42, 57, *Antigone*, 924.

16 J. Milton, *Paradise Lost*, ix, 423–57, LLI 85; R. Browning, 'The Pied Piper of Hamelin' (1842), LLI 127, 143; LLI 8, A. Tennyson, *Idylls of the King*, 'Lancelot and Elaine', lines 27, 16–17, LLI 7, 9.

17 A. Tennyson, *Enoch Arden*, lines 116, 146, LLI 116; *Enoch Arden*, line 222, Amos, 4: 11, LLI 125.
18 A.G. Swinburne, *Poems and Ballads*, 'Les Noyades', lines 11, 55–6, LLI 165; 'Laus Veneris', lines 375–6, LLI 82.
19 LLI 25, 81, 115, 142.
20 Two stories: 'The Melancholy Hussar of the German Legion' (1890) and 'A Tradition of Eighteen Hundred and Four' (1882), transferred to WT in 1912; Prefatory Note, LLI x; LLI 203, 29, 149.
21 LLI 77, 191; 87; 160, 106; 174.
22 WWR 218; LW 239.
23 LW 268.

Notes to Chapter 18

1 CL ii 46; Preface, JO xxviii.
2 LW 265, 209, 215, JO 206, 28; LW 215, JO 29–30; M 107, JO 154, 160.
3 M 346, *The Times*, 28 April 1888, p. 9.
4 LW 216; JO 29.
5 CL i 194; P 89; G1 34, 306, illustration No 14b (TH's sketch for Antell's tombstone), M 347–8; G2 84.
6 LW 265, 272–3, 267; JO 76, CP No 487.
7 DKR 157; LW 273.
8 CL ii 46; LW 279, 281, 282.
9 LW 274–5, JO 209, 239.
10 LW 279, 287–8, M 348–9; S. Gatrell, *Hardy the Creator*, 238; LW 283; M 359, F. Chalfont, 'Hardy's Residences and Lodgings', Part Two, THJ February 1993, No 1, p. 55.
11 M 359; serialized first as *The Simpletons*, then as *Hearts Insurgent*, Harper's *New Monthly Magazine*, December 1894 – November 1895, P 87–8; JO 50, 46, 123; *Harper's*, xci, 128; JO 155, 286, *Harper's*, xci, 593; JO 338; CL ii 70.
12 M 363; LW 285 (90 Ashley Gardens, Westminster); CL ii 84; LW 286.
13 P 91; LW 286–7; E. Gosse, *St James's Gazette*, 8 November 1895, CL ii 93–4; G2 114; M 368; G2 114; M. Oliphant, *Blackwood's Magazine*, January 1896, clix, 135–49, CH 256–62; LW 288; G2 118, M 372.
14 E. Gosse, *Cosmopolis*, January 1896, i, 60–9, CH 262–70; G2 119; LW 288–9; Aristotle, *Poetics*, 13; 1453a 29–30; CL ii 97.
15 LW 289; JO 11, LW 20; JO 13, LW 476; JO 8, 9, 179, 279, LW 289.
16 LW 290; LW 32, JO 26; JO 26, WRR 21–2; JO 31, LW 34; JO 26, LW 35; JO 21.
17 JO 211, LW 152; JO 7, LW 265; JO 253; JO 233, 'Midnight on the Great Western', CP No 465, P 203; JO 116; M 351; JO 297, CL i 286.
18 JO 141, 142, 174; CL ii 23, P.B. Shelley, *Epipsychidion*, 149–61.
19 1 Esdras 4: 17–18, cf. Part First epigraph, JO 1; JO 44; Esther 14: 236, Part Sixth epigraph, JO 273; History of Susanna 4, 8, 20, JO 314, 307.
20 JO 20, Genesis 11: 8; JO 34, 55, 322, Judges 16: 4–19; JO 76, Genesis 3: 7; Joshua 6: 20; JO 62, Genesis 21: 14, 19, JO 343; JO 115, Genesis 16: 12; JO 327.
21 JO 172, Genesis 37: 5–19; Genesis 37: 24, JO 343; Genesis 45: 1–5, JO 315; JO 97, Job 12: 3; JO 232, Job 3:3; JO 343, Job 3:3, 4, 7, 11, 13, 18, 20; Job 42: 12, 14.

22 Jude, verses 16, 19, Acts 10: 34, JO 96, 330, iii, 2 Corinthians 3: 6, 1 Corinthians, ch. 13.

23 JO 260, Mark 1: 10–11, JO 27; *Harper's New Monthly Magazine*, xc, 350, Mark 1: 21; JO 102, John 4: 16–18; JO 108; John 11: 53–4, JO 261; JO 203, 280, 271, 281, John 19: 28.

24 Revelation 21: 2, 19–20, JO 12–13, 149, 100.

25 Homer, *Odyssey* x, 337–8, JO 27; JO 239; JO 289, Aeschylus, *Agamemnon*, 60–8.

26 JO 288, Sophocles *Oedipus Tyrannus* 1320–30; Sophocles *Oedipus Coloneus* 1224– 7; Sophocles *OT* 1263–4; JO 236, LW 230, Sophocles *OT* 1365, JO 102.

27 Euripides, *Heracles*, 1023, R. Browning, *Aristophanes' Apology*, 4683, JO 286; Euripides, *Medea*, 1325–1414; JO 306, Virgil, *Aeneid*, vi, 168f; JO 23–4, Horace, *Carmen Saeculare*, 6; Ovid, *Metamorphoses* iv, 55–66, JO 59.

28 Spenser, *Faerie Queene*, II, xii, 42, 86–7, JO 98, 301; JO 13, 345, J. Bunyan, *Pilgrim's Progress* (1678), World's Classics edn, Oxford, 1984, pp. 46, 260, JO 13, 345; S. Johnson, *Rasselas, Prince of Abyssinia*, 1759; JO 57, 209; E. Gibbon, *Decline and Fall of the Roman Empire* (1776–88), 1820 edn, iv, 77, ii, 323, ii, 325, JO 78, 189.

29 LN ii 107 (No 2083), JO 287; P.B. Shelley, Notes on *Queen Mab*, v, 189, JO 187; *Epipsychidion*, 149–59, 5–7, 77–9, JO 156; Shelley, *Prometheus Unbound*, I. 192–4, JO 120.

30 A. Tennyson, *In Memoriam*, lxiv, JO 58; JO 13, Tennyson, 'Gareth and Lynette', 194–93; Hallam Tennyson, *Memoir*, 1897, ii 127–30, JO xxviii; JO 179, Tennyson, 'Geraint and Enid, 721–3.

31 JO 307, R. Browning, 'The Statue and the Bust', line 138; JO 68; A.C. Clough, *Adam and Eve*, i, 40–53, iv, 21, JO 297; M. Arnold, Preface to *Essays in Criticism*, SUP iii 290, 'To a Gipsy Child by the Sea-Shore', lines 37–40, JO 236, 233; JO 284, Samuel Butler, *Erewhon* (1872), Everyman edn, 1932, pp. 112–13.

32 CL ii 93; JO 267–8, 303.

33 JO 29, 81.

34 CL ii 93; JO 17, 13, 20, 54, 68, 95, 157, 340.

35 JO 27, 46, 321, 341, 345, 233.

36 JO 11, 51, 261, 185, 269.

37 CL ii 97.

Notes to Chapter 19

1 LW 304; LN i 45–7, 294–5 (Nos 442–60); B. Jowett, tr. *The Dialogues of Plato*, Oxford, 1871, 1892 edn, i, 252–8, Plato, *Phaedrus*, 245–51; *Illustrated London News*, 1 October 1892, p. 425 etc.; *Dialogues*, i, 561, Plato, *Symposium*, 191 d 7.

2 CL ii 169; LW 140, CL i 73, 97; T.W. Woolner, *Pygmalion*, 1881, p. 112; Woolner to W.E. Gladstone, 26 December 1881, in A. Woolner, *Thomas Woolner: Life and Letters*, 1917, pp. 311, CL ii 156; P.B. Shelley, *Alastor*, line 205; A. Woolner, *Pygmalion*, p. 332 and facing illustration.

3 LW 271, WB 30, 167; LW 226, 'Heredity', CP No 363; CL i 196, WB 99.

4 P 94; M 129–30; LW 234, CP 62, WB 162; LW 235, 239; CL ii 152; P 95.

5 CPW iii 358; LW 292–3; CL iv 33; CL ii 122; CL ii 128, LW 293, P 78, CL ii 150.

6 CL ii 111, 112, 117; CL ii 106, 128, 136.

7 LW 73, SR 57; LW 301–2; CL ii 141.

8 CL ii 140, 138; P 95; M 382, CL ii 155n, *The World*, 24 March 1897, pp. 13– 14; CL ii 156.

9   ILN 1 October 1892, p. 121, cf 427, 459; WB 164, ILN 1 October 1892, p. 426; LW 29, ILN 8 October 1892 p. 459, WB 24; LW 249, 286, 'Concerning Agnes', lines 7–12, CP 878; ILN 19 November 1892, p. 612, WB 99; LW 37.

10 LW 117, CL ii 167; ILN 1 October 1892, p. 425, WB 3; LW 190, 'The Last Signal', line 7, CP 472, WB 55; LW 244, WB 49, MCN 300, E. Hardy, *Thomas Hardy: A Critical Biography*, London, 1954, p. 145.

11 WB 13; ILN 15 October 1892, p. 481; ILN 17 December, p. 775, WB 191; DKR Plate 10, between pp. 128–9; WB 30; ILN 17 December 1892, p. 775, WB 191.

12 ILN 15 October 1892, p. 481, WB 166.

13 WB 69, Homer, *Odyssey*, vi, 93–101; WB 8, Sappho, 'To Aphrodite', line 2; ILN 15 October 1892, p. 471, WB 166–7, Virgil, *Aeneid*, i, 8–11, 135; iv, 114–27, WB 15; WB 4, DC 30.

14 J. Donne, 'Aire and Angels', lines 1–2, 5–6; R. Crashaw, 'Wishes to his Supposed Mistresse', lines 1–15, 106–8, 112–14, CL i 114, WB 1; WB 86; ILN 17 December 1892, p. 775, WB 190; conclusion to Voltaire, *Candide*, 1759: '*il faut cultiver notre jardin*'.

15 WB 8, P.B. Shelley, *Alastor*, line 151, *Epipsychidion*, lines 190–1, 267–8; ILN 17 December 1892, p. 744, WB 187, *Alastor*, lines 299, 305.

16 ILN, 3 December 1892, p. 710, WB 121, *Alastor*, lines 462, 469–71; LW 265; P 94.

17 J.H. Newman, *Apologia pro Vita Sua* (1864), ed. C.F. Harrold, New York, 1947, pp. 104, 211, WB 22.

18 C. Patmore, *The Angel in the House*, Book I, Canto ii, Section 3, WB 3, ILN 1 October 1892, p. 426, WB 164; R. Browning, 'Nympholeptos', in *Pacchiarotto, and How He Worked in Distemper: With Other Poems*, 1876, CL ii 153; CL ii 235. H. Rider Haggard, *She*, 1887, pp. 199, 294.

19 Preface. WB xxii; LW 303; 'The Well-Beloved', CP No 96.

20 CL ii 154; *The World*, 24 March 1897; LW 304, 10; WB 6, 19, 26; ILN 10 December 1892, p. 742, WB 176, 3.

21 ILN 1 October 1892, p. 426, WB 4; WB 3; A. Tennyson, *Maud*, I, 268–9; WB 123; *Chronica Jocelini de Brakelonda*, 'Jocelin of Brakelond', T. Carlyle, *Past and Present* (1843), Everyman edn, pp. 38–9.

22 ILN 17 December 1892, p. 773, WB 181; WB 95 ('Red-King'); Lewis Carroll, *Complete Works*, ed. A. Woollcott, London, 1939, pp. 173–4, WB 26; WN 104, ILN 19 November 1892, p. 643, WB World's Classics edn, 1986, p. 227.

23 ILN 17 December 1892, p. 773; WB 123, 114.

24 WB 3; Horace, *Ars Poetica*, lines 140–8.

Notes to Chapter 20

1   CL ii 156; LW 241, Keats, 'Ode to a Nightingale', line 33; 'Wessex Heights', lines 8, 13, CP 319; CL ii 166; EHD 205.

2   LW 302; CL ii 207; M 375 (Mrs Patrick Campbell).

3   LW 323, 309; LW 302, Plato, *Ion*, 542 b 2, B. Jowett, (tr.), *Dialogues of Plato* (1871), 1992 edn, i, 511.

4   LW 309, 300.

5   LW 302; CL ii 204, 217, 190, 193, 104, 147.

6   'Wessex Heights', line 8, CP 319; CL ii 109, 181, 188.

7   LW 317; E. Hardy, 'The Egyptian Pet', *The Animals' Friend*, March 1898, pp. 108–9.

8 LW 317; E. Hardy, 'The Egyptian Pet', *Animals' Friend*, March 1898, pp. 108–9; E. Hardy to Elspeth Grahame, 20 August 1899, DKR 175–6; J.S. Mill, *Three Essays on Religion*, 1878, pp. 37, 176–7, 179, 243, LW 317.

9 DKR 175; P 106, LW 325; CL ii 197, 200, 201–2, 203, 205; P 106.

10 CL ii 139, *Saturday Review*, 7 January 1899, lxxxvii, 19, CH 319–22; *Athenaeum*, 14 January 1899, p. 41, CH 326; *Academy*, 14 January 1899, lvi, 43–4, CH 322–3; LW 310, CL ii 214, 208; LW 325.

11 R. Browning, Preface to *Collected Works*, 1868, Preface to WP, CP 6; 'The Temporary the All', line 24, CP 7; 'Confession to a Friend in Trouble', CP 11–12, P. 97; 'She to Him', I–IV, CP 14–16, M 84–5.

12 Preface, WP, CP 6; 'The Temporary the All', line 11, CP 7; 'The Ivy-Wife, CP No 33, E. Hardy to R. Owen, 27 December 1899, JOB 91; 'Thoughts of Ph —— a, WP1, 163–4, cf CP No 38; 'Ditty', CP No 18, *Academy*, 14 January 1899, lvi, 44, CH 324; WP1 137–8, 140, CP 52–3, M 304n, CPM i 364; 'At an Inn', CP No 45, M 339–40.

13 'The Dance at the Phoenix', CP No 28, LW 28, 286; 'Heiress and Architect', CP No 49; 'The Impercipient', CP No 44, WP1, 183, LW 315, 294, P 102; 'In a Eweleaze at Weatherbury', CP No 47; 'I look Into My Glass', CP No 52, LW 265.

14 LW 322; CL ii 161–2, 84, H.T. Wharton, *Sappho: Memoir, Text, Selected Renderings, and a Literal Translation*, 1898 edn; CL ii 158, Wharton, *Sappho*, No 68, p. 113, No 3, p. 71; 'The Temporary the All, lines 11–12 (my italics), 10, WP1, 2, CP 7.

15 P 258; LW 240; J.W. Mackail, *Select Epigrams from the Greek Anthology*, 1890, p. 131, No ii, 23, *Palatine Anthology*, vi, 1, 18, 19, 20.

16 'I Look Into My Glass', line 8, CP 81, Horace, *Odes*, II, iii, 1–2; LW 51, Horace, *Odes*, I, v, 10, 1–3, 'Amabel', lines 13–16, CP 8; LW 241, Horace, *Odes*, III, xxvi, 1, 12, 'In a Eweleaze near Weatherbury', line 21, CP 71.

17 WP1 201, CP No 48, as 'The Bride-Night Fire', CPW i 365; LW 424–5; G. Chaucer, *Canterbury Tales*, 'The Marchantes Tale', line 2353, CP 72.

18 CP No 10, W. Shakespeare, *Hamlet*, I, ii, 78, III, 1, 70–2; 'Revulsion', line 7, CP 13–14; Shakespeare, *Sonnets*, cxxix, 2; 'Confession to a Friend in Trouble', CP No 8, line 12, Shakespeare, *Sonnets*, lxii, 1.

19 LW 326; 'Friends Beyond', line 4, CP 59; WP1 iv, T. Gray, 'Elegy in a Country Churchyard', line 1.

20 LW 302; G. Crabbe, *Tales, 1812*, Cambridge, 1967, 'The Lover's Journey', lines 28–9, 166–72, 1–2, 'My Cicely', lines 33, 2–4, 81–4, 110–12.

21 W. Wordsworth, 'I wandered lonely as a cloud', line 1, 'Middle-Age Enthusiasms', lines 1–2, 5–6, CP 63; G.G. Byron, *Don Juan*, VIII, xci, 1, xcv, 8, xcvi, 1–6, 'San Sebastian', CP 21–2, J. Keats, 'La Belle Dame sans Merci', lines 1–2.

22 CL ii 144; P.B. Shelley, *Alastor*, lines 81–94, 'A Sign-Seeker', lines 9–12, 42–5, CP 49–50; Shelley, 'Hymn to Intellectual Beauty', line 49–54; 'Her Initials', CP 13, Shelley, *Prometheus Unbound*, I, 737–8; A. Tennyson, *In Memoriam*, lxvii, 5–9.

23 CL ii 183; 'Amabel', lines 21–2, CP 8, A. Tennyson, *Maud*, III, 235–8; 'A Sign-Seeker', lines 27, 37–40, CP 49–50, *In Memoriam*, xii, 16, xcv, 37–44, cxxvi, 9–12, 'The Impercipient', lines 15–16, CP 67.

24 LW 322; 'The Burghers', lines 39, 67–9.

25 WP1 1, F. Chalfont, 'Hardy's Residences and Lodgings', THJ February 1993, IV, i, 57; WP1 30, 32, 53, 48, 61, 78, 115, 123, 197, 195; TM 280.

26 LW 309; CL ii 208; LW 110; Preface to WP, CP 6; 'Her Dilemma', line 15;
    CP 14; CP Nos 35, 52.
27 *Athenaeum*, 14 January 1899, 41, CH 325; CL ii 207, W. Archer, *Daily Chronicle*,
    21 December 1898; 'Friends Beyond', line 6, CP 60.
28 Horace, *Odes*, III, xxx, 1; 'Thoughts of Phena', CP No 38, LW 234; 'The Dance
    at the Phoenix', line 69, CP 45; 'Valenciennes', CP No 20, 'Valenciennes' in
    Hardy's book of folk-dances, DCM.
29 CL ii 208; LW 325; 'Nature's Questioning', lines 17–18, CP 66; 'The Sign-
    Seeker', line 27, CP 50.

Notes to Chapter 21

1   CL ii 229; W. Archer, *Real Conversations*, 1904, p. 40.
2   CL ii 209, 263; LW 328; 'Lines to a Movement in Mozart's E-Flat Symphony',
    CP No 388, P 196; 'A Second Attempt', CP No 720, P 239.
3   CL ii 256, 270–2; ELH to R. Owen, quoted DKR 173; M 399; CL ii 226,
    A. Grove, 'Objections to Woman Suffrage Considered', *The Humanitarian*,
    August 1899, xv, 90–100; E. Hardy, 'Spring Song', *Sphere*, 14 April 1900, i, 393;
    B. Newcombe, March 1900, quoted G2 138, M 397.
4   LW 328; CL ii 248.
5   CL ii 248, 247 spelt 'kahki'), 236, 233, 236, 269 (my italics), 232.
6   CL ii, 227–8, 238, 248, 256, 271–2; CL ii 288, 238, 283.
7   LW 333; Eduard von Hartmann, *Philosophy of the Unconscious*, tr. W.C. Coupland,
    London, 1884 (HPU), LN i 395, ii 520; W. Archer, *Real Conversations*, 1904,
    pp. 37–9, 46; Compact *OED*, i, 1764; LW 332–3.
8   CL ii 292–3, 298, P 118; *Saturday Review*, 11 January 1902, xciii, 49, CH 329–
    31; *The Times*, 21 December 1901, CH xxviii; T.H. Warren, *Spectator*, 5 April
    1902, p. 56, CH 332–5; P 119.
9   Preface to PPP, CP 84; 'War Poems', CP 86–99; 'The Embarcation', CP No 54,
    CL ii 233, 232; 'Going of the Battery', CP No 57, CL ii 238; 'At the War Office,
    London', CP No 58, CL ii 241; 'Souls of the Slain', CP No 62, CL ii 266;
    'Colonel's Soliloquy', CP No 56, CL ii 258; 'Sick Battle-God', CP No 64,
    W. Archer, *Real Conversations*, 1904, p. 47.
10 'Poems of Pilgrimage', CP 100–10, LW 194–204, 310–13; 'Rome: Building
    a New Street', CP No 69, CL i 163; 'Shelley's Skylark', CP No 66, lines 9–10,
    LW 479; 'Bridge of Lodi', CP No 74, LW 203–4, S.P. Bayard, ed., *Dance to the
    Fiddle, March to the Fife*, Pennsylvania State University Press, 1982, pp. 353–4;
    'Rome: On the Palatine', CP No 68, lines 11, 13–14.
11 'Retrospect', CP 184–7; 'Miscellaneous Poems', CP 111–80; 'In Tenebris III',
    CP No 138, lines 13–16; 'A Wasted Illness', CP No 122, LW 149, M 214–15;
    'The Self-Unseeing', CP No 135, LW 19; 'An August Midnight', CP No 113;
    'The Puzzled Game-Birds', CP No 116, LW 121; cf Nos 86, 114, 115, 117,
    119; 'In Tenebris II', line 14, CP 168.
12 'V.R. 1819–1901', line 13, CP 85, HPU ii, 246; 'The Bedridden Peasant', line
    32, CP 125; 'The Sleep-Worker', CP No 85; 'The Mother Mourns', CP No 76,
    LW 169.
13 'The Lacking Sense', lines 11, 28–9, CP 117–118; 'Doom and She', lines
    22–3, 10, CP 119, LW 227.
14 W 64, LW 317, TD 74; 'Doom and She', lines 1–2, 11, CP 118–19, J. Keats,
    Hyperion, i, 5, 20, 26, 34–6, *Fall of Hyperion*, i, 275, 264–71.

15 R.W. Emerson, *Essays*, 1841, Everyman Edn, London, 1906, p. 35; LW 309, 331.
16 'The Tenant-for-Life', lines 21–4, CP 162, Homer, *Iliad*, xxi 106–7; *Odyssey*, xxiv 5–11, 'The Souls of the Slain', lines 1–5, 14, 16, 20, 86–90; 'Sapphic Fragment', lines 1–2, CP 181, H.T. Wharton, *Sappho*, 1895, No 68, p. 113; Euripides, *Herakles*, 1089–1133, 'The Sleep-Worker', lines 1–10, CP 121–2; 'To an Unborn Pauper Child', CP No 91, Plato, *Republic*, x, 617 d 6 -e 5, Sophocles, *Oedipus Coloneus*, 1225.
17 'Embarcation', lines 9, 13, CP 86, Virgil, *Aeneid*, vi, 305–10; 'The Tenant-for-Life', lines 3–4, CP 161, Horace, *Odes*, II, xiv, 21–8, PW 187.
18 LW 240; 'God-Forgotten', lines 1–4, 29–30, CP 123–4; L 83, 'The King's Experiment', CP No 132.
19 'The Going of the Battery', CP No 57, *Saturday Review*, 11 January 1902, xciii, 49, CH 329; *Academy*, 14 January 1899, lvi, 434, CH 322; 'The Respectable Burgher', CP No 129; CP Nos 101, 103, 107, 115, 116, 117; 'The Puzzled Game-Birds', lines 1, 4, 7, CP 148.
20 'The Sick Battle-God', lines 17–20, 3, 7, 8, 20–4, CP 97–8.
21 'The Sick Battle-God', lines 42–4, CP 99; 'The Lacking Sense', lines 1, 7, 12, 20, 30, CP 116–18; Romans, 8: 22; W 64.
22 'V.R. 1819–1901', lines 3, 8, CP85; CP 184–7, 86–99, 100–10, 180–4, 111–80.
23 'On a Fine Morning', lines 1, 3, 5, CP 129; 'Song of Hope', CP No 95; 'The Well-Beloved', lines 51–2, 66, CP 134; 'The Dream-Follower', CP No 108; 'Her Reproach', CP No 97; 'The Church-Builder', CP No 139; The Lost Pyx', CP No 140.
24 'The Mother Mourns', CP No 76; 'The Puzzled Game-Birds', line 5, CP 148, 'The Bedridden Peasant', line 15, CP 125; 'Birds at Winter Nightfall', line 5, CP 148; 'The Darkling Thrush', lines 31–2, CP 150; 'The Bullfinches', lines 3–5, 12–15, 28–30, CP 122–3.
25 'V.R. 1819–1901', line 12; '*AGNOSTOI THEOI*', lines 4, 14–15, Acts 17: 23.
26 'Drummer Hodge', lines 6–12, CP 90–1; 'To an Unborn Pauper Child', line 23, CP 128; 'Shelley's Skylark', line 8, CP 101; 'The Bridge of Lodi', line 31, CP 108; 'An August Midnight', line 12, CP 147; 'I have lived with Shades', lines 21–2, CP 184; 'To Lizbie Browne', lines 50–4, CP 132; 'The Dame of Athelhall', CP No 124; 'The Last Chrysanthemum', CP No 118; 'The Levelled Churchyard', lines 5–8, CP 158.
27 'The Self-Unseeing', lines 9–12, CP 167.

Notes to Chapter 22

1 CL iii 5, 53, 51, 41, 6–7.
2 CL iii 5, HPU iii 196; CL iii 21; LW 340, G2 150; CL iii 99.
3 'One We Knew', lines 13–20, CP 275; LW 16, 21, 24, 53; D xi; E. von Hartmann, *Die Philosophie des Unbewussten*, 1868; LW 109, 110; WRR 100; LW 114, 117, 132.
4 Preface, D 3; LW 150, 152, 158; Fore Scene line 14, D 21.
5 A. Fouillée, 'L'Homme Automate', *Revue des Deux Mondes*, August 1886, pp. 548–71; LN i, 395, Nos 1443–4; LW 183, D 17, 27–8.
6 LW 203, 212, 224, 235, 231.
7 LW 245, D 27, 123; LW 261, Compact *OED*, p. 2151, D 116–17.
8 LW 293, EHD 208, LW 265; LW 317, D 27–8; LW 301; Preface, D 4, CL iii 81; LW 340.
9 CL iii 53, 116.
10 CL iii 23, LW 341; LW 340, 96, Thomas Hobbes, *Leviathan*, 1651, ch. 13.

11 LW 341, CL iii 116; CL iii 85–6, 87, 90, 74; P 122–3.
12 LW 343; A.B. Walkley, '*The Dynasts*: A Suggestion', *TLS*, 29 January 1904, TH, '*The Dynasts*: A Rejoinder', TLS, 5 February 1904, pp. 36–7, PW 141–4; Max Beerbohm, *Saturday Review*, 30 January 1904, xcvii, 137–8, CH 336–40; John Buchan, *Spectator*, 20 February 1904, p. 292, CH 341–5; CL iii 99, 'To an Unborn Pauper Child', lines 1–3, CP 127.
13 *Part First*, D 21; Preface, D 4; LW 27, D 61; MAT2 102, D 103; D 82; CL iii 8, D 100, 104; D 86, M 256; DFB 12.
14 D 60, 68–9, 141–2.
15 D 30; CL iii 43, D 21.
16 D 40, 187, 41–2; John 4: 5–19.
17 LW 110; D 5, 17; Homer, *Iliad*, i, 197, D 63; *Iliad*, i, 5, D 21; D 57, Virgil, *Aeneid*, iv, 173–95.
18 Sophocles, *Oedipus Coloneus*, 1224–5, D 39; *Trachiniae*, 1266–72, D 147; Plato, *Republic*, vii, 514–17, LW 183; L 90–1.
19 *Poetry and Prose of William Blake*, ed. G. Keynes, London, 1848, pp. 166–7, 225, D 27; PW 141; P.B. Shelley, *Prometheus Unbound*, I, 191–202, II, iv, 2–6, I, 236–634; J.H. Newman, *Dream of Gerontius* (1865), lines 392–474.
20 HPU i 2–5, ii 27, 245.
21 HPU ii 27, 247, 8–9, 360.
22 HPU iii 1–2, iii 133–6.
23 Homer, *Iliad*, xiv, 285–355.
24 CL iii 202, D 21, 30.
25 P 119; CL iii 91; D 30, 122.

Notes to Chapter 23

1   CL iii 135, 143; H.J. Moule, 13 March 1904; L. Stephen, 22 February 1904, see *Life and Letters* by F.W. Maitland, 1906, LW 348; CL iii 141, M 436; Dr E.H. Gifford, LW 349; CL iii 119, LW 344–5; 'After the Last Breath', lines 15–16, 18, CP 270, D 288.
2   CL iii 120; *saeva indignatio* (savage indignation), Swift's epitaph, in Prior's *Life of Malone* (1860), p. 381; J. Swift, *A Modest Proposal* (1729), CL iii 110.
3   CL iii 119, 98, D 277.
4   CL iii 135–6; 'Shut Out that Moon', lines 21–2, 17–18, CP 216; CL iii 134; CL iii 117, 'The Revisitation', line 140.
5   CL iii 135; LW 348, 346, 348; CL iii 179, 193.
6   P 126, LW 351; CL iii 182, 183, 166, 176, 182, 175.
7   CL iii 187, 191; M 441, P 126, LW 354.
8   A.H. Clough, 'Say not the struggle nought availeth', line 5; CL iii 199; LW 354; CL iii 198.
9   LW 501, D 401, 428; LW 479, D 417; D 289, CL iii 153; CL iii 135, D 290.
10 D 482, 292; CL ii 288, D 286; D 407, 367.
11 'Confession to a Friend in Trouble', lines 10–13, CP 12; D 279–80.
12 D 237, 225; D 236. Horace, *Satires*, II, iii, 243–5; R. Browning, 'Two in the Campagna', lines 52–4, D 281.
13 D 435–6, Daniel 5: 1–5, 25–31, cf. 1 Samuel 31: 4–8; Aeschylus, *Agamemnon*, 6, WRR 34, CL iii 197, Luke 1: 52–3.
14 HPU ii, 1f, 8–9, D 219, 249, 21, 315, 265.
15 W. Archer, *Real Conversations*, 1904, pp. 45–6; HPU ii 246–7, 358–60.
16 LW 487–8; HPU iii, 1–2, 133–6; WRR 100; D 437.

17 CPW iv 407; D 407.
18 D 299, 319, 409, 400–1, 413, 417.
19 D 265; CL iii 91; D 203, 236, 261, 383.
20 D 239–40, 358, 335, 382, 416, 426.
21 D 362, 348, 386.
22 D 231, 234; D 410–11, A. Tennyson, 'The Ballad of Oriana' (1830); D 335, Horace, *Odes*, I, ii, 23–4.
23 D 210, 272, 396.
24 D 343–4; A. Tennyson, 'The Vision of Sin', lines 33–45, 179–90, D 354.
25 A. Tennyson, 'Vision of Sin', lines 179–82, 60, 103–70, 220–4, D 437.
26 D 379, 276.

Notes to Chapter 24

1 CL iii 193; 'After the Visit', lines 1, 13, CP 309; CL iii 282; P 131.
2 SMH 9–10, 13–19, 22–9; CL iii 179, 205–6; A.H. Hyatt, *The Pocket Thomas Hardy: Being Selections from the Wessex Novels and Poems* (1906).
3 CL iii 190, 205, 240; J.-E. Blanche, G2 148.
4 CL iii 216; LW 356; CL iii 269, 218.
5 CL iii 220, 261–2; 'The Apotheosis of the Minx', *Cornhill Magazine*, May, 1908, CL iii 251, 274, DMH 32; 'On the Departure Platform', lines 4–6, CP 221; SMH 19–21; CL iii 261.
6 SMH 29; CL iii 253.
7 CL iii 213; LW 359; CL iii 231.
8 CL iii 231.
9 S.T. Coleridge, 'Work without Hope', line 13; CL iii 218, 223; LW 359; CL iii 267, 275, 277–8; G.G. Byron, 'The Prisoner of Chillon', xiv, 10–27.
10 P 134; TLS, 27 February 1908, CH 370; *Edinburgh Review*, April 1908, ccvii, 421, CH 385, 375 381; CL iii 305.
11 CL iii 205, D 462–7; D 469; D 519, CL iii 130; D 621–2, LW 19.
12 LW 28, D 671–2; M 153–4, LW 98, FBP 113, D 653.
13 D 605–7, LW 26; D 495, LW 122; PN 21–3, D 563; D 484, LW 163.
14 D 702; A. Tennyson, *In Memoriam*, cxxvi, 12, cxxvii, 1, 20, cxxviii, 23–4, cxxiv, 16, lv, 20, D 707.
15 D 478–80, Exodus 16: 14; D 516, 511, Matthew 24: 15.
16 D 596, Homer, *Iliad*, vi, 394–496; D 485; D 542, *Iliad*, vi, 486–8; D 558, *Iliad*, vi, 350–1; LW 110; *Iliad*, v, 335–380, D 685.
17 D 705–6, Aeschylus, *Agamemnon*, 478, 432–44, 472; Lucian, *Icaromenippus*, LUC 123.
18 D 706, Horace, *Epistles*, I, xii, 19; D 549–50, Horace, *Odes*, II, x, 9–12; LW 32.
19 LW 32, 21; Virgil, *Aeneid*, ii, 270–3, 276–7, D 675; *Aeneid*, vi, 617–18, Juvenal, *Satires*, x, 204–6, D 484, 486–7.
20 D 459, W. Shakespeare, *Macbeth*, V, i, 74; D 561, G.G. Byron, *Manfred*, III, iv, 150; JOB 588, G1 254; Byron, *Childe Harold*, III, xxi–xxxv, D 613–25; D 461, A. Tennyson, *Princess*, i, 96–9, 'The Brook', line 23.
21 D 468, 482–3, 523, 673, 675, 695.
22 D 693, 474, 480, 490; CL iii 298, D 650–1.
23 D 524, 624–5, 643, 525, 627, 675.
24 D 705, 22, 450, 445, 689–9.
25 D 657, 661, 492, 477, 493, 687.
26 W. Shakespeare, *Othello*, V, ii, 338–59, D 700–1.

27 D 447, Aeschylus, *Persae*, 402–5; D 620, 517, 648, 655, 670.
28 Title page, D iv; CL iii 305.
29 D 454, 496–7, 519.

Notes to Chapter 25

1 CL iii, 306; *Select Poems of William Barnes*, Oxford University Press, 1908; CL iii 307, 348, 346, 350, CL iv 16–20.
2 CL iii 333, 335, 343, 347.
3 CL iii 339, 333, 335, 339, 308, 331.
4 CL iii 327; LEF 41, 45; CL iv 9, iii 360.
5 CL iii 316, iv 29, iii 353; DKR 206, LEF 42, CL iv 21.
6 LW 374; M 462; *Tess* opera by Baron Frédéric d'Erlanger, Covent Garden, 14 July 1909, LW 374, CL iv 30, 32, 35; SMH 49–50 (with photograph; CL iv, 41, M 463; 'Eminent Authors on the Mud', *Aldeburgh, Leiston and Saxmundham Times*, 21 August 1909.
7 CL iv 35; M 463, LW 374–5, CL iv 51; P.B. Shelley, 'Lines written among the Euganean Hills', lines 1–2; CL iv 65.
8 CL iv 4, 26, 43–4, 42, 66.
9 Preface to TL, CP 190; 'On the Departure Platform', CP No 170; 'One We Knew', CP No 227; 'After the Last Breath', CP No 223; 'George Meredith', line 1, CP 287, LW 62–4; 'Aberdeen', CP No 242, LW 347.
10 'The Revisitation', line 140, CP 195, M 464; 'The Curate's Kindness', line 36, CP 209; 'He Abjures Love', CP No 192; 'The Dead Man Walking', lines 29–32, CP 218.
11 LW 479, 'The Reminder', line 9, CP 269; DFB 13–14, CL iii 52, 'The Night of the Dance', lines 8–9, CP 231; LW 28, 'The Fiddler', CP No 207; LW 45, 'Reminiscences of a Dancing Man', CP No 165; CL iii 308, 'John and Jane', lines 13–16, CP 208.
12 'A Church Romance', CP No 211; 'The Dead Quire', CP No 213; 'The Rash Bride', lines 19, 56–60, CP 253–4, CPW i 385; 'Autumn in King's Hintock Park', CP No 163, CL iii 235.
13 'Autumn in King's Hintock Park', lines 5, 9–11, 17, 21–4; P.B. Shelley, 'Ode to the West Wind', line 3, Virgil, *Aeneid*, vi, 305–10, Homer, *Iliad*, vi, 146–8.
14 LW 303, 'A Wife and Another', CP No 217, 'The Burghers', line 68, CP 26; Plato, *Republic*, 619 e 6–620 a 2, 'The Unborn', lines 1–3, 22–4, CP 286–7.
15 Theocritus, *Idylls*, i, 64, 70, 73, 76, 79, 84, 'the Ballad-Singer', line 5, CP 239; *Anthologia Palatina*, V, lxxxi, 'The Market-Girl', CP No 197; Horace, *Odes*, iii, xxvi, 1–8, 'He Abjures Love', CP No 192; D.G. Rossetti, 'The Blessed Damozel', lines 6, 67–8, 104–8, J. Bunyan, *The Pilgrim's Progress*, World's Classics edn, ed. N.H. Keeble, Oxford, 1984, p. 260, 'One Ralph Blossom Soliloquizes', line 25–6, CP 289.
16 R. Browning, 'Soliloquy of the Spanish Cloister'; 'Panthera', line 101, CP 282, R. Browning, 'An Epistle containing the strange medical experience of Karshish, an Arab Physician'; 'The Flirt's Tragedy', lines 26, 59, CP 210–11, R. Browning, 'A Light Woman'; R. Browning, 'Porphyria's Lover', line 60, 'A Wife and Another', line 70, CP 264.
17 'The Revisitation', lines 27, 64, 68, 74, 111, 115, 140, CP 191–5, R. Browning, 'Love among the Ruins', lines 3–4.

18 CL iv 5; A. Tennyson, 'Aylmer's Field', lines 846–9, 'The House of Hospitalities', lines 15–16, CP 206; A. Tennyson, 'The Vision of Sin', lines 171–182, 'Reminiscences of a Dancing Man', lines 25–9, CP 217; 'In the Mind's Eye', lines 7–8, 11–12, CP 226, A. Tennyson, *Maud*, ii, 195, 200; 'The Man He Killed', lines 13–16, CP 287, A. Tennyson, 'Charge of the Light Brigade', line 14.

19 A. Tennyson, *The Princess*, iv, 492–3, 496–500, vii, 243, 252; CL iii 360, LEF 6; 'The Orphaned Old Maid', lines 3–4, CP 244.

20 'The Revisitation', CP 194–5; 'God's Education', lines 12–15, CP 279; G.M. Hopkins, 'The Leaden Echo and the Golden Echo', published 1918.

21 'A Trampwoman's Tragedy', line 35, CP 196; 'A Sunday Morning Tragedy', line 65, CP 203; 'The Flirt's Tragedy', lines 26, 65, 214, CP 210–13.

22 'The Self-Unseeing', line 11, CP 167; 'The Farm-Woman's Winter', lines 9–12, CP 214; 'She Hears the Storm', lines 3–4, CP 275; 'Bereft', line 2, CP 206.

23 'The Dead Man Walking', lines 11, 39, CP 218–19, CL iii 308; TL Preface, CP 190.

24 CL iii 58–9, 135, LW 341, 517; CL iv 28.

25 'Before Life and After', CP No 230; 'New Year's Eve', line 20, CP 278; 'God's Education', CP No 232, CL iii 244; 'Wagtail and Baby', CP No 241, CL iii 74.

26 'Autumn in King's Hintock Park', CP No 163; CL iv 28; 'After the Last Breath', lines 11–12, CP 270.

Notes to Chapter 26

1 CL iv 28, 177; CM 30; LEF 75.

2 The Wessex Edition, London, Macmillan, 1912–; CL iv, 284, LW 390; *The Three Wayfarers*, Little Theatre, London, 21 November 1913, P 79; CL iv 312, 217, 184.

3 LW 278–9, 390, 52–3, 44, M 79–80; LW 385, M 477.

4 M 477; LEF 39–40, 38.

5 LEF 60n.; SR 61.

6 LEF 66, 234, 72, 68.

7 CL iv 211, 216, 'The Convergence of the Twain', lines 25–30, CP 307; CL iv 212.

8 LW 386–8; A. Harvey, 'I was Emma Lavinia's Personal Maid', THYB, 1973–74, pp. 6–9; DKR 227; M 485.

9 A. Harvey, THYB, 1973–74, pp. 6–9; CL iv, 243, 240.

10 CL iv 248, 245, 247, 243, 260, LW 389–90.

11 DKR 220; CL iv 239; A. Harvey, THYB 1973–74, p. 9; SMH 71; CL iv 257.

12 CL iv 300, 265, 297; P 156; CL iv 300, 306.

13 P 151–5; CM 17, M 33; CM 7, M i4; CM 102–13; P 155, CL iv 208; CL ii 43.

14 LW 23, 43; CM 247, EL 27, LW 478–9; CM 1, 3, 8, 19, LW 149–52; CM 149.

15 CM 143; Aeschylus, *Agamemnon*, 1–39; Sophocles, *Oedipus Tyrannus*, 754–64, 836–45, 1044–52; *Oedipus*, 264, CM 154; Aristotle, *Poetics*, 1449a 16–19, CM 147; H.G. Liddell and R. Scott, *A Greek–English Lexicons*, 1890, p. 1397, M.C. Howatson, *Oxford Companion to Classical Literature*, 2nd edn, Oxford, 1989, p. 560.

16 M. Arnold, 'On the Modern Element in Literature', SUP i 33, Lucretius, *De rerum natura*, iii, 1060–70, CM 236; CM 66, Virgil, *Aeneid*, vi, 314; CM 141,

Horace, *Odes*, I, x, 7–8; G. Chaucer, *Canterbury Tales*, 'The Marchantes Tale', CM 220; CM 270, 274.

17 H. Vaughan, 'They are all gone into the world of light', lines 1–2, CM 69.
18 CL iv 220; M. Arnold, 'The Study of Poetry', Ward's *English Poets*, 1880, I, xix; 'A Mere Interlude', CM 226–8; Master John Horsley, Knight', CM 187; 'The Grave by the Handpost', CM 108, 109, 113.
19 CL iv 315, 297; PW 127–8; 'Romantic Adventures of a Milkmaid', CM 317.

Notes to Chapter 27

1 Euripides, *Medea*, 1204; LW 394.
2 LEF 77, 78, 86.
3 LEF 96, 75, 87, 92–3, CL v 10, 21.
4 CL v 15–16, 9, 19.
5 LEF 93, 101–2.
6 LEF 95, 99, 102.
7 M. Arnold, *Culture and Anarchy*, SUP v, 229; 'The Sick Battle-God', CP No 64; LW 394–5; LEF 100.
8 CL iv 52; LEF 100, LW 395; LW 396, 'Men Who March Away', CP 493, LW 396; H. Granville-Barker, abridgement of *The Dynasts*, Kingsway Theatre, 25 November 1914–30 January 1915, P 135, 172–3; CL v 42, 57, 66, 59.
9 CL v 45, 37 (where 'some of them' = some of the pieces written after TL was published).
10 CL v 41–2; 'Satires of Circumstance', *Fortnightly Review*, April 1911, pp. 579–83; P 164, 172; CL v 70, 72; LW 396.
11 CL v 70; G. Lytton Strachey, *New Statesman*, 19 December 1914, CH 437; review reprinted in Strachey's posthumous *Characters and Commentaries*, London, 1933, pp. 195–201.
12 CL v 37, FMC 272, G.G. Byron, *Childe Harold's Prilgrimage*, IV, cxxxvii, 9; 'The Going', CP No 277; 'Your Last Drive', line 13, CP 339, LW 387; 'The Walk', lines 5, 7–8, CP 340; 'I Found Her Out There', CP No 281; 'Pain on a Grave', lines, 4–15, 30–6, CP 341–2, SR 3, JOB 296; 'Without Ceremony', CP No 282, M 438; 'The Lament', CP No 283, cf. SR 11; 'The Phantom Horsewoman', CP No 294, SR 50, cf. 'Beeny Cliff', line 14, CP 351; 'The Voice', CP No 285.
13 CP Nos 246, 249, 254, 255; 'The Torn Letter', lines 28–9, CP 314; CP Nos 250, 251; 'After the Last Lamp', lines 26, 7, 13–14, 32, CP 315.
14 HE 68, LW 382, 296.
15 CP No 269; LW 396.
16 Plato, *Symposium*, 189 e 5–7, 190 d 1–8, 191 d 5–7, 'The Convergence of the Twain', lines 30–3, CP 307; Lucretius, *De rerum natura*, iii, 945, 'Channel Firing', lines 9–12, CP 305; Horace, *Epistles*, I, xi, 27, 'Starlings on the Roof', lines 10–12, CP 390.
17 CP 338, Virgil, *Aeneid*, iv, 23.
18 Lucian, *Dialogues of the Dead, Dialogues of the Gods*, 'The Coronation', 'Aquae Sulis', CP Nos 307–8; J. Donne, 'The Apparition', 'The Wistful Lady', CP No 298; J. Milton, *Samson Agonistes*, line 1758, 'In Front of the Landscape', line 46, CP 304; W. Wordsworth, 'Lucy: Strange fits of passion have I known', 'The Face at the Casement', CP No 258, 'Lucy: She dwelt among the untrodden ways', lines 11–12, 'The Difference', CP No 252; A. Tennyson, 'Merlin and the

Gleam', 'God's Funeral', lines 60–7, CP 328–9; R. Browning, 'The Grammar-ian's Funeral', 'God's Funeral', CP No 267; D.G. Rossetti, 'Inclusiveness', 'The Re-Enactment', CP No 301; A.C. Swinburne, 'Hymn to Proserpine', lines 35–44, 'Aquae Sulis', lines 17–20, CP 376, cf. 'A Singer Asleep', CP NO 265; 'The Going', CP No 277, C. Patmore, 'Departure'; R. Browning, 'The Lost Leader', D.G. Rossetti, 'The Blessed Damozel', lines 20–3, 'The Voice', line 13–16, CP 346.

19 CL iv 151; 'In the Moonlight', lines 1, 6, 13–15, CP 423, P 164–5.

20 'At Tea', line 7, CP 416; 'At a Watering-Place', line 8, CP 418; 'In the Cem-etery', line 12, CP 418; 'At the Altar-Rail', line 13, CP 420; 'In the Nuptial Chamber', line 7, CP 421; 'At the Draper's', line 2, CP 421; 'The Going', lines 39–42, CP 339; 'Your Last Drive', lines 14, 16, 19, CP 339–40; 'Lament', line 20, CP 344; 'The Haunter', lines 2, 10, 26, CP 345–6; 'A Circular', line 12, CP 348; 'After a Journey', lines 5, 25, CP 349; 'Beeny Cliff', lines 14–15, CP 351.

21 'A Circular', CP No 287; P 171; M. Arnold, 'To Marguerite – Continued', line 4; 'Exeunt Omnes', lines 11–15, CP 414.

Notes to Chapter 28

1 CL v 80–1.
2 CL v 206; LEF 111; CL v 214, 220, 207; 'Moments of Vision', lines 9–10, CP 427.
3 LEF 104–5; CL v 16
4 LEF 110, 134, 111, 107; M 513, LEF 135; SMH 87; LEF 118, 136; CL v 212, 205.
5 CL v 118, 123, 116; CL v 203, LEF 129; CL v 107; CL v 203, LEF 130; CL v 121, 52, 123.
6 CL v 147; P 187; CL v 94, 156–7, 102–4.
7 CL iv 234–5; F.A. Hedgcock, *Thomas Hardy: penseur et artiste*, Paris, 1911, M 517n, CL vi 138–40; LEF 113–5; E. Clodd, *Memories*. London, 1916; FEH to Rebekah Owen, 3 December 1915.
8 LEF 133; LY 179, LW 408; for the whole process by which the 'biography' was produced see LW, Introduction, pp. x–xxix.
9 CL v 223; P 207–8; i.e. 'her', 'We Sat at the Window', line 7, CP 429.
10 WB 121; 'Moments of Vision', lines 1–2, CP 427; 'We Sat at the Window', lines 10–11, 14–15, CP 429; 'Near Lanivet, 1872', lines 10, 27, 31, CP 436; LW 403; 'On Sturminster Foot-Bridge', lines 9–10, CP 484; 'Overlooking the River Stour', lines 19, 22, CP 482.
11 'The Oxen', CP No 403, C.J.P. Beatty, *Thomas Hardy and the Restoration of Rampisham Church, Dorset*, Dorchester 1991, p. 13, Plate 4; 'Afternoon Service at Mellstock', lines 9, 11, CP 429; 'Apostrophe to an Old Psalm Tune', CP No 359, P 194; 'Quid Hic Agis?', CP No 371; 1 Kings 19: 4–12, LW 503, 162; JOB 354–5, CPW ii 497; 'To My Father's Violin', CP No 381, LW 28; 'The Last Signal', line 11, CP 473, RG1 69; 'Logs on the Hearth', CP No 433, CL v 135, 137.
12 'Copying Architecture in an Old Minster', lines 1–2, CP 438; 'To the Moon', lines 2, 7, 26–7, CP 427–8; 'Quid Hic Agis?', lines 47–52, CP 470–1; 'In the Garden', lines 9, 13, CP 531; 'The Clock of the Years', lines 2, 21, 26, CP 528–9.

13 'Midnight on the Great Western', lines 1, 6, 11, 16–19, CP 514; 'To My Father's Violin', lines 2, 8–9, 30, CP 451–2, Virgil, *Aeneid*, vi, 441, 687–9, 695, vii, 325.

14 Horace, *Odes*, II, v, 14–16, 'Timing Her', lines 1, 13–14, 17, 33, 49, 65, 72, CP 443–5; 'Great Things', lines 27–32, CP 475, Horace, *Odes*, III, xxix, 41–3; *Odes*, III, i, 40, 'The Interloper', lines 1, 13, CP 488; P 200; JOB 386–8.

15 'The Upper Birch-Leaves', lines 11–12, CP 507, S.T. Coleridge, 'Christabel', lines 44–7; 'His Country', lines 1–2, CP 539; S.T. Coleridge, 'The Rime of the Ancient Mariner', lines 125–6, 609–10, 'His Country', lines 28–30 (only in MV 1st edn, see MV, ed. A. Shelston, Keele University Press, 1994, p. 226), P 204.

16 'The Wind's Prophecy', line 1, CP 494, A. Tennyson, 'The Brook', lines 23–34, 39–50, 'The Tree and the Lady', CP No 485, A. Tennyson, 'The Talking Oak', lines 133–48; 'The Statue of Liberty', lines 57, 60, CP 454; 'The Something that Saved Him', lines 29–30, CP 523, CL v 203–4 and note, W. Morris, *The Story of Sigurd the Volsung* (1876), 1887 edn, p. 337.

17 LW 408; 1 Kings 19: 3–13; 'Quid Hic Agis?', line 68, CP 442; LW 396, 'Men Who March Away', lines 11, 22–3, 28, CP 538; 'A Call to National Service', Line 13, CP 546.

18 'Quid Hic Agis?', lines 65–74, CP 442.

19 1 Corinthians 13: 4–7, JO 308, 'The Blinded Bird', lines 15–20, CP 446.

20 CL v 213, 237; 'Jubilate', line 22, CP 511; 'The House of Silence', CP No 413; 'Heredity', CP No 363; 'The Pity of It', CP No 498; 'The Wind Blew Words', CP No 376; 'Transformations', lines 5–6, CP 472.

21 'A Merrymaking in Question', lines 1, 8, CP 465; 'At Madame Tussaud's in Victorian Years', lines 1–2, 13, CP 492, LW 13; 'Old Furniture', lines 21–5, CP 486; 'The Last Performance', CP No 430, LW 386–7.

22 'Moments of Vision', CP No 352; 'The Pedigree', lines 4, 15, 30, CP 460–1; 'Old Furniture', lines 6, 11–15, CP 485–6; 'Honeymoon Time at an Inn', CP No 466.

23 'In Time of "The Breaking of Nations" ' (cf. Jeremiah 51: 20), CP No 500, LW 81–2, 408, P 176.

24 CL v 151, 'The Last Performance', lines 1–5, CP 487; 'On Sturminster Foot-Bridge', lines 1–5, CP 426; P 199.

25 'At a Country Fair', lines 19–20, CP 504; 'The Caged Goldfinch', CP No 436, CPW ii 234, MC 276–81; 'Midnight on the Great Western', CP No 465, JO 231–3; 'The Clock-Winder', lines 28, 29–44, CP 520, P 203; 'The Sunshade', lines 1, 17, CP 490.

26 'Copying Architecture in an Old Minster', lines 31–5, CP 439.

27 LEF 104; 'The Royal Sponsors', lines 23, 31, CP 485; 'The Choirmaster's Burial', lines 21–34, LW 17.

Notes to Chapter 29

1 LEF 140; 'In the Seventies', lines 1–6, CP 459; LEF 152, 170–1, 152.

2 LEF 139; LW 408–9; M 544.

3 CL v 253, 241; LW 413, 414; CL v 246, 253; LW 425.

4 LW 417, CL v 267, M 523; CL vi, 38, 44; LW 427; LEF 172, 182–5; CL vi 93; CL v 303, 308, vi 56.

5 CL vi 24; LW 422; CL v 336, 338; LW 432, 436–7; CL vi 24.

6 CL vi 1–2; CL v 338; CL v 270, 314–15; CL vi 70–1, 79, 31.

7 CL v 292–3; LN ii 226–7 (No 2443), T.S. Eliot, 'The Love Song of J. Alfred Prufrock', lines 99–110, 120–31, D 27–8; CL vi 77, LEF 180.

8 M 542; LEF 180; CL vi 115; CL v 311; M 533.

9 LEF 165–6; CL vi 104; P 227; CL vi 177.

10 LEF 180; M 529, *Fortnightly Review*, February 1920; CP 560–1; LY 176, LW 407; M 539.

11 LW 425; 'I Sometimes Think (for F.E.H.)', CP No 520; 'A Jog-Trot Pair', line 24, CP 571, FEH to E. Clodd, 12 February 1914, Leeds University, Brotherton Collection; CL v 241, SMH 97, M 531, 'The Two Houses', lines 12, 42, CP 595.

12 'The Old Gown', lines 13–16, CP 585; JOB 447, M 451; 'A Duettist to Her Pianoforte', lines 7, 17, 28, CP 586–7; LW 78; cf JOB 447, CPW ii 512; 'Penance', lines 1, 4, 21–3, CP 630–1; 'If you had known', liens 1, 8, CP 632–3.

13 CL iii 218, 'The Opportunity', CP No 577; LW 247, 'The Woman I Met', line 29, CP 593; LW 30, 'The Passer-By', CP No 627; 'The Rake-Hell Muses', lines 47–8, CP 692.

14 'On One Who Lived and Died Where He Was Born', lines 1, 24, CP 659, LW 262, P 223; M 257, 'The Old Workman', lines 2, 5–6, 17, 20, CP 663.

15 'Weathers', line 5, CP 563; LW 122, 'The Maid of Keinton Mandeville', CP No 513; 'Barthélémon at Vauxhall', line 14, CP 568, LW 447; 'The Curtains Now Are Drawn', CP No 523, CPW ii 511; 'The Strange House (Max Gate A.D. 2000)', line 2, CP 580; 'The Chapel-Organist', lines 71, 83, 84, CP 635–6.

16 J. Vera Mardon, née Stevens, 'Thomas Hardy as a Musician', Toucan Press, Beaminster, Dorset, 1964, pp. 11–12; LW 45; 'Haunting Fingers', lines 1–5, 41, CP 590–1; 'Two Serenades', lines 13–14, 21, CP 604; 'In the Small Hours', lines 1–2, 6, CP 648; 'The Country Wedding', lines 3, 9–10, 25, 29–31, CP 651; 'At the Railway Station, Upway', lines 3, 8, 11, CP 607.

17 M 134, 116; TH to E. Gosse, 20 January 1920, quoted M 51; LW 19; CP Nos 604, 652, 659, 661; 'Surview', lines 6–10, 11–18; Philippians 4: 8, 1 Corinthians 13: 4–13.

18 CL v 300; Apology, CP 557, Luke 10: 32; LW 407; CP 558–9, Acts 17: 16–21; '"And There Was a Great Calm"', title, line 42, CP 588–90, Matthew 8: 26, Mark 4: 39; Luke 2: 14; CL v 72.

19 LEF 180; CPW ii 509; CL v 253; Plato, *Apology of Socrates*, ix, 23 b 3–23 c 2.

20 Apology, CP 557; 'Where Three Roads Joined', line 1, CP 587; JOB 447, CPW ii 512; Sophocles, *Oedipus Tyrannus*, lines 716, 730, ed. R.C. Jebb, 1887, pp. 100–1; Horace, *Odes*, I, xi, 8, 'A Young Man's Exhortation', CP No 555; LW 51, 53, Horace, *Ars Poetica*, 388.

21 LW 51, CL vi 155; 'Drawing Details in an Old Church', lines 9–12, CP 690, J. Donne, *Devotions*; P.B. Shelley, 'Ozymandias', 'The Children and Sir Nameless', CP No 584; A. Tennyson, *Idylls of the King*, 'Merlin and Vivien', lines 388–93, 'The Rift', CP No 579; R. Browning, 'An Epistle . . . of Karshish' 'The Wood Fire', CP No 574; D.G. Rossetti, 'The Blessed Damozel', lines 21–3, 'A Night in November', lines 5–10, CP 586; 'The Chapel-Organist', lines 7, 24, 27, 49, CP 633–5.

22 'A Woman's Fancy', CP No 531; 'On Stinsford Hill at Midnight', lines 2–3, CP 597, LW 278; 'The Sailor's Mother', CP No 625, LLI 124–5; 'She Who Saw Not', lines 14–15, CP 662; 'The Fallow Deer at the Lonely House', CP No 551.

23 'The Temporary the All', CP No 2, 'Weathers', lines 15–18, CP 563; 'Voices from Things Growing in a Churchyard', CP No 580.

24 'I Was the Midmost', line 13, CP 666; 'The Garden Seat', lines 5–8, CP 567; J. Keats, 'Ode to a Nightingale', line 62; Horace, *Odes*, II, xvi, 26–7 (*amara lento temperet risu*), 'An Ancient to Ancients', lines 57–60, 62, 66–70.

Notes to Chapter 30

1 CL vi 160, v 1; LEF 78; H.M. Moule, 'Ave Caesar', *London Mercury*, October 1922, p. 631, P 321; CL vi 120; LW 452, PN 69; LW 452, PN 64.

2 LW 81; CL v 179; P 229.

3 CL vi 194, 144.

4 CL vi 168–9, 151; CL iv 37, vi 146; Professors Samuel Chew and Ernest Brennecke Jr., CL vi 153–7, 259; Rev. E.J. Bodington, CL vi 182; CL v 218.

5 CL vi 167, 136, 149; LEF 197, CL vi 204–5, LW 455, M 548.

6 LEF 186, 197n; E.M. Forster, ed., Virgil, *Aeneid*, tr. E. Fairfax Taylor, 1906; T.E. Lawrence, tr. Homer, *Odyssey*, 1932; CL vi 170; CL vi 201–2, LW 455.

7 LW 454; CL vi 166; LW 452; CL vi 208.

8 CL vi 204, 220; M 551; CL vi 221, LW 456.

9 CL vi 219; P 230; LEF 205; LW 457; CL vi 224, 232.

10 LEF 205; CL v 179; LW 81, CL vi 224; QC 219, 208; T. Malory, *Le Morte d'Arthur*, Everyman edn, 1906, i, 239–40, LW 20; LW 452, LEF 194.

11 T. Malory, *Le Morte d'Arthur*, 1906, i, 290; LEF 203, 141.

12 P 229; Dedication, QC 185: LEF 182; 'Last Words to a Dumb Friend', CP No 619.

13 QC 202, 213–14, 238–9, PBE 274, CL iv 288.

14 *Morte d'Arthur*, 1906 edn, i, 330–1; CL vi 209; Thomas of Britain, *The Romance of Tristram and Ysolt*, tr. R.S. Loomis, New York, 1923, pp. 186, 293, P 227; A. Tennyson, *Idylls of the King*, 'The Last Tournament', 1871, M. Arnold, *Tristram and Iseult*, 1852, A.C. Swinburne, *Tristram of Lyonesse*, CL vi 221, 226.

15 QC 221–2, W. Shakespeare, *Julius Caesar*, III, i, 258–61; Prologue, QC 189, R. Browning, *The Ring and the Book*, i, 778, 824–5; Epilogue, QC 225, W. Shakespeare, *The Tempest*, IV, i, 148–56; J. Keats, 'The Eve of St Agnes', x, 5, xxix, 9, QC 208; QC 223, C. Dickens, *Oliver Twist*, chapters 13, 50 (possibly included in 'readings by Charles Dickens' that TH 'frequented' in 1865–7, LW 54).

16 QC 223; TD 360–2; SR 42; LW 32; Ovid, *Heroides*, xv, 219–20; 'A singer Asleep', lines 28–31, CP 324.

17 CL vi 221, 224.

18 QC 204; A.E. Housman, 'Fragment of a Greek Tragedy', lines 2, 10; reprinted in *Parodies: An Anthology from Chaucer to Beerbohm – and After*, ed. D. Macdonald, London, 1961; QC 205, 214–15.

19 QC 189, 196, 201, Sophocles, *Trachiniae*, 584; QC 223, *Trachiniae* 772–80; QC 222, *Trachiniae*, 813; QC 221, *Trachiniae*, 1090–1102.

20 QC 1st edn, title page, P 227; D 1.

21 RN 128, 130, 138; Horace *Ars Poetica*, 182–8; Aeschylus, *Agamemnon*, 1–39; QC 222.

Notes to Chapter 31

1 M 552; CL vi 233, 283–4, 318–19, LEF 222; PN 79, CL v 336, vi 242; G. Moore, *Conversations in Ebury Street*, 1924; J.M. Murray, 'Wrap me up in my Aubusson carpet', *Adelphi*, April, 1924, pp. 951–8; M 553.

2 CL vi 272, 274, 280; PN 84; M 554, FBP 371; 'Nobody Comes', CP No 715.

3 CL vi 248, 315, 307, 363, LEF 210.

4 LW 357, 361; CL vi 300, 276; LW 460, PN 84.

5 CL vi 344, 234, LEF 208, LW 458–9; CL vi 237, 263, 270.

6 PN 83; LW 282, 293, 460–2; CL vi 287; LEF 226.

7 PN 84; E.E. Titterington, 'Afterthoughts of Max Gate', MAT2 342; CL vi 292; TD 109, 196, 200, 227.

8 LEF 226, 219; G. Bugler, 'Personal Recollections of Thomas Hardy', 1964, MAT1 Monograph 1, pp. 9–10, 13.

9 CL vi 363; *John o' London's Weekly*, 24 October 1925–July 1926, P 70; LEF 226; PN 80; CL vi 307, 338, 341, 347; P 247, 227.

10 CL vi 252–3; LW 464.

11 'Waiting Both', line 8, CP 701, Job, 14: 14; 'Why Do I', lines 1, 5, CP 831, CL vi 359; LEF 233, 182, 'A Popular Personage at Home', CP No 776.

12 'When Dead', lines 5, 7, CP 721, LEF 210; 'Tragedian to Tragedienne', line 24, CP 824, 'The Waiting Supper', CM 30; 'Why She Moved House', CP No 806; 'Nobody Comes', CP No 715, PN 84.

13 'The Years Since', lines 12–14, CP 722, G. Herbert, 'Easter Wings', 'The Altar'; cf. illustration of 'the distant urn', 'The Casterbridge Captains', line 27, CPW i 64; 'The Monument-Maker', lines 15–16, 20, 22–3, CP 708, LW 389, 403–4; 'Every Artemisia', lines 17, 29–30, 32–3, CP 723; CL v 37.

14 'Louie', CP No 739, LW 30; 'Circus-Rider to Ringmaster', CP No 672, LW 172–3; 'The Mock Wife' CP No 728, PN 38, PW 228–30; 'On the Portrait of a Woman about to be Hanged', CP No 748, CL vi 178, CPW iii 315; 'Alike and Unlike', CP No 962, LW 270; P 242, 345; JOB 546–7.

15 LN ii 544, 228–9, LW 453.

16 'The Absolute Explains', lines 65, 17, 24, 76, CP 755–7; 'The Six Boards', lines 13–30, CP 821.

17 CL v 232–3, Lucretius, *De rerum natura*, iii, 840–2; Virgil, Aeneid, vi, 309–10, 431–3, 557–72, 'Last Week in October', lines 6–8, CP 709; 'Genitrix Laesa', lines 10–13, CP 771, Horace, *Epistles*, i, xii, 9.

18 Aeschylus, *Agamemnon*, 136–9, 'Compassion', lines 7, 23, 25–8.

19 J. Keats, 'Bright star, would I were stedfast as thou art', lines 1, 3, 'Waiting Both', CP No 663; A. Tennyson, 'the Charge of the Light Brigade', line 14, 'Horses Aboard', lines 3–4, 6, 9, 12.

20 M. Arnold, 'Stanzas from the Grande Chartreuse', lines 72, 69, 'A Cathedral Façade at Midnight', lines 5, 11, 20–1, CP 703; Arnold, 'East London', lines 2, 5, 13, 'An East-End Curate', lines 17–18, CP 713.

21 'At a Fashionable Dinner', lines 10, 20, 21, 25, 20, CP 721–2, G. Meredith, *Modern Love*, xvii, 1, 4, 6–7, 15–16; 'The Last Leaf', lines 26, 28–30, CP 745; 'A Watering-Place Lady Inventoried', CP No 781.

22 M 560–1; 'At Wynyard's Gap', CP No 718; 'The Sexton at Longpuddle', lines 9–14, CP 777; 'Farmer Dunman's Funeral', CP No 744; 'The Six Boards', lines 10–12, CP 821; 'In the Evening', lines 4–5, 25, CP 820.

23 'Lady Vi', lines 17–24, CP 799; 'Bags of Meat', lines 35–8, CP 808; JOB 502; CL vi 262, 'A Refusal', lines 48–54, CP 803.

24 'A Bird-Scene at a Rural Dwelling', line 10, CP 701; HS title, CP 699; 'The Aërolite', lines 1, 4, 5, 22–3, CP 769; 'Known Had I', CP No 785; 'Not Only I', line 28, CP 783; 'An Inquiry', CP No 724; 'The Aërolite', lines 34–5, CP 758.
25 'Epitaph on a Pessimist', CP No 779; J.W. Mackail, *Select Epigrams from the Greek Anthology*, 1911, P. 172, *Anthologia Palatina*, vii, 309; CL vi 360, vii 4; P 244, Greek text in CPW iii 318; 'Any Little Old Song', lines 1–2, 7–12, CP 702.

Notes to Chapter 32

1 CL vii 7; LW 485.
2 CL v 246; LEF 262; WW, 'Introductory Note', CP 834.
3 LEF 238; CL vii, 7, 9; CL vii 8, TD 47; LW 466; CL vii 25, 1–2, 14.
4 LW 459; V. Woolf, 'How It Strikes a Contemporary', TLS, 5 April 1923' (reprinted in *The Common Reader*, 1925), CL vi 190–1; V. Woolf, *Diary*, ed. A.O. Bell, London, 1980, iii, 96–101.
5 LW 466, 467, PN 94; CL vii 45.
6 M 562; LEF 243, 245; LW 468.
7 LW 468, 286; CL vii 51, 54, LW 469, PN 96.
8 LEF 243; LW 471; 'The Ancient Cottages of England', PW 233–5; P 323–4; CL vii 57–9, 63.
9 LW 472–3; CL vii 13, 61; PW 235–7.
10 LEF 249; CL vii 78–9; CL vii 79, PN 292–3.
11 LEF 253, 254–5; LW 479; CL vii 89; 'A Wish for Unconsciousness', CP No 820; FEH to E. Clodd, 18 January 1928, Brotherton Collection, Leeds University; W. Shakespeare, *King Lear*, V, iii, 315–16.
12 LW 479–81, E. Fitzgerald, *The Rubáiyát of Omar Khayyám*, 4th edn, lxxxi.
13 LEF 274; M 571; 'Epitaph for G.K. Chesterton', CP No 946, CPW iii 339n.; 'Epitaph for George Moore', lines 5–6, CP 954, PN 79; Proverbs 25: 21–2.
14 LW 481; M 571–2; E.E. Titterington, 'The Domestic Life of Thomas Hardy' (1921–28, MAT1, Monograph 4, p. 16; PN 287, LW 543; RG2 280, 307, DFB 55.
15 LEF 264; CL vi 298; M 574–5, cf LEF 266, 304.
16 M 575; E.E. Titterington, MAT1, No 4, p. 16; LW 285–6.
17 For the history of the 'biography' see PN 189–202, LW x–xxix; LEF 268.
18 LW xxi; PN 288–9; LW xxv; LEF 274; p 265–7, 272–3.
19 LEF 263; CPW iii 321; p 262; WW Introductory Note, CP 834, CL vi 221.
20 LEF 274, 277, 'The New Dawn's Business', lines 13–14, CP 835; 'He Resolves to Say No More', CP No 919; 'To Louisa in the Lane', line 21, CP 840, LW 30; 'A Forgotten Miniature', line 21, CP 900, EL opposite 96, LW Illustration No 4, JOB 486.
21 CP Nos 818, 855, 890, 916, 873; 'Not Known', lines 5–8, CP 917; 'The Aged Newspaper Soliloquizes', lines 2, 8, CP 913.
22 CP Nos 862, 907; LW 463, 468; CP Nos 870, 849, 839; PN 292–3, 'The Brother', lines 3, 9, CP 880.
23 After the Death of a Friend', line 1, CP 861; RG1 254, JOB 588; 'Standing by the Mantelpiece', CP No 874, P 257; for suggested interpretations, see JOB 602–4.
24 'A Philosophical Fantasy', lines 26–39, CP 694; 'The Mongrel', line 6, CP 877.

25 'Concerning Agnes', lines 8, 21–2, CP 878; Homer, *Odyssey*, i, 14–15; 'The Bad Example', line 8, CP 839; Meleager, *Anthologia Palatina*, xii, 54, J.W. Mackail, 'Selections from the Greek Anthology', p. 226, CPW iii 323; 'Faithful Wilson', CP No 882, Strato of Sardis, *Anthologia Palatina*, xii, 248, Mackail, p. 128, CPW iii 329.

26 Pausanias, *Description of Greece*, IV, ix, 4–8, 'Aristodemus the Messenian', line 84, CP 853, CPW iii 324; D 573, V. Puccitta, *Aristodemo*, based on V. Monti, *Aristodemo*; CL vii 14, 29; LEF 277; D. Taylor, *Hardy's Metres and Victorian Prosody*, Oxford, 1988, pp. 265–6.

27 'An Evening in Galilee', CP No 864; 'The Poet's Thought', lines 5–8, CP 865; A. Tennyson, 'The Poet', lines 24, 33–4; 'The Flower', lines 23–4.

28 'Squire Hooper', lines 13, 18, CP 882; 'Throwing a Tree', CP No 837; Lying Awake', CP No 863; 'Liddell and Scott', lines 50–7, CP 845; LEF 275, LW 481.

Bibliography

Primary Sources 1: for Hardy's life, work, and thought

Hardy, Florence Emily, *The Early Life of Thomas Hardy 1840–1891*, London, 1928.
——, *The Later Years of Thomas Hardy 1892–1928*, London, 1930.
Hardy, Thomas, *The Life and Work of Thomas Hardy*, ed. Michael Millgate, London, 1984.
——, *The Collected Letters of Thomas Hardy*, ed. Richard Little Purdy and Michael Millgate, Oxford, 1978–88.
——, *One Rare Fair Woman: Thomas Hardy's Letters to Florence Henniker 1893–1922*, ed. Evelyn Hardy and F.B. Pinion, London, 1972.
——, *The Personal Notebooks of Thomas Hardy*, ed. Richard H. Taylor, London, 1978.
——, *The Literary Notebooks of Thomas Hardy*, ed. Lennart A. Björk, London, 1985.
——, *Thomas Hardy's Personal Writings*, ed. Harold Orel, London, 1990.
——, *The Complete Poems of Thomas Hardy*, ed. James Gibson, London, 1976.
——, *The Variorum Edition of the Complete Poems of Thomas Hardy*, ed. James Gibson, London, 1979.
——, *The Complete Poetical Works of Thomas Hardy*, ed. Samuel Hynes, Oxford, 1985–96.
——, *Collected Short Stories*, introduced Desmond Hawkins, ed. F.B. Pinion (New Wessex Edition), London, 1988.
Hardy, Emma, *Some Recollections*, ed. Evelyn Hardy and Robert Gittings, London 1961.
——, *Emma Hardy Diaries*, ed. Richard H. Taylor, Ashington, Northumberland, 1985.
——, and Florence Hardy, *Letters of Emma and Florence Hardy*, ed. Michael Millgate, Oxford, 1996.
Hardy, Florence, unpublished letters in Brotherton Collection, Leeds University.

Primary Sources 2: related to Hardy's reading

Aeschylus, *Agamemnon, Choephori, and Eumenides* with translation by Herbert Weir Smyth, London, 1926.

—— , *The Tragedies of Aeschylus*, tr. T.A. Buckley, London, 1849.

—— , *Agamemnon: A Tragedy, Taken from Aeschylus*, by Edward FitzGerald (1876), reprinted in *FitzGerald: Selected Works*, ed. Joanna Richardson, London, 1962.

—— , *Agamemnon Transcribed* by Robert Browning, London, 1877.

—— , *Persae*, and *Prometheus Vinctus*, with tr. by Herbert Weir Smyth, London, 1922.

Apocrypha: Translated out of the Greek and Latin Tongues, The (1894), Oxford, 1926.

Apollonius Rhodius, *Argonautica*, with tr. by R.C. Seaton, London, 1912.

Aristotle, *Poetics*, with tr. by W. Hamilton Fyfe, London, 1927.

Arnold, Matthew, *The Complete Poems*, ed. Kenneth Allott, London, 1965.

—— , *The Complete Prose Works*, ed. R.H. Super, Ann Arbor, 1960–77.

Austen, Jane, *Northanger Abbey*, introd. R. Brimley Johnson, London, 1906.

Barrett, Elizabeth (Mrs Browning), *Poems*, London, 1850.

—— , *Aurora Leigh* (1857), London, 1890.

Bede, *Historia Ecclesiastica Gentis Anglorum*, tr. L. Gidley, London, 1870.

Bible, The Holy, Authorized Version (1611), introd. Alfred W. Pollard, London, 1911.

—— , *New Testament in the Original Greek, The*, ed. B.F. Westcott, J.A. Hort, London, 1901.

—— , *Biblia Sacra Vulgatae Editionis*, Rome, 1959.

Blake, William, *Poetry and Prose*, ed. Geoffrey Keynes, London, 1948.

Braddon, Mary E., *Lady Audley's Secret: A Novel* (1862), new edn, Thomas Downey, London, n.d.

Brontë, Charlotte, *Jane Eyre* (1847), London, 1969.

Browning, Elizabeth Barrett, *see* Barrett, Elizabeth.

Browning, Robert, *The Poems*, ed. John Pettigrew, 2 vols, Harmondsworth, 1981.

Bunyan, John, *The Pilgrim's Progress*, ed. N.H. Keeble, Oxford, 1984.

Butler, Samuel, *Erewhon* (1872), London, 1932.

Byron, George Gordon, *Poetical Works*, ed. Frederick Page, rev. John Jump, London, 1970.

Carlyle, Thomas, *The French Revolution: A History* (1837), London, 1906.

—— , *Past and Present* (1843), London, 1960.

Carroll, Lewis (C.L. Dodgson), *Complete Works*, ed. Alexander Woollcott, London, 1939.

Chaucer, Geoffrey, *The Canterbury Tales*, in *Complete Works*, ed. Walter W. Skeat, London, 1933.

Clough, Arthur Hugh, *The Poems*, ed. F.L. Mulhauser, Oxford, 1973.

Coleridge, Samuel Taylor, *Select Poetry and Prose*, ed. Stephen Potter, London, 1950.

Common Prayer, The Book of, London, 1662.

Comte, Auguste, *A General View of Positivism*, tr. J.H. Bridges, London, 1865.

Crabbe, George, *Tales, 1812 and Other Selected Poems*, ed. Howard Mills, Cambridge, 1967.

Crashaw, Richard, 'Wishes to his Supposed Mistress', and 'Hynn to the Name and Honor of the Admirable Saint Teresa', in *The Oxford Book of Seventeenth Century Verse*, ed. H.J.C. Grierson and G. Bullough, Oxford, 1934.

Dante Alighieri, *Divina Commedia*, ed. and tr. John D. Sinclair, 3 vols, Oxford, 1971.

Darwin, Charles, *The Origin of Species* (1859), introd. W.R. Thompson, London, 1928; ed. J.W. Burrow, Harmondsworth, 1968.

Dickens, Charles, *Oliver Twist* (1838), ed. Humphrey House, London, 1949.

Donne, John, *The Poems*, ed. H.J.C. Grierson, London, 1933.

Dowden, Edward, *Life of Percy Bysshe Shelley*, London, 1886.
English Plays of the Nineteenth Century, ed. M.R. Booth, Oxford, 1973.
'Ethics of Suicide, The', *Saturday Review*, xli, 770 (17 June 1876).
Eton Latin Grammar, The, ed. T.W.C. Edwards, 24th edn., London, 1850.
Euripides, *Alcestis, Medea*, with tr. by David Kovacs, London, 1994; *Hercules Furens*, with tr. by A.S. Way, London, 1912; *Hippolytus*, with tr. by David Kovacs, London, 1995.
Fielding, *The History of Tom Jones*, ed. A.R. Humphreys, 2 vols, London, 1963.
———, *The History of Tom Jones*, ed. G.S. Haight, Oxford, 1981.
Fitzgerald, Edward, *Selected Works*, ed. Joanna Richardson, London, 1962.
Fouillée, 'L'Homme Automate', *Revue des deux mondes*, lxxvi, 548–71 (1 August 1886).
Gibbon, Edward, *Decline and Fall of the Roman Empire* (1776–88), 12 vols, London, 1820.
Gilbert, William Schwenk, *Plays*, ed. George Rowell, Cambridge, 1982.
Gray, Thomas, *Poems*, in *The Poetical Works of Johnson, Parnell, Gray, and Smollett*, ed. George Gilfillan, Edinburgh, 1855.
Haggard, H. Rider, *She*, London, 1887.
Hartmann, Eduard von, *Die Philosophie des Unbewussten* tr. W.C. Coupland as *The Philosophy of the Unconscious*, 3 vols, London, 1884.
Herbert, George, *Poems*, ed. F.E. Hutchinson, Oxford, 1941.
Hogg, T.J., *The Life of Percy Bysshe Shelley*, London, 1856.
Homer, *Iliad*, tr. Theodore Alois Buckley, London, 1854.
———, *Iliad*, with translation by A.T. Murray, London, 1924.
———, *Odyssey*, with translation by A.T. Murray, London, 1919.
Horace, *Odes and Epodes*, with tr. by C.E. Bennett, London, 1914.
———, *Satires, Epistles and Ars Poetica*, with tr. by H. Rushton Fairclough, London, 1926.
Hutchins, John, *The History and Antiquities of the County of Dorset*, 3rd edn., 1861–73.
Huxley, Thomas Henry, 'Literature and Culture', *Collected Essays*, London, 1893.
Jerrold, Douglas William, *Mrs Caudle's Curtain Lectures*, London, 1846.
Jeune, Mary, 'Saving the Innocents', *Fortnightly Review*, September 1885.
———, 'Helping the Fallen', *Fortnightly Review*, November, 1885.
Johnson, Samuel, *Rasselas Prince of Abyssinia, The History of*, in *Prose and Poetry*, ed. Mona Wilson, London, 1950.
Keats, John, *The Poetical Works*, ed. H.W. Garrod, 1956.
Lemprière, J., *Classical Dictionary of Proper Names mentioned in Ancient Authors*, ed. F.A. Wright, London, 1963.
Longus, *Daphnis and Chloe*, with tr. by George Thornley, rev. J.M. Edmonds, London, 1916.
———, *Daphnis and Chloe*, tr. Angel Day, 1587; repubd ed. Joseph Jacobs, London, 1890.
———, tr. Paul Turner, Harmondsworth, 1956, London, 1989.
Lucian, with tr. by A.M. Harmon, *Icaromenippus, Charon, Auctio Vitarum*, London, 1915, *Reviviscentes sive Piscator*, London, 1921, *Menippus*, London, 1925; *Dialogues of the Dead, Dialogues of the Gods*, with tr. by M.D. Macleod, London, 1961.
———, *Satirical Sketches*, tr. P. Turner, Harmondsworth 1961, Bloomington and Indianapolis, 1990.
Lucretius, *De rerum natura*, with tr. by W.H.D. Rouse, London, 1924.
Mackail, J.W., *Select Epigrams from the Greek Anthology*, London, 1890, 1911.
Malory, Thomas, *Le Morte d'Arthur*, introd. John Rhys, 2 vols, London, 1906.
Marcus Aurelius Antoninus, *Meditations*, with tr. by C.R. Haines, London, 1916.

—— , *Thoughts of the Emperor Marcus Aurelius Antoninus,* tr. George Long, London, 1862.

Marvell, Andrew, *Poems,* ed. H.M. Margoliouth, 1927.

Meredith, George, *Modern Love,* London, 1862.

Mill, John Stuart, *On Liberty* (1859), *Utilitarianism* (1861), London, 1910.

—— , *The Subjection of Women* (1869), London 1929.

—— , *Three Essays on Religion,* London, 1874.

Milton, John, *Poetical Works,* ed. H.C. Beeching, 1938.

Morris, William, *The Earthly Paradise: A Poem,* London, 1868–70.

—— , *Sigurd the Volsung* (1876), London, 1887.

Moule, Horace, 'The Story of Alcestis', *Fraser's Magazine,* November 1871, pp. 575–85.

Newman, John Henry, *Apologia pro Vita Sua* (1864), ed. C.F. Harrold, New York, 1947.

—— , *The Dream of Gerontius,* London, 1866.

Nineteenth-Century Plays, ed. G. Rowell, Oxford, 1953.

Ovid, *Heroides,* with tr. by Grant Showerman, London, 1921.

—— , *Metamorphoses,* with tr. by Frank Justus Miller, rev. G.P. Goold, 2 vols, London, 1994.

Pater, Walter, *The Renaissance: Studies in Art and Poetry* (1873), ed. Louis Kronenberger, New York, 1959.

—— , *Marius the Epicurean* (1885), London, 1934.

Patmore, Coventry, *Poems,* introd. Basil Champneys, London, 1928.

Pennie, J.F. (Sylvaticus), *The Tale of a Modern Genius,* London, 1827.

Plato, *Apology, Phaedrus,* with tr. by Harold North Fowler, London, 1914.

—— , *Symposium,* with tr. by W.R.M. Lamb, London, 1925.

—— , *Republic,* with tr. by Paul Shorey, London, 1930, rev., 1937.

—— , *The Dialogues of Plato,* tr. B. Jowett, 4 vols, Oxford, 1871.

Plautus, *Aulularia, Mostellaria, Miles Gloriosus,* with tr. by Paul Nixon, London, 1924.

Proctor, R.A., *Essays on Astronomy,* London, 1872.

Rabelais, François, *Gargantua and Pantagruel,* tr. J.M. Cohen, Harmondsworth, 1955.

Richardson, Samuel, *Pamela or Virtue Rewarded* (1740–1), introd. M. Kinkead Weeks, 2 vols, London, 1962.

Robertson, T.W., *Six Plays,* ed. M.R. Booth, Ashover, Derbyshire, 1980.

Rossetti, Dante Gabriel, *Poems,* ed. Oswald Doughty, London, 1961.

Saint-Pierre, Bernardin de, *Paul et Virginie* (1788), ed. J. van den Heuvel, Paris, 1984.

—— , *Paul and Virginia,* Thomas Nelson, London & Edinburgh, 1849 (Hardy's copy, at Dorset County Museum).

Sappho, in *Greek Lyric, Sappho and Alcaeus,* ed. and tr. David Campbell, London, 1990.

—— , *Sappho: Memoir, Text, Selected Renderings, and a Literal Translation* by H.T. Wharton, London, 1895.

Shakespeare, William, *The Complete Works,* ed. W.J. Craig, London, 1905.

Shelley, Percy Bysshe, *The Complete Poetical Works,* ed. Thomas Hutchinson, London, 1934.

Sheridan, Richard Brinsley, *The Plays,* London, 1906.

Sophocles, *Oedipus Tyrannus,* ed. and tr. R.C. Jebb, Cambridge, 1883.

—— , *Antigone,* ed. and tr. R.C. Jebb, Cambridge, 1888.

—— , *Trachiniae,* ed. and tr. R.C. Jebb, Cambridge, 1892.

—— , *Oedipus Tyrannus, Antigone, Trachiniae, Oedipus Coloneus,* ed. and tr. Hugh Lloyd Jones, London, 1994.

Spenser, Edmund, *Poetical Works,* ed. J.C. Smith and E. de Selincourt, London, 1935.

Swift, Jonathan, *Gulliver's Travels and Selected Writings*, London, 1968.
Swinburne, Algernon Charles, *Atalanta in Calydon*, 1965.
——, *Poems and Ballads*, London, 1866.
——, *Tristram of Lyonesse* (1882), London, 1915.
Tennyson, Arthur, *Poems and Plays*, London, 1965.
Theocritus, *Idylls*, in *The Greek Bucolic Poets*, with tr. by J.M. Edmonds, London, 1912.
Thomas of Britain, *The Romance of Tristram and Ysolt*, ed. R.S. Loomis, New York, 1923.
Virgil, *Eclogues and Aeneid*, with tr. by H. Rushton Fairclough, London, 1965.
——, *The Works of Virgil*, tr. John Dryden (1697), Oxford, 1903.
Voltaire, *Candide*, tr. John Butt, Harmondsworth, 1947.
Ward, Thomas Humphrey, *The English Poets: Selections with Critical Introductions*, 4 vols, London, 1880–1.
Woolner, Thomas W., *Pygmalion*, London, 1881.
Wordsworth, William, *Poetical Works*, ed. Thomas Hutchinson, Oxford, 1936.
——, Preface to *Lyrical Ballads* (1800) in *English Critical Essays: Nineteenth Century*, ed. Edmund D. Jones, Oxford, 1916.

Secondary Sources: besides editorial material in Primary Sources

Alvarez, A., Introduction to *Tess of the d'Urbervilles*, London, 1978.
Archer, William, *Real Conversations*, London, 1904.
Bailey, J.O., *The Poetry of Thomas Hardy: A Handbook and Commentary*, Chapel Hill, 1970.
Barber, D.F., ed. *Concerning Hardy: A Composite Portrait from Memory*, London, 1968.
Barber, Giles, *Daphnis and Chloe: the markets and metamorphoses of an unknown bestseller*, London, 1988.
Barrineau, Nancy, annot. *Tess of the d'Urbervilles*, Oxford, 1988.
Beatty, C.J.P., introd. *Desperate Remedies*, London, 1975.
Blythe, Ronald, ed. *Far from the Madding Crowd*, London, 1978.
——, introd. *A Pair of Blue Eyes*, London, 1975.
Boone, Colin C., 'Hardy's Poem "Lines to a Movement in Mozart's E-FLAT Symphony" – Which Symphony?', *Thomas Hardy Journal*, February 1990 (vi, 1, 61–9).
Brake, Laurel and Ernest Hardy, annot. *The Trumpet-Major*, London, 1974.
Brown, Douglas, *Thomas Hardy*, London, 1961.
Bullen, J.B., *The Expressive Eye: Fiction and Perception in the Work of Thomas Hardy*, Oxford, 1986.
Caless, Bryn, annot. *The Mayor of Casterbridge*, London, 1974.
Chalfont, Fran, 'Hardy's Residences and Lodgings', *Thomas Hardy Journal*, October 1992, February 1993, May 1993 (viii, 3, 46–56; ix, 1, 41–61; ix, 2, 19–38).
Coleman, Terry, ed. *An Indiscretion in the Life of an Heiress*, London, 1985.
Cox, J. Stevens, *Thomas Hardy: Materials for a Study of his Life, Times and Works*, St Peter Port, Guernsey, 1968.
——, *Thomas Hardy: More Materials for a Study of his Life, Times and Works*, St Peter Port, Guernsey, 1971.
Cox, R.G., ed. *Thomas Hardy: The Critical Heritage*, London, 1970.
Dalziell, Pamela, ed. *An Indiscretion in the Life of an Heiress and Other Stories*, Oxford, 1994.
Deacon, Lois and Terry Coleman, *Providence and Mr Hardy*, London, 1966.
Draper, R.P., and Martin S. Ray: *An Annotated Critical Bibliography of Thomas Hardy*, New York and London, 1989.

Draper, Jo, *Thomas Hardy: A Life in Pictures*, Stanbridge, Wimborne, 1989.
Ebbatson, Roger, ed. *The Trumpet-Major and Robert his Brother*, Harmondsworth, 1984.
Evans, Ray, introd. *The Trumpet-Major*, London, 1974.
Furbank, P.N., annot. *Tess of the d'Urbervilles*, London, 1974.
Furbank, P.N., annot. *Jude the Obscure*, London, 1975.
Gatewood, Jane, ed. *A Laodicean*, Oxford, 1991.
Gatrell, Simon, and Nancy Barrineau, ed. *The Return of the Native*, Oxford, 1990.
——, ed. *Under the Greenwood Tree*, Oxford, 1985.
——, *Hardy the Creator: A Textual Biography*, Oxford, 1988.
Gibson, James, introd. *Tess of the d'Urbervilles*, London, 1974.
——, introd. *Far from the Madding Crowd*, London, 1974.
——, *Thomas Hardy: A Literary Life*, London, 1996.
Gittings, Robert, introd. *The Hand of Ethelberta*, London, 1975.
——, *Young Thomas Hardy*, Harmondsworth, 1978.
Gittings, Robert, and Jo Manton, *The Second Mrs Hardy*, London, 1979.
Gittings, Robert, *The Older Hardy*, London, 1980.
Goode, John, *Thomas Hardy: The Offensive Truth*, Oxford, 1988.
Grigson, Geoffrey, introd. *Under the Greenwood Tree*, London, 1974.
Grindle, Juliet and Simon Gatrell, ed. *Tess of the d'Urbervilles*, Oxford, 1988.
Hands, Timothy, *A Hardy Chronology*, London, 1992.
Hardy, Evelyn, *Thomas Hardy: A Critical Biography*, London, 1954.
Hardy, Barbara, introd. *A Laodicean*, London, 1975.
Hardy, Ernest, notes to *A Laodicean*, London, 1975.
Hetherington, Tom, ed. *The Well-Beloved*, Oxford, 1986.
Hilton, Timothy, *The Pre-Raphaelites*, London, 1970.
Hynes, Samuel, ed. *Thomas Hardy*, Oxford, 1984.
——, 'Mr Hardy's Monster: Reflections on *The Dynasts*', *Sewanee Review*, Spring 1994 (cii, 2, 213–32).
Ingham, Patricia, ed. *Jude the Obscure*, Oxford, 1985.
Jesty, Vera, *Hardy's Wessex Today: Modern photographs and texts by Vera Jesty, Original photographs by Hermann Lea*, introd. Michael Millgate, Mellstock Press, Belper, 1990.
Johnson, Trevor, ed. *Wessex Poems and Other Verses*, Keele, 1995.
Kay-Robinson, Denys, *The First Mrs Thomas Hardy*, London, 1979.
——, *The Landscape of Thomas Hardy*, Exeter, 1984.
King, Kathryn R., ed. *Wessex Tales*, Oxford, 1991.
Kramer, Dale, ed. *The Woodlanders*, Oxford, 1981.
——, ed. *The Woodlanders*, Oxford, 1985.
——, ed. *The Mayor of Casterbridge*, Oxford, 1987.
Lodge, David, annot. *The Woodlanders*, London, 1974.
Manford, Alan, ed. *A Pair of Blue Eyes*, Oxford, 1985.
Mardon, J. Vera. *Thomas Hardy as a Musician*, Beaminster, 1964.
May, Derwent, annot. *The Return of the Native*, London, 1974.
Mendelson, Edward, annot. *The Well-Beloved*, London, 1975.
Miller, J. Hillis, introd. *The Well-Beloved*, London, 1975.
Millgate, Michael, *Thomas Hardy: His Career as a Novelist*, London, 1971.
——, *Thomas Hardy: A Biography*, Oxford, 1982.
Orel, Harold, ed. *The Dynasts*, London, 1978.
Pinion, F.B., introd. *The Mayor of Casterbridge*, London, 1974.
——, introd. *The Woodlanders*, London, 1974.
——, introd. *Two on a Tower*, London, 1975.

Pinion, F.B., ed. *Wessex Tales*, London, 1976.

——, ed. *The Queen of Cornwall*, London, 1977.

——, *A Hardy Companion: A Guide to the Works of Thomas Hardy and their Background*, London, 1984.

Purdy, Richard Little, *Thomas Hardy: A Bibliographical Study*, Oxford, 1954.

——, introd. *Our Exploits at West Poley*, Oxford, 1978.

Reynolds, Graham, *Turner*, London, 1969.

Rutland, William R., *Thomas Hardy: A Study of his Writings and their Background* (1938), New York, 1962.

Seymour-Smith, Martin, *Hardy*, London, 1994.

Shelston, Alan, ed. *Moments of Vision and Miscellaneous Verses*, Keele, 1994.

Skilton, David, ed. *Tess of the d'Urbervilles*, London, 1978.

Stewart, J.I.M., *Thomas Hardy*, London, 1971.

Taylor, Dennis, *Hardy's Metres and Victorian Prosody*, Oxford, 1988.

Temblett-Wood, J.C.S., introd. *The Return of the Native*, London, 1974.

Tunks, Brenda, *Whatever Happened to the Other Hardys?*, Canford Heath, Poole, 1990.

Wightman, T.R., introd. *Jude the Obscure*, London, London, 1975.

Winfield, Christine, annot. *Far from the Madding Crowd*, London, 1974.

Wing, George, '*A Group of Noble Dames*: "Statuesque Dynasties of Delightful Wessex"', *Thomas Hardy Journal*, May 1991 (vii, 2, 24–45).

Woodcock, George, ed. *The Return of the Native*, Harmondsworth, 1978.

Woodward, Sir Llewellyn, *The Age of Reform*, Oxford, 1962.

Index